The Philosophic Roots
of Modern Ideology

THIRD EDITION

The Philosophic Roots of Modern Ideology

Liberalism, Communism, Fascism, Islamism

DAVID E. INGERSOLL
University of Delaware

RICHARD K. MATTHEWS
Lehigh University

ANDREW DAVISON
Vassar College

 Upper Saddle River, New Jersey 07458

Library of Congress Cataloging-in-Publication Data

INGERSOLL, DAVID E., [date]
  The philosophic roots of modern ideology: liberalism, communism, fascism, Islamism
  / DAVID E. INGERSOLL, RICHARD K. MATTHEWS, ANDREW DAVISON.—3rd ed.
    p. cm.
  Includes bibliographical references and index.
  ISBN 0-13-109075-5
    1. Political science—History. 2. Liberalism—History 3. Communism—History 4.
  Fascism—History. 5. Islam and state—History. I. Matthews, Richard K., [date] II.
  Davison, Andrew, [date] III. Title
  JA83 .I55 2001
  320.5'09—dc21   00-028483

VP, Editorial Director: *Laura Pearson*
Executive Editor: *Beth Gillette Mejia*
Assistant Editor: *Brian Prybella*
Editorial/production supervision: *Edie Riker*
Prepress and Manufacturing Buyer: *Benjamin D. Smith*
Director of Marketing: *Gina Sluss*
Cover Director: *Jayne Conte*

This book was set in 10/12 New Baskerville by East End Publishing Services, Inc., and was printed and bound by Hamilton Printing Company. The cover was printed by Phoenix Color Corp.

Printed in the United States of America

10 9 8 7 6 5 4 3 2 1

ISBN   0-13-109075-5

Prentice-Hall International (UK) Limited, *London*
Prentice-Hall of Australia Pty. Limited, *Sydney*
Prentice-Hall Canada Inc., *Toronto*
Prentice-Hall Hispanoamericana, S.A., *Mexico*
Prentice-Hall of India Private Limited, *New Delhi*
Prentice-Hall of Japan, Inc., *Tokyo*
Pearson Education Asia Pte. Ltd., *Singapore*
Editora Prentice-Hall do Brasil, Ltda., *Rio de Janeiro*

To
our students at
Delaware, Lehigh, and Vassar
who remind us
why . . .

Contents

PREFACE xiii

1 THE ORIGINS OF POLITICAL IDEOLOGIES 1

THE CAVE: THE ILLUSION AND THE REALITY OF EDUCATION 2

What Is Ideology? 4
Ideology's Distinguishing Features 5

MASS MOVEMENTS 9

Leadership Roles 11
Why Study Ideologies? 11
The Competition for Hearts and Minds 16
Why Unpopular Ideas? 17
Mill on Toleration 18
Become a "True Believer" 19

SUGGESTED READINGS 20

2 INDIVIDUALISTIC (MARKET) LIBERALISM 21

PRELIBERAL SOCIETY AND THE RISE
OF LIBERALISM IN RELIGION AND SCIENCE 22

Luther, Bacon, and Descartes 25
Thomas Hobbes: Individualistic Roots of Liberalism 27
John Locke 32

HOBBES AND LOCKE RECONSIDERED 38

Self-Interest Motivation 39

LIBERALISM BECOMES LIBERAL DEMOCRACY 40

Conservatism 42

SUGGESTED READINGS 47

3 LIBERALISM IN THE UNITED STATES   48

THE AMERICAN CONTEXT: "BORN EQUAL"   49

Participation: A Basic Value   51

JAMES MADISON AND THE CONSTITUTION OF 1787   52

Madison's View of Humanity   54
The Problem of Factions   55

MADISONIAN POLITICS: AMBITION
COUNTERACTING AMBITION   57

Restraints on Majority Tyranny   58
Control Through Representation   60
Control Through Institutions   62
Other Devices of Control   63

MADISON'S REMEDY: LIBERAL OR LIBERAL DEMOCRATIC?   65

Criticisms of Madison's System   66
Madison's View of Suffrage   67

THE RISE OF THE IMPERIAL PRESIDENCY   70

THE RISE OF MAJORITARIAN LIBERALISM   70

Avoiding Instability and Revolution   71
Majoritarianism in the British Tradition   73

MAJORITARIAN LIBERAL DEMOCRACY IN AMERICA   74

The Tension Between Liberty and Equality   75

ELITE THEORY IN MODERN LIBERAL THOUGHT   77

Power-Elite Analysis   79
Normative Democratic Elitism   81
The "Irony of Democracy"   83

JOHN RAWLS: A CONTRACT FOR JUSTICE   84

SUGGESTED READINGS   86

4 LIBERALISM: ALTERNATIVE VISIONS   87

Rousseau's State of Nature   88

The Social Contract   92

Jefferson's Self-Evident Truths   96

Jeffersonian Government   97

Property: Economic and Political Freedom   100
Happiness: The Ultimate Good   101
Jefferson's View of Humanity   102
Jeffersonian Politics   104

JOHN DEWEY AND THE LIBERAL TRADITION   106

Economics and the Common Man   110

FINAL THOUGHTS ON LIBERAL DEMOCRACY   111

SUGGESTED READINGS   112

5   MARXISM   113

MARX'S LIFE   114

Marx's Writing and the "Real" Marx   117

HEGEL'S PHILOSOPHY AND POLITICS   118

Transforming Logic   120
Hegel on Labor   121
Hegel's Political Theory   123

CRITICS OF HEGEL: FEUERBACH AND MARX   124

Marx on the Human Condition   125

HISTORY AND THE DEVELOPMENT OF CAPITALISM   130

The Progress of Humanity   133
Marx's View of the Bourgeois Class   134

THE CAPITALIST ECONOMIC SYSTEM: ITS DECLINE AND FALL   135

The Surplus Value of Labor   137
Increasing Profits at Worker Expense   137
Beyond Capitalism   139

SUGGESTED READINGS   142

6   MARXISM AND LENINISM   143

THE DIVISIONS WITHIN MARXISM—PEACEFUL
OR VIOLENT REVOLUTION?   144

Marxism of the Center   145
Marxism of the Right   146
Marxism of the Left   147
The Readiness of the Proletariat   147

TWENTIETH-CENTURY RUSSIA   148

LENIN'S LIFE   149

   Lenin's Years in Exile   150

THREE THEMES FROM LENINISM   152

   Revolutionary Leadership and the Party   152
   The Doctrine of Permanent Revolution   154

THE STATE AND REVOLUTION   155

   Dictatorship of the Proletariat   156

THE THEORY OF IMPERIALISM   159

   Wars of National Liberation   161

SUGGESTED READINGS   162

7   MARXIAN *PRAXIS:* THE SOVIET EXPERIMENT   163

STALIN'S RISE TO POWER   164

   Stalin's Life   166
   Lenin's Distrust of Stalin   167

MARXISM-LENINISM-STALINISM   169

   The World's First Totalitarian State   170
   Interests of the Soviet State Come First   171
   The Problems of Directing World Revolution   172

SOVIET MARXISM AFTER STALIN   173

   Denunciation of Stalin   175
   Changes in the International Movement   176
   The Doctrine of Peaceful Coexistence   178

PERESTROIKA   179

   Boris Yeltsin and Post-Soviet Marxism   185

SUGGESTED READINGS   187

8   CHINESE *PRAXIS:* THE POLITICAL THOUGHT OF MAO ZEDONG   189

CHINESE MARXISM   190

   The Life of Mao Zedong   191
   Imperialism and Mao's Rural Strategy   192

CHINA'S PATH TO SOCIALISM   195

    Mao on Contradiction   196

THE PRC AND THE USSR   198

    Revisionists and "Paper Tigers"   200

MAO ZEDONG AS A SYMBOL   201

CHINA AFTER MAO   203

    The Rise of Deng Xiaoping   204
    The Fall of Deng Xiaoping   207
    Concluding Thoughts   208

SUGGESTED READINGS   210

9   **FASCISM   211**

EVOLUTION OF THE DOCTRINE   215

    Benito Mussolini   215

CHARACTERISTICS OF FASCISM:
THE NATION-STATE, ANTI-LIBERALISM,
ANTI-BOLSHEVISM, CORPORATIVISM   217

    The Nation-State   218
    Anti-Liberalism   219
    Anti-Bolshevism   221
    Corporativism   222

NATIONAL GOALS, ELITISM, AND LEADERSHIP   224

    Fascism and Race   227
    Fascist Traits   228

SUGGESTED READINGS   230

10   **NATIONAL SOCIALISM   231**

GERMAN ROMANTICISM   232

    Emotionalism versus Rationalism   234

RACISM   236

    Influence of Richard Wagner   237
    Emphasis on Aryan Leadership   238
    The Struggle Between Aryans and Jews   240

ADOLF HITLER: RACE, LEADERSHIP,
AND THE NATIONAL-SOCIALIST STATE   241

    Mystical Exchange of Spiritual Energy   244
    Use of Propaganda   245
    Racist Internationalism   246

SUGGESTED READINGS   248

11   THEOPOLITICS AND ISLAMISM   250

THE ISLAMIC REVIVAL   251

    The Abrahamic Monotheistic Background   253
    Basic Beliefs and Values of Islam   257
    Politics and Struggle (Jihad) in Early Islam   259
    Leadership and Authority after Muhammad   261
    The Growth of Islam   263
    Theopolitics and Modern Ideology   266
    Reasons for Islamist Resurgence   268
    Puritanical and Reformist Tendencies   275
    Revolutionary, Participatory, and Socialization Strategies   279

COMPARATIVE IDEOLOGICAL REFLECTIONS
AND THE QUESTION OF ISLAMIC "TOTALITY"   284

SUGGESTED READINGS   287

**12   IDEOLOGICAL CONFLICT
IN THE TWENTY-FIRST CENTURY   289**

SOME THOUGHTS RECONSIDERED:
LIBERALISM'S CHALLENGE   291

    Competing Ideological Claims   293

SHADOWS OF THINGS THAT WILL (OR COULD) BE:
SOME FINAL THOUGHTS   294

SUGGESTED READINGS   299

INDEX   301

Preface

It has been less than a decade since publication of the earlier, second edition of *Philosophic Roots of Modern Ideology*. During that brief time, dramatic changes—some unforeseeable—have occurred and significantly altered our world. Among the most significant events was the surprising and rapid collapse of the Soviet Union, bringing to a conclusion, at least for the time being, this particular experiment in building a socialist state. When that superpower disintegrated, so too did the "Cold War" between the Soviet Union (*cum* Russia) and the United States, leading some political thinkers to assume *Pax Americana* would soon become the global reality or that we were witnessing the end of ideology itself. This, however, has yet to happen. Military actions around the world—from the Middle East to Somalia, from East Timor to Yugoslavia, to name just a few—show that global peace under American hegemony remains elusory. Moreover, the recent detonation of nuclear devices in India and in the Islamic Republic of Pakistan call further into question just how stable the world is, even with only one superpower. Influential analysts suggest that with the Cold War now over we have entered an age characterized by a clash of civilizations. Others suggest fundamental and irreconcilable conflicts exist among the forces of the global free market, those of ethnonational tribalism, and those of democracy.

Meanwhile, the People's Republic of China, the other great experiment in building socialism, found itself simultaneously enjoying the fiftieth anniversary of its founding while trying to learn to plot a course for itself without the presence of a helmsmen who can trace his roots back to its revolution. With the death of Deng Xiaoping, the last of China's celebrated founding generation, its new leaders must define China's place in a global economy where China is not only the most powerful communist nation but also seen by capitalists as an extraordinary market for future investment.

The fall of the USSR led to events that poignantly illustrate the fragility of the absolute sovereignty of states. Governments appear to be threatened on two fronts: the political and the economic. For the first time in modern history, in 1999 the sovereign right of a nation to govern itself was challenged as NATO, acting on behalf of other powerful states, elected to force its policies on Yugoslavia.

Regardless of one's views on the appropriateness of NATO's actions, there is no doubt that this event will have enormous consequences for the very concept of state sovereignty. In a less dramatic fashion, the European Union can tell its member nations what are acceptable social policies; and the United Nations, through sanctions and military actions, can try to force its mandate on any nation it perceives as a threat to world security. In a less obvious, but perhaps more effective manner, huge transnational corporations have been created; some have more money, power, and influence than many of the smaller nations, calling into question the ability of states to control individual economic entities. Who knows, perhaps like the city-state that preceded it, the nation-state may be in the process of undergoing profound changes that may lead to its transformation into a new form of political organization.

Finally, the world has witnessed the emergence of politically significant religious movements. The deadly actions of the Aum Shinrikyo in Japan and Heaven's Gate in California signify the provocative character of the smaller movements. On the larger scale, the resurgence of mass-based religiopolitics has played an increasingly visible role in the West, most obviously seen in the Christian Coalition's influence on American politics. It is also profoundly visible in the modern states of the Muslim world, where Islamists argue that God's way is the only way to social justice and they challenge both domestic and foreign governments that stand in their path. These religious activists challenge another fundamental assumption about modern state sovereignty, namely that matters of faith and politics should remain separate.

All of these factors have already altered the geopolitical landscape and produced important, sometimes tragic, human and political effects. More importantly, all will continue to change the world of politics profoundly and—if they are to be fully comprehended—must be understood within an ideological context.

This book is designed as an overview for readers who have little or no knowledge of the basic political idea systems of modern times. Given that purpose, we have constantly found ourselves in the frustrating position of oversimplifying, ignoring interesting side issues, and avoiding topics that in a longer work would surely be essential. What follows is original scholarship in the sense that the emphases of interpretations are dependent to a large extent on our own backgrounds and interests. We have, however, often relied heavily on the work of other scholars and will be happy if we have provided a partial synthesis of their work. In trying to accomplish this, we are acutely conscious of at times seeming to "parrot" the work of others—if this occurs too often we are sincerely apologetic. Along the same lines, it is difficult to sort those interpretations that are ours and those that have resulted from the hard work of others. We have benefited tremendously from the writings of scholars in these areas—many of whom we have never met. Our simple hope is that we have assisted in their endeavors by presenting these idea systems in a form whereby beginning students can more easily understand them. Our fondest hope is that this book will stimulate readers to explore idea systems in all of their complexity and richness, and that they will see the importance of ideas in themselves as well as in relation to what too often passes for the "real world." In short, we hope to initiate a process that will promote *political literacy*.

Much of the intellectual groundwork for what follows is to be found in David E. Ingersoll's 1971 *Communism, Fascism, Democracy*. In comparison, *The Philosophic Roots of Modern Ideology, 3rd Edition*, contains interpretations that are radically different from the former book, treats numerous topics not covered in the earlier work, addresses some of the same issues differently, and benefits from the major contributions and insights of co-authors Richard K. Matthews and Andrew Davison. We should also acknowledge that our treatment of American liberalism—particularly regarding Thomas Jefferson and James Madison—is largely based on Matthews's *The Radical Politics of Thomas Jefferson* and his *If Men Were Angels: James Madison and the Heartless Empire of Reason*. Similarly, the conceptual bases for our discussion of religious revivalism and theopolitics are drawn significantly from Davison's *Secularism and Revivalism in Turkey: A Hermeneutic Reconsideration*.

A final explanatory note concerning the use of footnotes and bibliography seems in order. We have used footnotes sparingly, and we have appended a brief bibliography to each chapter. This is in keeping with the nature of the work, which purports to provide an overview of an extremely complex subject matter and to stimulate students to explore further on their own. To that end it seemed desirable to avoid copious footnoting while leading the student directly to the primary sources and to other, more detailed works in the field. We are certain that many excellent books are absent from the bibliography, either because of a lack of knowledge or because of space limitations. We hope that the ones that are included will be sufficient to assist the student in the pursuit of further knowledge.

We would like to acknowledge the contributions, both direct and indirect, of the many persons who have made this book possible. Our students at the University of Delaware, Lehigh University, and Vassar College have contributed enormously, if often unwittingly, through their reactions to ideas we have presented. Our respective classrooms have often served as experimental laboratories for sections of this book. Matilda DiDonato and Dorothy Windish have provided typing assistance at various stages in the process. The following scholars have read and commented on the manuscript, and we have benefited from both their critiques and their encouragement: Katherine Restuccia, Ronald Hill, Yaroslav Bilinsky, Mark Miller, Norman Girardot, Caleb Elfenbein, Don Barry, Nicole Kieler, and especially the Prentice Hall reviewers: Gregory White, Smith College; Isaac Kramnick, Cornell University; and Asher Horowitz, York University.

Despite all this assistance, there are, no doubt, errors of omission and commission in what follows; if so, they are our responsibility.

D. E. I.

R. K. M.

A. G. D.

Acknowledgments

Displayed quotations in the text are from the following sources:

Opening Quote   Walter Kaufman, ed., *The Portable Nietzsche* (New York: The Viking Press, Inc., 1954; renewed 1982 Viking Penguin, Inc.), p. 91. Reprinted by permission of Viking Penguin, Inc.

Chapter 1   John Stuart Mill, *On Liberty* (Baltimore, Md.: Penguin, 1974), p. 95.

Chapter 2   Thomas Hobbes, *Leviathan*, C. B. Macpherson, ed. (Baltimore, Md.: Penguin, 1968), pp. 189–90.

Chapter 3   James Madison, *The Federalist*, Jacob E. Cooke, ed. (Middletown, Conn.: Wesleyan University Press, 1961), p. 374 ©1961 by Wesleyan University.

Chapter 4   John Dewey, *The Public and Its Problems* (Chicago: The Swallow Press, 1954), p. 149. Reprinted with the permission of Ohio University Press.

Jean-Jacques Rousseau, trans. by Allan D. Bloom, *Politics and the Arts*. Reprinted with permission of The Free Press, a Div. of Simon & Schuster, Inc. Copyright ©1960 by The Free Press.

Chapter 5   Karl Marx, "Theses on Feurerbach," in *The Marx-Engels Reader*, 2nd ed., Robert C. Tucker, ed. (New York: W. W. Norton & Company, 1978), p. 145.

Chapter 6   V. I. Lenin, "What Is to Be Done?" in *The Lenin Anthology*, Robert C. Tucker, ed. (New York: W. W. Norton & Company, 1975), p. 19.

Chapter 7   Mikhail Gorbachev, *Perestroika: New Thinking for Our Country and the World* (New York: Harper & Row, Publishers, 1987), p. 35.

Chapter 8   Mao Zedong, *Selected Works of Mao Tse-tung*, 4 Vols. (Peking: People's Publishing House, 1960), Vol. 1, p. 28.

Chapter 9   Benito Mussolini, "The Doctrine of Fascism," in *Social and Political Philosophy*, John Somerville and Ronald E. Santoni, eds. (Garden City, N.Y.: Doubleday and Company, 1963), p. 427.

Chapter 10   Adolf Hitler, *Mein Kampf,* trans. Ralph Manheim (Boston: Houghton Mifflin Company, 1971), p. 296.

Chapter 11   Imam Khomeini, *Islam and Revolution: Writings and Declarations of Imam Khomeini* (Berkeley, Calif.: Mizan Press, 1981), p. 275.

Jalal Al-e Ahmad. *Gharbzadegi (Westtruckness)*, trans. by John Green and Ahmad Alizadeh (Costa Mesa, Calif.: Mazda Publishers, 1982 [1964]), pp. 15–16, and 169.

Chapter 12   G. W. F. Hegel, *Reason in History* (Indianapolis: Bobbs-Merrill, 1977), p. 27.

The Philosophic Roots
of Modern Ideology

The surest way to corrupt a youth is to instruct him to hold in higher esteem those who think alike than those who think differently.

Nietzsche

The Origins of Political Ideologies

No one can be a great thinker who does not recognize that as a thinker it is his first duty to follow his intellect to whatever conclusions it may lead. Truth gains more even by the errors of one who, with due study and preparation, thinks for himself than by the true opinions of those who only hold them because they do not suffer themselves to think.

John Stuart Mill

THE CAVE: THE ILLUSION AND THE REALITY
OF EDUCATION

Think of Plato's cave. Perhaps the most powerful and frightening of all metaphors in Western political philosophy, it is an insightful allegory about the potential of domination and oppression, but ultimately about education and liberation.

Plato ingeniously compares the effect of education, and the lack of it, upon people to the following situation: Imagine a place where humans are living in an underground, cavelike dwelling. The cave contains a way out and up to the sun, but it is rather far removed from the people. They have been here from birth; their necks and legs are in bonds, so that they remain in place and can see only what is directly in front of them. Light inside the cave is provided by a fire burning somewhere behind and above them. Between the fire and our contented prisoners, somewhere behind and on a higher level, there is a path across the cave and along this a low wall has been built. It is similar to the screen at a puppet show in front of the performers who display their puppets above it. Imagine also that these puppeteers carry all kinds of objects, statues of people and animals, so that the figures are above the screening wall. Imagine also that some of the puppeteers are talking while others are silent.

In such a situation, our prisoners could see only the shadows that the fire casts upon the wall of the cave in front of them. Moreover, they would believe that the sounds (echoes) they hear are coming from these shadows. Since they can see neither their own bodies nor the bodies of the other people, they inevitably assume reality to be nothing else than the shadows and sounds of the puppeteers and their artifacts.

"Preposterous!" you say. "How could such people be either so stupid or so foolish as to be tricked by shadows on the wall?" And yet Plato claims this is precisely the human condition. We are all born into a type of comfortable slavery where it is extremely difficult for us even to become aware of our slavery, our ignorance, let alone become capable of discovering the difference (assuming there is a difference) between truth and illusion.

Continuing his tale, Plato asks us to imagine what would happen if one of the prisoners, suddenly released from bondage, turned around and looked into the light of the fire. Would that person not be temporarily blinded by the light? It would be impossible to see either the shadows or the things that produced them. Even though reality was now closer in that the person was at least looking in the right direction, one would be frightened, disoriented, and in pain. The world of comfortable illusions has been shattered: The fire has been seen. Yet our observer is in a state of confusion. Undoubtedly, one would prefer to retreat to the prior condition, having one's back securely pressed against the familiar wall. The desire to return to bondage is so strong that Plato claims that the prisoner may have to be dragged, by physical force, out of the cave and into the sunlight—the entire journey producing considerable physical pain and mental anguish. Once out of the cave, our prisoner again is incapable of seeing or understanding the simplest things even though surrounded by the light of day. Slowly, the eyes adjust, the senses become aware of their new surroundings, and the prisoner begins to differentiate among things in this new world. In time, according to the story, even the sun itself will become an object of attention and comprehension. Although this odyssey is no easy task, it too is part of becoming human. We all long for the comfort and security of a world filled with few questions, readily comprehensible answers, and universally accepted, seemingly correct values—the original paradise of the prisoners in the cave. Yet such a situation is both an illusion and, if paradise, the paradise of fools.

Originally, we said that Plato's allegory of the cave was a story of domination and oppression as well as education and liberation. It is appropriate to explain these terms and why they are important in Plato's tale. Domination is a peculiarly human condition of self-enslavement where individuals (mis)perceive their condition to be one of freedom. In Plato's story, the people in their original state think they are free; they think that they understand the nature of their world. He even suggests that games and prizes be devised for those best able to follow the shadows. As external observers of this situation, we, the readers, are aware of the more genuine reality. Nevertheless, the prisoners continue to hug their chains, believing that they are experiencing reality. Education is a slow, often painful process of exposing individuals to the truth, and the first step in that process is a recognition of the incomplete nature of the shadow world. In their original confines the prisoners had *a* way of looking at the world, and, at least for them, this manner of viewing reality made sense. However, it made more sense to view the situation from outside the confines of the cave. As the angle of vision was enlarged, so too was the freedom of our prisoner–cum–fully conscious human being. Liberation and education are thus intimately connected. In the experience of becoming educated, in developing knowledge about self and the world, our prisoner is being liberated from a condition of ignorance.

Plato's ultimate goal in *The Republic,* as well as his purpose in using the allegory of the cave, is to describe the process whereby human beings come to know the objective Truth—to contemplate, to the extent they are capable, the sun. Our concern in what follows is not with Plato's search for the sun, but with the initial process of breaking the shadowlike chains of conventional wisdom, believing that such a questioning process is the beginning of education and liberation.

Finally, we stated that the allegory of the cave is also a story of oppression, that is, direct, obvious physical control of people over others. This aspect is not as readily apparent in Plato's allegory. It occurs when the first prisoner, anxious to return to the comfort and security of the chains, is forcibly dragged out of the cave and into the sunlight.

Who might want to do this? Who is capable, either through force, persuasion, or influence, of leading others out of the cave? It is logical to assume that this person would have to possess knowledge of the way out of the cave if that person is to lead others to the sun. This person, then, would have to be a philosopher!

Since earliest times, political philosophers have often provided society with warnings of potentially disastrous courses of action. Like those of the mythical figure Cassandra, prophesies of doom, although true, are fated to fall on deaf ears.

Plato's allegory, as we understand it, contains such a portent. It warns against the inevitable attempts of humans—*armed with their vision of truth*—who feel compelled, for *our* own good, to drag by force their fellow humans out of the cave and into the "light." Each of the ideologies examined in this book contends that it understands reality and it knows what is best for humanity; each is militantly committed to help us see the light. Even though Plato believed that finding one's way out of the cave is an important part of being human and that other humans called philosophers will play a crucial role in this undertaking, he also knew that the process is extraordinarily difficult, exceedingly dangerous, and impossible with force.

Still, like it or not, all of us either have been, or presently are, in a position similar to the prisoners in Plato's cave. From our first days, we have been taught by well-intentioned puppeteers—parents, teachers, religious leaders, politicians, authority figures—what is best for us. What we must attempt to accomplish is to be able to differentiate between shadows and puppets, truths and illusion, so that we will be in a better position to understand the differences among what various people believe to be true, just, beautiful, and good.

What Is Ideology?

Contemporary students of modern idea systems have been unable to agree on a common definition of the term *ideology*. Some see an ideology as a rather loosely organized folk philosophy encompassing the totality of ideals and aspirations of a people. Others describe it as a weapon to be used in a battle, a club designed to flatten opponents. There are perhaps as many definitions of ideology as there are definers. The following discussion is offered with little hope of clearing up the confusion surrounding this term (desirable as that clarification may be), but to indicate initially what seem to be some of the salient differences between ideologies and other types of idea systems. First, some distinctions between traditional political philosophy, modern scientific (empiricist) theories of politics, and ideology are in order. While all three share the conviction that their task is to offer compelling interpretations about the existing environment, they differ in the scope of both their individual activities and their ultimate goals.

Traditional political philosophy—encompassing philosophers such as Plato, Augustine, Locke, Hegel, and Mill, to name a few—attempts to construct philosophic systems that are all-inclusive; it strives to explain every dimension of political reality—including making explicitly moral judgments about the range and scope of political power, the role of the state, and the meaning of liberty, justice, equality, and citizenship. Modern scientific approaches to political analysis attempt to be comprehensive as well, but in a different way. Their purpose is to describe and predict human behavior based on knowledge of "facts" and testable propositions (hypotheses) that link them together. Such analyses may even have the aim of altering political conditions to create certain focused outcomes in politics, such as increasing voter turnout. But modern empiricists purposefully restrict their endeavors to specific, empirically testable questions. They explicitly desire to avoid judgments of value, and they do not attempt to create grand theories of ideal political communities. Despite their differences, modern (empirical) political theory and classical political philosophy share one goal: the development of propositions that, taken together, are not contradictory and provide accurate descriptions of politics and political activity.

An important difference between the classical tradition and modern analysis is that classical philosophers felt compelled to go beyond mere description, to self-consciously judge the world as it is, and to propose remedies for perceived insufficiencies in it. Thus a Plato, while developing a theory of human nature and social interaction based upon his observation and insight, believed it necessary to set forth an ideal society wherein human beings would achieve their ultimate potential. As he saw it, his task was both descriptive (to explain how humans *do* live) and prescriptive (to explain how humans *ought* to live); he sought both to explain and to reform existing conditions.

Ideology's Distinguishing Features

In many respects, an ideology has more in common with traditional political philosophy than it does with modern political theory. An ideology also attempts a meaningful analysis of the existing environment to discover real truths concerning humanity. Although its analysis is frequently far less rigorous and less systematic than modern political theory or political philosophy, this is not always true. Marxism, for example, is certainly systematic and attempts to be quite rigorous. Whatever the case, a major distinguishing feature of ideology, as opposed to modern political theory, is its *action* orientation.

Ideologies provide a picture of a better, perhaps the best, life for humans—a *goal culture*. Moreover, they encourage mass political action to attain it. The kind of action differs according to the existing relationship between a given ideology and a given political context. If the goal culture already exists, then the ideology encourages action to sustain the status quo. Ideologies, therefore, often support the existing state of affairs by advocating activities to "stay the course." (Of course, if ideological insiders believe that the current goal culture is in the process of decay, there may be sharp calls for a return to the fundamental values of the ideology's founders.) On the other hand, if the goal culture of an ideology does not yet exist, then the ideology articulates a desire for massive changes in the existing environment based upon its picture of humanity as it *should* be. At some point in time, therefore, all ideologies take (or have taken) this form, finding fault with existing conditions and demanding changes in the immediate future. Remember, even liberal democratic capitalism has a history: It too went through a time when it was a newly emerging ideology that was not in power, was portrayed as a corrupting influence of the status quo, and sought to change the world.

Ideologies thus share with political philosophy the desire to shape significantly the world to conform to their conception of a goal culture. Indeed, it can be argued that what is often called the Age of Ideology came about as a reaction to classical philosophic thought and its apparent lack of concern with the processes by which change could be effected. Karl Marx put it quite nicely: "The philosophers have only *interpreted* the world; the point is to *change* it." A focal point for our ideologue is the realm of action, as opposed to the classical political philosophers who tended to spell out grand theories without demanding anyone take action.

Our ideologue, furthermore, is more concerned with the issue of time: When will the change occur? Immediacy frequently is crucial. These ideologies demand not simply change, but change now! While humans are surely capable of working toward a better society for their sons and daughters, the revolutionary fervor found in many ideological movements is more easily sustained if adherents believe utopia is attainable within their own lifetime. It is possible, however, to have an ideology that advocates gradual change in pursuit of the goal culture—democratic social-ism and much of the tradition of liberalism are examples. And you may recall, it is also true that ideologies may be highly supportive of the existing state of affairs. Still, it is our belief that a fundamental trait shared—in varying degrees, to be sure—by the ideologies largely discussed in this book is a desire for *change,* fre-quently massive change.

Many reasons can be cited for the extreme *action orientation* that character-izes modern ideologies. Such ideological movements are similar to the religious crusades of the Middle Ages. Adherents believe their ideal state to be possible (indeed, sometimes inevitable) on earth rather than in some heavenly kingdom. Ideological movements can be seen as political outgrowths of the tremendous sense of possibility generated by the Industrial Revolution, an optimism that believed humanity for the first time in history was capable of truly controlling its environment. Undoubtedly, such ideologies are part of the historic rise of the masses to political consciousness and participation, making them essentially twen-tieth-century phenomena. Whatever the reasons behind the revolutionary orien-tation of these modern ideologies, there is little doubt that we are dealing with a phenomenon quite different from the political thinking of the classical philoso-phers. Some of the preconditions for an ideological movement will be discussed throughout this book, but first it is necessary to explore some other general char-acteristics of ideologies.

As systems of ideas based on certain assumptions concerning humans and their relationship to the world, ideologies in general perform at least three func-tions: (1) They simplify the view of the world into select categories; (2) they demand action either for (when out of power) or against (when in power) change; and (3) they attempt to justify the course of action taken as well as the view of the world established. Each of these functions is dependent upon and gains support from the other two; therefore, it must be kept in mind that none of these can be understood, in the final analysis, in isolation from the other. A discussion of each function will be helpful.

1. To simplify: Ideologies attempt to make verifiable statements about real-ity by specifically focusing on human beings, and their relationship to other humans, as well as to the past and future world. Although ideologies are often backed by political philosophy, ideologies are usually (here Marxism may be the exception) neither as detailed nor as sophisticated as philosophic systems. Since their goal is to prescribe action, they must make an increasingly complex world more readily understandable. Ideologies tend to suspend the intellectual intricacies of the grand philosophical systems of an Aristotle or a Hegel, and make simple—if not simplistic—observations about the world. Consequently, the ideological system need not be terribly concerned with logical coherence. The emphasis is placed on presenting credible interpretations, ones that people will be willing to believe even in the face of evidence to the contrary; empirical verifiability based on rational thought processes is of secondary importance. What matters is not so much "what is," as what people *believe* to be the situation. So strong is this emphasis on belief, or faith, that one of the more common contemporary definitions of ideology is *belief system.*

Because of their desire to enlist mass support, ideologies in general are less concerned with logical niceties than are traditional political philosophy and modern political theory. Relying greatly on faith and belief, ideology is much less bothered by logical inconsistencies within the system of ideas. Indeed, it can be argued that for purposes of attracting dedicated followers, inconsistency is desirable in that it requires total belief. Reflection can stall action, which runs counter to the fundamental purpose of ideology. If individuals cannot rationally understand a system of ideas but nevertheless choose to become members of the movement, they can accept additional, even contradictory, changes in the idea system. Total belief in the validity of an ideology, however contradictory it may seem to another person, can produce a creature who will carry out any action that seems necessary to ensure success. Political ideologies, then, may be evaluated more in terms of their success in persuading individuals to embrace them rather than in terms (important to both political philosophy and modern political theory) of either accuracy or logical coherence.

In their attempt to simplify reality, ideologies make statements about the political world that are often presented in critical black-and-white terms of what is "right" and what is "wrong" with humanity, the world, and the future. In addition, change-oriented ideologies usually locate some fatal flaw(s) in the world that their converts must struggle to overcome to swing the balance away from the dark, evil side of humanity toward forces that will bring about its betterment. For Karl Marx it was alienation and the oppression of the proletariat by a capitalist economic system. For Adolf Hitler it was modern materialism and the unnatural domination of the Aryan race by the "Jewish menace." For James Madison it was the rise of sociopolitical factions and the difficulty of governing masses of people without creating tyranny or anarchy. For politically motivated religious revivalists, it is contempt for the perceived degeneration of traditional social morals. And, tied to the fatal flaw is usually a body of "sacred literature" that followers are expected, more or less, to embrace: the *Communist Manifesto, Mein Kampf,* The Constitution of the United States.

2. To demand: With their stress on action rather than mere comprehension, ideologies demand certain courses of behavior from their adherents. Toward this end, ideologies generate goal cultures, that is, ideal visions of conditions under which human beings can truly fulfill themselves. These goal cultures serve as guideposts toward which humanity must move. When the ideology is out of power, it demands active, continuous pressure—sometimes lawful, but not necessarily so—to bring about a change in the status quo. When the ideology is the status quo, it attempts to use its position to maintain its following and to help it move toward the appropriate goal, if that goal has not been as yet fulfilled.

3. To justify: One of Plato's more brilliant, but often forgotten, observations concerning humanity is his comment that people can love the beautiful. In the present context, we understand Plato to mean that all humans want to think of themselves as good, or just, or beautiful beings. How they define the good, the just, or the beautiful is subject to heated debate and sometimes armed conflict. Indeed, in many ways this very conception is at the heart of every ideological system. In spite of this subjective aspect, Plato's insight is of paramount importance to understanding ideologies: It shows, however defined, the motivating factor behind the clarion call for action.

To understand—or, more appropriately, to empathize with—each ideology, it is crucial to keep foremost in mind the fact that each of these ideologies believes that it alone knows the beautiful, it alone knows what is best for humanity. People do not want to believe themselves the creators of evil; rather, we all want to be thought of as agents of good. Difficult as it may appear at first, it is important to realize that Marx, Lenin, Madison, Jefferson, Mussolini, Hitler, and Khomeini all believed that their systems were best for those for whom they were addressing. Thus armed with their vision of the beautiful, each ideology uses its vision to justify and to support its own and its members' action.

In terms of this book, then, an ideology is any more or less systematic set of ideas about human nature, history, society, economics, government, and the relationships among these things. Each of these sets of ideas, moreover, explicitly or implicitly makes certain assumptions about reality, and on the basis of these assumptions demands action in support of its position. Once these assumptions are granted, or, as is more often the case, left unexamined, there is little left to debate: The conclusions drawn from the initial premises normally follow given the traditional rules of logic. It is important, then, both to expose and to examine the postulates upon which each of these ideological systems is constructed. To aid in this endeavor, it is important for you the reader to ask certain crucial questions of each idea system, questions that relate to people, history, society, and political economy. Among these questions are the following:

1. What is the ideology's concept of humanity? Is the nature of the species fixed? Is it variable? Evolutionary? Are people emotional and passionate creatures who must be led to fulfill themselves? Or are they both reasonable and sensitive beings who could be free and human only if allowed self-government? Are people selfish? Altruistic? Self-interested? Are they a combination of each?
2. What is society? Is it an artificial creation inevitably in conflict with individual self-interest? Or is it a natural and beneficial by-product of human development?
3. What is government? Is it a necessary arbitrator of competing interests? Is it the very embodiment of God's rational presence on earth? Or is it the agent of oppression of the ruling class? And if government is either necessary or desirable (a proposition anarchists would challenge), who should rule? People of property because they are more rational and have a greater stake in society? Or an all-powerful, mystically selected leader whose presence guarantees the destiny of a race?

4. What is the relationship between politics and economics? Are these separate, independent arenas in which people can find a meaningful existence if the political can be kept out of the economic? Or do these two areas automatically intertwine to the point where it becomes utter nonsense to talk about the one without the other?
5. What is history? Does history proceed through recurring cycles? Or is it more of a linear progression? Are people the fated pawns of God's will or of inevitable laws of history? Or does individual will and volition play a crucial part in human development?

Each of the idea systems examined will provide specific answers to these questions. Before discussing reasons for and approaches to studying these ideologies, we must briefly examine some of the factors that permit many people to call this the Age of Ideology.

MASS MOVEMENTS

If, as has been argued, the ideologies to be discussed are distinctive in their demand for and ability to bring about change in the existing state of affairs, they must develop a vehicle for effecting that change. While a discussion of the highly complex phenomena of revolutionary change is not possible within these brief confines, the enlisting of mass numbers of people in pursuit of a new society is such a central part of the Age of Ideology that it cannot be overlooked.

There have been numerous attempts to define the conditions that are conducive to the development of revolutionary movements. Classical Marxism contends that the major factor in revolutionary development is an ever-increasing discrepancy in the amount of wealth in modern society—the rich get richer and fewer, the poor poorer and more numerous, and the latter eventually revolt. Other theories contend that the inability of political leaders to respond to demands arising in the society results in a decline in support for the regime and provides the preconditions for revolution. Still others assert that the inability of a society to fulfill the ideals of its culture produces a tension between those ideals and actual practice, leading to growing dissatisfaction with the existing conditions. We know also that the revolution of rising expectations, whereby the lot of once poverty-stricken groups in society is significantly improved, does not automatically produce contentment but can lead to demands for greater improvement. Whatever theory or combination of theories is correct, most students of the phenomenon would agree that a vital element in producing revolutionary change is the development of an ideology that coordinates the various dissident elements in the unstable society, gives direction to their frustrations, and provides leadership for their cause.

Why do people become members of a revolutionary movement? Is there a particular type of individual who is attracted by a mass movement? Does the content of the ideology really matter or is the relief that a person apparently feels in joining a mass movement of prime importance? These are but some of the important questions that the student of mass movements must ask; the answers, unfortunately, do not come easily. There does seem to be agreement that converts to an ideology experience a tremendous feeling of exhilaration, a discovery of a new, more important identity when they enter the ranks. There is evidence that people who see their status in the present society declining are prime recruits. The petite bourgeoisie, the shopkeepers and small merchants in Nazi Germany whose status was severely shaken by the Depression of the 1930s, provided one of the important groups for the Nazi movement. Others have theorized that people who are unable to succeed in the existing society are a major source of potential revolutionaries. Because of this inability to succeed, they experience overwhelming feelings of personal guilt, which can be relieved only by attacking the society or particular, powerful groups within it; if it is the existing society and its values that are wrong, the unsuccessful person need feel no guilt. In joining a revolutionary movement the individual renounces the old self and all the failures attached to it to become a member of a group and attain a new identity. Most observers agree that this "giving up of self" is a prime characteristic of a revolutionary and that the selflessness often produced by membership is a truly remarkable phenomenon. Hannah Arendt in her classic study of *The Origins of Totalitarianism* puts it this way:

> The disturbing factor in the success of totalitarianism is rather the true selflessness of its adherents: it may be understandable that a Nazi or a Bolshevik will not be shaken in his conviction by crimes against people who do not belong to the movement or are even hostile to it; but the amazing fact is that neither is he likely to waver when the monster begins to devour its own children and not even if he becomes a victim of persecution himself, if he is framed and condemned, if he is purged from the party and sent to a forced-labor or a concentration camp. On the contrary to the wonder of the whole civilized world, he may be willing to help in his own prosecution and frame his own death sentence if only his status as a member of the movement is not touched.[1]

If this is the case—if it is the emotional catharsis that accompanies group membership that is most important—one must ask whether the content of the ideology really matters at all. Would, for example, our "true believer" be as eager to join a revolutionary communist group as he would a fascist movement? We know that some of the world's most committed anticommunists are former party members whose "god" failed. Further, Hitler at one time asserted that communists were the easiest people to win over to the doctrines of Nazism, implying that the capacity for belief was more important than the actual goals of the movement. While there may be some truth to these assertions, in all probability the content of the ideology establishes certain limits for the potential revolutionary. It is a bit difficult, for example, to conceive of a well-established capitalist joining a movement that vows to destroy capitalism or a Jew embracing the Nazi doctrine of anti-Semitism, although such situations have occurred. A person's culture and the values the person holds dear probably should not be antithetical to the goals of the revolutionary movement. Indeed, a perceived assault on one's culture has proven to be a cause for solidarity around revolutionary goals as in the case of Iran during the 1970s. Here, cultural changes generated by Shah Reza Pahlavi's determined Westernization campaign were condemned by his opponents as culturally imperialistic, "Westoxication," and thus became part of the dynamic that culminated with the 1979 Islamic revolution led by forces claiming to be more culturally authentic. To be sure, whether the motivation is cultural or otherwise, it may be easier to convert a true believer to another ideology once that individual has developed

[1] Hannah Arendt, *The Origins of Totalitarianism* (New York: Meridian Books, 1958), p. 307.

the capacity for total belief in any set of ideas. Whatever the case, this discussion is not meant to support the notion that all people committed to ideological goals are somehow demented or emotionally unstable—surely idealism and a desire to find some meaningful course of action in one's life can be both honorable, in and of itself, as well as prime motivating forces in the development of a progressive movement.

Leadership Roles

Even if we can support the concept of a true believer who gives up everything in life to be a member of a revolutionary group, there are important figures active in ideologies who, while totally dedicated to the cause, are also quite aware of more pragmatic goals. As mentioned earlier, most ideologies seem to have a priesthood or a small circle of leaders who can manipulate the ideology to conform to environmental changes as well as formulate revolutionary strategy. While the truly modern element of contemporary ideological movements is their ability to enlist masses of people in the cause, the leadership role of a small cadre of adherents is nevertheless quite essential.

Lenin's concept of the role of the Communist party in fomenting and carrying out a revolution is probably the best example of the relationship between leaders and masses. Although Lenin did not believe it would be possible to have a coup d'état staged by a small group of dedicated Bolsheviks, and insisted that mass support was a prerequisite for successful revolution, his manipulation of Marxist ideology to give it immediate appeal to the Russian peasant clearly showed that the followers were being used by the leadership elite. Moreover, the tendency of revolutionary movements to develop one individual as the personification of the movement (Hitler, Mussolini, Lenin, Mao Zedong, Khomeini) generally gives that person great latitude in interpreting the ideology. Perhaps the safest summary of ideological movements is to say they are essentially phenomena of the modern age, potentially involving masses of dedicated people, and they seem to be an essential element in producing revolutionary change. While the content of the ideology seems to be important in eliciting mass support, we are not, from the ideological perspective, quite sure just how much it matters.

Here, then, are some indications of the problems involved in the study of idea systems, as well as some reasons that show why such a study is worthwhile. The phenomena of the revolutionary personality and the general subject of the role of mass movements, while they are very important aspects of the investigation of idea systems, are subjects that are somewhat tangential to our main topic.

Why Study Ideologies?

Anyone who attempts to write a brief survey of the intellectual foundations of major modern ideologies will probably be greeted by great cries of laughter from a whole host of sincere students and colleagues. The complexity of the subject matter is such that one is open to all sorts of possible criticism. The expert on the development of Marxian thought immediately may declare the task impossible, students of Nazi Germany may deem it superficial, committed liberals may assert that it is unneeded, and the pragmatist may scream that it is worthless, for ideas have little effect in the real world of action. While all of these criticisms may be in part correct, and some finally just, the fact remains that a general knowledge of a subject matter is better than no knowledge at all.

What follows is an attempt to provide that general knowledge of the major systems of political ideas of modern times. What is desired is a presentation that is simple but not simplistic, and which makes no claims to be comprehensive, yet satisfactorily explains central themes. Such a purpose is easily stated, but even a superficial examination of the existing literature will indicate how difficult it is to achieve. There are, for example, almost as many ways of approaching the thought of Karl Marx as there are Marxian scholars. Many people believe that fascism is best seen as a phenomenon peculiar to the period between World Wars I and II and is hardly contemporary; or, conversely, that religious revivalisms are merely momentary blips in history that will conclude by inevitably escorting the clergy out of the halls of political power. Finally, others maintain that it is impossible to speak, in general, of either liberal or democratic thought because both are diverse and changing traditions.

A further complication is the common identification of these systems of ideas with particular nation-states. When the average American speaks of communism, the referent normally is the former Soviet Union or China, while fascism brings forth dark images of the Holocaust and Nazi Germany. Yet it is quite appropriate to see these nation-states as highly imperfect attempts to realize sets of ideals that transcend the political systems that invoke them. That is, these states attempt to apply the ideas advanced in the ideology, but the ideology itself exists independently of them. One of the underlying assumptions of this book is that ideologies are capable of being profitably studied as systems of ideas—regardless of their applications in the "real world." Obviously, when a major contributor to the development of an ideology is also the head of a political system, as, for example, in the case of Lenin, or, in a certain sense, Madison, the ideological contributions may have a quite direct effect in political action. Even so, Lenin's contributions to Marxism may be studied as an effort to keep Marx's thought and vision relevant in a new historical context. In the same light, Madison the politician may be separated from Madison the theoretician and his contributions in each area judged separately, even while we realize that they were very much interrelated in his personal life.

Although the complex question of the relationship of ideas to action is beyond the scope of this book, a few tentative remarks on that subject are in order. It is extremely difficult if not impossible to prove a cause-and-effect relationship between ideas and action. When someone declares he or she acted in a particular way because the principles of Marxism-Leninism commanded it, how are we to respond? Obviously, the person could simply be lying, using the ideological argument as a rationalization to disguise the real reasons for action. Again, the person could be deluding himself or herself, being unaware of the actual motivation for action—a German SS officer exterminating Jews for the good of the Fatherland while actually giving vent to his own latent anti-Semitism. Most often, the real reasons for any action are so complex that it is impossible to single out any particular factor that triggered the action. Having said all this, it still seems obvious that idea systems do affect human behavior in some way, even if the exact relationship cannot be conclusively proven. The persistence of the Soviet Union in retaining for many years the obviously incorrect genetic theories of Lysenko because they supported the ideological goal of producing a new proletarian generation, the absurd tenacity of Hitler in following minute details written in *Mein Kampf,* the radical democrat's enduring belief in the essential goodness of the common person in spite of much evidence to the contrary are but some examples of the effects of ideology. When we recognize the tremendous impact particular cultures and values have upon individual development we cannot doubt the importance of ideas in influencing action. This, then, is an initial reason for studying ideologies: They seem to have a good deal to do with influencing and constituting human behavior such that certain actions, policies, and institutions would not be what they are without them.

The attempt to understand the relationship between idea systems and political reality characterizes a field of political analysis called *hermeneutics.* As an alternative tradition of social inquiry that focuses on the nature of interpretation, its goals differ from those of classical political theory and modern scientific theory. Hermeneutics maintains that to understand either individual or collective political action, we must first understand the concerns and purposes of those who are participating in that action. It assumes that human action is meaningful precisely because human beings have specific ideas, concerns, and goals in mind when they act. To be sure, unconscious motivations may be a complicating factor, but the initial interpretative step must be to try to understand what the political actors think they are doing and why they are doing it.

Unlike modern scientific theory, which seeks to ascertain causal relationships between facts (like income level, or years of education, and voting patterns), hermeneutics aims to provide interpretations of the purposes of human political action as they are expressed in language—words, texts, symbols, and other forms of communication. In addition, hermeneutics assumes that to understand either individual or collective political experience, one must understand the concepts and symbols that *"constitute"* experience for the actor(s). That, after all, is what significantly makes the experience what it is. Consequently, hermeneutic interpretation frames the core analytical interests of ideological analysis. A few examples may help clarify this matter.

Karl Marx, for example, would not have organized communist workers to overthrow capitalism without the ideas he and Friedrich Engels articulated in *The Communist Manifesto* calling directly for such action. If Marx had not conceived of capitalism as ultimately a destructive social system, why would he advocate its overthrow? Put differently, if Marx had been convinced by Adam Smith's views of the liberating effects of free enterprise, would he still have dedicated his life to ending human alienation? Probably not. In order to understand both Marx's own revolutionary activities and those of the larger communist movement, one must understand the concepts, goals, and purposes that constituted them. The relationship between the ideas Marx held, and the actions he (and others) took, is constitutive; without those formative ideas, Marx as well as many other people—including both those who followed and those who attacked him—probably would have done something entirely different with their time and lives. Similarly, the activities associated with the Holocaust cannot be fully understood without understanding the doctrines of the Nazi ideology that constituted them. Nor, of course, can actions taken against Marxists or Nazis by liberals or fascists be understood without understanding their respective ideas and concerns. Hermeneutics maintains, then, that the way to grasp ideological concerns is by understanding the concepts and their meanings in the minds of those who carried them out. And the way to do this is by studying the languages of their politics. Ayatollah Khomeini, for instance, would not have become the leader of a new Islamic government were it not for his concept of "Governance by the Grand Jurist"; similarly, global capitalists might not invest in the world market without their particular conception of "profit maximization." These concepts make various aspects of political life what they are to such a degree that without those ideas, the participants in political life might well be doing something entirely different. Who knows, Khomeini may have become a counterrevolutionary (which, from the liberal perspective, he was) and Mussolini a liberal! As an alternative to modern scientific inquiry, then, hermeneutics requires that political analysts provide interpretations of the concepts, concerns, and purposes constitutive of political life as expressed through language.

Hermeneutic interpretations do not enable the kinds of precise predictions that modern scientific theory aims to achieve, but they do help us to understand one of the most significant bases for political change—the human capacity to give meaning to experience. Hermeneutics does not expect to provide strong predictions about political phenomena precisely because it recognizes that human beings are capable of conceptualizing, and more importantly, *reconceptualizing* their experiences and concerns. It keenly recognizes that change, even unpredictable change, is a permanent feature of life. As purposive creatures, human beings can act with different purposes, both across different cultures and within the same culture. Indeed, individual human beings can, and often do, act with different purposes in a single lifetime. Mussolini, for instance, started as a dedicated socialist before he reconceptualized the political landscape and transformed himself into a fascist. When change occurs, individuals may coin new terms for their experience or assemble previous ideas in innovative ways. When the concepts and goals that constitute life change, most often the actions and relationships of life change as well. Prediction in ideological analysis is extremely difficult for the simple reason that human beings may alter their purposes, goals, and concerns in unexpected ways; consequently, the direction or content of conceptual change may be close to impossible to identify in advance. It may be helpful to think of it this way. Predictability would be more probable *if* it were possible to rule out change. *If, in a given situation,* we knew that no significant change had occurred relative to actor(s) x, y, and/or z, then we could predict how, in all likelihood, the actor(s) would behave in the given context. This is similar to the disclaimer *ceteris paribus*—"other things being equal"—of which economic theorists are so fond. Hermeneutic analysts are critically aware that "other things being equal" is rarely the case.

While ideological analysis in the tradition of hermeneutics will not replicate the precision of a natural scientist, it nevertheless does enable us to understand certain conceptual patterns and to anticipate why, in a given ideological setting, certain political actions may be more likely to occur than others. For example, by understanding the full meaning of the concept of imperialism, we may be able to anticipate possibilities for national liberation struggles against foreign exploitation under conditions of colonialism; and, from the perspective of the other side of this ideological coin, to be able to understand the conceptual rationale for capitalism within liberal democracy, we may be able to anticipate Western advocacy of globalized markets as a means of political and economic reform and growth.

The different hermeneutic assumptions may be illustrated in the hypothetical case of a radical Marxist activist who, at some point in his or her life, decides to become a stockbroker. At some crucial moment, he or she must have altered his or her conception of goals and purposes. Perhaps she decided that the workers' revolution would never come; or perhaps he needed a lot of money to cover unexpected medical expenses. The point is that with an alteration of purposes, comes an alteration in behavior. The person who may have once organized workers outside company gates may now go through an entirely different set of activities. Where meanings change, so too, do actions. Meanings are constitutive of activity in this sense. Similarly, think of a married woman who reconceptualizes her place in the family and social structures from one of "housewife" to one of "equal and independent contributor to society." Just as former secularists have become religious revivalists, the former "housewife" may become the head of a major social institution. Hermeneutics suggests that both the content and the direction of these changes are rather difficult to anticipate in advance: Human purposes change in the context of life in ways that may not be knowable in advance.

This seems particularly true concerning any future changes in an ideology itself, for to be able to anticipate the next set of ideas relevant to vast numbers of individuals is precisely to articulate those ideas. The only thing that is knowable in advance is that a change of mind, heart, and action is always possible. This is the starting point for hermeneutical analysis. It is, furthermore, the reason why prediction is not very likely and why accurate predictability is of secondary concern to understanding the constitutive terms of political life. In fact, it often is the goal of the leading ideologues to change the attitudes of the average person by altering the content of his or her understanding about society, government, and political possibilities. Ideologists seek to make sense of life for large numbers of people and to mobilize them for particular purposes (as we have said, either in defense of, or against, the status quo). Whether these ideologists are the famous founders of the ideologies or those who, like Mikhail Gorbachev or John Dewey, have innovated from within them, ideologists share a desire to give conceptual shape to unattained goals. In doing this, they seek to redirect the energies shaped by one set of ideas to those shaped by another. They seek to change society by changing the ideas and thereby the actions of its inhabitants. For Marx, workers should cease to view themselves as competitive beneficiaries of capitalism. For Locke, the king's subjects should no longer view his power as an authorized grant of God. Ideologists want to shift human understanding in order to change human behavior. Indeed, what makes the ideologists whose ideas we analyze here profoundly important in the modern world is that they offered new interpretations of life that captured the hearts and minds of millions of people. They expressed widespread concerns, articulated goals, and described ways of achieving those goals that masses of people have made their own. As such, the ideologists have articulated ideas according to which masses of human beings have acted to change the world.

Ideological analysis, as we understand it, is therefore part of the broader hermeneutic tradition of political inquiry concerned with interpretation of the various languages of politics that constitute political reality—as it has been, as it is, and as it inevitably changes under the direction of new and powerful ideas. This leads us to additional reasons for exploring idea systems.

As already indicated, it is worthwhile to study systems of ideas irrespective of their effect in producing action in the real world. The ideological systems under discussion are all attempts to say meaningful things about humans and their environment. Thus, we may judge the accuracy of their descriptions. Are humans, as Karl Marx believed, inevitably in a condition of alienation under a capitalist system? Does the fragmentation and depersonalization of a modern liberal democratic society produce human beings who are stunted in their growth, unable to be truly human, as Mussolini would have us believe? Are these accurate portrayals of reality? Does the democrat's belief in humanity's capacity for self-governance ring true in light of the discoveries of modern psychology and sociology? Are secular styles of living essentially and inevitably unethical as *theopolitical* ideologists assert? Whatever the ultimate answers to these questions may be, their descriptions of humans and the human condition may be subjected to tests of their validity and found either sufficient or wanting. Since each of the ideologies ultimately seeks converts, their ability to make correct statements about reality may be influential in their achieving the desired mass support.

The Competition for Hearts and Minds

The final reason that can be advanced for this type of study is that all ideologies are in present-day competition for the "hearts and minds" of humanity. Whether stated in terms of the "free world" versus "atheistic communism" or "holy wars" against "imperialistic capitalism," the war for converts has waxed and waned ever since the beginning of the twentieth century. This makes the task of the student of ideologies extremely difficult. While the ultimate objective must be the understanding of ideologies, the student is already either disposed toward or committed to one of them. The classical problem that social science faces in suspending particular judgments about its subject matter is thus particularly difficult in the study of idea systems. Can a person who believes that one particular ideology is better than another temporarily free himself or herself of that belief to attempt to understand another? This book tries to do precisely that, and it supplies specific suggestions as to how this might be attempted.

Ultimately, of course, we will fail in this attempt, for impartial investigation is seldom achieved, and in this area it seems an impossible ideal. Yet the attempt must be made, for the reflexive anticommunist, the unthinking anticapitalist, and the unreflective martyr do a disservice to human intelligence by not attempting to understand the phenomena they are trying to combat. Indeed, they weaken their own cause by knowing little of their enemy. Even the most committed liberal democrat must admit that some sort of vaguely defined communism has been attractive to many people during the past century, just as an avowed communist must realize that people continue to flock to and die under the banner of liberal democracy. The intelligent response to such facts is to ask why; to attempt to understand what it is in these idea systems that accounts for their continuing viability; or, in the face of their demise (apparent or real), why they have been rejected. It is clear that the apparent collapse of communism in the Soviet Union did not entail either the end of Marxian politics or the inevitable and total triumph of liberal democracy. The end product of sincere attempts at understanding may well be a renewed dedication to fight the enemy, but the combat will be more effective with a knowledge of the opponent's strengths and weaknesses. For this reason, the book devotes a larger amount of space to the presentation of nonliberal ideologies: It will, after all, be read primarily by those who believe that liberal democratic ideas are, if not absolutely correct, at least the best possible in an imperfect world. It is these persons who must try to understand the appeal of the other ideologies and must decide whether the criticisms of democratic liberalism are just.

Why then, one might ask, include liberal democracy at all? Primarily because it is only by comparing and contrasting all the different portrayals of reality that one can come to a fuller understanding of each. As the following discussion will show, in spite of their marked differences, the ideologies are also related in many ways. And finally, we have a vague suspicion that our "committed democrat" (or "committed capitalist") is not as fully aware of the strengths and weaknesses of liberal democracy as is possible, and knows little of the phenomena of Marxism, fascism, national socialism, and religious fundamentalism and their relationship to liberalism.

Here, then, are some initial reasons for studying ideologies as well as some of the difficulties to be encountered. Before moving to a presentation of the specific ideologies, we want to reemphasize a few crucial points.

Why Unpopular Ideas?

Earlier in our discussion, Plato, through the allegory of the cave, served as our guide in explaining why it was necessary for humans to break the chains of conventional wisdom and see the "shadows" on the wall of the cave for what they were—imperfect copies of a more fundamental reality. However, as we noted, in Plato's mind this was but the initial step in an arduous process of discovering objective truths (the puppets themselves, and ultimately the sun), which he believed were universally correct. Proper education, at least for some, would lead to the discovery of ultimate reality. Sure of his truth (or, at least, the appropriate process for discovering it), it became Plato's task to instruct others as to the true nature of reality. We make no such claim for what follows. Rather, it is our belief that the processes of education and liberation are most effectively accomplished—at least in the beginning—through an examination of alternative views of reality. In a sense, we will be examining differing perspectives of the shadows on the cave wall, always holding out the possibility that one perspective, or a combination of them, may provide at least a glimpse of the sun. This is, we understand, somewhat of a liberal bias in that it presupposes no "objective truth" to be communicated to the reader, no absolute knowledge to be conveyed. Plato, in that he presupposes the existence of such truth, is therefore an inadequate guide for the remainder of our journey. A far better one is the liberal British philosopher John Stuart Mill (1806–1873), who with extraordinary effectiveness describes the desirability of trying to understand ideas that may seem foreign or are unpopular.

Mill on Toleration

By the middle of the nineteenth century, England was well into the Industrial Revolution: Industry, business, and finance were developed; a working class was evolving; and a fear of what Mill and the French student of democracy Alexis de Tocqueville called the "tyranny of the majority" was commonplace. Beyond the reaches of the coercive power of government to control the opinions and beliefs of its citizens, Mill was alarmed by the potentially threatening power of public opinion to stifle, if not silence, the flowering of divergent viewpoints and lifestyles. Out of the social context of this modern, industrialized world, Mill, in the second chapter of his classic book *On Liberty*, stated what has become the cornerstone of the liberal democrat's arguments for toleration and freedom of expression:

> If all of mankind minus one were of one opinion, mankind would be no more justified in silencing that one person, than he, if he had the power, would be justified in silencing mankind.[2]

Mill begins his defense of free thought and open discussion with these ringing words; he follows this with a fourfold argument for toleration of unpopular ideas: (1) The opinion that is being suppressed may possibly be true. Of course, those who are attempting to suppress the opinion deny its truth, but they themselves may be wrong. Hence, Mill concludes that any silencing of discussion is an assumption of infallibility. The history of the famous Italian astronomer Galileo Galilei is illustrative of Mill's point. In 1633, when papal authorities forced Galileo to recant his support of Copernicus's heliocentric theory of the universe, they simultaneously attempted to rob humankind of the opportunity to exchange falsity for truth.

Mill's first case, then, assumes the unorthodox opinion to be the correct view. But what if the new opinion is in error? On this point (2) Mill maintains that, although the opinion may for the most part be incorrect, it may nevertheless contain a portion of truth. It is rare, he argues, that an opinion is wholly true or wholly false. It is therefore important to allow the less correct opinion to see the light of

---

[2] John Stuart Mill, *On Liberty* (Baltimore, Md.: Penguin, 1974), p. 76.

day, to challenge and to refute the erroneous portion of that view, and thereby allow humankind the chance to accept and to embrace the grain of truth it may contain. Mill reasons that truth is often found in a delicate balance between two or more contrasting positions. Pushing his argument to its extreme, Mill claims that (3) even if the commonly held opinion is not only true, but the whole truth, unless it is continually and vigorously challenged and tested, it risks the danger of being held in the manner of prejudice, rather than the end result of a rigorous thinking process based on rational grounds. And, if this occurs, it is but a matter of time until (4) "the meaning of the doctrine itself will be in danger of being lost or enfeebled." In place of a vital truth, humanity will have unwittingly substituted a dead dogma. So grave are the consequences of losing the dynamic process of critical dialogue, Mill argues, that if none is present the society should appoint an advocate of the minority view.

> So essential is this discipline to a real understanding of moral and human subjects, that if opponents of all important truths do not exist, it is indispensable to imagine them, and supply them with the strongest arguments which the most skillful devil's advocate can conjure up.[3]

Mill argues that we, as individuals, should struggle to identify and to empathize with those opinions we initially find unacceptable so that we may test our own truths and determine if our rejection is based on reason or prejudice. Mill urges us to emulate Cicero—philosopher, politician, and the greatest of all Roman orators.

> What Cicero practiced as the means of forensic success, requires to be imitated by all who study any subject in order to arrive at the truth. He who knows only his own side of the case, knows little of that. His reasons may be good, and no one may have been able to refute them. But if he is equally unable to refute the reasons on the opposite side; if he does not so much as know what they are, he has no ground for preferring either opinion.[4]

Become a "True Believer"

In the wisdom of Plato and Mill (strange bedfellows, some would say), we find reasons for attempting to liberate ourselves from the ghosts of our past, warnings about the perils of the education/indoctrination process, and guidelines on how to proceed in this Herculean journey to humanness.

Although it is no small task to attempt to walk the line between Plato's warning of indoctrination and Mill's guidelines for open inquiry, this is precisely the position taken by this book. Although our presentation of each ideological system is inevitably skewed by the authors' individual backgrounds and personal beliefs, we will strive to present in as persuasive and favorable a manner as possible each of the ideologies under discussion. It is the reader's task not only to attempt to

[3] Ibid., p. 99.
[4] Ibid., p. 98.

understand the systems presented but also to empathize with and to become, at least a few hours a week, a "true believer." Specifically, this means you must try to be Karl Marx when communism is the focus of the discussion, James Madison when American liberalism is under examination, Benito Mussolini when Italian fascism is being presented, and Ayatollah Khomeini when Iranian Islamic theopolitics is the center of our attention. To be sure, this is hard. And, yet, we too are persuaded by the powerful imagery of Plato's cave and the compelling logic of Mill's arguments for free discussion. Like Aristotle, Plato's student, we believe people are political, are uniquely human, when they exercise their capacity of *logos:* reasoned speech. Aristotle believed that it was humanity's species-specific capacity to communicate with one another about what is good and what is bad, what is just and what is unjust, about, in short, how we *ought* to live. We will, therefore, consciously attempt to provide an atmosphere where you will be able to carry on a rational dialogue about political ideology, where you will be able to present many of the arguments *for,* rather than against, each of the ideologies presented. If this position is openly embraced and practiced for each ideology, the critical perspective will take care of itself; for in the final analysis, each ideology is the refutation of its competing system. Once again, it may not be the case that any one of the systems contains the whole truth, for Mill may indeed be correct when he argues that the truth may be contained in a delicate balance of the cases presented.

SUGGESTED READINGS

ARENDT, HANNAH, *The Origins of Totalitarianism.* New York: Meridian Books, 1958.

BALL, TERENCE, JAMES FARR, and RUSSELL L. HANSON, eds., *Political Innovation and Conceptual Change.* Cambridge: Cambridge University Press, 1989.

BELL, DANIEL, *The End of Ideology: On the Exhaustion of Political Ideas in the Fifties.* New York: Collier Books, 1962.

CHADWICK, OWEN, *The Secularization of the European Mind in the Nineteenth Century.* Cambridge: Cambridge University Press, 1975.

DALLMAYR, FRED R., and THOMAS MCCARTHY, eds., *Understanding and Social Inquiry.* Notre Dame: University of Notre Dame Press, 1977.

DUNN, JOHN, *The History of Political Thought and Other Essays.* Cambridge: Cambridge University Press, 1996.

FREIRE, PAULO, *Pedagogy of the Oppressed.* New York: Continuum Press, 1982.

MACPHERSON, C. B., *Democratic Theory: Essays in Retrieval.* Oxford: Clarendon Press, 1973.

MANNHEIM, KARL, *Ideology and Utopia.* New York: Harcourt Brace and World, 1936.

MILL, J. S., *On Liberty.* Baltimore, Md.: Penguin, 1974.

2

Individualistic (Market) Liberalism

And because the condition of Man . . . is a condition of Warre of every one against every one; in which case every one is governed by his own Reason; and there is nothing he can make use of, that may not be a help unto him, in preserving his life against his enemyes; It followeth, that in such a condition, every man has a Right to every thing; even to one another's body.

Thomas Hobbes

Although *liberty* is obviously at the root of *liberalism*, it is not, nor has it ever been, precisely clear what is meant by liberty. The word has had different meanings to different people. Liberalism is a diffuse system of ideas and values that has been associated with such widely divergent thinkers as Thomas Hobbes, James Madison, John Stuart Mill, and John Rawls. Since there appears to be considerable liberty in the very use of the word *liberalism*, it is important to identify those common characteristics that are embraced by most of its proponents.

American liberals often tend to assume that all people are in favor of liberty or freedom and are sometimes surprised to discover that such is not the case. When the Tory party in early nineteenth-century England first attached the Spanish label *liberales* to its opponents, it was meant in a negative sense. The Tories were directly linking the opposition with a foreign political movement, thereby suggesting that there was something un-English in their new ideas. This illustrates the historic fact that in its beginning, liberalism played a revolutionary, sometimes destructive, role in Europe by challenging, altering, and often smashing the values, customs, habits, and opinions of the traditional culture. In fact, liberalism was received originally, by some segments of European society, without much enthusiasm.

In this section of the book we will take an extended look at liberalism. In the present chapter, we hope to show the radical character of the doctrine as it first appeared in the realm of ideas by contrasting it to the ethos of *preliberal* society. A historical approach to liberalism will accomplish this and help clarify the distinction, too often overlooked, between liberalism and democracy. The simple truth of the matter is that mankind first devised a liberal society that, with the pressure of time, developed into a liberal democratic society. In the subsequent chapter we will continue this discussion by examining how liberalism began and ultimately developed in the United States. Finally, in the third chapter on the topic, we will explore the historical background and theoretical framework of what we believe to be a second, distinct brand of liberal thought that we call *alternative liberalism.*

PRELIBERAL SOCIETY AND THE RISE
OF LIBERALISM IN RELIGION AND SCIENCE

During the greater part of the Middle Ages, Europe operated under a social system known as *feudalism*. The word itself developed from the Germanic *fehu-od*, referring to property in land. Founded upon an agriculturally based, locally oriented economic system, feudalism established pockets of interconnected communities where hierarchy, order, and harmony were the valued goals. The system itself involved a complex series of interrelationships, obligations, and bonds among individuals. This produced communities that were rigidly structured, hierarchically organized, and, for a very long period of time, quite stable. The land-dominated system had a profound organic and natural orientation pervading it. It valued the good of the ordered community, where individuals had neither independent rights nor independent meaning. Tied to these attributes was the omnipresent sense of tradition. People rarely conceived of questioning the feudal order because it appeared to be both ordained by God and to have been in existence from the beginning of time. Given the cohesiveness of this complex, hierarchical system where each person had a place and everything had its own unique function, to question any single part was to threaten the entire structure.

In spite of its incredible stability for centuries, feudalism eventually gave way to the onslaught of liberalism and modernity. Modernity initiates the notion that all human beings possess reason equally; liberalism puts forth the idea that human beings are best conceived of as "individuals" and not parts of an organic whole. Together, these ideas radically challenged the hierarchical order. Modern liberalism claimed that human beings are rational individuals who can use their reason to understand and to alter the world for the better. In practice, this justified and secured the emerging needs of the individual as well as the collective goods of society such as liberty, equality, and universal justice—goods that were not secured by the old, hierarchical, feudal order.

Over the course of decades, two powerful forces continued to develop and to batter down the old order. One of these was the deliberate political actions of an increasingly powerful, increasingly centralized, and increasingly secularized modern state; the other, was the rise of the capitalist economic system. Together, these complimentary forces brought down the old tradition-bound, community-oriented society and established in its place the modern market society erected upon a radically individualistic (and economic) concept of humanity.

Perhaps it might be helpful to pause momentarily to present two paradigms, or models, of preliberal and liberal society. As models, they are designed to help us understand the current discussion. They are not intended either to be the only possible models of feudalism or liberalism or to be based on actual societies. They are, rather, metaphoric devices that may explain more clearly the ultimately significant differences between a feudal and a liberal social order.

Feudalism	Liberalism
priority of community	priority of individual
"**partness**"	"**a-partness**"
tradition	reason
authority	liberty
hierarchy	equality
cooperation (as organic)	competition (at times friendly)
government as burden	government as necessary,
of aristocratic dignity	but necessarily evil

Each of the six comparative characteristics highlights the differences between these social formations. In feudalism, the emphasis is on community, tradition, authority, hierarchy, cooperation, and government by the natural elite. In contrast, liberalism emphasizes the individual, reason, liberty, equality, competition, and government as a necessary evil. In many, if not most ways, a feudal society meant the inverse of the principal characteristics of a liberal model of society. Whereas the priority of the individual is fundamental to the liberal schema, feudalism accepted the priority of the community. Individuality itself must always be understood as an expression of a particular form of society. In feudalism, it is tacitly accepted and felt that the individual is a dependent part of a whole. The individual celebrates his or her "partness" within the society. The person's purpose and abilities are only to be realized within a set of social relationships, traditions, and institutions that do not themselves depend on a separate, "natural," individual will. The best, most complete people are those who most adequately fulfill the highest functions in the organic social whole.

Since the community is prior to the individual, the source of individual obligation is not to be found in the reason that can be exercised by separate subjects. Divine or divinely inspired traditions supply the authoritative codes of behavior that organize and guarantee all of the tasks, functions, roles, and relationships that characterize such societies. Since the community is taken absolutely to precede the individual, it makes little or no sense to think of individuals as fundamentally equal. Since individuals do not exist apart from highly specific and interrelated social roles, they are relatively subordinate by nature. Tradition and authority take the place of rationality and liberty. Competition between individuals is understood as the primary source of disorder and equality is understood to mean nothing other than chaos and a reversal and degradation of the natural order of things. Here government is necessarily not an evil, but both a burden and responsibility assigned to those parts of the community divinely appointed as best suited to carrying out the requisite tasks. One final point. In the feudal model, it is the organic whole—the community—that matters. Those at the top as well as those at the bottom exist in a meaningful manner only insofar as they fulfil their duties and obligations to society (and therein all parts benefit).

In the liberal model of society the individual is taken to be prior to society. The individual is an atom who accepts "a-partness" to such a degree that being a subordinate part never enters the mind. It is not necessary to examine the society of which that individual is a part to know what the individual is because the essential humanity of that individual is contained within him or her as a rational creature. To say that the individual is rational means that he or she can discover and learn the fundamental principles that govern the material and moral universe and become, as an adult, self-directed. Reason liberates individuals from any unquestioned authoritative traditions; it liberates them from being identified with only a specific, narrow and compulsory social role, and it liberates them from any natural social hierarchy. Reason belongs to the free subject. It enables that subject to determine and pursue self-defined ends, independent of the authority and will of others. This instrumental, but not necessarily amoral, reason is given to each person to be a servant to the individual's wants and needs. It makes each individual free and makes all individuals equal. They are equal in a fundamental sense, and not in a substantive sense. There may be a thousand differences between them, but none of these differences touch the essential freedom of the rational creature to be its own master, and in this sense to be the equal of all other rational creatures. Society is understood to be nothing but that set of arrangements and relationships freely entered into by the individual to further personal ends. In society, liberty means the relative absence of external impediments to rationally willed activity. A society of rational, fundamentally equal and free individuals will necessarily be plural and competitive, because individuals are not restrained by the nature of their inescapable social roles and are, at bottom, each their own judge of the good life. Since competitive, equal individuals must see in each other's freedom and equality not only the essential dignity of all individuals but also a potential threat to their own freedom, government is a necessity and its essential function is to protect the freedom of individuals in their competitive relations with their equals. Yet government itself is essentially an instrument rather than even a part of the ends of human life, and it is an instrument which, since it must be more powerful than what it controls, is necessarily an object of suspicion. It must be controlled by those whom it is to control in turn—otherwise it defeats its own purpose.

Some of these differences will reappear when we discuss the other nonliberal ideologies. For now, it's enough to repeat that the feudal tradition lacked any notion of the individual separated from special functions within the overall structure of society; and that any particular person was such a small, insignificant part of this system that sacrifices at the altar of the common good were easily made. It is a small wonder it lasted for so long. Nevertheless, in religion, science, and political theory the idea of *individualism* broke through these traditional norms of thought. A brief look at Martin Luther, Francis Bacon, and René Descartes will help clarify the role of individualism in smashing the remnants of the feudal order in the European Christian world. These thinkers questioned the traditional hierarchies by expressing a new understanding of the relationship between the individual, rational believer and the Judeo-Christian Creator God. A fuller discussion of Thomas Hobbes will expose the modern epoch's interest in economic and political individualism.

Luther, Bacon, and Descartes

On October 31, 1517, the day Martin Luther nailed his 95 theses on the church door at Wittenberg, he simultaneously sounded the beginning of what eventually became the death knell for the prior tradition. In spite of his reactionary political beliefs, Luther's actions called into question not only the position of the Church in the realm of religion but also the entire traditional society. Under the religious practices of the day, salvation could be attained only through the mediation of the Church's earthly representative. To Luther, authentic religious experiences could have no intermediary; the relationship between God and the individual was extremely personal, and no outside party could interfere. Luther also attacked the notion that the Scriptures were under the total interpretive jurisdiction of the clergy. He maintained that since the pope and his lieutenants were human, they could err in matters of theology. Each person, therefore, had to be free to understand God's word in an individual manner. Similarly, Luther called the monopoly control of the sacraments by the Church "oppressive," in that it denied each believer's "right" to full participation in the exercise of religion. At the foundation of Luther's theology was the "priesthood of all believers," which held that grace was a gift from God given freely to each individual on the basis of faith alone. As individuals, each stood alone before God; and, in this regard, all people were equal.

Luther's theological egalitarianism, like his understanding of freedom, however, was solely an inner matter. Given his perception of the persistence of the sinful human condition and the ongoing chaos of the fallen world of humanity, the individual was still subject to the system of worldly powers and was still a tiny fragment of a social hierarchy that Luther accepted as both natural and necessary. Luther accepted the Pauline and Augustinian notion that even corrupt worldly power had a divine role to play in keeping peace and order. Nevertheless, by defining the individual's self-determined relation to God as right, Luther set into motion certain ideas that in time would ripen in the political realm. After all, if a person as an isolated individual must stand alone before God, why should that person kneel before an earthly lord?

The rise of individualism is also evident in the scientific philosophies prevalent at that time. Even though Galileo's verification of Copernicus's hypothesis dramatically altered human knowledge about the universe, it is in the ideas of Francis Bacon (1561–1626) that the scientific spirit found its modern beginnings. Bacon believed that science had given humanity the means to create, literally, a new world. The desire to control, command, subdue, and dominate nature through the use of science is at the heart of the Baconian dream. "For man by the fall fell at the same time from the state of innocency and from his dominion over creation. Both of these losses however can even in this life be in some part repaired; the former by religion and faith, the latter by arts and sciences," Bacon declared.[1] Through the abandonment of prejudice, the adaptation of experimentation, and cooperative investigation, humanity could turn away from superstitious cosmology and return to the idyllic state prior to humankind's Fall: The objective of human knowledge is "a restitution and reinvesting (in great part) of man to the sovereignty and power (for whensoever he shall be able to call the creatures by their true names he shall again command them) which he had in his first state of creation."[2]

In René Descartes (1596–1650), scientific knowledge as power is again a central theme as he too encouraged humanity to "make ourselves the masters and possessors of nature."[3] However, in Descartes's writing the emphasis on individualism is explicitly evident. Starting from the philosophic premise that everything must be questioned, he attempted to ground his theory on a more certain base than did past thinkers: *"Je pense, donc je suis"* ("I think, therefore I am").[4] With these famous words, Descartes plays the role of a god as he places himself (and all thinking individuals) at the center of a world in which he—as an isolated individual—is both discoverer and creator. No longer a mere fragment in a larger, more important

---

[1] Francis Bacon, "The New Organon," in *The Works of Francis Bacon*, J. Speeding, R. L. Ellis, and D. D. Heath, eds. (New York: Hurd and Houghton, 1869), Vol. 4, pp. 247–48.

[2] *Works of Bacon*, Vol. 3, p. 222.

[3] René Descartes, *Discourse on Method*, trans. Laurance J. Laffleur (Indianapolis: Bobbs-Merrill, 1950), p. 40.

[4] Ibid., p. 21.

whole that is governed by the mystical laws of an unknowable God, humans were now conceived of as creators of their own selves, their own world, and owing allegiance only to their individual selves.

Thus in religion and science, individualism combined with rationalism to confront traditional society with some exceptionally threatening ideas. As the economic arena began to witness the breakup of the traditional moral rules against profit, commercialization, and usury (lending money and charging interest), the final vestiges of the feudal order toppled to earth. Secularization, individualism, rationalism, and power are all central themes in the political theory of the English philosopher Thomas Hobbes (1588–1679), who developed what can perhaps be called the first modern theory in political science. For our purposes, Hobbes's view of human beings in their most natural condition illustrates graphically the individualistic liberal conception of the nature of humankind. Hobbes developed a theory of the role and function of politics that most would call distinctly illiberal— indeed, perhaps authoritarian. In spite of this, the boldness and clarity of his thought, along with the economic basis of his prescriptions, makes him particularly important in the history of individualistic liberalism. Quite simply, he laid the groundwork for those who followed.

Thomas Hobbes: Individualistic Roots of Liberalism

> The Value, or Worth of man, is as of all other things, his Price; that is to say, so much as would be given for the use of his Power. . . . And as in other things, so in men, not the seller, but the buyer determines the Price. For let a man (as most men do), rate themselves as the highest Value they can; yet their true Value is no more than it is esteemed by others.[5]

As in any philosophical endeavor, Hobbes attempted to take a fresh look at humans and human nature. As we shall see in later chapters, this is a common project for ideologists: Karl Marx described the evolution of humanity from a condition he called primitive communism, and Benito Mussolini asserted that people were by nature social animals. In a similar fashion Hobbes tried to envision what human relationships would be were no governmental power present. He was the first in a series of political theorists who attempted this feat using an intellectual device, a heuristic fiction, called the *state of nature*. State-of-nature theorists tried to imagine an environmental setting where people were unencumbered by governmental power and consequently acted in ways that were basic to their very nature. Although some state-of-nature theorists had a tendency to write as though this setting actually existed in human history, somewhere back before civilization— this was not an attempt by Hobbes at a theory of history; rather, it was simply a method of discovering how people would act in their most basic condition in order

---

[5] Thomas Hobbes, *Leviathan,* C. B. Macpherson, ed. (Baltimore, Md.: Penguin, 1968), pp. 151–52.

to theorize on what were the necessary foundations for political obligation and legitimate governance.

What did Hobbes view as the qualities basic to human nature? In *Leviathan*, a book containing the most complete formulation of Hobbesian politics, Hobbes began his analysis on a sure-footed, Cartesian-like base. He advised his readers to follow his example and "*Nosce teipsum, Read thy self.*"[6] Hobbes believed that his political theory was so reasonable that if people would but look inside themselves, they would agree with his premises on human nature and would accept his conclusions on how to construct a political order. From his individualistic starting point, Hobbes proceeded to deduce political rights and obligations. Explicitly rejecting all prior attempts to erect a political theory based upon an externally imposed sense of purpose, order, or harmony to the universe, Hobbes elected to construct his theory on a secure, scientific foundation of empirical observation. He closed the door on the feudal ethos by attacking the classical notions of justice. In response to the feudal norms of exchange based on equality of value and equality of benefit, Hobbes scoffingly responded: "As if it were Injustice to sell dearer than we buy; or to give more to a man than he merits."[7] Fully aware that the opposite situation comprised the reality to be shunned, Hobbes declared that, as in all matters, the market mechanism determined what is genuinely the just value of anything. Hobbes sharpened his assault on the tradition of an ordered and just universe by boldly declaring that in the state of nature "no law can be Unjust." In Hobbes's world, humanity is the creator of all things.

By observing the actions of both himself and others, Hobbes believed he had uncovered the basic traits of human nature. All humanity moves by appetite and aversion. Some appetites and aversions are innate, but most are acquired; they are subject to alteration, and are different in degree and character in different people. Moreover, our appetites are incessant, keeping people in constant motion: "Life itself is but Motion, and can never be without Desire, nor without Feare, no more than without Sense."[8] In order to stay in motion, everyone needs some amount of power, and Hobbes believed that this naturally resulted in a situation where the power of every individual—by definition—resisted and hindered the power of every other person. My power, then, is always relative to, and in conflict with, the power of others. Hobbes further believed that the desire for power, although necessary to the life of each individual, was limited in most humans, but limitless in some. From this he concluded:

> So that in the first place, I put for a generall inclination of all mankind, a perpetuall and restlesse desire of Power after power, that ceaseth only in Death. And the cause of this, is not alwayes that a man hopes for a more intensive delight, than he has already attained to; or that he cannot be content with a moderate power: but because he cannot assure the power and means to live well, which he hath present, without the acquisition of more.[9]

---

[6] Ibid., p. 82.
[7] Ibid., p. 208.
[8] Ibid., p. 130.
[9] Ibid., p. 161.

Given this universal competition for power, which, as must be recalled, is power over others, Hobbes asked, somewhat rhetorically, what human interaction would be like if there were no governmental power to keep people in check. In one of the most famous passages ever written in the history of political theory, he described the natural condition of humanity in the prepolitical state of nature.

> In such condition, there is no place for Industry; because the fruit thereof is uncertain, and consequently no Culture of the Earth; no Navigation, nor use of the commodities that may be imported by Sea; no commodious Building; no Instruments of moving, and removing such things as require much force; no Knowledge of the face of the Earth; no account of Time; no Arts; no Letters; no Society; and which is worst of all, continuall feare, and danger of violent death; And the life of man, solitary, poore, nasty, brutish, and short.[10]

Two things are particularly worth noting in this quotation. First, Hobbes indicated that he assumes, above all else, that people do not want to die. Second, he has given an additional indication of the kind of society he implicitly holds in his mind as being the model of, and for, human interaction: a society pervaded by, and constructed upon, industry, agriculture, commerce, and knowledge.

To this point, we have spelled out Hobbes's premises on human nature: (1) People are inevitably involved in a power struggle with others, and (2) they want to avoid death. In his secular description of the sinful character of humanity, Hobbes nevertheless found these premises to be factually true and assumed his readers would be in agreement. He also introduced into his argument the idea of *natural right.* Hobbes claimed that all people have rights simply by virtue of their humanness; neither providence nor society grants them. These are rights that individuals have in the state of nature, where there is no political power to protect people from each other. To Hobbes, the most fundamental right of nature was "the Liberty each man hath, to use his own power, as he will himselfe, for the preservation of his own Nature; that is to say . . . of doing any thing, which in his own Judgement, and Reason, hee shall conceive to be the aptest means thereunto."[11]

The Social Contract. In the state of nature, this right to self-preservation is fully operative; any individual can "do anything" to anybody: "It followeth, that in such a condition, every man has a Right to everything; even to one another's body." Furthermore, Hobbes believed that all possessed this right and, in that sense, they were equal. Hobbes's postulate on human equality, similar to the rest of his theory, was not based on an ethical principle but rather on what he believed to be empirical reality. Hobbes reasoned that all people are equal in that they are capable of killing each other. Even if one individual is particularly gifted with natural power, Hobbes assumed that others are capable of using their reason to form a temporary alliance to "do in" the strongest. So even though we are equal in terms of natural right, it is a useless situation since it results in a condition of war of all against all.

---

[10] Ibid., p. 186.
[11] Ibid., p. 189.

Hobbes paired his natural rights argument with a notion of *natural law* where humans, aided by reason, can discover certain general rules of conduct that will help them preserve themselves. Because all want to avoid death, it is natural that people are forbidden to do anything that is destructive of their own lives. In addition, they must look for a reasonable way out from under the condition of war in the state of nature, for that situation is intolerable. Through reasoning, Hobbes uncovered two fundamental *laws of nature* that all individuals should embrace: (1) "to seek Peace" and (2) "to lay down this right to all things; and be contented with so much liberty against other men, as he would allow other men against himselfe."[12] Briefly, Hobbes thought it reasonable that individuals would find it to their personal advantage to give up their right to everything provided others reciprocated. They would, in effect, form a *social contract* with each other and relinquish their claim to everything. And yet, given what we know about human nature, only a fool would uphold the contract without some mechanism to enforce the agreement.

The Hobbesian solution came in the form of a self-perpetuating, authoritarian government that possessed virtually unlimited power over its subjects. It must be understood that the social contract was among individuals—not between the individuals and the sovereign. It was the function of the government, the Leviathan (which means *monster*), to enforce—by whatever means it deemed necessary—the contract among these individual power competitors. In effect, Hobbes's individuals join together and transfer their powers over others to an all powerful sovereign who in turn has unlimited power over them. Individuals give up and transfer all their natural rights except one: the right to self-preservation. Since this was *the* factor that originally led them to create the contract, it would make no sense to give up this right. But even here there are qualifications concerning the right of self-preservation. People were, for example, obligated to give up their lives in defense of the state as long as the sovereign remained in clear command.

It is through this mechanism of a social contract that humans secured the "right to govern their own bodies; enjoy air, water, motion, ways to go from place to place; and all things else without which a man cannot live, or not live well."[13] Thus, they learned to control some of the effects of their contentious nature. The human desires to stay in motion and to dominate one another never disappear; the war of all against all continues to rage; however, in this new context the energy gets channeled into more socially constructive outlets: industry, commerce, agriculture—activities that produce what Hobbes called "commodious living." Government's function, then, is to establish rules of conduct that will allow people the liberty to pursue their own self-interest while prohibiting certain other types of behavior. This leads to another crucial aspect of Hobbesian politics. Hobbes, in spite of his intentions, seems not to be describing a "natural" universal human condition valid across time and place, but rather is analyzing a particular type of society with its particular mode of human interaction and its

---

[12] Ibid., p. 190.
[13] Ibid., p. 212.

particular conception of human beings: bourgeois society with market relationships conducted by modern consumers. No wonder we find Hobbes so painfully convincing—he is describing us!

Possessive Market Society. Hobbes's political theory was constructed to confront the economic and social reality of seventeenth-century England, a society that experienced the horrors of civil war between those who claimed to be the Leviathan. Given his depiction of "commodious living" and the human desire "to live well," it is obvious that he was analyzing an economically advancing civilization. However, through his description of power—and the relationships among people—it is also clear that he was describing a society where power was constantly and continuously being exchanged. He believed that people naturally desire power over others; even though individuals contract not to kill one another, any individual may nevertheless still gain power over others provided that person can get others to transfer—in exchange for something, for example, money—their power to that person. "The Value, or Worth of a man, is . . . his Price; that is to say, so much as would be given for the use of his Power. . . ," Hobbes declared. In order to heighten the contrast between this particular type of society with other economically based societies, the political analyst C. B. Macpherson has called Hobbes's society a "possessive market society." It differs from societies where both work and rewards for work were distributed by those in authority; and it also differs from a society of independent producers where only goods are exchanged. In contrast with these societies, a possessive market society has a market in human power, that is, a *market in labor.* Macpherson describes the situation in this way:

> If a single criterion of the possessive market society is wanted it is that man's labour is a commodity, i.e., that a man's energy and skill are his own, yet are regarded not as integral parts of his personality, but as possessions, the use and disposal of which he is free to hand over to others for a price. It is to emphasize this characteristic of the fully market society that I have called it the *possessive* market society. Possessive market *society* also implies that where labour has become a market commodity, market relations so shape or permeate all social relations that it may properly be called a market society, not merely a market economy.[14]

Possessive market societies, of which capitalism is the most developed form, emphasize the degree of economic penetration into the very fiber of human relationships. Virtually every aspect of social interaction is conceived in market terms wherein individuals are conceived of as "rational" self-interested calculators of their own welfare. The market has become the measure of all things.

Many of the central concepts of what will become liberal thought are present in the Hobbesian view of human nature and the origin of the state even though, as we have noted, his "solution" to these problems of natural man can hardly be called liberal. The innate individualism, radical freedom, natural rights, relative equality, and passion-based motivation are all part of the human condition. Furthermore, we see society and government formed as a creative act

---

[14] C. B. Macpherson, *The Political Theory of Possessive Individualism: Hobbes to Locke* (Oxford: Claredon Press, 1962), p. 48.

of human rationality—institutions designed to serve the selfish interests of individuals; both society and its institutions are conceived of as being *artificial*—human constructs. Only out of an urgent sense of necessity do people agree to live together, and only for as long as the Leviathan is present, and peace and order maintained.

This paints quite a different picture of human nature and social relation than those found in ancient and medieval political philosophy as well as in the ideologies of Marxism and absolutism. Still, what is significant is that Hobbes has shown us a rather dark side of the liberal tradition. People, although naturally free, independent, and equal, are forced to establish institutions that limit their behavior in the name of self-preservation. The prospect of a return to the state of nature is so menacing that all are willing to subject themselves to tremendous limitations in the name of order and the prospect of commodious living.

Finally, the Hobbesian view of people as dominated by passion, always attempting to maximize their own self-interest—even if it is at the expense of others' rights—is an early indication of one of the central themes and major problems in what will become liberal democratic theory. We shall meet this problem later in the form of the ongoing conflict between majority rule and minority rights. In Thomas Hobbes, then, we find perhaps the first, most certainly the boldest expression of the modern, individualistic liberal concept of humanity. Given his concept of the natural human condition, his conclusion as to the necessity of a powerful sovereign seems to follow inexorably. If, however, Thomas Hobbes outlined the theoretical basis for the liberal conception of human nature, it received its most famous modern embodiment in the hands of John Locke.

John Locke

The Lockean view of the state of nature contains many of the same elements we observed in Hobbes, but there are also significant differences worthy of note. Both theorists see people as distinctly individual, free, equal, and possessed of certain natural rights. In Hobbes's theory, all of these attributes were deduced from observation in an effort to give his approach the weight of scientific rationality. However, in Locke, God is introduced as a central factor in politics, giving Locke's theory a far more palatable flavor than Hobbes's secularizing tendencies. For Hobbes, humans can reason about means to secure peace; for Locke, they can reason about their moral obligations to each other as children of God.

John Locke (1632–1704) was an English philosopher, physician, and student of politics who is widely regarded as the founder of liberal democratic thought. In Locke's thought, all people possess certain natural rights to "life, liberty, and estate," for example—which they hold prior to, and independent of, either government or society—by virtue of the fact that all people are created by God. This common, divine origin is also the reason why people are equal by nature, rather than subjects of absolutist kings who claim divinely ordained natural hierarchies. It is not surprising, then, that seventeenth-century readers found Locke's political theory far more appealing than Hobbes's.

Following Hobbes's lead, Locke used a state-of-nature argument to make his case. At times, his description of the state of nature sounds rather idyllic, even though he eventually comes around to a position reminiscent of Hobbes: "To avoid this State of War . . . is one great reason of Mens putting themselves into society, and quitting the State of Nature."[15] In this passage, Locke considered the state of nature to be a state of war, and he assumed people would like to remove themselves from this condition. Even so, Locke argued that there were moral imperatives present in the state of nature that required humans, even without the presence of government, to respect the rights of others, including their mutual right to acquire property. In a sense, it seems appropriate to speak of a primitive, protocommunity in the state of nature where God acts as the creator and sovereign.

Locke found this theological connection helpful in the economic basis of his argument as well. He believed that God had "given the Earth to the Children of Men, given it to Mankind in common." From the two additional assumptions that, (1) every individual has "a right to . . . [self-]Preservation" and (2) "every Man has a Property in his own Person [which] . . . no Body has any Right to but himself," Locke deduced an individual's natural right to property.[16] By approaching this issue from a theological angle, Locke could not ignore the feudal restrictions on property accumulation. He specifically discussed two natural law restrictions on this individual property right: (1) An individual must leave enough property for others to use (after all, the earth was given, by God, to all people in common); and (2) an individual must not allow anything to spoil (God's grant was to make use of the earth, not to allow it to "rot"). Having respected these prohibitions, an individual could claim property rights over anything out of the common with which one mixed one's labor. These property rights, then, were both *inclusive* and *exclusive.* Within Locke's frame, they were inclusive because all individuals had an equal claim to part of the common; and yet, they were simultaneously exclusive insofar as Locke established property as one's own—a right which may not be restricted without the individual's consent. Locke denied the absolutist royalists their claim to total dominion over the lives and labors of their subjects, and he maintained that the Bible could not be used to justify authoritarian absolutism. To the contrary, it supported the concept of natural human rights and of limited government whose function was to secure and to protect those rights.

Locke's liberalism coincided with the evolving historical dynamics of capitalism. Indeed, long before G. W. F. Hegel and Karl Marx, Locke presented one of the earliest arguments on behalf of the relationship between property and human personality. As a person invests labor in something, part of the self is placed in that object; this expenditure of personal energy gives that person rights of ownership that are independent of, and prior to, civil society. Indeed, individual property rights are part of providence's plan for humanity, for "God, when he gave the world

[15] John Locke, *Two Treatises on Government,* Peter Laslet, ed. (New York: New American Library, 1960), p. 323.

[16] Ibid., pp. 327–28.

in common to all mankind, commanded man also to labour."[17] In an ingenious manner, Locke continues his argument on natural rights, demonstrating not only how people have the right to individual accumulation of property but also how humanity has circumvented the natural law restrictions on property accumulation and substituted the right—and obligation—of *unlimited* property accumulation, all as part of a divine design.

 The Invention of Money. Locke's argument proceeds along two stages. Originally, a person could accumulate only as much property as could be used personally, without spoilage and with sufficient property remaining for others. However, with the invention of money, Locke argued that humanity unanimously agreed to alter the rules of the original situation. At this point Locke introduces the notion of a tacit agreement or *tacit consent* among people in the state of nature. They agree to the usage of money as a medium of exchange. In addition to functioning as a medium, money serves an even more valuable purpose of allowing people a mechanism to circumvent the natural law prohibition against spoilage. Gold and silver do not spoil. Of course, goods still could not be permitted to spoil, but with the invention of money this burden shifted from the producer to the consumer. As for the second limit of allowing sufficient property for others to use, Locke explicitly argued that when people agreed to use money they simultaneously and unanimously agreed to the right of "disproportionate and unequal Possession of the Earth."

> This I dare boldly affirm, That the same Rule of Propriety (viz.) that every Man should have as much as he could make use *of*, would hold still in the World, without straitening any body, since there is Land enough in the World to suffice double the Inhabitants had not the *Invention of Money*, and the tacit Agreement of Men to put a value on it, introduced (by Consent) larger Possessions, and a Right to them.[18]

 Furthermore, as succeeding generations continue to use money to serve their needs, they reaffirm their commitment to the right of individual, unlimited accumulation.

 Locke's Views of Property. Before examining Locke's argument for limited government, two final points concerning his view of property must be examined. First, throughout his analysis of humanity in the state of nature, Locke assumes that it is natural for people to sell their labor to others: One may sell to another "for a certain time, the Service he undertakes to do, in exchange for Wages he is to receive."[19] When this exchange takes place, the laborer also transfers any property claim over the goods produced to the buyer. Therefore, to Locke, property ownership can be established through both direct, personal labor, or through indirect, purchased labor.

---

[17] Ibid., p. 332.
[18] Ibid., p. 335.
[19] Ibid., p. 365.

Thus the Grass my Horse has bit; the Turfs my Servant has cut; and the Ore I have dig-g'd in any place where I have a right to them in common with others, become my *Property*, without the assignation or consent of any body. The *labour* that was mine, removing them out of that common state they were in, hath *fixed* my *Property* in them.[20]

The second point concerning property is Locke's assumption of qualitatively different levels of rationality in people. Immediately after arguing that God gave the "World in common to all Mankind," he refines his position, asserting that given the "penury" of the human condition, God "commanded" people to labor on the earth. Labor then, is critical not only to human survival but also to the human soul. In the next paragraph of his famous *Second Treatise*, Locke further qualifies the commonality of this grant by stating: "He gave it to the use of the Industrious and Rational. . . ; not to the Fancy or Covetousness of the Quarrelsom and Contentious."[21] The hidden premise for Locke is that all of God's creatures should be industrious and rational, but the distinctions of kinds of people carries along with it clear inegalitarian implications. These serve to justify emerging class distinctions within capitalism and its inherent goal of unrelenting capital accumulation. Simply put: Some people are industrious and rational; others are quarrelsome and contentious. The former act in accordance with natural law, the latter against it. Thus, it follows that the former should be rewarded for their good work and money makes this possible. By permitting the industrious and rational to accumulate more property than they individually can use, Locke grants them not only material rewards but also the right to infinite accumulation. The virtue of this system of added material incentives for the industrious, Locke argues, is that all of humanity benefits from their efforts.

There cannot be a clearer demonstration of any thing, than several Nations of the *Americans* are of this, who are rich in Land, and poor in all the Comforts of Life; whom Nature having furnished as liberally as any other people, with the materials of Plenty, i.e., a fruitful Soil, apt to produce in abundance, what might serve for food, rayment, and delight; yet for want of improving it by labour, have not one hundredth part of the Conveniences we enjoy: And a King of a large fruitful Territory there feeds, lodges, and is clad worse than a day Labourer in *England*.[22]

Here, Locke presents an early form of the "trickle-down theory." By rewarding those who are industrious, the whole society benefits as the fruits of the labor of those at the top make their way down to those at the bottom. The industrious and rational will employ those considered less industrious and less rational, so that the most efficient use of labor is achieved.

We have quoted Locke extensively because his arguments establish the basis for a capitalist market society against a society like the Native Americans' where no private property rights exist. A person at the top of the social stratum of a society where land is still held in common is—given Locke's materialistic criteria—worse off than a person at the lowest point in a market society.

[20] Ibid., p. 330.

[21] Ibid., p. 333.

[22] Ibid., pp. 338–39.

Finally, Locke extends this bias in rationality among people into his arguments on governing society. Those who have fulfilled their duties to God—have demonstrated their rationality by owning property and, by virtue of their ownership, have a stake in the maintenance of social order—may also participate in the governing of society. Those who possess nothing but their labor may not participate in the governing of society. The former may vote; the latter may not. Because the laborers nevertheless are still subject to the laws of society, even though they cannot participate in the making of those laws, they are said to be *in*, but not *of* civil society. If at some point the laborer acquires sufficient property, that person will be admitted into the ruling class.

Dramatically, Locke has turned the arguments of traditional society concerning unlimited property accumulation on their head. What in the feudal tradition was once considered morally reprehensible behavior is, in a market society, now virtuous. In like manner, the old arguments in favor of traditional government have been jettisoned, to be replaced by Locke's limited, majoritarian government.

By returning to Locke's state of nature and the transition from it into civil society, we recognize some of the differences between Locke and Hobbes that result in Locke's somewhat more benign conception of the role of government. Locke spoke not merely of one social contract in the tradition of Hobbes, but of two agreements, one appropriately called a *contract* and the other more of a *trustee relationship*. The initial contract was called the *contract of society* (civil society) whereby people agree to relinquish the total freedom of the state of nature and to establish a society. The society as an entity then proceeds to the establishment of a disinterested third party, absent from the state of nature. This action, resulting from the second agreement, is the origin of government. However, the type of agreement here is substantially different from the earlier contract of society. Initially, it is not properly called a contract, for the two parties to the agreement (civil society and government) are not equals, each possessing certain rights. Government possesses no independent rights whatsoever, thereby making the agreement process simply one of society's imposing obligations upon the government.

The designation of a trustee relationship is used by Locke to describe this situation since, in a trust arrangement, the manager of the trust operates solely in the interest of a client (in this case civil society) and possesses no legal rights in the relationship. To speak of governmental rights in the Lockean political philosophy is simply incorrect. Government has no rights; it simply incurs obligations, namely to protect the natural rights of the individuals who comprise civil society.

In addition to this, the agreement to constitute a government is not made by unanimous decision, but by a majority of the property owners who are, after all, the only fully rational members of society. From civil society the government is given certain powers to perform limited duties, such as providing for defense of the community and contributing to the general welfare. The extent of the powers granted government is a subject of continuing controversy among students of Locke's philosophy, and it will become a major concern of our future discussion. For the moment, however, the important fact is that the society, which by *majority rule* (of the property holders) establishes a government, may also remove it by a negative majority vote. Further, if a government is overthrown in this fashion there is no Hobbesian-like fear of a return to a chaotic state of nature, because the contract of society remains intact, and only the majority-initiated government is replaced.

The majority (of the men of property), not the individual, becomes then the central unit in Lockean politics: Locke grants the majority of civil society the power to *unmake* government, and with this power "the people," whom Locke thinks of as the men of property, will be able to hold the government accountable to their wishes. Power, in Locke, ultimately resides with "the people," although not all adults count as part of this political category. In Hobbes there is no such grant: The Leviathan is checked by itself alone.

The Lockean notion of a dual agreement that occurs in the process of leaving the state of nature introduced an important element in the liberal tradition. In the Hobbesian state there was no distinction between the political system (sovereign) and the individual member of the state. While for Hobbes, people did retain the right of self-preservation as individuals, there was no intermediary body to act as a mitigating force or as a check on state power. In the Lockean system there is a three-tiered relationship. The individual is at one and the same time a private person, a possible member of a societal majority, and the subject of a limited government. With such a scheme, Locke provides for a clear differentiation between the general and the particular, or, better, between the *public* life and *private* life. There is a sphere of human existence that is not subject to political action, namely, the area encompassed by Locke's notion of individual rights—those areas that the majority decides are not appropriate subjects for governmental policy making.

A Plea for Toleration. In *A Letter Concerning Toleration* (1689), Locke drew this crucial public versus private distinction in terms of provinces where governments may or may not intervene. In this letter, Locke argues that, in its very essence, religion is a subject of belief rather than of science or reason; humanity, therefore, could never be absolutely certain of the truthfulness of any particular interpretation of Christianity. In light of this uncertainty, then, Locke argues that government may not interfere with any individual's religious beliefs. Furthermore, he calls for toleration not only by government but also by all people to respect others' beliefs. Here Locke establishes two essential liberal values: toleration and a separation of the public from the private. The public-private dichotomy eventually develops the groundwork for the creation of civil rights; that is, individual rights with which neither the state nor society may interfere. In the United States this idea of civil rights finds its clearest and more secularized expression in the first ten amendments to the United States Constitution, usually called the Bill of Rights.

As we shall see in the subsequent discussion, the exact delineation of these areas of appropriate governmental and societal concern is one of the most crucial problems of the entire liberal democratic tradition. For present purposes, however, the Lockean distinction between public and private spheres provides another direct contrast with Marxism and absolutism. As we shall see, in non-liberal ideologies all areas of individual action may be viewed as the appropriate concern of the state or society. Under fascism for example, the individual achieves fulfillment as a human being by contributing to national greatness, thus making all actions the direct concern of the state. Under the "transfer culture" of modern Marxism, the individual is viewed as a builder of socialism and all of that person's activities are public matters. And in Islamism, there is no distinction between the public and the private.

HOBBES AND LOCKE RECONSIDERED

In both Hobbes and Locke the one feature of human existence that stands out most noticeably is *individuality*. People are viewed as atomic units, sufficient unto themselves and interacting with other individuals primarily in pursuit of their own selfish interests. True, there are differing degrees of this individualism expressed by the assorted members of the liberal school. Whereas Hobbes saw people as completely self-contained entities, contacting others only when they desired similar things, Locke saw a connection between basically self-interested people since they are all subject to the constraints of the natural law of God. Despite these differences, the liberal tradition of Hobbes and Locke can be characterized only by its emphasis on radical individualism; people exist, prior to the establishment of society, as self-contained individuals.

We should immediately anticipate a great difference between British liberalism and the other ideologies we will be discussing. To the fascist, for example, people are viewed as human in their natural condition insofar as they are members of the group or the race. Their interaction with that group defines in large part their very existence. To a Marxist, "natural" humans are gregarious, members of a community governed by shared values; humanity's historic difficulties are economic. While in Islamism, if humans would actively and totally submit to the word of Allah the ideal Islamic community could be created. But in British liberalism the individual is supreme. Further, people possess certain rights—natural rights—that are granted them by the very nature of their humanity. These rights are not dependent for their existence upon their recognition by a state, or by any other human institution, but are inherent in human nature itself. To some members of the liberal tradition, people possessed the right to acquire anything they wanted—even a right to another person's body. Such unlimited rights were, however, constrained by the fact that all other individuals possessed them. Despite differences in physical and mental ability, all human beings were similarly endowed with these natural rights, leading to a position of relative *equality*. People were equal to the extent that they all possessed the right to a great many things. Granted, I have the right to attempt to take away property that you have acquired, but you have a corresponding right to defend that property from any attack. Thus, we may say that the British liberal tradition viewed people in the state of nature as relative equals, whether that equality derived from a common parenthood in God or from the ability of one individual to deprive others of their rights. Implicit in this notion of equality is the fact that all possess the *freedom* necessary to secure their natural rights. While at times that freedom may be constrained by the presence of other people or by certain natural laws of God, in general, humans are endowed with the freedom to secure the objects they desire.

Here then is a brief sketch of the attributes of humanity in its natural condition: free to pursue ends; relatively equal; possessed of rights that are not subject to the authority of any other human being; and, above all, dependent only upon themselves, or God, for their existence. Of particular note in the liberal concept of the natural human condition is what modern social theorists would call the lack of *shared values*. There is no natural human community which sets up standards of behavior for the individuals in it. Indeed, the concept of a community or society is conspicuous by its absence in early liberal thought. Even Locke, whose view of the natural state is somewhat less individualistic than those of other liberals, believed that people merely shared a common origin through their creator and were governed by natural laws that were difficult to apply to particular cases. This lack of shared values is underscored if we look more carefully at individuals in the state of nature and, in particular, at the forces motivating their behavior.

Self-Interest Motivation

People are motivated largely by selfish desires, often to acquire things. They are interested primarily in satisfying their desires, in fulfilling the needs that their self-interest dictates. Throughout the liberal tradition there is an emphasis on the passionate basis of human motivation, and a consequent deprecation of human morality as a major force in governing behavior. Human rationality, furthermore, is conceived in narrow, instrumental, means-ends terms; people are dominated by their own selfish interests (the ends), and reason serves the function of instructing them how to secure those desires most efficiently (the means). This orientation is nicely summed up by the Scottish philosopher David Hume, whose view of reason was that of a "scout" for the more basic human passions. Obviously the most prevalent way these passions find their expression is through the acquisition of objects taken from the environment, and all of the individualistic liberals were most concerned with the notion of *private property*. Given what we know of the relative equality of people combined with the freedom they possess, it follows that the liberals thought that humans had a right to acquire property for their own selfish interests. Indeed, it is probably correct to assert that British liberalism as a whole was preoccupied with humans as essentially economic beings. The mere mention of Adam Smith's name among their number indicates that. Inventing the *labor theory of value*, which we will encounter again in Marxian thought, the liberals argued that, when people mixed their labor with an object in the environment, the object became an extension of the person and therefore could be legitimately owned by that person. Indeed, there is much in liberalism that viewed property as the natural expression of human potential and an indication of personal creativity. Given all of this, it is appropriate to speak of a natural right to the unlimited acquisition of property in the state of nature. The state of nature, therefore, is hardly an idyllic setting and instead is equally definable as a state of war in both theories.

Conflict arises because selfish interest leads people to desire the same objects, and there are simply no rules of the game to determine whose interest is more legitimate. Insofar as all people had a natural right to acquire anything, it was inevitable that their desires would lead them to concentrate on similar objects, producing disagreement as to legitimate ownership. As long as an unlimited right existed, people could not feel secure in their possessions or, for that matter, in their own continued existence. It is this conflict in the state of nature that leads people to use their reason to discover ways by which their selfish interests may be better served. This leads them out of the state of war and into society. Although Hobbes and Locke disagreed over the desirability of holding the government accountable for its actions, they did not disagree over the necessity for a strong, authoritarian sovereign who possessed virtually unlimited power—when so endowed by the people.

Locke's political theory contained within it a theological dimension that undoubtedly distinguished it from Hobbes's more naked statement. However, in the final analysis, it is the similarity of the two theories, rather than any minor differences, that is important. Both theorists, beginning from the assumption of an evolving capitalist society with ("fallen") acquisitive humans as its component, erect political structures designed to fit the needs of this radically individualistic, highly competitive society. This again emphasizes the fact that in terms of its origin, there is not much democracy in liberalism. Indeed, it is only by looking to Jeremy Bentham and James Mill that we can see why and how liberalism decided to become democratic.

LIBERALISM BECOMES LIBERAL DEMOCRACY

As we have seen in the discussion of Hobbes and Locke, liberalism arrived on the scene at the same time as did capitalism, providing an explanation of and a justification for this new economic system. By rewarding those individuals who use their reason and industry in pursuit of personal gain, everyone in the society benefits: Private vice becomes public virtue. As the noted satirist Mandeville put it, "Thus every part was full of vice, yet the whole mass a paradise."[23] Be that as it may, it was also clear that not all members of civil society had equal rights: Locke argued for majority rule, but only the fully rational, those who owned property, were permitted to vote. As decades passed and class divisions began to harden in this economic universe, it seemed unlikely that those people who composed a clear majority of society were going to remain satisfied being ruled by the propertied class. Hence, out of a sense of practical power politics, liberal theorists began to make a case for extending the franchise to all males.

In 1818 Jeremy Bentham proposed that the franchise should be extended to all males of mature age, and of sound mind, who shall have been resident as either householders or inmates within the district or place in which they are called upon to vote. Shortly thereafter, James Mill, John Stuart Mill's father, made a similar argument for universal male suffrage. Mill's position is straightforward: The vote

[23] Bernard Mandeville, *The Fable of the Bees*, 2 Vols. (Oxford: Clarendon Press, 1924).

gave political power and given human nature, every person needed the vote for self-protection. In his 1820 *An Essay on Government,* Mill describes the human condition in bold terms reminiscent of Hobbes.

> That one human being will desire to render the person and property of another subservient to his pleasures, notwithstanding the pain or loss of pleasure which it may occasion to that other individual, is the foundation of government. The desire of the object implies the desire of the power necessary to accomplish the object. The desire, therefore, of that power which is necessary to render the persons and properties of human beings subservient to our pleasures is a grand governing law of human nature. . . . The grand instrument for attaining what a man likes is the actions of other men. Power . . . therefore, means security for the conformity between the will of one man and the acts of other men. This, we presume, is not a proposition which will be disputed.[24]

Given this position, "one person, one vote" was logically necessary in order to keep these invading individuals at bay. In spite of his own logic, Mill was willing to exclude many groups in society—for example, women—from voting. Nevertheless, he presents the most basic case for democracy, and it now becomes historically appropriate to speak of liberal democracy.

Jeremy Bentham and James Mill were part of a movement in nineteenth–century British liberal thinking called *Utilitarianism.* The most famous member of that movement, however, was undoubtedly James Mill's son, John Stuart Mill. The latter's writings on politics constituted significant contributions to the advance of liberal thinking in Britain and, as we have already noted, his classic work, *On Liberty,* remains required reading for any student of liberalism.

Without going into an extensive examination of Utilitarian thinking, we must take note of an important result of its advocacy of extending the franchise from its original Lockean base. We have established that, with philosophic support from Utilitarianism, liberalism was becoming more democratic, including, at a minimum, non-property-holding males in its definition of citizens. As such, male non–property holders (and eventually women) came to constitute a majority of the citizenry, and the political system increasingly had to take their wishes into account in the formulation of public policy. John Locke's "Industrious and Rational" men of property were being supplanted in political power by, again in Locke's words, the "Quarrelsom and Contentious." This led, perhaps inevitably, to a clash between the desires of the new majority and the rights of individuals—particularly with respect to private property. If the non-property-holding majority wished to use its newly constituted political power to place governmental restrictions on the fundamental rights of individuals (again, primarily property rights), there was little in Locke's scheme to stop them. After all, the legislature, as a trustee, should be responsive to, and ultimately responsible only to, majorities.

The problem of *majority tyranny,* or at least the potential of it, was to bother greatly John Stuart Mill and, in the United States, James Madison. In Great Britain with its parliamentary system, there were few structural barriers to prevent tyrannical

---

[24] James Mill, *An Essay on Government,* Currin V. Shields, ed. (Indianapolis: Bobbs-Merrill, 1955), p. 56.

actions on the part of majorities, leading John Stuart Mill, for example, to place great weight (some would say "faith") on processes of education which would make propertyless majorities more respectful of traditional liberal conceptions of rights. As we shall see in the subsequent chapter, however, it was the American James Madison who designed a "structural" remedy for the potential evils of tyrannical majorities.

Conservatism

Before examining the American "solution" however, we must briefly mention the existence of a political tradition generally called *conservatism*. As should be obvious from both the title of this book and the subject matter of the ensuing chapters, our primary concern is with the broadly defined tradition of liberalism. Nevertheless, a discussion of conservatism, however brief, seems necessary at this point if only to outline its central ideas and to show its development alongside of, and its comparability with, liberalism. Moreover, a central theme of conservative thinking, particularly that of Edmund Burke, involves the protection of individual rights from potentially tyrannical actions by majorities. If John Stuart Mill and James Madison were worried about controlling the reactionary tendencies of majoritarian liberal democracy, Burke was genuinely terrified by its revolutionary potential.

Conservatism, in its specifically political context, is a relatively modern phenomenon, gaining its official usage in England in the 1830s. It developed into a political movement in reaction to progressive forces in Europe. The noted sociologist Karl Mannheim draws a useful distinction between two meanings of *conservatism*. The first he calls *traditionalism*: It reflects the almost universal tendency in humans to "cling to the old ways." Largely an unconscious character trait, traditionalism need not have a specific, political component. Indeed, since traditionalism is a rather subjective factor, it is possible to have a traditionalist who is also a political progressive; that is, a person who desires social and political innovation but prefers the status quo in his or her private life. Political conservatism, in contrast, is the conscious choice to stick with the status quo. In a sense, it is traditionalism become self-conscious of itself, and then specifically imposed on politics. Mannheim's point is twofold: first, to create terms that help to separate private inclinations or dispositions from political movements; and second, to demonstrate the ubiquity of humanity's resistance to change and the resultant widespread appeal of conservatism. It should be obvious, then, that in a very important sense conservatives are associated with every political ideology; it is appropriate to speak of conservative Marxists, as well as conservative liberals. This being said, we will nevertheless turn to Edmund Burke as our principal spokesperson for this conservative movement inside the liberal democratic tradition.

Edmund Burke. Born in Dublin, Ireland, in 1729, Burke spent almost thirty years of his life as a member of parliament in the British House of Commons. While contemporary conservatives still consider him to be a profound political thinker of a deservedly high reputation, Burke himself disdained abstract theorizing about politics. Instead, he preferred to deal with specific, concrete situations where it would be possible for him to bring tradition and history to bear on the issue. His most celebrated work, *Reflections on the Revolution in France and on the Proceedings in Certain Societies in London Relative to That Event* (1790), reflects this attitude. The latter part of the title shows Burke's concern not with hypothetical speculations on revolution in a foreign country but rather with the political impact of a foreign revolution on England.

Burke did not share liberalism's optimistic sense of the potentiality of rational individuals. Indeed, there is a distinctively feudal flavor to Burke's entire viewpoint. He believed that humanity can realize itself only in history and only through conventional institutions; that is, institutions that have withstood the rigorous tests of time. "For man," he writes, "is a most unwise, and a most wise, being. The individual is foolish. The multitude, for the moment, is foolish, when they act without deliberation; but the species is wise, and when time is given to it, as a species it almost always acts right."[25] Tradition—the collected history of custom, opinions, prejudice, and wisdom—is the appropriate vehicle for achieving justice, even though it cannot be the ultimate standard of justice. Blind obedience to precedent would be as foolish a practice for humanity to follow as it would be for humanity to turn its back on the past; change, slow and gradual, is also a part of history, and Burke advocates prudential development through social reform based on the lessons of history. Nothing was more dangerous to Burke than the doctrine "liberty always."

Society is an organism; it is both ordered and hierarchical in nature. The purpose of society is to help promote the good of the community and of every individual who comprises it. Burke understands the community to be larger than the sum of the individuals who live in it. It is much more than a loose collection of atomized units. "In a state of rude nature," he wrote, "there is no such thing as a people. A number of men in themselves have no collective capacity. The idea of a people is the idea of a corporation."[26] Men do not enter civil society in order to protect their natural rights. Society *precedes* individuals and should actively aim to shape and form them, not vice versa. Burke argued that upon entering civil society individuals give up all such claims.

> Society requires not only that the passions of individuals should be subjected, but that even in the mass and body as well as in the individuals, the inclinations of men should frequently be thwarted, their will controlled, and their passions brought into subjection. This can only be done by a power out of themselves; and not, in the exercise of its function, subject to that will and to those passions which it is its office to bridle and subdue.[27]

Like other political thinkers, Burke was willing to see society as a kind of contractual arrangement, and he discussed the relationship among three groups of

[25] Edmund Burke, *Works*, 16 Vols., Rivington ed. (London: F. C. J. Rivington, Publishers, 1803–27), Vol. 10, pp. 96–97.

[26] Ibid., Vol. 6, pp. 210–11.

[27] Edmund Burke, *Reflections on the Revolution in France*, Connor Cruise O'Brien, ed. (Baltimore, Md.: Penguin, 1969), p. 151.

people, two of which are not living. Here the notion of society as an organic, historic community is again evident.

> Society is indeed a contract. . . . It is to be looked on with other reverence; because it is not a partnership in things subservient only to the gross animal existence of a temporary and perishable nature, it is a partnership in all science; a partnership in all art; a partnership in every virtue, and in all perfection. As the ends of such a partnership cannot be obtained in many generations, it becomes a partnership not only between those who are living, but between those who are living, those who are dead, and those who are to be born. Each contract of each particular state is but a clause in the great primeval contract of eternal society, linking the lower with the higher natures, connecting the visible and invisible world, according to a fixed compact sanctioned by the inviolable oath which holds all physical and all moral natures, each in their appointed place.[28]

By reason alone, history should not be changed. One generation should respect the legacy of previous generations and should exercise considerable caution in its attitude toward "progressive" change.

Although Burke rejected *natural* rights, he nevertheless argued that contemporary humans, now that they are born into civil society, have certain *inherited* rights; rights they possess by virtue of their participating in the social processes and traditions that are cultivated and passed along by successive generations.

> Men have a right to live by that rule [of law]; they have a right to justice; They have a right to the fruits of their industry; and to the means of making their industry fruitful. They have a right to the acquisitions of their parents; to the nourishment and improvement of their offspring. . . . Whatever *each* man can separately do, without trespassing upon others, he has a right to do for himself; and he has a right to a fair portion of all which society, with all of its combinations of skill and force, can do in his favor. In this partnership all men have equal rights; but not to equal things. He that has but five shillings in the partnership, has as good a right to it, as he that has five hundred pounds has to his larger proportion. But he has not a right to an equal dividend in the product of the joint stock.[29]

Here it plainly can be seen how easily Burke employs economic terms to discuss political concepts. Burke, the bourgeois theorist, is fully compatible with Burke the conservative: While Burke was in favor of traditional English society, by the time he began his political career, England was already capitalist, and that Burke should see this as the natural, good, and traditional society is understandable. The example of Burke, moreover, helps to demonstrate how individualistic liberalism and conservatism easily blend together. Conservatives, although they may criticize some of the consequences of the rapid social and cultural transformations introduced by evolving capitalism, overall accept as an unquestioned presumption the presence of a capitalist market as the base of the good society.

Burke, then, sees society as an organized, structured entity. All political power in society is, as in John Locke, a trust. As a trust, it is possible—though usually highly undesirable—for citizens to revolt against their government.

---

[28] Ibid., pp. 194–95.
[29] Ibid., pp. 149–50.

"Governments must be abused and deranged," Burke wrote, "before [revolution] can be thought of; and the prospect of the future must be as bad as the experience of the past."[30]

An important aspect of the trust is Burke's idea of a mixed and balanced constitutional government. Burke conceived good government as being composed of three groups: the monarchy, the aristocracy, and "the people." Although the people play a central role in Burke's theory, the term should not be understood as applying to very many individuals. On one occasion Burke numbered the people as roughly 400,000, comprising the upper-class property holders in Scotland and England: "the great peers, the leading landed gentlemen, the opulent merchants and manufacturers, the substantial yeomanry." Yet even the people are incapable of self-rule; they are to serve as a counterbalance to the court. The core of good government resides with the *natural aristocracy,* who, by birth, custom, and habit, know how to rule wisely on behalf of all. Given their economic status and social conditioning, the aristocracy serves as the bulwark of liberty between the pressures of monarchical despotism and of popular tyranny. In addition to the political functioning of these groups, Burke discusses the role of the British parliamentary system in terms of good government.

Burke's position on the role of parliamentary representation complements the above position. It is the duty of a member of parliament to watch out for the good of the society as a whole. Burke explained his model of representation thusly to his own constituents at Bristol.

> Your representative owes you, not his industry only, but his judgement; and he betrays, instead of serving you, if he sacrifices it to your opinion.
>
> If government were a matter of will upon any side, yours, without question, ought to be superior. But government and legislation are matters of reason and judgement, and not inclination. . . .
>
> Parliament is not a *congress* of ambassadors from different and hostile interests; which interests each must maintain, as an agent and advocate, against other agents and advocates; but parliament is a *deliberative* assembly of *one* nation, with *one* interest, that of the whole; . . . You Chuse a member indeed; but when you have chosen him, he is not a member of Bristol, but he is a member of *parliament.*[31]

Since representatives are not instructed delegates who represent specific interest groups, but are members of parliament who must reason for the whole, it is not essential that all individuals or groups have the vote. Burke called this idea "virtual representation." Although this form of representation is possible in a homogeneous society, Burke thought it had practical limitations. For example, he flatly rejected the claim that the American colonists had virtual representation in parliament: They were too far removed from England and had fundamental interests at odds with it. Still, with the theory of virtual representation the issue of suffrage becomes one of minor import because, in theory, all groups—whether or not they have the vote—are represented by all members of parliament.

[30] Burke, *Works*, Vol. 5, p. 73.
[31] Ibid., Vol. 3, pp. 19–20.

The role of the United States Constitution in the American political system is an excellent example of Burke's notions of good government and social obligation. Although many years have passed since the Constitution of 1787 was ratified, it continues to be the fundamental law of the land. The American people can alter it, but it requires significantly more effort than majority rule. Moreover, as time passes, it rightly becomes increasingly difficult to alter the basic principles contained in it because of the *presumption* against tampering with an institution where the weight of time and experience continually reestablish the wisdom contained therein. In a 1782 speech on reform, Burke could almost have been speaking about the American Constitution today when he stated:

> . . . our constitution is a prescriptive Constitution; it is a Constitution, whose sole authority is, that it has existed time out of mind. . . . It is accompanied with another ground of authority in the constitution of human mind, presumption. It is the presumption in favor of any scheme of government against any untried project, that a nation has long existed and flourished under it. . . . A nation is not an idea only of a local extent, and individual momentary aggression, but it is an idea of continuity, which extends in time as well as in numbers, and in space. And it is not the choice of one day, or one set of people, not a tumultuary or giddy choice; it is a deliberate election of ages and generation, it is a Constitution made by what is ten thousand times better than choice.[32]

Edmund Burke, then, not only demonstrates how conservatism and individualistic liberalism are compatible in their manifestations but he also presents us with the rudimentary outlines of conservative thought: Society is an organism; good government is based on order, structure, and a natural aristocracy; the aristocracy, with *noblesse oblige*, rules on behalf of all; custom and tradition, not momentary insight, are to guide decision making; and humankind should *conserve* the best of the species by paying careful attention to the wisdom of the past.

Many of the tendencies associated with conservatism are evident in the American political tradition. Within the broadly defined tradition of liberalism, there is a real concern with the value of stability. Further, as we shall see, James Madison's conception of the role and function of a representative is in many respects similar to that of Burke's, and Thomas Jefferson's preoccupation with a cohesive political community might be seen as an expression of a fundamental conservative value. To make sense of such observations, however, we must now return to our primary concern—the individualistic liberal tradition, primarily as manifested in the United States.

---

[32] Ibid., pp. 96-97.

SUGGESTED READINGS

BARKER, SIR ERNEST, ed., *Social Contract.* New York: Oxford University Press, 1960.

BERLIN, ISAIAH, *Four Essays on Liberty.* New York: Oxford University Press, 1969.

KRAMNICK, ISAAC, *The Rage of Edmund Burke: Portrait of an Ambivalent Conservative.* New York: Basic Books, 1977.

LASKI, HAROLD, *The Rise of European Liberalism.* London: George Allen and Unwin, 1936.

MACPHERSON, C. B., *The Political Theory of Possessive Individualism: Hobbes to Locke* Oxford: Clarendon Press, 1962.

POLANYI, KARL, *The Great Transformation.* Boston: Beacon Press, 1957.

TAWNEY, R. H., *Religion and the Rise of Capitalism.* New York: Mentor Books, 1947.

WOLIN, SHELDON, *Politics and Vision: Continuity and Innovation in in Western Thought.* Boston: Little Brown and Co., 1960.

Liberalism in the United States

Had every Athenian citizen been a Socrates; every Athenian assembly would still have been a mob.

James Madison

"In framing a government which is to be administered by men over men, the great difficulty lies in this: You must first enable the government to control the governed; and in the next place, oblige it to control itself."[1] These words from James Madison sum up a central dilemma of the individualistic liberal democratic tradition. Once one accepts the *democratic notion* that all people ought to have a voice in their governance, the task becomes one of devising a process of decision making that will translate *only* the legitimate, liberal wishes of the people into public policy. As we have seen in British liberalism, however, considerable difficulty lies in attempting to define the word *people*. Originally, "the people" was restricted, as in the writings of John Locke, to include men of property. It took considerable time, until around the middle of the nineteenth century, for liberal theorists to conceive of giving the vote to all white males; it required even more time for theorists to think about including nonwhites and women. If it is appropriate to view a society as being a legitimate democracy only at the point where it moves from the idea of universal suffrage to the reality of universal suffrage by actually extending the franchise, then it becomes questionable to discuss liberalism becoming liberal democratic in the United States until well into the twentieth century.

In addition to the suffrage problem there is the historical fact that preliberal governments, like the Greek *polis*, seemed inherently unstable, quickly degenerating into either mob rule or dictatorship. The task for political theory, therefore, was to develop a stable political system that fulfilled three functions: protect the inherent rights of individuals and minorities; respond to the expressed, legitimate wishes of majorities of its citizens; and lastly, control itself. The examination of these questions as they were debated and resolved in the American context will occupy a large portion of this chapter. Before addressing these issues, however, we must briefly examine the political and social context of America in the late 1700s, largely as a means of discussing some of the presuppositions of a liberal democratic society.

THE AMERICAN CONTEXT: "BORN EQUAL"

The egalitarian premise of British liberalism was very much part of the intellectual tradition in the American colonies. The removal of overt distinctions between classes (titles and so forth) and the influence of British libertarian rhetoric had produced a situation where political equality was taken to be the basic presupposition of all government. One need not delve too deeply into America's past to recall that this idea of political equality initially and historically was quite restrictive in practice—all were created equal except natives, black slaves, women, non–property holders, and so on. Nevertheless, the acceptance of the concept of

[1] James Madison, *The Federalist*, Jacob E. Cooke, ed. (Middletown, Conn.: Wesleyan University Press, 1961), p. 349.

political equality as an ideal, if nothing else, is an important presupposition for any regime that deems itself democratic.

America's egalitarian genesis has been an often-noted feature of its unique history. As long ago as the 1835 publication of the classic *Democracy in America,* Alexis de Tocqueville emphasized this point: "The great advantage of the Americans is that they have arrived at a state of democracy without having to endure a democratic revolution; and that they are born equal, instead of become so."[2] Indeed, Tocqueville went so far as to maintain that in the United States "the equality of conditions is the fundamental fact from which all others seem to be derived, and the central point at which all my observations constantly terminated."[3] What he found significant was that America did not have to go through the kind of economic and cultural revolutionary ferment that had rocked European society. The American colonialists had fought a lengthy war against the British Empire over the right of self-determination, but they did not suffer the throes of a social revolution. In terms of our prior discussion of feudalism, this egalitarian origin means that the United States did not pass through the feudal stage of development; it did not have to spend decades battering down the legal and psychological barriers to egalitarian thought. Lacking a feudal experience, America also lacked the community or corporate memory of a feudal past. The American experience seemed to be, quite simply, the fulfillment of Lockean liberalism in an isolated political environment; isolated, that is, from the counter ideological pressures of the right and left located in Europe.

The United States, then, was founded by men and women who fled from the feudal *ethos* of Europe and brought with them the liberal *ethos* of John Locke. While Locke's thought unfolded on both sides of the Atlantic, in Europe it had to contend with other political worldviews: feudalism and eventually socialism to name but two. And, if we can use England as an example, the early British liberals (Bentham, Mill, and others) had to battle constantly against a conservative monarchical establishment. Consequently, liberalism in Europe underwent important changes as it adjusted itself to the political environment there. The American situation was far different. Here, there was no need of fundamental compromise for there were, at that time, no major competing ideologies. Remember, during the Revolutionary War the conservative Tories who lived in (British) Colonial America had few choices: They could flee to Canada, return home to England, convert to the revolutionary cause, or stay and suffer the consequences (which sometimes meant, at a minimum, having their property confiscated). Whatever option they chose, Tory thought was eventually banished from American consciousness. As a result, any thought that did not fit into the broadly defined Lockean liberal perspective was considered un-American and had no political impact.

At least one additional factor helped produce the peculiar American experience with liberalism. America was blessed with vast expanses of "free" land. Given this economic base, an individual could become a property owner with relative

---

[2] Alexis de Tocqueville, *Democracy in America,* 2 Vols., trans. Henry Reeve (New York: Schocken Books, 1961), Vol. 2, p. 122.

[3] Ibid., vol. 1, p. lxviii.

ease. And, for a considerable period of time, no obvious economic class division developed in America as it had in Europe. Rather, the distinction existed between large property owners and small property owners, not between propertied and propertyless. All of these factors helped produce a cultural environment in which the individualism of Lockean liberalism flourished to the point of myopia: the "American Way" being considered, by Americans, to be the *only* way.

Participation: A Basic Value

The liberal idea of participation in government was also present in the American environment. Citizens had indeed participated in colonial government and, more importantly, felt they ought to participate in making decisions that affected their lives. Although many people viewed government with a good deal of suspicion, it was not thought of as the exclusive prerogative of some ruling class, elected or hereditary. It is too easy to generalize from the active political participation that characterized the propertied classes in places like Virginia and assume mass participation throughout the states: We simply do not know the extent to which a common laborer, for example, participated in political decision making. However, in the minds of those who had the greatest influence on the making of the American political system, the concept of participation in public affairs was a basic value.

Similarly, the notion that the ideas of another person ought to be tolerated even though they were deemed wrong was a major value, at least in intellectual circles. Again, much of what was practiced in the colonies did not live up to this ideal, as evidenced in a good deal of religious persecution. Still, the principle existed and eventually became incorporated into the Constitution of 1787 with the adoption of the Bill of Rights. One might go on to speak of other factors that made the climate conducive to some sort of liberal regime. A large land space, a relatively homogeneous English tradition, a country removed from the immediate threat of major military powers—all of these things combined to produce an environment that made experimentation with liberal government possible.

One of the scholarly fads of recent years has been an attempt to draw up a list of preconditions necessary for the establishment of a stable democratic government. Thus we are told that there must be a rather well-developed industrial economy (or the potential to create one), widespread literacy, a homogeneous culture, toleration of political opposition, and so on. Whether the construction of such lists is helpful in predicting the possibility of a viable liberal democratic regime is a subject that need not concern us here. What is important from an ideological perspective is that in general the *values* held by the founders of the American political system conformed to those of the liberal tradition. There is no doubt that the imperfect application of those values had important, even horrifying, consequences for individuals—if one, for instance, happened to be a native, female, or black. It may be, therefore, more helpful to look at the values embodied in the various American political documents as ideals to be achieved rather than descriptions of reality: As such, the entire American political tradition can be viewed as an attempt to actualize these ideals for all.

JAMES MADISON AND THE CONSTITUTION OF 1787

In 1776, the *Declaration of Independence* provided an eloquent statement of the ideals and aspirations of a liberal democratic society. The now familiar themes of equality, freedom, government by consent, and the right of resistance to arbitrary authority formed the ideological framework for the American revolution. But this statement of ideals, however lofty, neither provided a solution to the type of problems in democratic theory of which we have been speaking, nor attempted to establish a workable framework of government for the new nation. Having operated under the mainly *ad hoc* rules of the *Articles of Confederation* for almost a decade, the country had reached a point where few of the political elite were satisfied with its ability to control the state governments, and many committed liberals began to despair of the possibility of having an enduring republic in America. This concern became crystallized when news of a taxpayers' revolt in Massachusetts spread throughout the Eastern United States.

The significance of the 1786–1787 Massachusetts taxpayers' revolt, which historians have dubbed Shays' Rebellion, can scarcely be overrated. What Daniel Shays and some Massachusetts debtors actually did remains unimportant; what matters is what George Washington, James Madison, Alexander Hamilton, and others believed were the intentions of the rebels. For this information, they relied on Henry Knox's imaginative report. Acting as Superintendent of War under the *Articles of Confederation*, Knox constructed a fabricated but frightening account of the rebellion. He claimed that between twelve and fifteen thousand men were part of Shays' forces and that they endorsed the following, radical leveling position: Since the property of the United States had been protected from British confiscation by the joint exertions of all Americans, it therefore ought to be the common property of all Americans! To achieve those ends, therefore, Knox believed the Shaysites hoped to capture Boston, loot the Bank of Massachusetts, gain additional supporters, and march southward redistributing property along the way. (In fact, Shays' force of approximately twelve hundred men was soundly defeated by early 1787.) Nevertheless, the impact of Shays' uprising and its enormous contribution to the constitutional cause was recalled by James Madison as late as 1821: "the recent & alarming insurrection headed by Shays, in Massachusetts . . . [produced a] very sensible effect on the public mind."[4] Thus, the Constitutional Convention of 1787 provided an opportunity to reconstruct a new government along more viable lines and a group of bold men made sure that the opportunity did not pass.

The Convention has become many things to many people: To the patriot, it is the birthplace of the American form of democracy; to the student of political coalitions, it is a fascinating study in political bargaining; to those interested in political ideas, it provides a forum for the discussion and resolution of enduring problems in democratic theory. We cannot delve into all of the personalities attending the Convention nor discuss the ideas they presented—one must

---

[4] Madison, quoted in Richard K. Matthews, *If Men Were Angels: James Madison and the Heartless Empire of Reason* (Lawrence: University Press of Kansas, 1995), pp. 132–33.

tread lightly in the preserve of historians. But if we are forced to find a figure who approximated an authoritative interpreter of the principles embodied in the Constitution, there is little doubt that James Madison must be the choice. The Madisonian conception of the nature of the American system as articulated at the Constitutional Convention and later formalized in *The Federalist* papers provides the closest thing to an authoritative interpretation that we possess. Following other writers on American political thought, our presentation will largely be confined to Madison's viewpoint, particularly though not exclusively as it is developed in *Federalist 10*. Before moving to that presentation, however, let us note some additional effects on popular thinking wrought by the *Articles of Confederation*.

The American revolution was fought in the name of resistance to arbitrary authority and in defense of the traditional rights of Englishmen. The colonialists, after all, were British Americans. Naturally the symbol of capricious authority became the English monarchy. Whether that was a correct assessment of the situation or not is unimportant in this context, but it did produce a widespread distrust of a powerful head of state. This fear of monarchy was, of course, reflected in the *Articles of Confederation*, which provided for little effective national leadership, much less a powerful head of state. In the language of democratic theory, the primary fear was tyranny by one individual or by a minority, and the resulting political arrangements reflected that apprehension. Experience with the *Articles of Confederation*, however, convinced many of those who gathered at Philadelphia that the prime threat to the American experiment no longer existed in the form of a tyrannical individual or minority; rather, it resided in the capricious moods of democratic majorities that increasingly controlled the thirteen state governments. This distrust of uneducated, mob-like majorities fit in nicely with the elitist attitudes of many of the founders. Although Tocqueville described the egalitarian base of the early United States, there still existed—especially in the eyes of the elite—a great horizontal divide between extraordinary and ordinary people, between gentlemen and commoners. This attitude itself provided some balance to controlling unwarranted authority. The central question of American liberalism became, then, how to establish a popularly based government that would avoid the excess of tyranny whether imposed by a minority or a majority. This problem Madison addressed in *Federalist 10*, one of the most famous theoretical writings to emerge from the constitutional period.

The brainchild of Alexander Hamilton, *The Federalist* papers were written by Hamilton, John Jay, and James Madison. They originally appeared as individual newspaper pieces designed to convince the people of the state of New York to support the recently completed Constitution. While their major purpose was persuasion, the papers also provided a defense of the philosophical presuppositions and institutional framework provided for in that document. In particular, Madison's tenth paper addressed itself directly to the classic political problem of tyranny, and it claimed to have found a "Republican remedy for the diseases most incident to Republican Government."

Madison's View of Humanity

Madison began his discussion by presupposing the desirability of some form of popular government. There is little in the way of systematic analysis of other possible governmental types; this, of course, had to be expected given the recent war for independence. Madison simply asserted that a government that denied a significant, albeit indirect, degree of popular sovereignty would be incompatible with the character of the American people. Indeed, there seemed to be almost universal agreement that some sort of popular government was what was needed, but the problem lay in devising one that would avoid the difficulties of all prior democratic regimes. Madison's analysis of all past experiments with democratic governments indicated that they were constantly subject to instability. The most common cause of this instability was a majority of the citizens who, for whatever reason, attempted to impose their will through the government upon the rest of the society and in the process deprived them of their rights. Simply stated, prior democratic forms had a marked tendency to degenerate into mob rule. Sensing its inability to govern, the mob would then elevate a single person to assume dictatorial powers in the name of the people, and once that happened that particular democratic experiment was finished.

The cycle of tyranny of the majority leading to dictatorial rule and the consequent loss of freedom was all too familiar to students of history. Some even contended that it was impossible to create a stable and enduring democratic government. This tendency of a group of citizens, whether a majority or a minority of the whole, to seize power and deprive other citizens of their rights was the cardinal difficulty with democracies; a solution to the problem would have to be found before the system could work. One must take note of a distinctly Hobbesian attitude in Madison's analysis of human nature. Human passions are such that, in the absence of constraints, people will naturally seek to dominate one another. "Ambition must be made to counteract ambition," Madison boldly stated. "But what is government itself but the greatest of all reflections on human nature? If men were angels, no government would be necessary."[5]

People are not angels. They must be held in check, or they will tyrannize each other. And yet, Madison notes an interesting characteristic of humanity that Hobbes apparently missed. As an individual, isolated from other individuals, people are reasonable, timid, and cautious. However, a person inevitably comes into contact with other individuals, forms into groups Madison called *factions*, and at that point human behavior begins to change. "The reason of man, like man himself is timid and cautious, when left alone; and acquires firmness and confidence, in proportion to the number with which it is associated," observed Madison.[6] When this occurs, as it must, passion—not reason—rules. In one of the most uncharitable observations ever penned on human nature, Madison, in the quotation cited at the beginning of this chapter, eloquently captures the essence of the situation. It bears repeating: "Had every Athenian citizen been a Socrates;

---

[5] Madison, *The Federalist*, p. 349.
[6] Ibid., p. 349.

every Athenian assembly would still have been a mob." Madison believed that even Socrates, historical symbol of the most wise and most just individual, will turn into a member of a tyrannical mob when he becomes associated with like-minded individuals.

The Problem of Factions

Political philosophers and constitution makers must take this concept of humanity into account or their efforts will be for naught. This made the American framers' task even more difficult in that popular governments seemed most susceptible to this disease of factions. Democracies, to a greater extent than any other governmental form, permitted the individual liberty that led to the development of factions. Liberty was the air that spread the fire of faction, but to remove that air, Madison argued, would be to deny the basic premise of liberal government. Popular sovereignty would mean little if there were no liberty to form and articulate opinions. One cannot, then, solve the problem of factions by removing the liberty that permits them to exist, for, as Madison observed, the cure would be worse than the disease. Madison advanced and rejected one other possible cure for the causes of faction. Factions would not exist if it were not for the diversity of human interests, which forces people into competition for dominance. In theory, then, we might be able to remove the cause of faction by insuring that all the citizens have similar opinions, passions, and interests. If everyone agreed on everything, there would be no need for any group to attempt to dominate another. Madison quickly dismissed this cure by declaring that diverse interests are a necessary part of human nature and that it would be impossible to give everyone the same opinions. Again, we must stop and note that Madison raised an important point. Although his answer is consistent with his own philosophical premises, more contemporary democratic theorists pay considerable attention to the very real possibility of "giving everyone the same opinions." In an age like ours where the control of information and the use of propaganda through the mass media are everyday realities, the possibility of controlling or heavily influencing the opinions of an entire society cannot be so easily dismissed. Indeed, we shall see that, at times, ideologies attempt to do precisely that. Consistent with the premises of his individualistic liberal heritage, however, Madison specifically rejected that possibility even as he despaired of finding a cure for the causes of faction.

Factions are ubiquitous, contentious, and dangerous. Adapting Scottish philosopher David Hume's (1711–1776) prescriptions primarily from "Parties" and "Idea of a Perfect Commonwealth," Madison established his own basic dichotomy between factions. Some factions are based on "passion," like those established on religious or political beliefs; others are based on "interest," that is, economic factors. The latter are not only more reasonable, their multiplicity becomes the "grand elixir" to social instability. The former, less predictable and more volatile, require a particularly cunning scheme to control them and we will return to them momentarily. But Madison, as did Karl Marx less than a century later, found a crucial correlation between factions and economic interests.

> From the protection of different and unequal faculties of acquiring property, the possession of different degrees and kinds of property immediately results: and from the influence of these on the sentiments and views of the respective proprietors, ensues a division of society into different interests and parties.[7]

To Madison, then, the "most common and durable source of faction has been the various and unequal distributions of property." Since the unequal distribution of property resulted from the differences among individuals in their capacities to labor, what Madison calls their "unequal faculties," he followed Locke and accepted the inevitable socioeconomic consequences.

> Those who hold, and those who are without property, have ever formed distinct interests in society. Those who are creditors, and those who are debtors, fall under a like discrimination. A landed interest, a manufacturing interest, a mercantile interest, a monied interest, with many lesser interests, grow up of necessity in civilized nations, and divide them into different classes, actuated by different sentiments and views.[8]

It becomes "the principle task of modern legislation" to regulate "these various and interfering interests." Why does Madison think modern legislation can regulate these competing interests? To begin with, economic factions have a specific interest, a tangible thing which governments can, using a variety of means from taxation to confiscation, take from the owner. Furthermore, utility maximization underlies all economic activity; this means that humans can logically (even mathematically) understand and predict the behavior of others. But how can a society deal politically with an intangible religious or political belief? And since beliefs do not have a rational or logical foundation, nor do their reward structures lend themselves to the calculus of utility maximization, predicting their behavior can be extremely problematic—especially when individuals believe they are divinely authorized in their actions. After all, how can a secular power genuinely punish an individual or group who are motivated by divine sanction? Madison, then, was particularly concerned over the possible blending of politics and religion. His solution, consequently, was to draw a wall of separation around the religious sects, keep them out of the political arena, and play them off against each other in civil society. This ingenious strategy, however, cannot be employed quite so directly on political groups. For obvious reasons, Madison cannot a priori ban factions from politics; he can, however, permit them free reign to establish any form of government they want to—provided it is republican. He can also utilize the advantages of geographic space in combination with multiple political hurdles—like separation of powers, federalism, and representative government—to impede the progress of impetuous factions. But more on this at a later moment.

At first glance, the antagonisms resulting from property differences seem to be the sole cause of domestic unrest. But on closer examination, it can be seen that the root of human antisocial behavior runs far deeper and wider. Beyond property divisions are other causes of animosity. The destructive behavior of

---

[7] Ibid., p. 58.
[8] Ibid., p. 59.

passionate factions based on religion or politics is clear in one of his bolder statements on this point:

> A zeal for different opinions concerning religion, concerning government, and many other points, as well of speculation as of practice; an attachment to different leaders ambitiously contending for pre-eminence and power; or to persons of other descriptions whose fortunes have been interesting to the human passions, have turned mankind into parties, inflamed them with mutual animosity, and rendered them much more disposed to vex and oppress each other, than to co-operate for their common good. So strong is this propensity of mankind to fall into mutual animosities, that where no substantial occasion presents itself, the most frivolous and fanciful distinctions have been sufficient to kindle their unfriendly passions, and excite their violent conflicts.[9]

Given that the causes of faction are latent in human nature, the only possible solution to the problems that factions generate is to attempt to control their evil effects. While human nature cannot be changed, it might be possible to devise a set of social and political institutions that would work to counter these tyrannical tendencies. It is in his proposed system of control of factions that the genius of the Madisonian solution is to be found.

MADISONIAN POLITICS: AMBITION COUNTERACTING AMBITION

Initially and in a rather cavalier manner, Madison dismissed the dangers of *minority* factions. These present no difficulty because their evil designs can be controlled by the basic principle of majority rule. If a minority of citizens band together to seek to deprive others of their rights, the vast majority of citizens will realize the threat and deny the minority access to power. One can call this a summary treatment of the problem, for it presupposes to begin with that the majority of citizens will recognize a threat when presented. It further assumes that access to political decision-making organs is the only means by which one group can oppress another.

In the discussion of modern theories of democratic elitism presented later in this chapter, we shall encounter the question of minority faction presented in a much more graphic manner. However, for Madison, the ability of the majority to control the minority through the ballot box was a sufficient control over a factional minority. Disposing of that issue, he addressed himself to the classical problem of *majority tyranny*. It is obvious that the control of the vote that blocked minorities will have no effect here, for majorities can elect their leaders to positions of power. This being the case, Madison had to depend on other devices; his solutions fall into three general categories. First, there is a reliance on a particular type of political and economic environment; second, there is the introduction of a specific concept of representation; and third, there is the development of a series of institutions—a divided but powerful central state, a

[9] Ibid., p. 59.

federal system of governance, and a written constitution—that will make it exceptionally difficult for a tyrannical majority to assume political power. Let us examine each of these aspects of the Madisonian solution.

Restraints on Majority Tyranny

Prior to Madison, it was a commonplace assumption in classical theory that the democratic form of government was best suited to small states. In that the translation of popular preferences into public policy was one of the major goals of that type of regime, it was understandably thought that the most accurate presentation of the people's views would occur if citizens gave voice to their own thoughts. This type of *direct democracy*, while guaranteeing that the people's views were accurately portrayed, necessarily limited the size of the state. While notions of including some scheme whereby certain people were elected to represent the views of other citizens had been advanced, the conventional wisdom held that democracies or republics should be small, the ideal being a modern variation of the Greek *polis*. As we shall discuss briefly, Madison's idea of a republic involved such a scheme of representation as one of its essential elements, but his real break with the tradition came with his advocacy of creating a political system for governing a very large territory and population.

Turning the classical position around, Madison argued that one of the major causes of instability in prior republics was that their small size made it easy for a tyrannical majority to form and gain control of the government. In the close quarters of a *polis* or small state, human passions could easily become embroiled at a moment's notice and for the wrath of the majority to be unleashed upon innocent citizens. If the physical area of the state was much larger and its population more numerous, the formation of a majority faction would be a far more difficult enterprise. While the majority in one area of the state might be engulfed by a factional impulse, the spread of such views might well be contained by the sheer size of the country. Furthermore, given what he assumed about the diversity of human passions, Madison argued that a large number of citizens would tend to produce a whole series of small interest groups, thereby making it very difficult to form a majority that was bent on depriving others of their rights. The diversity of human interests would at worst lead to the formation of numerous minority factions that could then be controlled through majority voting rules. In *Federalist 10* Madison wrote:

> Extend the sphere, and you take in a greater variety of parties and interests; you make it less probable that a majority of the whole will have a common motive to invade the rights of other citizens; or if such a common motive exists, it will be more difficult for all who feel it to discover their own strength, and to act in unison with each other.[10]

Rather than attempt to prevent the formation of these self-interested and factional groups, governments ought to tolerate them, for the effect of many interests would be to ensure that no one group could gain sufficient power to be

[10] Ibid., p. 64.

tyrannical. "Society itself will be broken into so many parts . . . that the rights of individuals . . . will be in little danger from interested combinations of the majority," Madison observed.[11] The existence of a multiplicity of factions would have the effect of achieving a balance or equilibrium, thereby mitigating against the possibility of a majority faction. Of course, it remains crucial to remember that Madison's real fear is not some abstract, unspecified majority faction, but in Martin Diamond's words "*the* majority faction, i.e., the great mass of the little propertied and the unpropertied." In fact, to operate successfully Madison's political theory assumes a "modern commercial republic" where "the commercial life must be made honorable and universally practiced."[12] Diamond's point is well taken. When Madison described the virtues of an extended political space, he had in mind a particular type of economy, a *commercial* republic where power acquisitive individuals could pursue their own economic self-interest and, as John Locke and Adam Smith promised, the entire society would economically benefit. More importantly, if individuals could find meaning pursuing economic matters they would have less interest in interfering in political matters.

Here, then, is the Madisonian notion of an *extended republic.* We must stop and note both how well the argument flows from his premises and the ingenuity of the solution. People are selfish and power seeking by nature, and those drives have historically led to the downfall of regimes based upon popular sovereignty. Instead of attempting to change people so that they behave in a more benign fashion (an improbable task at best), government should take these selfish motives and use them to produce a situation where they cancel each other; the private, selfish vices will unintentionally produce public, selfless virtue. This is a clear statement of the idea that twentieth-century political theorists call *pluralism.* Because of the inability of any one group to dominate the others, there will be plural centers of power within the society and these will tend to balance each other to produce a society that is both stable and enduring. Madison accomplished this feat without removing the freedom that permits factions to form, thus ensuring that individuals will at least have the opportunity to pursue their own selfish interests. Finally, with an eye toward future discussion, it should be remembered that Madison thought the major source of faction was the human desire for economic goods. It is well known that competition for scarce resources is a major cause of conflict in any state, and as Karl Marx observed, the state was designed primarily to protect economic privilege. Recognizing the economic basis of most factions, Madison proposed to control their detrimental effects by allowing the formation of a great number of factions and putting them in competition with one another. We have, then, in the political realm, the equivalent of some form of economic *laissez faire*, whereby Madison assumed that multiplicity and competition lead to equilibrium and ensure that no one group gains political ascendancy. Indeed, the entire system is designed to avoid the political equivalent of monopoly in much the same way as classical economic theory sought to accomplish the same

[11] Ibid., p. 351.

[12] Martin Diamond, "The Federalist," in *The History of Political Philosophy*, Leo Strauss and Joseph Cropsey, eds. (Chicago: Rand McNally, 1974), pp. 647, 648, 650.

end in the economic arena. As a preliminary observation, then, we should note that the Madisonian political system—like both the Hobbesian and Lockean systems—seems to be quite compatible with some form of free market, capitalist economy where the state plays the minimalist role of umpire to competing factions. We shall explore the relationship between political systems and economic systems at a later point in the book; for the moment let us move on to Madison's concept of representation, the second device that he proposed for controlling factions.

Control Through Representation

It should be noted that Madison carefully distinguished between the terms *democratic* and *republican*, specifically calling his proposed regime a *republic*. To his mind a republic differed from democratic forms not only in that it preserved liberty, but was also larger both physically and numerically, and that it included a scheme of representation. This last distinction has largely been lost in modern times, where we tend to think of all democracies as possessing some scheme of representation. The term *representative government* is very close to the Madisonian republic. Whether or not it is appropriate to call Madison's system democratic is an important question that we will confront shortly. For the present, let us examine further the Madisonian notion of republican government.

In *Federalist 39* Madison defines a republic to be "a government which derives all of its powers directly or indirectly from the great body of the people."[13] A few things should be said about this definition. First, although power must ultimately come from "the people," it may be authorized by indirect methods. As will become clear, Madison tried to keep the relationship between the people and the government as indirect as possible. Indeed, in his concluding contribution to *The Federalist*, Madison boasted that "the true distinction" between the ancient republics and his proposed experiment "*lies in the total exclusion of the people in their collective capacity.*"[14] Second, just who comprises the category of "the people" is not readily apparent. What at first appears to be a rather open and popular basis of government eventually turns out to be rather restrictive. Perhaps more important, it is also evident that Madison tried to keep suffrage as limited as political reality would permit. In a similar manner, Madison's system of representation was designed to serve functions other than the mere reflection of popular opinion: He viewed it as an additional curb on potentially tyrannical factions.

In many respects the term *representative* contains built-in ambiguity. Common language as well as philosophical tradition employs it with two rather different meanings. On the one hand, a representative can be viewed as a person whose task is to discover the preferences of those whom he or she represents on a particular matter and to cast votes in accordance with the wishes of a majority of those constituents. In this meaning the representative is seen as the accurate

---

[13] Madison, *The Federalist*, p. 251.
[14] Ibid., p. 428; Madison's emphasis.

reflector of the constituency, simply a *delegate* to collect, synthesize, and report opinions. Modern technology has the capability of replacing this type of representative with a computer programmed to record and transmit majority preferences.

The other meaning of the word has the representative standing, as it were, in the place of the constituents and making decisions deemed in the best interests of those represented—as well as the total community. Here the representative acts as the *trustee* of the constituents, exercising judgment to the best of his or her ability, as each of them presumably would do in a situation of direct democracy. In this meaning of the word, it is quite possible that the representative will act contrary to the opinions of a majority of the constituents, feeling that he or she, in a Burkean manner, has more information, possesses a broader vantage point, or simply knows better.

These are two rather different notions of what it means to be a representative, and presumably any conception of representative democracy will vary depending on the meaning given to the initial term. The most common resolution of this difficulty is to use the word with both meanings; in effect, to assign two separate, and perhaps contradictory, roles to the legislator. Where the representative is normally the transmitter of majority opinion, at times we expect that person to assume the role of statesman and to ignore constituent wishes if those wishes are believed to be wrong. It is in performance of this role that one can write about "profiles in courage," where a representative suffers electoral defeat as the result of a principled stand. In the Madisonian scheme, the legislative role occasionally is seen in this dual fashion, but the Madisonian representative is usually perceived in the statesman role, providing a check against majority tyranny. Madison is rather explicit about the matter:

> The effect of the first difference [representation] is, on the one hand to refine and enlarge the public views, by passing them through the medium of a chosen body of citizens, whose wisdom may best discern the true interest of their country, and whose patriotism and love of justice, will be least likely to sacrifice it to temporary or partial considerations. Under such a regulation, it may well happen that the public voice pronounced by the representatives of the people, will be more consonant to the public good, than if pronounced by the people themselves.[15]

There will be times, perhaps quite a few, when the Madisonian legislator will be expected to ignore the temporary or partial considerations of the people represented, thereby denying the supremacy of the popular will. One of the reasons for the complexity of the process of elections described in the Constitution, as well as the staggered terms of office and varying length of term, is to provide for some distance between the representative and the constituency. Perhaps, given sufficient time to think the matter over, the cooler heads among the constituents will realize that their representative's act of frustrating the immediate popular will was the best course of action after all. Still, representatives must eventually submit themselves for reelection and too many such acts of courage will surely lessen their chances of reelection.

---

[15] Ibid., p. 62.

Control Through Institutions

The Madisonian concept of representation is sometimes described as an antidemocratic device, and in a sense that is correct. If we use a more majoritarian definition of democracy, there is little doubt that this legislative role is designed on occasion to frustrate majority will. Still, Madison could argue that it is but a temporary check on majorities and ultimately consistent with the principles of popular sovereignty, for the constituents have the last word at election time. It is rather difficult to speak of the Madisonian conception of the legislator in *vacuo* (in a vacuum) for it is part and parcel of the elaborate framework of institutions devised to provide additional safeguards against tyranny. Insofar as this third general category of mechanical or legal checks involves the entire structure of the United States Constitution, our discussion must, of necessity, be limited; still, we can hardly ignore the political framework that was to make the whole system function correctly.

We have seen that the effect of Madison's first defense against tyranny (it is sometimes called the *size principle*) was to produce a society in which varied interest groups were free to pursue their designs while ensuring that no one group could achieve sufficient dominance to become tyrannical. The framework of legal rules and governmental institutions advanced in the Constitution was designed to implement the size principle by providing access to major interests while assuring that there were appropriate checks on all the groups concerned. In a sense the entire Constitution, with its elaborate *federal* system, *separation of powers*, and *checks and balances*, is but a political reflection of the size principle discussed earlier. Presupposing a multiplicity of interests, government must give these interests access to political power so that they may press their claims effectively and, correspondingly, have sufficient defensive power so that they may block potentially tyrannical actions by other groups.

The initial device designed to accomplish this was the written constitutional document itself. It granted to the government certain *enumerated powers*, restricting governmental involvement to only those activities explicitly or implicitly granted to it. Equally important, the Constitution expressly prohibited the government from taking certain action. As the supreme law of the land, the Constitution would prescribe the powers and limitations of the government. Over the course of time, the Supreme Court embraced the concept of judicial review and thereby became the ultimate arbiter of claims regarding the powers and limitations set forth in the document. This firmly established the principle of limited government and ensured a legalistic framework of operation. Tocqueville, as early as 1835, observed that every matter in the United States eventually becomes a legal issue. Even if this was never intended by many of the framers, firmly established legal remedies for the resolution of conflicts have slowly become the norm. The other two major institutions of the federal government—the presidency and the Congress—were specifically designed to give representation to large interests within the country. The president, although supposedly "above faction," was viewed as particularly responsive to the propertied classes, and the veto power provided a means to check the excesses of the legislative branch. This is readily apparent if we recall the method of presidential election as originally detailed in the Constitution, wherein that person was chosen by a group of electors who were acting as representatives of their respective states.

Given the closer proximity of the legislative branch to the people and remembering Madison's concept of humanity, it seems natural that Madison should fear this branch the most. In order to control the most popular branch, which has the power to create laws, Madison divided the legislature into two houses—an upper and a lower chamber, each with similar but not identical powers, thus giving access to other interest groups. Representation in the Senate was by states, thereby ensuring that the interests of the large populous states would not overshadow those of the smaller ones. Granted, the existence of relatively independent states would have dictated some sort of federal arrangement in any case, but if we assume with Madison that certain types of interests can be geographically defined (that is, by state boundaries), the Senate affords them an important voice. The House of Representatives served as the voice of the people, and through the requirement of frequent elections it would presumably remain closest to the everyday wishes of the population. At that time the House of Representatives, designed to provide representation for the more populous states and urban centers, was the *only directly elected* institution in the entire Madisonian scheme. But with a minimum of 30,000 constituents per district, even this body would be composed of representatives rather removed from the potential excesses of the people.

Thus, these three major institutions—the executive, judicial, and legislative, the latter being further divided into two—are separate, each with unique powers; they are, however, also interconnected through the necessity of gaining the acquiescence of the other branches before public policy can be formed. In certain exceptional instances, of course, it is possible for the will of one branch to dominate over another—as in the case of overriding a presidential veto—but the general principle is nicely summed up by the old phrase of "checks and balances." To add an additional impediment to the force of faction, Madison utilized a federal system of government. This meant that not one, but fourteen governmental systems—each with its own system of competing branches of power, checking and balancing each other—had to be circumnavigated if any fundamental issues were to become law.

Other Devices of Control

In a similar fashion, the practice of staggering elections and terms of office acted as another restraint against potentially factional majorities. While members of the House of Representatives are elected every two years and presumably reflect rapid changes in public opinion, control of the Senate and the presidency requires a minimum of four years. It would take that long for a majority bent on tyranny to assume control of sufficient magnitude to put its design into effect. But we must not overlook the Supreme Court's roll in all of this. The justices are not elected; rather they are appointed to serve (assuming good behavior) for life. This immunity from the electoral process serves as yet another check on tyranny. Presumably a majority could be frustrated for as long as it took a certain number of older justices to die or retire. It must be emphasized, however, that these are only structural limitations on majority power; in the real world a Supreme Court that did not somewhat follow the election returns would undoubtedly endanger the legitimacy of the institution.

Similarly, in a system that is to a significant extent based on the self-interest of representatives in being reelected, even a senator not up for immediate reelection would be foolish to ignore completely a powerful shift in popular will among constituents. And, it is probably impossible to sustain a presidential veto over legislation strongly desired by a clear majority over a long period of time without sacrificing the idea of popular sovereignty. Minimally, what Madison hoped to achieve with the combination of institutional checks and balances and other mechanical devices was *delay*—a period of time in which members of a majority faction might rethink their actions and change their behavior. In this context we should note the emergence of a slightly more optimistic side to the Madisonian view of human nature.

Earlier it was stated that Madison's assumptions concerning the essential selfishness of human beings were in line with Hobbes's view. Although true, Madison was sophisticated enough to see that there were different types of selfish interests, some more disruptive of political systems than others. He was particularly impressed with how rapidly some popular passions—most notably those based in religion—could infect a majority and result in some precipitous action that, upon further reflection, would have led even selfish people to avoid. We already noted that Madison was influenced by the political writings of David Hume (much of *Federalist 10* is borrowed from Hume's work) and that a major focus of Hume's thought was a distinction between *calm* and *violent* passion. Although both types of passion were based upon individual self-interest, the latter was more volatile and temporary while the former looked to long-range selfish concerns. The violent passions of people might tell them to try to take away the natural rights of members of the community for some offense against popular opinion, but their calm passion would warn them that on some future occasion they too might be subject to the wrath of some new irate majority. Note that both of these passions are based upon selfish interest, but they would lead to quite different kinds of behavior. If institutional checks and balances could produce a delay in which tempers were allowed to cool, long-range self-interest, or as Madison called it, "enlightened self-interest," might prevail.

One of the reasons why many of the founders were preoccupied with processes of education involved an attempt to ensure that citizens would adopt this long-range view of their interests. While Madison paid too little attention to such matters of habit and education in *The Federalist*, one of the later concerns of the leadership of the country was the production of a well-educated citizenry. Some commentators argue that if Madison had been more concerned with developing democratic habits in the populace and with ensuring the existence of a liberal value structure, he need not have been so concerned with institutional checks on majority tyranny. Whatever the case, the institutional checks were intended at least in part to encourage the ascendancy of enlightened self-interest.

MADISON'S REMEDY: LIBERAL
OR LIBERAL DEMOCRATIC?

"In the extent and proper structure of the Union, therefore, we behold a Republican remedy for the diseases most incident to Republican Government."[16] These words, from the concluding paragraph of *Federalist 10,* are Madisonian shorthand for summarizing the entire endeavor of the framers as well as their claim to fame. We have attempted to describe the "extent and proper structure" remedies of the Madisonian republic using the threefold distinction of *size, representation,* and *institutional checks.* Madison's system is brilliant. Through the structure or design of the system itself, all but the most intense factions will automatically be thwarted. A mechanical system of government, employing nonhuman factors wherever possible, was "the remedy" to factions. Hobbes's *Leviathan* relied too heavily on humans; less subject to human frailty, Madison's system attempted to utilize nonhuman factors. Through an extended commercial republic, itself divided into a federal system of governments, with each component having a degree of power, Madison hoped to create equilibrium. The division of the central government into three branches, each one step further removed from the people, provided an additional safeguard. Limited suffrage and a trustee model of representation created more checks. Lastly, a written constitution that delegated limited and enumerated powers while it prohibited others, comprised the final bulwark. Thus, Madison strove to build a machine-like system, a structure of government that would automatically divert and diffuse factions. Furthermore, the system would check itself by not allowing its human operators to become too powerful. Madison created an ideal, self-perpetuating Leviathan that would provide the prerequisite social stability for the attainment of commodious living.

It should be reemphasized that the Madisonian system is specifically designed to impede governmental change. If any single federal political institution says "no" to new legislation, that policy is defeated. Put differently, when there is governmental gridlock, the system is functioning exactly as designed. When it seems as if "nothing is happening" in Washington, that conclusion is wrong for whenever the government refuses to change public policy, it simultaneously reinforces the status quo. Those who like things the way they are think government is working just fine. Clearly, the Madisonian design itself is quite conservative in nature; it privileges the past over the future.

Two questions remain unanswered: (1) Does Madison meet his own standard of a "republican remedy"? (2) Can this system be considered democratic? To address the first query, the answer appears to be in the affirmative. Madison desired a government based upon the principle of popular sovereignty, which avoided the tyrannical excesses of past forms of popular government. But it must be remembered that in Madison's conception of a republic, popular sovereignty could be exercised either "directly or indirectly" by the "great body of the people." Madison's reliance primarily on indirect controls, therefore, remains consistent with his definition of republican government. However, this facet to Madisonian

---

[16] Ibid., p. 65.

government is more problematic when examining its claim to being democratic. Still, in permitting individuals the liberty to acquire property, form interest groups, and press demands on government, the system had to be capable of accommodating the constantly changing desires of people while avoiding the excesses of instability. To form a stable and enduring republic, Madison believed it would be necessary to compromise the basic principle of popular sovereignty to the extent necessary to ensure that people did not abuse each other's rights. Yet the question remains whether the constraints he instituted were sufficient to prevent tyranny. Or, did they so constrain majority will as to violate the basic principle of popular sovereignty?

Criticisms of Madison's System

Many individuals, particularly after the constitutional system had been in operation for a period of time, believed that Madison's efforts to check majority faction had not been completely successful. He had, it was argued, made no provision whatsoever for the development of the political party system that emerged early in the history of the republic. That being the case, even if one granted that his system controlled the development of *natural* majority factions, it did not stop the formation of the *artificial* and enduring majority factions produced by political parties. Indeed, Madison was one of the initial founders of the Republican (now Democratic) party. Parties were capable of forging temporary alliances among quite disparate minority factions for the purpose of securing control of the political structure, whereupon they might try to achieve minority goals at the expense of the rights of others. Although this type of faction was not the natural majority type that Madison so feared, it was equally capable of tyrannical action.

This general position was most eloquently advanced by John C. Calhoun, the major spokesman for southern interests in pre–Civil War days. In the name of further defense of individual and states' rights, Calhoun argued for an extension of the control mechanisms on majorities, largely by giving any major interest group (states, sections) veto power over any legislation affected by it. Such a position would have further diminished the power of the national political system and greatly expanded the sphere of private action. Whatever the details of Calhoun's proposals, he is an excellent representative of those who believed that Madison correctly identified the major problem of majority faction but that his control devices were only partially effective and would have to be supplemented.

On the other side of the coin, many individuals, some of whom we shall meet in the next section, asserted that Madison had been so preoccupied with the potential of majority tyranny that he produced a system that so constrained majorities that it made a mockery of the principle of popular sovereignty. From this perspective, the sociological and political checks against majorities made it very easy for a small group of people to frustrate legitimate majority desires, thereby producing a government by minority. Minimally, the minority in control of the political system at any particular time could deny legitimate popular claims, but it also could produce the opposite of Madison's great fear—that is, tyranny by the minority.

Finally, in an extension of the foregoing argument, there are those who contend that Madison achieved precisely what he intended. From this vantage point, Madison was a Virginia aristocrat, terrified of the possibility of majority power over the propertied interests of his class, yet sufficiently sophisticated to realize that some form of popular government was inevitable in America. As such, he devised an ingenious system that gave some power to popular majorities, sufficient to permit them to "blow off steam" and to believe they were actually governing, while making it virtually impossible for them to achieve enough control to initiate basic change in the emerging capitalist economic system. As Madison explained it, "A government like ours has so many safety-valves, giving vent to over heated passions, that it carries within itself a relief against the infirmities from which the best of human institutions cannot be exempt."[17]

Controversy surrounds the Madisonian claim of having found a "republican remedy" to the unrest of factions. Needless to say, we are as yet in no position to evaluate these varying interpretations of the Madisonian enterprise. However, the types of questions raised here do comprise a loose conceptual framework for the debate concerning the nature and success of the American "democratic" experiment, a debate that continues to this day. Thus, the final question regarding Madison can at last be addressed: Was he a democrat?

Madison's View of Suffrage

As we have already noted, Madison carefully separated himself from democratic movements of the past. He found them unstable and preferred his republican system, which required only "indirect" control from "the great body of the people." Just who, then, comprised "the great body of the people"? We can get some idea by examining Madison's view of suffrage.

Like many liberals of his day, Madison recognized the importance of the franchise question and was concerned with the impact non–property holders might have if given the vote. At the Constitutional Convention, he argued for a property qualification for electors to the House of Representatives: "the freeholders of the Country would be the safest depositories of Republican liberty." When the issue of voting for the Senate arose, he again advocated that "Landholders ought to have a share in the government, to support" their "invaluable interests." The voting pattern must be drawn up, he stated, "to protect the minority of the opulent against the majority."[18]

Although no property qualification for voters or officeholders appears in the body of the Constitution, a motion was carried at the Convention instructing a committee to fix property qualifications for voting. Failing to agree upon the nature of the qualifications to be imposed, delegates to the Convention dropped the issue. The Convention established a few guidelines and returned the question to the individual states. Madison knew that by giving the states the power to establish voting standards the immediate result would probably be that not even all white males

---

[17] Madison, quoted in Matthews, *If Men Were Angels*, p. 173.

[18] Max Ferrand, ed. *The Records of the Federal Convention of 1787*, 3 Vols., (New Haven: Yale University Press, 1966), Vol. 2, p. 203, Vol. 1, pp. 143–44, and 432.

would have the vote since many states would impose property qualifications. At the time of the Constitutional Convention, then, Madison was no democrat: He did not accept the equal right of every human to participate in the governing of society. Some years later, however, he changed his mind.

In 1821, while correcting and expanding his own Convention notes from other recently printed accounts of the Constitutional Convention, Madison recorded a modest—but highly significant—change in his views on suffrage. Commenting on his Convention speech of August 7, 1787, he noted: "These observations . . . (of 1787) . . . do not convey the speaker's more full and matured view of the subject, which is subjoined. He felt too much at the time the example of Virginia." Now more than three decades after arguing his freeholder's position, Madison explicitly rejected any voting conditions that would, either then or in the future, exclude the mass of society from political participation.

In this 1821 revision of his Convention position, Madison warned: "Allow the right [of suffrage] exclusively to property, and the rights of persons may be oppressed. . . . Extend it equally to all, and the rights of property or the claims of justice may be overruled by a majority without property, or interested in measures of injustice." Madison reviewed several qualification schemes on which suffrage could be based, but he rejected a categorical property qualification because "It violates the vital principle of free Government that those who are to be bound by laws, ought to have a voice in making them. And the violation would be more strikingly unjust as the lawmakers become the minority." Still, Madison ended up endorsing a system very similar to his original 1787 position: "Confining the right of electing one Branch of the Legislature to freeholders, and admitting all others to a common right with the holders of property, in electing the other Branch." This system will suffice, he argued, until "the non-freeholders should be the majority."[19] Recognizing the inevitability of the majority eventually becoming nonfreeholders, Madison was forced to accept the inevitable. In tones and logic similar to that of James Mill, whom we discussed in the prior chapter, Madison endorsed white male suffrage:

> Under every view of the subject, it seems indispensable that the Mass of Citizens should not be without a voice, in making the laws which they are to obey, & in chusing the Magistrates, who are to administer them, and if the only alternative be between an equal & universal right of suffrage for each branch of the Government and a confinement of the entire right to a part of the Citizens, it is better that those having the greater interest at stake namely that of property & persons both, should be deprived of half their share in the Government; than that those having the lesser interest, that of personal rights only, should be deprived of the whole.[20]

Hardly a ringing exultation in support of democratic principle, the preceding passage does, nevertheless, show that Madison recognized the necessity of individualistic liberalism becoming democratic. The answer to our question, then, is twofold. At the time of the Constitutional Convention, Madison cannot be considered a

---

[19] James Madison, *Mind of the Founder*, Marvin Meyers, ed. (Indianapolis: Bobbs-Merrill, 1973), pp. 502, 503, 506, and 507.

[20] Ibid., pp. 508–9.

democrat: an individualistic liberal to be sure, but not a democrat. Sometime in the first quarter of the nineteenth century, however, Madison "backed into liberal democracy" as he recognized the political impossibility of denying the vote to the ever-growing propertyless class.

We have attempted to present James Madison as the primary spokesman for the individualistic liberal tradition of Hobbes and Locke in the early years of the United States. It should now be clear that his enterprise involved much more than merely "fitting" that tradition to the unique conditions that prevailed in America. His "republican solutions to the evils inherent in republican government" constituted a real and lasting contribution to the ongoing dialogue concerning the appropriate nature of a liberal democratic society. Finally, Madison's scheme, because of its embodiment in the Constitution, in many ways set the context for the aforementioned dialogue, at least in its American context. In effect, Madisonian politics became, in the words of George Beam, "usual politics"; and triumphs and failures, critiques and proposals for reform in the American system have been generally advanced within the intellectual context formulated by Madison.

Many students of American history view the Constitution of 1787 and the Madisonian political philosophy it embodied as a conservative reaction to the more majoritarian ideals expressed in the *Declaration of Independence.* Where the *Declaration* recognized equality, freedom, and the supremacy of popular will as the ultimate goals of government, Madison's system compromised on equality, attempted to restrict freedom through competition, and placed severe checks on the power of popular majorities—all in the pursuit of stability. One need not agree with such an assessment of the enterprise of the founders and framers to recognize that the overall pattern of development of the American political system since 1787 has been toward increasing majoritarianism. The expansion of the franchise led the way. Slowly but surely, all segments of the populace— non–property owners, Native Americans, blacks, and women—were granted the vote, so that universal suffrage became the hallmark of late twentieth-century American democracy.

We have already noted that the early development of a political party system provided focal points for groups interested in attaining power, and to a certain extent mitigated the balance which Madison thought would be achieved through a multitude of diverse interest groups. Although American political parties remain rather weak in contrast to their highly disciplined European counterparts, the existence of a two-party system did make it possible for majorities to gain access to the government. However imperfect the American political system of today might be, it functions in a far more majoritarian fashion than its eighteenth-century ancestor. Structural changes such as the popular election of senators and the evolution of the role of the presidency gave greater power to the people at the expense of states and propertied interests. The extent of that evolution toward majoritarianism and some reactions to that process comprise much of the subject matter of contemporary liberal thinking. To some degree we must delve into American political history to explain the ideological changes that accompanied the evolution of the institutions after 1787. To avoid extensive historical discussion, however, let us concentrate on the changes in the presidency as a sort of case study.

THE RISE OF THE IMPERIAL PRESIDENCY

It has been noted that the presidency was in part designed to ensure that the person who occupied the office was above politics. The election of a president was left to an Electoral College, a collection of presumably distinguished people appointed by the states, who would gather and choose the best person for the office. George Washington, the first to hold the office, succeeded somewhat in retaining the image of nonpartisanship, but the advent of the party system in reaction to his regime ultimately made this an impossible task. Further, despite the rhetoric advocating a nonpartisan leader, the method of presidential election ensured that, to a certain extent at least, he or she would be the representative of minority interests. Insofar as the members of the Electoral College were appointed by the legislatures of the varying states, and those legislatures were dominated by property owners, it is appropriate to view this office as a further check against propertyless majorities. The next 200 years in the history of the presidency were marked by a sporadic but continual movement toward majority control of that office.

The first major change in the presidency is commonly seen as occurring with the election of Andrew Jackson in 1828 as a self-styled "man of the people." While the nature and extent of Jacksonian democracy remains a matter of some controversy, there is little doubt that the representation of the office as being responsive to popular wishes marked a significant change from the intention of most of the framers. Once begun, the pattern of greater and greater influence of popular majorities on the presidency became a dominant theme in the development of American democracy. The facts of expanding presidential leadership in response to popular wishes and societal needs are familiar even to those with only a superficial knowledge of American history. Some examples are Abraham Lincoln's assumption of near-dictatorial power as commander in chief during the Civil War, Woodrow Wilson's role as an international force in World War I, Franklin D. Roosevelt's aggressive behavior on the economic and military fronts, and William Clinton's leadership in using NATO against "international threats." One could cite other examples, but these make it clear that the American presidency in the twentieth century, largely as a result of foreign and domestic crises, became the prime focus of popular opinion, and as such became increasingly responsive to the wishes of popular majorities.

Changes in this one institution reflect in a graphic manner an alteration in the concept of the entire governmental enterprise in the United States and parallel a changing view of the nature of liberal democratic government itself. Largely through the expanded scope of presidential action, the traditional individualistic liberal ideal of limited government gradually eroded.

THE RISE OF MAJORITARIAN LIBERALISM

Recall that the entire American experiment with liberal democracy was initiated in a period of profound fear of the power of states. Drawing on the ideas of classical British liberalism, the framers produced a system intended to ensure that the individual possessed a large sphere of action that was not subject to governmental involvement. To use the standard terminology, speech, religion, assembly, movement, and economic activity were areas largely removed from political interference. It was this emphasis on the essential privacy of individual action that made the American experiment consistent with the highly individualistic ideals of the mainstream liberal tradition. However, the system was also predicated upon the assumption that individuals and groups would press their demands upon the government in an attempt to produce policies that maximized their private interests. In a real sense there was a built-in conflict between the liberal emphasis on highly limited government and the realization that groups would attempt to use the system for their own aggrandizement.

The Madisonian solution of an extended commercial republic with built-in checks and balances was in part intended to assure that there would be no governmental action unless a broad consensus existed on a particular matter. In his pursuit of protection from the dangers of majority and minority tyranny, Madison helped produce a political system that reinforced the liberal ideal of limited government by making it quite difficult for majorities to form on any issue. If the multiplicity of interest groups and the checks and balances performed their function of balancing competing interests, there would be little in the way of a mandate for action of any sort on the part of the political system. That being the case, the scope of government would be limited not only by law but also by the absence of a widespread call for action of any type. It was in this way that the Madisonian system reinforced the inherent individualism of the tradition, because it tried to ensure a large private sphere of interaction. The gradual evolution of the presidency toward majoritarianism, combined with the other democratic changes mentioned earlier, in many respects undermined the check-and-balance functions of the system.

Although there is currently a good deal of disagreement as to the extent of majoritarianism in America (as will be obvious from the ensuing discussion of democratic elitism), let us for the moment accept the statement that changes in institutions as well as advances in communications made it easier for cohesive majorities to form and ensured that government would be more responsive to them. If that were the case, what were the consequences for the traditional liberal democratic conception of government? Two of the immediate and far-ranging consequences were that the sphere of private action dear to individualist liberalism was inevitably diminished and that the entire question of the legitimate extent of democratic majority action arose once again.

Avoiding Instability and Revolution

In order to discuss the shrinking area of private action in a system with growing majoritarian tendencies, we must recall several points made earlier. It was stated that all governments, irrespective of their ideological goals, had to satisfy certain minimal demands that arose from the citizenry if they were to avoid instability and revolution. No series of demands sought by large numbers of citizens could be ignored by any political system for a long period of time without risking social upheaval. As we shall see, in the transfer culture of communism, and in other nonliberal ideologies as well, concerted attempts are made to control the types of demands advanced by the citizenry. Thus in all nonliberal regimes there is extensive use of propaganda and censorship in an effort to mold popular opinion and give the leadership the widest possible latitude to pursue their goals. If the types of demands placed on the political system could be limited at their source, societal instability could be avoided. In democratic governments, however, this type of control and censorship of opinions cannot be openly attempted—although propaganda may be used to influence opinion—for one of the basic presuppositions of democratic philosophy is that information is public and that individuals must be free to develop and pursue their interests.

This is the same problem in a somewhat different form that Madison raised when he discussed and dismissed the possibility of limiting factions by giving all members of the population the same opinions. If the liberty that permits the development of myriad demands on government cannot be abridged, we must then be prepared for a constant clamoring among groups in the society who wish to secure the passage of legislation beneficial to their interests. Realizing this, Madison erected the types of checking devices already discussed. Since the growing majoritarianism of the American system meant a more rapid translation of popular wishes into public policy, it was probably inevitable that government would expand its scope of action so as to be able to respond to those demands. Indeed, if it did not respond to them, it would be constantly risking instability. Faced with such a situation, one would naturally expect legislation to satisfy the demands of significant portions of the population whenever these demands arose. Thus, whenever the informal and customary control mechanisms of the private sector seemed insufficient to solve problems or to contain conflict, a demand was inevitably pressed on the political system to solve the problem through political rules, that is, to pass laws. As soon as this occurred, government had, in effect, turned a matter formerly private in nature into a subject of public policy. To clarify this process let us refer in an admittedly superficial way to the Depression crisis in 1929.

Although the American government had been involved in the economic sector to a considerable extent prior to the onset of the Great Depression, the myth that the free enterprise system contained a self-control mechanism through supply and demand was still very much part of the conventional wisdom. Ever since John Locke had declared that property was something inherent in the individual and subject to only minimal regulation by government, the notion of a free market economy had been something of an individualist liberal dogma. Faced with the crisis of the Depression and the apparent inability of the informal market mechanisms to solve that crisis, the political system was immediately bombarded with demands that it step in and legislate the Depression out of existence. It could not help but respond to those demands if it valued the continued existence of not only a particular regime but also the entire form of government. Note that we are not discussing whether governmental actions during the Depression solved that particular economic crisis. We are only saying that the political system had little choice but to take some sort of public action to alleviate private suffering.

One can duplicate this example in many other areas. A decline in the cohesiveness of the family structure has led to demands that the government support the children of unstable or broken families; a decline in the status of religious institutions as keepers of the public morals has led to demands that laws be passed prohibiting deviant behavior or controlling the types of art people are allowed to enjoy. All of these actions have the effect of greatly increasing the scope of public action and reducing the area that was formerly private.

Again, we must insert a caveat to the effect that the transference of a particular subject matter from the private to the public sphere does not necessarily mean that the freedom of the individual to do as he or she wants is greatly lessened. The informal control mechanisms of religious institutions can be just as restrictive of individual action as any formal law, and local committees formed to ban textbooks or "pornographic" magazines and musical CDs can keep them off shelves as effectively as any governmental edict. What is important here is that we are chronicling a distinct change in the conception of the appropriate role and function of political institutions. The highly limited government of the liberal tradition of Locke and Madison is a thing of the past in America. The emergence of something that we shall call *majoritarian liberalism,* and alongside of it the *positive state,* lends a quite different character to modern American liberal democratic thought.

Before exploring that theme, however, it might be helpful to take a brief excursion outside of the American context to explore the effects of increasing majoritarian pressures on other liberal democratic systems. England's parliamentary system provides a good example because, as noted earlier in this chapter, it did not possess the type of antimajoritarian political structures instituted by Madisonianism.

Majoritarianism in the British Tradition

We have already mentioned that in England, James Mill and other early individualistic liberals had, however grudgingly, accepted the extension of voting rights to all males—and women were soon to follow. The implications of the extension of the franchise were, however, considerably different in England (as well as in some Continental democracies) than in the United States. The absence of Madisonian checks designed to mute the potential power of majorities have made non-Madisonian liberal systems much more responsive to the wishes of majorities in the twentieth century. In England the rise of the mass-based Labor party provided a vehicle for the transference of majoritarian preferences into public policy.

Moreover, the English tradition of responsible parties (highly centralized and disciplined, in contrast to their American counterparts) ensured that, upon election, the preferences expressed in the parties' programs were transferred into public policy. The checking and balancing of competing interests engendered by the Madisonian system provided no barrier in England. For this reason many critics of the American system, who believe that it is insufficiently responsive to majoritarian preferences, cite England as an alternative model of a stable liberal democratic regime. John Dewey, whom we will meet in the next chapter, exemplified this position when he argued that Madisonianism had produced a condition whereby competing interest groups precluded both the possibility of achieving and the possibility of conceiving a truly *public* interest in America.

In this context we should also mention that responsiveness to majoritarian preferences has frequently led not only to increasing governmental policy making in areas heretofore considered "private" (the welfare state, for example), but in the eyes of many it has loosened, if not broken, the traditional tie between individualistic liberalism and capitalist economics. And this loosening may provide a bridge between majoritarian democracy and socialist economics. As we shall see in our discussion of communist thought, some Marxists early in the twentieth century (called "revisionists") viewed the extension of the franchise in places like England and Germany as providing the possibility of peacefully legislating a socialist economic system, rendering the violent revolution that Karl Marx foresaw unnecessary. If majorities desiring socialism possessed political power, they could use the government to evolve into a socialist society. In the majoritarian liberal tradition of the twentieth century, we have one of the possible bases for a doctrine of *democratic socialism*. While we shall address that point in the next chapter, for the moment let us return to our discussion of the question of majoritarianism in the United States.

MAJORITARIAN LIBERAL DEMOCRACY IN AMERICA

The idea that government ought to play a more positive role in the lives of its citizens developed gradually in the United States. Early liberalism conceived of the state's function being essentially minimal and *negative*. It would use the least amount of power to protect individuals and their property. If one wanted to attach a time period to the emergence of the *positive state*, one could point to the earlier part of the twentieth century, when the political system became actively involved not only in the protection of individuals and property but also in the control of the economy and in the expansion of functions that occurred from World War I to the aforementioned Great Depression. The date one might choose is somewhat immaterial. From the point of view of Madisonian liberalism, the significant fact is that the one hundred years between 1850 and 1950 marked a profound change in the processes of American government; it now had to take positive action to improve the general welfare of its citizens.

Although the core values of the liberal tradition remained relatively intact, certain of their number were given greater emphasis while others moved to a lower position in the value hierarchy. We have already noted that the trend toward majoritarianism had a great effect on the individualistic liberal conception of limited government. Instead of viewing the political system as an umpire, balancing the competing claims of private interest groups, the majoritarian liberalism of the twentieth century envisioned government as an active force in producing a better life for its citizens. The impartial third party of Lockean theory is replaced by attempts to institute a modern welfare state. Perhaps the most important value change that occurred in the evolution from individualistic majoritarian liberalism was in the status of the individual.

We began our discussion of the tradition initiated by Hobbes and Locke by emphasizing that the idea of the free, relatively isolated individual was the one concept shared by the first liberal theorists. While that value is retained by American majoritarian liberalism, its force is considerably altered. Inevitably, as government began to expand its sphere of activity, it generated rules that necessarily constrained the freedom of some individual action. To use a rather crude example, the freedom of the tobacco industry to advertise its product in a glamorous manner on television is reduced to the extent that it not only is prohibited from using that medium but it must also post a health warning on its packages. The old notion of *caveat emptor* (let the buyer beware) is replaced by the legal responsibility of the producer to warn consumers of potential health risks.

Note that there is no need to attach any sort of moral judgment to these changes in values; we are simply attempting to describe an evolution in the conception of the individual as well as the role of the state. One may heartily approve of governmental legislation to prohibit shoddy business practices or one may feel such action is interfering with individual rights; the fact remains that freedom to act is being constrained. It should also be noted that governmental legislation to limit individual action was very much a part of individualist liberal democratic thought. Humans, after all, limit themselves merely by becoming members of a society. The controversy arises regarding the appropriate scope of legislation by political systems that call themselves liberal democratic regimes.

The Tension Between Liberty and Equality

Paralleling the reduction in importance of the unconstrained individual in majoritarian liberalism is the rise in importance of the old democratic value of equality. Indeed, some commentators see a necessary interrelationship between the values of liberty and equality or note a tension between these two cardinal values of the mainstream tradition. Minimally, one can assert that equality was the most ill-defined and limited of the values of individualistic liberalism. Recall that Thomas Hobbes saw people as equal only in the negative sense that they all possessed the ability to kill one another. The major question involving the interrelationship between the values of liberty and equality, however, arose first in the economic area.

Beginning around the turn of the twentieth century, people began asking how one could be free without the means to exercise that freedom. To use an obvious example, a person residing in the United States possesses a theoretical freedom or right to leave the country for other places in the world. That theoretical right does not, however, put the money in his or her pocket that will permit the exercise of this right. Is not the person who possesses the means to exercise the abstract right of free movement actually more free than one who does not? Stated in a slightly more complex way, people were beginning to see that economic inequalities conferred greater power on some of their number and that the abstract values of liberty and equality meant little without the financial ability to fulfill them.

Similarly, the theoretical equality between black and white, male and female, is little more than meaningless rhetoric if minorities and women are systematically denied the opportunity to achieve economic equality. To return to our initial point, however, governmental legislation that is designed to achieve economic equality, or laws that attempt to ensure that people of color and women will be treated equally, both in fact and in theory, will undoubtedly constrain the freedom of other members of the community. This is precisely what is meant by the tension between freedom and equality. When my ability to discriminate on the basis of race, religion, or sex is abridged through the action of government, my personal liberty is indeed limited. While all right-thinking individuals might applaud such legislation on the grounds that such discrimination deprives others of their rights from the individualistic liberal point of view, it nevertheless reduces freedom. The response from majoritarian liberalism would simply be that the classical value of freedom is meaningless without relative equality. The hallmark, then, of the American majoritarian liberalism of the twentieth century is the attempt to use the political system to ensure greater degrees of equality or, at least, *equality of opportunity*. To use a popular sports metaphor, the government must create a "level playing field" so all citizens—even those disadvantaged at birth—have an equal chance to develop their individuality.

With the advent of majoritarian liberal democracy, a split in the ideology occurred over the meaning of both the liberal and the democratic components. The early liberals argued on behalf of those market freedoms necessary to allow individuals to pursue their own self-interest, even if this meant, as it usually did, that one person's gain was another person's loss. When the class inequalities produced by capitalism became rather obvious, other liberal theorists argued that the freedom that was necessary to human fulfillment was not market freedom but the *equal effective right* of individuals to develop their own capacities.

Similarly, liberal theorists disagreed over the nature of democracy. One group believed that democracy was essentially just a *political mechanism* for electing government. It was important in that it allowed individuals to protect themselves from each other as well as the government. Since this viewpoint embraced the market freedoms associated with capitalism, it desired a minimum amount of governmental influence so that in the private economic arena individuals could pursue their own advantage.

The second perspective viewed democracy not only as an electoral mechanism but also as a *way of life*, a type of society. Placing greater weight on the principle of equality, this side believes that participating in politics is not simply an activity to be engaged in out of self-protection but rather an endeavor that is beneficial in itself, part of living a fully human life. Since every person must have an equal effective right to develop his or her own individual powers and capacities, some of the so-called market freedoms will need to be restricted in the interests of social well-being.

We have explained earlier in the chapter how the nineteenth-century Utilitarian movement in England provided a justification for the increasing majoritarianism in British politics. In the twentieth century in the United States, a similar utilitarian intellectual movement functioned in much the same way. While it is difficult to generalize about American utilitarianism, it seems safe to say that it was united by the aforementioned desire to provide individuals with an equal effective right to develop their own individual capacities. Another way of describing it is to say that the increasing majoritarianism of liberal democracy, buttressed by Utilitarianism, was primarily concerned with the *general welfare* of the country. The rights of individuals—so dear to the early liberals—were still considered important, no doubt, but the overall concern of politics was to be the achievement of the general welfare.

Characteristic of perhaps all developments in the realm of ideas, the creation of majoritarian liberal democracy produced a reaction to it in the form of a revival of "rights-based" liberal theory during the second half of the twentieth century. We shall examine that revival and the effect that it has had on contemporary liberal thinking shortly. Prior to that, however, we must note the existence of a line of thinking that contends that majoritarian liberalism—desirable though it may be—is extraordinarily difficult to achieve in complex modern societies.

ELITE THEORY IN MODERN LIBERAL THOUGHT

We should note initially that while elitist analysis of modern liberal democratic society is directed primarily toward the United States, it has implications for all regimes as well as for democratic theory as a whole. Elitist analysis begins by attempting to assess realistically what the basic value of "rule by the people" really means in a complex modern society. Relying on the arguments presented by past thinkers such as Gaetano Mosca, Vilfredo Pareto, and Robert Michels as well as modern organizational theorists, these people assert that popular rule means very little indeed. It can be demonstrated conclusively that any large-scale organization, including government, is, of necessity, organized in a hierarchical fashion. That is, there are certain people, who, by the nature of the tasks they perform, possess far more power than others. Any organization can thus be divided into two groups of people—the elite, who make all of the basic decisions, and the mass that follows them. The reasons for such a division are many and varied. Obviously every member of a group, be it a government or a fraternal organization, cannot be expected to know all of the details involved in running the organization. In the case of political systems, people who are nominally citizens of the state are primarily concerned with earning a living for themselves and pursuing their individual interests. To expect the average person to be a full-time participant in the political process at the same time seems simply absurd. The complexity of modern society thus demands that we adopt a specialization of labor whereby some people become experts in running organizations and fulfill that task on a full-time basis.

We have seen that classical liberal democratic theory confronted a similar problem and solved it by introducing the concept of representation, so that democratic governments might exist in large states. To the elitist, however, such a solution really raises more problems than it solves, particularly in complex modern societies. A representative is, by the very nature of the position, cut off from those represented, elitists contend. The representative possesses far more information than the average constituent, pursues tasks as a professional politician, and in all probability has a broader perspective than any of those represented; in short, the concerns and position of both parties are quite different. One would not, after all, expect the chairman of the board of General Motors to submit a questionnaire to all of the stockholders of the company asking them how many cars they should build that year and then proceed to act on their recommendation. The average stockholder simply could not make an informed judgment on such a matter without spending a considerable amount of time studying the market for automobiles; that is, unless the person were willing to become an expert.

To return to political concerns, there is an even more pervasive phenomenon that colors the types of decisions that can be made. The representative's (and here we use the word to refer to any elected decision maker) position makes it possible to influence significantly even the types of questions that are submitted to the population. By posing two alternatives as the only possible courses of action in any situation, the representative can effectively preclude discussion of other alternatives that might be more desirable from the people's point of view. In effect, formidable limits can be set on the types of governmental action that can even be publicly considered. Robert Michels, author of the "*iron law of oligarchy*," discussed this phenomena and argued that organization gives birth to the domination of the elected over the electors, of the mandataries over the mandators, of the delegates over the delegators. With organization inevitably comes oligarchy, Michels declared.

This, then, is the cornerstone of the elitist position. The complexity and need for expertise in modern societies ensures that popular representatives are divorced from their constituents and are capable of making—and to a certain extent must make—decisions independent of popular wishes. The choice, then, seems to be between organization (which appears indispensable) and democracy (which may or may not be desirable). But, the elitist argues, you cannot have both!

We must note that as yet there is no moral judgment attached to such a position. From this descriptive perspective, the elitist simply asserts that, like it or not, this is the way it is, a fact of modern society. Confronted with such an argument, the defender of liberal democratic theory might admit that it is necessary to have this situation when the process of running a government is such a complicated business. Such a defender would, however, probably go on to assert that it really does not matter, for the representative's constituents can remove that person if they so desire when the next election occurs. If a person acting in the name of the people fails in their eyes to perform his or her tasks correctly, they can simply vote the person out of office. This is, in effect, the old Madisonian argument for the appropriate means of controlling minority tyranny.

Expanding on the type of reasoning used earlier, the elitist would respond that periodic elections provide no real popular control, because the choices to replace a bad representative are greatly limited. The existing elite controls the access to the political system, thereby ensuring that only candidates who possess elite values are offered as choices to the electorate. This is accomplished through the political party structure, through the necessity of having considerable amounts of money to wage a successful campaign, and through a series of legal rules and customs.

Further, even if a "common person" surmounted all of these obstacles and were elected to office, that person would have little power, for within the governmental institutions themselves there are additional control devices as exemplified by seniority and committee systems in Congress. These are dominated by the elite as well. Under such circumstances the only choice available to a voter at election time is between competing elite groups who possess basically the same values, which preclude the possibility of any real change in governmental policy. If this is political reality, what does the phrase "government by the people" mean? Before attempting to respond to that question, we must record a further extension of the elitist argument, which may make the phrase "popular government" even more inapplicable to modern American society.

Power-Elite Analysis

Up to now we have avoided mention of any particular individual advancing the elitist position, preferring to refer to a vaguely defined group of democratic elitists. The major reason for this is that it is a most diverse tradition and sufficiently current to make it difficult to single out leading representatives. However, one person, C. Wright Mills, is most closely associated with this position, and his analysis of modern American democracy provides a further extension of the basic elitist position.

Accepting as fact the notion that complex organizations are of necessity hierarchical in structure and that a clear distinction must be made between elite and mass, Mills went on to argue that economic factors in the United States had produced a two-class society wherein even the government was powerless to effect any basic changes in policy. Let us ignore for the moment the prior argument that elected representatives are by virtue of their positions divorced from the people and assume that they actually do reflect popular desires. What real power does the average representative or senator possess? Very little if any, Mills contended, particularly regarding the basic matters such as war and peace or significant changes in the economic structure. The elected representative is at best in a middle-range power position, for the great decision-making capability lies in the hands of an economically based *power elite*, which is largely outside the control of the political system. Membership in this group is defined by birth and wealth, although it is possible for a member of the nonelite to become part of it by adopting the values of that group. Elite members go to the same schools, belong to the same social clubs, intermarry, and in general share similar values. While there may be minor disagreements among members of the elite over the everyday matters of public policy, they share a firm commitment to preserving the existing value and class structure.

Franklin D. Roosevelt is frequently cited by scholars ascribing to this position as indicative of the overall cohesiveness of the power elite. Elected to the presidency in a period of severe economic crisis and equipped with an apparent mandate for massive social and economic change, Roosevelt succeeded with a series of patchwork measures (and a war) in avoiding any fundamental change in the nature of American society. In much the same fashion, President Eisenhower drew rather unexpected applause from power-elite theorists when he cautioned against the government becoming a captive of a "military-industrial complex," which sought to use the political system for its own selfish ends.

The sum of the power-elitist argument is that the government is largely controlled by a small group of people who owe their power to their economic and social position in the society. If this be the case, there can be no true change in the system, because the members of the elite group simply will not permit any decline in their status. Government and, consequently, the representatives of the people are reduced to making relatively unimportant decisions, which in the end can serve only to perpetuate the existence of the status quo.

Anticipating our discussion later in the book, we must note that there are distinctly Marxian overtones to this type of analysis in that it sees the economic variable as crucial in determining people's actions and it relies heavily on a class analysis. Further, it might also be termed Marxian in that it views government, in effect, as the tool of a capitalist class that seeks to use the political system to perpetuate and extend its class's power. Whatever one chooses to term the Millsian type of analysis, from the theoretical perspective its import lies in the fact that it makes explicit the necessity for a reevaluation of the concept of power in liberal democratic systems.

The Power of Money. Traditional democratic theory presupposed that by providing people with equal voting power one could keep the limited functions of government consistent with popular desires. In attempting to divorce political matters from the economic realm and by viewing the political system as an umpire between competing factions, individualistic liberalism and the Madisonian implementation of it paid insufficient attention to the power that money confers. From the power-elite perspective, the American political system has always involved tyranny by a *minority*, which derives its power from its economic position. Attempts to implement greater economic equality through the institution of majoritarian liberalism have provided, elitists assert, nothing more than sops to the people and perpetuated a class-based capitalist market society. Viewing the American political system as a device for perpetuating minority interests, the elitist thus calls for revolution in the system in the name of producing a true democracy. The only way the minority control of the system can be checked is through giving greater decision-making power to the people.

Similarly, the only way the norm of equality, which majoritarian liberalism purported to be trying to achieve, can actually be fulfilled is through increasing democratization of both political and economic decision making. Mills's form of democratic elitism, then, ends up as a critical analysis of existing American politics. There is present in his theory an implicit faith in the basic common sense of the average person, and in the ability of the American democratic experiment to solve all problems through increasing democratization. We shall see in the next chapter that many of these themes are central to the tradition of what we call "alternative liberalism."

Shortcomings of Elitist Analysis. Before moving to a brief discussion of the other form of the elitist responses to majoritarian liberal democracy, a position which accepts the elitist analysis of American politics but sees it as a positive virtue, we must point out some of the possible difficulties in the power-elitist position discussed thus far.

Initially, critics have contended that the elitists have been by no means able to demonstrate the existence of a distinct class of people who constitute the power elite. Indeed, even if one is able to show great similarity in background among major political and economic decision makers, does this mean that they automatically share similar values? Further, the elitist must be able to prove that there is no fundamental difference between competing elite groups, and this, so critics contend, has yet to be accomplished. If varying elite groups change their policies in an attempt to win popular support, then the elitist charge that the voter has no real choice during elections is refuted.

Other critics have contended that it can be demonstrated that numerous individuals of nonelite origins have risen to elite status with their values essentially intact and have been able to effect serious change in public policy. Finally, critics contend there is a distressful lack of precision in the elitist argument. We are told that some ill-defined elite groups constantly use government for their own purposes at the expense of popular wishes, and that they agree on fundamental matters. But what is meant by fundamental? If it is nothing more than retention of the essentials of the existing economic system, then the elite probably reflects public opinion accurately: There seems to be, after all, little call from the masses for an economic revolution.

These and similar matters are the material of current controversy and dialogue among students of American liberalism. Thus it would be both presumptuous and foolhardy to attempt to resolve them here. Let us instead follow a safer path and move to a discussion of the second form of elitist reaction to the prevalent majoritarian liberal democracy of the twentieth century.

Normative Democratic Elitism

Another even more loosely defined group of individuals who merit the term *elitist* deserve brief mention if only because they form somewhat of a modern equivalent of the old Madisonian position. Impressed (perhaps *depressed* is the better word) by the apparent potential of the modern democratic citizen for irrational action, and distrustful of the masses' ability to support traditional democratic values in the face of crisis, these thinkers advocate elitist control of the society in the name of preserving liberal democracy. If that seems a bit paradoxical, it serves only to show again the many uses of the words *liberal* and *democratic*.

This position, sometimes called *normative democratic elitism*, can, for our purposes, be represented by the thinking of Joseph Schumpeter. In his influential book *Capitalism, Socialism and Democracy* (1947), Schumpeter sketched the outline of his theory. His position has three main points. First, democracy is not a kind of society but simply a mechanism for selecting governments. Democracy is a political *method*; it is a certain type of institutional arrangement for arriving at political, legislative, and administrative decisions. The mechanism, second, consists of competition between at least two sets of self-chosen politicians (elites). And third, the voter's role is not to decide political questions but simply to elect the individuals who will decide both the questions and the answers. Thus, for Schumpeter, political participation has no intrinsic value; indeed, he did not think universal suffrage was a requisite of democratic politics. As he put it, "The electoral mass is incapable of action other than a stampede."

As an economist, it was perhaps easier for Schumpeter to view the political system as an approximation of the market, with voters as the consumers and politicians as the entrepreneurs. Schumpeter was clear, however, that this was no free market: "Party and machine politicians . . . attempt to regulate political competition exactly similar to the corresponding practices of a trade association."[21]

Concerning the will of the people, what in the market metaphor would be consumer demand, Schumpeter described the reality of an artificially created demand. "The ways in which issues and the popular will on any issue are being manufactured is exactly analogous to the ways of commercial advertising."[22] Arguing a position reminiscent of Madison, Schumpeter summarized his position: "democracy does not mean and cannot mean that the people actually rule in any obvious sense of the terms 'people' and 'rule.' Democracy means only that the people have the opportunity of accepting or refusing the men who are to rule them."[23]

Normative democratic elitism believes, in effect, that the mass must be protected from itself. It notes that research into the values held by members of modern democratic states shows that it is the well-educated and generally affluent minority that has the highest respect for traditional liberal democratic values. The average person seems far more prone to adopt authoritarian solutions to problems, is quick to attempt to silence dissent, and in general finds it difficult to live with individual deviation from accepted behavior.

There is a tendency in majoritarian democracies to attempt to standardize all forms of conduct and to punish any deviation from those norms. As the sphere of governmental activity expands, we have found that it establishes rules of behavior in areas formerly part of the private sphere of activity. In a majoritarian liberal democracy, what this means is that the wishes of a majority of the people gradually become the accepted standards of conduct for the entire society. What bothers the elitist is that these mass tastes seem inevitably to reflect the wishes of what they believe to be the lowest common denominator of individuals in the society. What develops is a *mass culture* composed of television programs designed to appeal to the greatest possible number of people, news programs that simplify complex events down to sound bites to make them understandable, architectural styles designed for broad appeal, and faddish clothing styles that reflect the fickle desires of the masses. One can go on and on.

Although the phenomenon of mass culture is not in and of itself a bad thing for democracies, the elitist sees it as inevitably discouraging individual deviation from the established norms. Thus, the individual who does not conform is far less successful than one who does, but the society loses the type of creative energy that seems to be generated most often by nonconformists. Put in terms of political values, mass democracy seems bent on destroying the individuality that is the core idea in liberal democratic theory. In a way, we are back to the points made earlier about the tensions between liberty and equality. In pursuit of egalitarian goals, majoritarian liberal democracies, as John Stuart Mill warned, tend to standardize

[21] Joseph Schumpeter, *Capitalism, Socialism, and Democracy,* 2nd ed. (New York: Harper & Row, 1947), p. 283.

[22] Ibid., p. 263.

[23] Ibid., pp. 284–85.

everything, creating a society with a homogenized culture which stamps out individual liberty.

The "Irony of Democracy"

It should be apparent now why one can call this elitist position somewhat equivalent to the old Madisonian stance. Both accept as given the presence of a capitalist economic system as well as a plural society; that is, society is composed of individuals who belong to various, often conflicting, interest groups. While the basic value of popular sovereignty is not denied, the elitist recognizes that the masses under the banner of majority rule will tend toward excessive use of their power, thereby depriving others of their liberty to act as they choose. Here then is a more modern equivalent to the Madisonian tyranny of the majority, where communications advances make it quite possible to give everyone the same opinions. Far from being unhappy with the fact that modern society necessitates some type of distinction between elite leadership and mass following, the normative elitist sees the leadership group as a prime bulwark against the excesses of majorities. If the people did indeed rule as the majoritarian liberal tells us they ought, the liberal individualistic values of the tradition would soon be lost. This sober conclusion has been referred to as "the irony of democracy."

It is the irony of American democracy that the elites, and not the masses, are most committed to liberal democratic values; and, if the masses ever did actually rule, they would wipe out all vestiges of these democratic norms in favor of more authoritarian values. Voter apathy, consequently, is seen as a positive benefit since it is primarily the masses who fail to participate. There is some question whether this view can legitimately be called liberal democratic in that it explicitly relies on elite control of the masses. If one insists on a more majoritarian definition of liberal democracy, it obviously cannot be. If, however, one defines liberal democracy in more individualistic terms while retaining an overall commitment to popular sovereignty, normative elitism is probably as "liberal" as the Madisonian variety. The elitist, while recognizing the desirability of ultimate control by the people, is very happy that complex modern organizations ensure that educated liberal elites control much of the day-to-day activity of the state.

By now the reader will no doubt realize that we have come almost full circle in our discussion of individualistic liberal democracy. The normative elitist's fear of excessive majority control leading to conformity and authoritarianism is quite similar to the Madisonian concern with majority tyranny. In describing the spectrum of liberal democratic thought as it became embodied in the American political tradition, we have tried to show the full range of possibilities given the uniqueness of the American experience. But this dialogue has been conducted largely within the confines of the individualist liberal tradition of Hobbes, Locke, and Madison. Another form of liberalism—an alternative vision—whose roots may be traced to the French thinker Jean Jacques Rousseau and which received its American expressions in Thomas Jefferson and John Dewey will advance a rather different picture of an *ideal* liberal democratic society. That is the subject matter of the next chapter. Before leaving the mainstream individualist tradition, however, we must attempt to describe briefly the aforementioned contemporary revival of "rights-based liberalism" initiated by the 1971 publication of John Rawls's *A Theory of Justice*.

JOHN RAWLS: A CONTRACT FOR JUSTICE

John Rawls serves as an example of a contemporary social contract theorist in the broad tradition of Hobbes, Locke, and Rousseau. In his enormously influential *A Theory of Justice*, Rawls's primary goal is not, however, to justify a particular view of politics and political authority. Nor are the actors in his scheme Hobbesian, essentially competitive, power-acquisitive individuals who must enter into a contractual relationship with others as a means of escaping the state of nature and thereby protecting their lives and property from the likes of their fellow beings. Rather, Rawls's project is to establish principles of justice grounded in liberal democratic values by people he assumes are rational and moral beings.

Rawls imaginatively constructs a state of nature setting called "the original position" wherein the contracting individuals are placed behind a "veil of ignorance." The original position is a kind of presocietal state wherein rational actors, deprived of all sorts of particular knowledge about their lives in society, must devise principles of justice that will govern their lives upon their return to society. Behind the veil, they are, more specifically, deprived of knowledge about their place in history and society; their race, sex, nationality, class, or age; their wealth; their conceptions of the good; and "their distribution of natural talents and abilities":

> The principles of justice to which all are forever bound are chosen in the absence of this sort of specific information. A veil of ignorance prevents anyone from being advantaged or disadvantaged by the contingencies of social class and fortune; and hence the bargaining problems which arise in everyday life from the possession of this knowledge do not affect the choice of principles.24

Rawls grants that these individuals will possess *general* knowledge about political affairs, economic theory, bases of social organization, and human psychology; he also believes they will prefer more, rather than less, of what he calls "primary goods": certain rights, liberties, opportunities, income, wealth, and bases of self-respect.

The veil of ignorance thus serves as Rawls's fictional device to prevent those in the original position from making political decisions based on a narrowly conceived self-interest that would protect only their personal property and abilities. Before the veil is lifted, the actors are typical self-interested and rational human beings; and yet, because they do not know their place in society, Rawls assumes that these individuals will recognize that they may be without talents or

---

24Robert Paul Wolff, *Understanding Rawls* (Princeton, N.J.: Princeton University Press, 1977), pp. 60–61.

social status—in essence, the "worst-off" members of society. This will lead them, Rawls believes, to construct principles for the contract so that the least privileged people of the society will be as well off as possible. Rawls reasons that because the contract will not be devised by a group of elite men who are working to ensure that their property and status are protected, the final product will be fundamentally more fair to the entire society at hand. Hence, Rawls has defended his approach as participating in the traditions of modern democratic thought.

Rawls argues that two principles of justice will emerge from behind the veil of ignorance. The first is that members are guaranteed the greatest possible civil liberties without infringing on others' rights in the society. This principle underscores Rawls's commitment to the central ideal of liberalism. In his words, "Each person is to have an equal right to the most extensive basic liberty compatible with a similar liberty for others." With regard to economic opportunities and social position, Rawls states that they "are to be arranged so that they are both (a) reasonably expected to be to everyone's advantage, and (b) attached to positions and offices open to all."[25] Rawls claims that the first principle on liberty takes priority: Liberty must be established before the second distribution principle becomes effective. Part (a) of the second principle—the difference principle—is especially significant. It requires that any inequalities in society should be arranged to secure the greatest benefit of the least advantaged. That is to say that inequalities should not be severe: The least well-off ought to have as much a share of income, wealth, and self-respect as possible. Justice thus means "fairness" for Rawls. Since anyone in the original position could find themselves in the condition of the worst off when returning to society, Rawls believes the contractors would want no one to be permanently disadvantaged and no one to be made worse off by the actions of others.

In essence, Rawls suggests that liberty can be made compatible with greater equality, that extreme forms of inequality under which any member of society suffers are unjust, and that universally applicable principles of justice may be arrived at through abstract reasoning. Since its publication in 1971, this theory of justice has occupied center stage in contemporary political theory, wherein Rawls has been criticized from all directions. Democratic theorists have questioned whether Rawls adequately considers the relation between economic inequality, which he sanctions as long as it serves the poor, and political inequality. (Those with more social and economic power often possess more political power.) Theorists of citizenship have criticized Rawls's emphasis on the economic rationality (the "more, rather than less" assumption) and inadequate attention to the more deliberative demands of citizenship. Finally, many have criticized Rawls for overlooking how preferences for justice often stem precisely from people's identities and conceptions of the good. Rawls suggests that people can think about justice without any particular identity, that the "self" may be conceived of prior to society. Perhaps it is the reverse: that the preferences and values people have about their world—including Rawls's—are shaped in and

---

[25]John Rawls, *A Theory of Justice* (Cambridge: The Belknap Press of Harvard University Press, 1971), pp. 60–61.

through their participation in communities, traditions, and sociocultural practices more broadly. Rawls seems to prefer a neutral uniformity as the basis for justice, rather than the more richly textured and diverse contexts of modern politics.

In favor of his project, however, Rawls's theory can be seen as a creative attempt to establish norms for justice derived exclusively from human reason—the capacity that modern democratic theorists like Rawls maintain is shared by all human beings independent of their various differences, that enables them to think beyond their own situations and consider what is good both for themselves and for others. In this light, Rawls departs from mainstream liberalism of Hobbes-*cum*-Madison by seeking justice beyond the class-divided society that the earlier liberals were trying to justify and protect. Given the latter aspects of his theory, Rawls may be seen as moving closer to the kind of societal democratic ends envisioned by the alternative liberalism of Rousseau, Jefferson, and Dewey. Indeed, Rawls can serve as yet another example of a modern liberal trying to tame market society; and it is interesting to note that either socialism or communism could fulfill all of his criteria for *A Theory of Justice.* But this is a topic for a later moment in the book.

SUGGESTED READINGS

BOORSTIN, DANIEL J., *The Genius of American Politics.* Chicago: The University of Chicago Press, 1953.

COLEMAN, FRANK M., *Hobbes and America: Exploring the Constitutional Foundations.* Toronto: University of Toronto Press, 1977.

COOKE, JACOB E., ed., *The Federalist.* Middletown, Conn.: Wesleyan University Press: 1961.

DAHL, ROBERT A., *A Preface to Democratic Theory.* Chicago: University of Chicago Press, 1963.

HARTZ, LOUIS, *The Liberal Tradition in America.* New York: Harcourt Brace and World, 1955.

MATTHEWS, RICHARD K., *If Men Were Angels: James Madison and the Heartless Empire of Reason.* Lawrence: University Press of Kansas, 1995.

MILLS, C. WRIGHT, *The Power Elite.* New York: Oxford University Press, 1979.

RAWLS, JOHN, *A Theory of Justice.* Cambridge: The Belknap Press of Harvard University Press, 1971.

TOCQUEVILLE, ALEXIS DE, *Democracy in America,* 2 Vols., trans. Henry Reeve. New York: Schocken Books, 1961.

4

Liberalism:
Alternative Visions

With liberty, wherever abundance reigns, well-being also reigns. Plant a stake crowned with flowers in the middle of a square; gather the people together there, and you will have a festival. Do better yet; let the spectators become an entertainment to themselves; make them actors themselves; do it so that each sees and loves himself in the others so that they will all be better united

Jean Jacques Rousseau

Laws and institutions must go hand in hand with the progress of the human mind. As that becomes more developed, more enlightened ... institutions must advance also, and keep pace with the times. We might as well require a man to wear still the coat that fitted him when a boy, as civilized society to remain ever under the regimen of their barbarous ancestors.

Thomas Jefferson

Fraternity, liberty, and equality isolated from communal life are hopeless abstractions.
John Dewey

U p to this point the discussion of liberalism has been restricted to that form of the phenomenon that is intimately connected with capitalism. There exists a second branch of liberalism which, realizing that there are large political and social costs to modern market societies, tries to construct a more egalitarian political community that is less subject to the never-ending competitiveness and crass materialism of the market. The political theorist who gave the clearest early expression to this alternative liberal ideology was the French philosopher Jean Jacques Rousseau (1712–1778). We will later explore two of the American manifestations of *alternative liberalism* in the thought of Thomas Jefferson and John Dewey. For the moment, however, let us examine in some detail Rousseau's effort to formulate a different vision of liberal society.

ROUSSEAU'S STATE OF NATURE

The third of the grand political philosophers to employ a state-of-nature metaphor to help convince his audience of the validity of his position, Rousseau consciously constructed a markedly contrasting portrait of humankind prior to government that strives to be both critical of, and superior to, the models of Thomas Hobbes and John Locke. While the latter two theorists' views of the state of nature were imaginative constructions of what "civilization" would look like if government vanished, Rousseau presented a historical, evolutionary description of humanity from prehistoric times to the relative present. In other words, Rousseau described how natural humans evolved into social beings, and then moved to civilization, while Hobbes and Locke restricted their discussion to people who were already quite civilized. By pushing back humanity's starting point thousands of years, Rousseau critically exposed many of the unexamined assumptions of the other two philosophers, questioned their conclusions, and presented an alternative political solution to the problems of his day.

Rousseau's chronicle of human evolution, titled *Discourse on the Origin and Foundations of Inequality Among Men*, begins with a description of the life of our proto-human ancestors. Asocial, amoral creatures blessed with sufficient food and natural shelters, they lacked any reason for sustained interaction among themselves. Having very simple needs, which the natural environment easily met, these creatures were lazy, contented, and peaceful. Rousseau believed that they functioned rather well and operated simply on two principles of motivation that were "*anterior* to reason": self-preservation and commiseration. Naturally, these primitives did everything necessary to survive. But given the low, animal level of wants and the relative bounty of nature, they were not required to struggle for scarce resources. In addition to self-preservation, these creatures also displayed commiseration (*pitié*): "a natural repugnance to see any sensitive being perish or suffer, principally our fellowmen."[1] By his careful wording, Rousseau seems to suggest that this innate impulse was extended to all

[1] Jean Jacques Rousseau, *The First and Second Discourses*, R. D. Masters and J. R. Masters, trans. and eds. (New York: St. Martin's Press, 1964), p. 95.

sensitive beings, which would have made our earliest ancestors vegetarians. It also suggests that this unreflective impulse produced "moral" behavior in the proto-human and it existed prior to the development of human rationality. No wonder Rousseau called this unsophisticated being a noble savage. Nevertheless, if necessity demanded it, the first principle of self-preservation would always take precedence over the second, and conflict between these noble savages would occur, albeit rarely.

Rousseau's model of humans therefore begins with the two interdependent characteristics of self-preservation and commiseration. His conception, however, is more complicated than that. He also believed that humans contain certain other species-specific characteristics that, in the course of time, would concretely develop from their mere potential in our proto-human ancestors. These additional capacities are free will, *perfectibilité*, and imagination. While each will be discussed in the sections that follow, it is important to note at this juncture that Rousseau presents a highly ambivalent attitude toward the capacity to reason. Indeed, his critique of the Enlightenment and human rationality anticipates many of the insights found in late twentieth-century critical theory. But that is a topic to be explored on another occasion; for now it is appropriate to follow his description of human development.

Over a period of many years, the primitive needs of the noble savages slowly began to expand, and it became necessary for these creatures to expend additional energy to meet the new, largely superfluous wants. As Rousseau put it, "The first man who made himself clothing or a dwelling, in doing so gave himself things that were hardly necessary."[2] Taking on a force of its own, a dynamic situation developed between human *needs* and *wants*. As these creatures began to want new objects and to work to secure what they desired, they became incapable of being satisfied or fulfilled, always desiring additional, more sophisticated things. While still in the garden, the noble savage's wants and needs were in perfect harmony, until the day came when one of them imagined having clothing or a dwelling and thus initiated the fall into a situation where wants always exceed needs. Slowly but surely, this capacity to "imagine" suggested distinct possibilities that mere logic and reason alone could not conceive. Perhaps more importantly, out of this process also developed the need for other people. In part, this need for other humans was psychological, but it was also economic: By laboring together they could produce more than by laboring alone. Thus, humans developed into social creatures. Originally *a*social, they evolved and needed other humans in order to survive and to fulfill themselves. Rousseau, in contrast to Hobbes and Locke, believed humanity to be a developing species that changes over time. Humans, moreover, are the only species who had the potential to participate knowingly in their own evolution! On the other hand, this also meant that if they participated *un*knowingly in their development, the consequences could be tragic. Here is the point where Rousseau introduces the two interdependent characteristics of free will and *perfectibilité*.

In explaining free will, Rousseau begins by challenging the ancient prejudice that it is reason that separates humans from the rest of the animal kingdom. "Every

---

[2] Ibid., p. 112.

animal has ideas," claims Rousseau; "it even combines its ideas up to a certain point, and in this regard man differs from a beast only in degree." Rousseau concludes that "it is not so much understanding which constitutes the distinction of man among the animals as it is his being a free agent." Humanity's free will and "consciousness of this freedom" are what separate us from other animals.[3] So too does "the faculty of self-perfection." In explaining what he means by this, Rousseau foreshadows Karl Marx's notion of humans as the species being. This faculty, Rousseau argues "resides among us as much in the species as in the individual" and is what enables us "*to perfect*" all of our other talents and abilities. While this faculty sounds like a wonderful capacity, Rousseau captures its bittersweet essence: "An animal is at the end of a few months what it will be all of its life: and a species is at the end of a thousand years what it was the first year of that thousand. Why is man alone subject to becoming imbecile?"[4] That specific, haunting question Rousseau answers in his chronicle of the human odyssey, to which we now return.

At first, temporary hunting-and-gathering associations were sufficient to meet the emerging needs of humanity. As psychological needs developed, more permanent relationships were desired, and families were formed. Believing this early familial stage gave "rise to the sweetest sentiments known to humans," Rousseau lamented its eventual passing and noted the transition into civil society caused by the creation of market property rights.

> The first person who, having fenced off a plot of ground, took it into his head to say *this is mine* and found people simple enough to believe this, was the true founder of civil society. What crimes, wars, murders, what miseries and horrors would the human race have been spared by someone who, uprooting the stakes or filling in the ditch, had shouted to his fellowmen: Beware of listening to this imposter; you are lost if you forget that the fruits belong to all and the earth to no one![5]

Prior to the invention of property rights that allowed individuals to exclude others, there occurred random, sporadic outbursts of violence, but this was the exception rather than the norm. With the creation of property, the generally peaceful existence of precivilized humanity came to a close, and constant, systematic, all-pervasive competition and exploitation of people by one another began.

> But from the moment one man needed the help of another, as soon as they observed that it was useful for a single person to have provisions for two, equality disappeared, property was introduced, labor became necessary; and vast forests were changed into smiling fields which had to be watered with the sweat of men, and in which slavery and misery were soon seen to germinate and grow with the crops.[6]

The sporadic, random violence of premodern society is exchanged for a constant, systematic, all-inclusive exploitation of individual by individual, where "smiles" are now extracted by the "sweat," enslavement, and "misery" of others. At

---

[3] Ibid., p. 114.
[4] Ibid., pp. 114–15.
[5] Ibid., pp. 141–42.
[6] Ibid., pp. 151–52.

this point, well into the narrative of *The Second Discourse,* Rousseau's account of human history has finally reached the point where Hobbes and Locke began their arguments. By this stylistic maneuver, Rousseau hoped to demonstrate how the prior state-of-nature theorists were actually describing their own contemporaries—seventeenth- and eighteenth-century English men and women—civilized beings who had already changed enormously from their natural condition.

As economic inequality and class divisions further developed between those who owned and those who did not own property, a general condition of war prevailed. Pressed by necessity, the rich devised a clever scheme to deceive the rest of the people into establishing a government designed to protect their property. In Rousseau's view, "Destitute of valid reasons to justify himself . . . the rich, pressed by necessity, finally conceived the most deliberate project that ever entered the human mind." The project was the creation of a *social contract* designed to protect the rich from the poor in the name of achieving justice for all. Presented with the contract creating government, Rousseau argued that, "All ran to meet their chains, thinking they secured their freedom."[7] The modern state, then, is constructed atop a fraudulent contract; and as such, it must be overthrown in order to establish a legitimate community.

One additional point concerning reason, civilization, and the creation of nation-states seems crucial. Rousseau suggests that through the processes of becoming citizens, including the socialization we all experience, humans have learned to forget what their natural inclinations would normally direct them to do. Rousseau's words describe "the first effects one glimpses of the division of the human race into different societies."

> The bodies politic, thus remaining in the state of nature with relation to each other, soon experienced the inconveniences that had forced individuals to leave it; and among these great bodies that state became even more fatal than it had previously been among the individuals of whom they were composed. Hence arose the national wars, battles, murders, and reprisals which make nature tremble . . . and all those horrible prejudices which rank the honor of shedding human blood among the virtues. The most decent men learn to consider it one of their duties to murder their fellow-men. . . .

Rousseau concluded this devastating account with the assertion that "more murders were committed on a single day of fighting . . . than were committed in the state of nature during whole centuries over the entire face of the earth."[8] What good was this so-called "Enlightenment" if it taught humans to betray their more moral, unreflective selves? These passages make it understandable how many people have misread Rousseau and assumed he was calling for a return to the original state of nature. But this solution, as he knew, was impossible: As developmental, or *becoming* creatures, humans do not have the capacity to go back, to *unbecome.* Rather, we must try to construct a different type of political community.

---

[7] Ibid., pp. 158–59.
[8] Ibid., p. 161.

The Social Contract

Rousseau begins his most celebrated work, *The Social Contract* (1762), by reminding us of both our past and the predicament of the present with this enigmatic observation: "Man is born free, and everywhere he is in chains. One believes himself the master of others, and yet he is greater slave than they."[9] Here Rousseau exposes the self-deceptive nature of modern life. People think they are free, yet they are not. The modern person is a creature of alienation, an alienation that is self-inflicted and self-endured. Individuals agreed to establish a state believing it would bring them freedom; instead, they established class inequality and the rule of the rich for the rich, but with the appearance of rule of all for all. Among the first of all modern political theorists to understand alienation, a direct consequence of free will, *perfectibilité*, and imagination, Rousseau understood the awesome power of domination when individuals enslave themselves—all under the guise of autonomy or freedom. Since the present situation was unacceptable, what prerequisites were necessary to create a legitimate community? Since neither fraud nor force can be resorted to, Rousseau had to create a condition in which all willingly and knowingly consent to live together. His prescription was threefold, involving property, positive freedom, and the full participation of individual citizens.

Recognizing the disruptive effects of class division among people, Rousseau argued that a moderate equality of property was necessary to a harmonious society. "It is therefore one of the most important functions of government to prevent extreme inequality of fortunes; not by taking away wealth from its possessor, but by depriving all men of the means to accumulate it; not by building hospitals for the poor, but by securing the citizens from becoming poor."[10] The role of government was to help combat the creation of antagonistic class relationships by passing legislation, income and luxury taxes for example, designed to redistribute wealth. "No citizen shall ever be wealthy enough to buy another, and none poor enough to be forced to sell himself," Rousseau explained.[11] In this specific prescription involving "citizens" who either "buy" other citizens or must "sell" themselves, Rousseau showed clearly that his concern was with the lack of freedom created by capitalist economic relations where one class of citizens purchases the services and freedom of another class of citizens.

Anticipating much of Karl Marx while drawing up short of reaching his conclusions, Rousseau was alarmed at the condition of wage slavery by which modern citizens were oppressed. To guard further against class conflict, Rousseau argued that everyone in society needed to own a *limited* amount of property. Calling this right to property "the most sacred" of all rights, Rousseau's position was that small ownership gave every individual an alternative to working for someone else. Limited property was instrumental in securing freedom; freedom remained the ultimate goal, but without the economic security provided by every citizen owning

[9] Jean Jacques Rousseau, *The Social Contract*, Charles M. Sherover, trans. and ed. (New York: New American Library, 1974), p. 5.

[10] Ibid., p. 271.

[11] Ibid., p. 85.

property, freedom for all could not be achieved. Hence, Rousseau wanted to create a *one-class* society where everyone had access to the means of sustaining him or herself. While specific public policies could be invoked to handle some of the evil effects of property, legislation alone could not bring about the type of change in individuals that Rousseau believed was essential to community.

Rousseau's proposed solution to the problems of modern existence has been the subject of considerable controversy. Some see him as an early advocate of modern forms of totalitarianism, while others view him as an intellectual father of the more radical side of the French revolution. We believe that much of the confusion surrounding Rousseau's thinking results from the fact that he was bound by the social contract terminology of the British liberal tradition even as he was attempting, in a sometimes confused way, to transcend that tradition. Lee McDonald has stated that Hobbes and Locke had made concepts such as individual rights and the social contract necessary categories for anyone who wished to talk about political philosophy—in a real sense, Rousseau remained a captive to the conceptual universe of British liberalism even as he attempted to both criticize and go beyond it.

Cunningly, Rousseau also termed his proposed agreement to form a political association a "social contract"; it was, however, to be a far different type of agreement since it would be based upon a different conception of human nature and a different type of society than that of Hobbes or Locke. Asher and Gad Horowitz have intriguingly described Rousseau's agreement as "a contract to end all contracts."[12] What, precisely, did he propose? He argued that people who have recognized the inhumanity of their condition in modern society ("the English people thinks it is free") could come together and bond themselves to one another in such a way as to produce a true community. In the language of Hobbes and Locke, they would give up *all* of their individual rights to the community. No wonder future commentators would brand Rousseau as the first modern totalitarian!

Let us look at his proposal more carefully. To whom are we transferring these rights? Rousseau argued that we are simply giving them to ourselves as members of a new, participatory community of which we are part of the composition of the sovereign. To put it too simply, the Hobbes/Locke language of "giving up rights" to another entity, be it the Leviathan or Civil Society, was not adequate to convey Rousseau's meaning. He was speaking of a new, moral entity, which would be the product of individuals pledging themselves to one another in an effort to govern themselves in a way that was best for all. They would reject their selfish, individual wills, and in community seek to govern themselves according to what Rousseau called the *general will.* The general will, Rousseau asserts, "cannot err"; and, by definition, it is in the true interests of the whole community and each of the individual parts. To further complicate matters, the general will would not necessarily be discovered by a simple tabulation of the views of participating members. If a majority of individuals believe that they have discovered the general will on a particular matter, this does not inevitably mean that they have actually done so. It is perfectly

---

[12] Asher Horowitz and Gad Horowitz, *"Everywhere They Are in Chains."* (Scarborough, Ontario: Nelson Canada, 1988), p. 62.

possible that a vast majority believes that they know the general will of the community, but that one member of the minority truly possesses it.

How, then, are we to proceed? How will we govern ourselves? When will we be ready to "contract" to "end all contracts"? Remember that the members of this community are people who have recognized the inhumanity and lack of meaning in modern society. Remember also that they have committed themselves to a continuing process whereby they constantly participate and interact to discover what the general will dictates in everyday matters. Given this, the task of finding what is good for the community might not be as difficult as it first appears. The community members' commitment is, after all, to always search for that which is good for all of them. Perhaps this task seems difficult to us because of our mainstream Hobbes/Locke assumptions concerning the primacy of egoism built into our nature! Still, Rousseau recognizes how difficult this process may be and offers yet another enigmatic proposal in the form of a central figure in *The Social Contract* called "the Legislator."

Rousseau introduces "the Legislator" into the discussion even though this character actually does not legislate. Without legislative power, it is not surprising that the Legislator was described by Rousseau as having "an authority that is mere nothing." And yet, the Legislator is to play the most important role in the development of community by helping individuals change their perceptions of themselves. The Legislator is to "transform," to "change human nature," to "alter man's constitution." Given this task of transforming humanity, it becomes clearer why legislation itself will not help. What is needed is a change in the internalized forms of control. The Legislator's function, then, is to lead individuals to a stage of self-awareness where they come to understand both their individual selves and their common history; they must rediscover that, from Rousseau's perspective, there is no self without other. Remember, Rousseau's model of human nature is not static; humanity changes and will continue to do so. Thus, the Legislator's task is to assist in this process of self-enlightenment, which is simultaneously an overcoming of our alienation.

> It is a grand and beautiful sight to see man emerge from obscurity somehow by his own efforts . . . rise above himself; soar intellectually into celestial regions; traverse with giant steps, like the sun, the vastness of the universe; and—what is even grander and more difficult—come back to himself to study man and know his nature, his duties, and his end.[13]

Exactly how Rousseau's charismatic leader will achieve this transformation need not detain us. Indeed, it remains the subject of much scholarly controversy. What is important is that for individuals to be free they must first "know thyself" and then rule themselves. "Obedience to a law one prescribes for one's self" is Rousseau's definition of freedom. Under this standard of consciously self-imposed laws, Rousseau rejected the possibility of representative government. Indeed, representative forms of government are usually among the most corrupt forms because the citizenry believe that they are free. From Rousseau's perspective, the

---

[13] Rousseau, Discourses, p. 35.

citizens of a representative government would be free only during the moment they voted for their representatives; as soon as that was accomplished, they would return to slavery because they allowed others to run their lives for them. For Rousseau, then, any form of government short of a direct, participatory democracy is an insult to and a denial of humanity. Hence, by actively participating in the political life of society, by making the laws they themselves will obey, all individuals achieve freedom—truly positive freedom. After all, the people are only obeying themselves.

Individual *participation* is crucial. Yet Rousseau's chronicle of human evolution must be kept in mind. As creatures, our development began as isolated, atomistic beings who owed no obligations to others even though there existed a natural repugnance to see others suffer. Eventually, we became social creatures whose need for others was at least as much psychological as material. Rousseau's human, then, becomes a social-individual. Above all, the Legislator must enlighten individuals to both the social and the individual components of human existence. Society is not an artificial creation of individuals as portrayed by Hobbes; it is material and necessary to human development. Once individuals come to view themselves as extensions of others, they will be able to participate actively in the creation of the general will. The *general will*, they will understand, must be in the best interests of society and *every* member of that society. Prior to transforming themselves from their bourgeois mentality, the citizens do not recognize this. However, after the moral transformation, individuals consciously construct public policies, recognizing both the individual and the social dimensions of their actions. And yet, the fundamental question remains: How will we know if we have successfully undergone this transformation? Rousseau suggests that we have indeed been morally transformed when we no longer need a "social contract" (as in Hobbes and Locke) to form a political community. Think about this. What is a contract? Is it not a sign of fundamental distrust, where some external authority is empowered to punish those who violate the contract? Must all communities be established on this notion? Is it possible to form a (non*bourgeois*) community by first agreeing that we do not need a social contract—"to contract," in a symbolic sense, to "end all contracts"? Rousseau thought that we could. He believed that when a community of social-individuals achieved such a level of coordination, that any individual from the community could be called upon to articulate the general will. As Rousseau put it, this individual will merely "give expression to what all have previously felt." After all, the individual's real *particular will* and the *general will* should be perfect correlatives in Rousseau's vision.

In Rousseau, then, we are presented with an alternative view of liberal democracy. It is liberal in that it begins with a view of people who, as radical individuals in the state of nature, have the liberty to pursue whatever their limited imaginations desire. As humanity develops, people become social beings who need moral freedom in order to lead a fully human life. Rejecting capitalism as antithetical to equality, freedom, and community, Rousseau argued for a simple one-class society where the citizens would own sufficient property to sustain themselves and where it would not be possible for a capitalist society to develop. Rousseau, then, is a liberal democrat in a dual sense: He conceives of democracy as a *kind of society* where everyone must have an equal chance to develop and democracy as an *electoral mechanism* whereby individuals—not their representatives—discuss and vote on public policy. Although Rousseau's theory was constructed to fit a small city or territory, Thomas Jefferson created his own alternative vision of liberal democracy, which in many ways was similar to that of Rousseau's yet designed to confront the needs of an entire continent.

JEFFERSON'S SELF-EVIDENT TRUTHS

> We hold these truths to be self-evident: that all men are created equal; that they are endowed by their Creator with certain inalienable rights; that among these are life, liberty, and the pursuit of happiness; that to secure these rights, governments are instituted among men, deriving their just powers from the consent of the governed; that whenever any form of government becomes destructive of these ends, it is the right of the people to alter or to abolish it.[14]

Those heady, opening words of the *Declaration of Independence* both contain a brief summary of the evolution of liberalism and present a unique addition to it. Concepts of liberal equality and natural rights go back to the time of Thomas Hobbes, and the ideas of consent of the governed and the right to overthrow government can be traced to John Locke. What is new to more modern political thought is Thomas Jefferson's introduction of the concept of "happiness" as a standard by which to evaluate governments. In the preceding quotation Jefferson argued that if a government does not protect people's life and liberty, people have a right to overthrow it. More importantly, he argued that if government does not allow people to pursue happiness—an abstract and ethereal notion itself—people again have the right to revolution. With the introduction of happiness, then, Jefferson introduced a higher standard for government to strive for, and in the process he began to articulate a view of American liberalism that transcended private property.

In the *Second Treatise on Government,* John Locke argued for rights to "life, liberty, and estate." But Jefferson demanded more. Although he too thought some amount of property was necessary to freedom and happiness, he did not think individuals had natural rights to it. Moreover, Jefferson did not believe that property acquisition was what individuals should pursue throughout their life. Instead, happiness was the end for which we were created. Jefferson's clear preference for happiness over property is evident on at least one other important occasion. While serving as the American minister to France during the earliest days of the French revolution, Jefferson was asked by the Marquis de Lafayette to review an early draft of the *Declaration of the Rights of Man.* Jefferson bracketed the words "right to property" and substituted the phrase "search for happiness" into the document. Throughout Jefferson's life he argued that it was happiness—not property—to which individuals have an equal, natural right.

---

[14] Thomas Jefferson, "The Declaration of Independence," in *The Portable Jefferson,* Merrill D. Peterson, ed. (Baltimore, Md.: Penguin, 1975), p. 235.

Jeffersonian Government

Thomas Jefferson was never very pleased with the United States Constitution of 1787. Although his reaction to it was usually cool, on a few occasions he voiced open hostility to it. Perhaps a brief passage written by Jefferson from France in 1788 can illustrate his attitude toward the new constitution:

> But I own that it astonishes me to find such a change wrought in the opinions of our countrymen since I left them, as that three-forths of them should be contented to live under a system which leaves to their governors the power of taking from them the trial by jury in civil cases, freedom of religion, freedom of the press, freedom of commerce, the *habeas corpus* laws, and the yoking of them with a standing army. This is a degeneracy in the principles of liberty to which I had given four centuries instead of four years.[15]

Throughout his life Jefferson drafted several model constitutions that present a clearer view of his idea of what a democratic government would look like and how it would function. In addition to having a bill of rights (which the Constitution of 1787 did not), Jefferson argued that suffrage was the most important single issue to democratic government. In an early draft of a model constitution for Virginia, Jefferson appeared to limit suffrage to males who owned one-fourth of an acre in town or twenty-five acres of land in the country. However, at another point in the same constitution, Jefferson wrote that every person who never owned fifty acres of land, would be entitled to an appropriation of that amount. In effect, then, Jefferson thought of land as being *instrumental* in securing both economic and political freedom; political, in that it gave all white males the vote; and economic, in that, like Rousseau, land gave individuals the freedom to reject wage-labor relationships should they so choose.

In addition to equal and universal white manhood suffrage, Jefferson—unlike the other founding fathers—wanted to create a public space where citizens could actively participate in politics. He believed politics was an activity that all should engage in as part of living a fully human life. Rather than an activity for a propertied few, Jefferson thought politics to be an ennobling activity in which all had a right and duty to participate. In hopes of creating an arena—a public space—for citizen participation, Jefferson argued the case for *ward-republics.*

"Divide the counties into wards of such size as that every citizen can attend . . . and act in person," suggested Jefferson. The ward-republics should have control of all local matters, for example, education, police, law. Jefferson called the wards "the wisest invention ever devised by the wit of man for the perfect exercise of self-government" and he constructed a scheme of government where these local units played a crucial role. The design is a four-tier pyramid structure: The national government forms the peak and is "entrusted with the defense of the nation, and its foreign and federal relations"; the next level, the state governments, are concerned with "the civil rights, laws, policy and administration of what concerns the state generally"; the lower quarter confronts "the local concerns of the

---

[15] Thomas Jefferson, *The Papers of Thomas Jefferson*, 20 Vols., Julian Boyd, ed. (Princeton, N.J.: Princeton University Press, 1950), Vol. 12, p. 558.

counties"; and the base, composed of the ward-republics, "direct[s] the interests within itself."[16] At the base, every official position is an elective one. Each division of the pyramid functions as a republic; each is dependent on the next subordinate level for its authority and guidance.

> The elementary republics of the wards, the county republics, the state republics, and the republic of the Union, would form a graduation of authorities, standing each on the basis of law, holding everyone its delegated share of powers, and constituting truly a system of fundamental balances and checks for the government. Where every man is a sharer in the direction of his ward-republic, or of some of the higher ones, and feels that he is a participator in the government of affairs, not merely at an election one day in the year, but every day; when there shall not be a man in the state who will not be a member of some one of the councils, great or small, he will let the heart be torn out of his body sooner than his power be wrested from him by a Caesar or a Bonaparte.[17]

Division and subdivision "until it ends in the administration of everyman's farm by himself," then, is the mechanism by which political freedom is guaranteed. As in Rousseau, mere periodic elections are insufficient for a democratic society: "Every day" individuals must be a "participator in the government of affairs," Jefferson wrote. The ward-republics provided the proper mixture whereby "the whole is cemented by giving to every citizen, personally, a part in the administration of the public affairs." Certainly, with his advocacy of requiring each citizen to give his vote *viva voce*, and his insistence on dividing "the counties into wards of such size that every citizen can attend . . . and act in person," Jefferson's views are in harmony with the ancient Greek conception of politics and citizenship.[18]

Purpose of Ward-Republics. The ward-republics are to fulfill a fourfold function: (1) to check the petty tyrants at home, (2) to maintain the revolutionary spirit of 1776, (3) to provide a base for general education, and (4) to ensure a space where the citizens could become proficient in the art of politics. This last function, often overlooked in Jefferson, has two distinct, but complementary, parts. The first, already discussed, deals specifically with the creation of a public space for the daily activity of local politics. The second concerns Jefferson's desire to provide for every generation the opportunity to create its own political community.

Hannah Arendt firmly grasped the importance of both aspects of the fourth function of the ward-republic in Jefferson's governmental system. She observed that he

> knew, however dimly, that the Revolution, while it had given freedom to the people, had failed to provide a space where this freedom could be exercised. Only the representatives of the people, not the people themselves, had an opportunity to engage in those activities of "expressing, discussing and deciding" which in a positive sense are the activities of freedom.[19]

[16] *Portable Jefferson*, pp. 556–57.

[17] Thomas Jefferson, *Writings of Jefferson*, 20 Vols., Albert E. Bergh, ed. (Washington, D.C.: The Thomas Jefferson Memorial Association, 1903–4), Vol. 6, pp. 543–44.

[18] *Portable Jefferson*, pp. 556–57.

[19] Hannah Arendt, *On Revolution* (New York: Viking Press, 1963), p. 238.

The "fresh start" Jefferson and his contemporaries had been given in the revolutionary experience must somehow be passed on to each succeeding generation. Each generation must be allowed to begin the world anew. Each generation must redefine its goals and ideals; each must recommit itself to one another. Jefferson believed it essential to a democratic community that each generation could have the chance to "depute representatives to a convention, and to make the Constitution what they think will be the best for themselves."[20] He recognized the necessity of recreating the constitutional congresses and conventions of the 1770s and 1780s: A mere reshuffling of the government would not do. Using the mechanism of the small ward-republics, Jefferson argued that all citizens could thereby be incorporated into the political processes of legislation and governance.

Through ward-republics, "the voice of the whole people would be thus fairly, fully, and peacefully expressed, discussed, and decided by the common reason of the society."[21] This participation alone, argued Jefferson, would make a "true democracy." Anything short of this process allows for the rule of the dead from beyond the grave.

The creation of a public place is intimately linked with the maintenance of a spirit of revolution in the society at large. In the foreground of several revolutions, Jefferson appeared to have found the experiences refreshing. His letters on revolution conveyed a sense of catharsis, of cleansing, of providing an opportunity to begin again. The year 1787 produced two of Jefferson's more famous observations on this topic. Eager to calm James Madison over the recent rebellion in Massachusetts, he wrote, "I hold it that a little rebellion now and then is a good thing, and as necessary in the political world as storms in the physical."[22] And to William Smith, once more on Shays's Rebellion, he explained,

> God forbid we should ever be 20 years without such a rebellion....We have had 13 states independent 11 years. There has been one rebellion. That comes to one rebellion in a century and a half for each state. What country before ever existed a century and a half without a rebellion? . . . The tree of liberty must be refreshed from time to time with the blood of patriots and tyrants. It is its natural manure.[23]

Permanent revolution, then, became a central Jeffersonian principle to maintaining a vital, democratic community. The ward-republics were to play the primary role in maintaining a public space for humans to govern themselves. Once again it was Hannah Arendt who accurately compared Jefferson's ward-republics to the Paris Commune, the Soviets, and Räte. In a sense, the ward-republics were created to institutionalize revolution. But to keep revolution a permanent part of American life, Jefferson also introduced an additional principle, "the earth belongs in *usufruct* to the living."

[20] *Portable Jefferson*, p. 560.
[21] Ibid., p. 561.
[22] Ibid., p. 417.
[23] Jefferson, *Papers*, Vol. 12, pp. 356–57.

Property: Economic and Political Freedom

Toward the last days of his tenure as U.S. minister to France, in the fateful year 1789, Jefferson sent James Madison one of the more illuminating of his political letters. Caught up, no doubt, in the excitement of the impending revolution in France, Jefferson took the opportunity to speculate openly on the nature of obligations between generations of humans. Specifically, can one generation of society bind, either legally or morally, the succeeding one? Jefferson considered this question both *sui generis* and important.

Echoing the style of the *Declaration of Independence*, Jefferson presented what he thought were two self-evident truths: (1) "that the earth belongs in *usufruct* to the living" (that is, the fruits of the earth may be used, but the earth must be passed on to the next generation in *at least as good* a condition as they received it); and (2) "that the dead have neither powers nor rights over it." From these truths, Jefferson boldly concluded that a new generation owes *no obligation* to its predecessor. Whenever a member of society dies, the control over the portion of land which that individual had a right to use while living reverts to society. Jefferson noted that inheritance laws may be socially established, but in the absence of such laws, appropriation would be based on first occupant. His point is that it is positive law, not natural right, that creates individual property rights. "But the child, the legatee, or creditor takes it, not by any natural right, but by a law of the society of which they are members, and to which they are subject," Jefferson declared.[24]

This position—terminating control over landholdings with the death of each individual—Jefferson extended to the passing of each generation. Put differently, Jefferson believed in a *natural, generational right to property*. Moreover, he also extended the principle beyond the boundaries of property; it included the repayment of any debts, public or private, as well as all positive laws—even the Constitution of 1787. Jefferson's principle, that "the earth belongs to the living," is, as he put it, "of very extensive application and consequence." Lest the full impact of his principle be misread, he posed to Madison the following hypothetical case as an example. Jefferson asked: What would be the obligation of the present generation of Frenchmen if Louis XIV and Louis XV had contracted 10,000 Swiss millards of debt on behalf of the nation? Would either the lands, or the revenues from them, be due to the creditors? He responded negatively. Realizing that this notion flew in the face of tradition and the "common sense" of the day, Jefferson stated that the payment of debts by succeeding generations was a matter of "generosity and not of right."[25] It also followed that if the nation decided to end "perpetual monopolies," compensation was similarly a matter of generosity. A fiscal conservative, Jefferson thought this principle a way of avoiding the crippling accruement of large national debts, usually incurred as the result of war. Each generation was responsible for its own monetary matters; if one generation contracted debts it could not repay, the succeeding generation (calculated by Jefferson on the basis of

[24] *Portable Jefferson*, p. 445.
[25] Ibid., p. 450.

mortality tables to evolve every nineteen years) was under no obligation to pay them. Furthermore, by making this principle a matter of public policy for the United States (that is, known to the world), both borrowers and lenders were liable for observing these rules or suffering the consequences.

In the nineteenth year, all the laws and constitutions of society are to be automatically terminated. Quite simply, this means that approximately every twenty years—if not sooner given the prominence of the ward-republics in his system— society must either reaffirm or construct anew all of its statutes and institutions. The doctrine of *tacit consent* made popular by John Locke and embraced by James Madison would not suffice; Jefferson wanted to institutionalize revolution in order to keep the spirit of 1776 perpetually alive. Seen from another perspective, it is as if Jefferson believed that every generation had a natural right to fail. If subsequent generations were denied this opportunity to create their own political society, even if it risked failure, then they would never be as free as the original founders.

Happiness: The Ultimate Good

Although Jefferson's principle extended to every legal facet of society, its impact on property is particularly important. While much of the liberal tradition followed Locke, who viewed property as a natural right and its accumulation as the fulfillment of human endeavors, Jefferson did not. His vision of humans and of humankind's goal was much grander. Happiness is the ultimate good. More importantly, every person has a natural right to pursue it. Property is merely an institution created by society to help people gain "life, liberty, and the pursuit of happiness." Hence, property laws could and should be altered at least every nineteen years to ensure that goal.

Politically, Jefferson struggled to change the property laws in his home state of Virginia by drafting legislation that put an end to the last feudal holdovers of *entail* and *primogeniture*. Entail and primogeniture guaranteed that the eldest son would inherit the father's estate *in toto* and thus perpetuated large landholdings. Inequality of property was viewed by Jefferson as the root of "numberless instances of wretchedness." Everything that is "practicable" must be done to equalize property holdings.

> I am conscious that an equal division of property is impracticable. But the consequences of this enormous inequality producing so much misery to the bulk of mankind, legislators cannot invent too many devices for subdividing property, only taking care to let their subdivisions go hand in hand with the natural affections of the human mind.[26]

He noted the impracticality, not the impropriety, of equality. Although he did not believe that it was politically possible to redistribute property equally, Jefferson did, as we have seen, argue that every male must be given some amount of property, at least fifty acres, to live. Like Rousseau, Jefferson wanted to create a one-class society where small property holdings become the instrument for

---

[26] Jefferson, *Papers*, Vol. 8, pp. 681–82.

ensuring economic freedom, but unlike Rousseau, Jefferson wanted a large repub-lic—which would be broken down into smaller ward-republics—where copious amounts of free land become essential for sustaining democratic communities. No wonder Jefferson could not pass up the purchase of Louisiana.

Jefferson believed that free land would provide for economic freedom; as long as individuals had the option of meeting their needs on their own land, they could freely choose to leave the land and enter into a wage-labor situation that was not automatically based on exploitation. Jefferson knew that in America,

> . . . every one may have land to labor for himself if he chooses; or, preferring the exercise of any other industry, may exact for it such compensation as not only to afford a comfortable subsistence, but wherewith to provide for a cessation from labor in old age.[27]

With the option of sustaining themselves on their farm, American laborers, unlike their European counterparts, could enter into a wage contract that was not inevitably exploitative. Land guaranteed economic freedom, and it was imperative for a democratic community.

From this brief discussion of property, some of the implications of Jefferson's political theory manifest themselves. First, there is no natural, individual right to property; such property rights are social grants, created to aid people in the pur-suit of life, liberty, and happiness. Insofar as economic freedom was necessary to a fully human life, every citizen had to be guaranteed the option of owning a small farm. Be that as it may, there is in Jefferson a natural, generational property right. To ensure further economic as well as political freedom, Jefferson advanced his principle that "the earth belongs in *usufruct* to the living." Once implemented, this principle would guarantee the required periodic alterations in property laws so essential to maintaining a society where all have the chance to pursue, if not always find, happiness. C. B. Macpherson has observed:

> [Jefferson's] justification of property rests, in the last analysis, on the right to life at a more than animal level: freedom from coerced labour and arbitrary government are held to be part of what is meant by a fully human life. At the same time this justification is an assertion of the right to the means of labour: the whole point is that by working on his own land or other productive resources a man can be independent and uncoerced.[28]

Jefferson's View of Humanity

Much like Rousseau, Jefferson believed that individuals were evolving creatures whose human essence could flourish if placed in an appropriate environment. Where Rousseau thought humans had a natural inclination toward commiseration, Jeffer-son believed humans had a "moral sense." This sense was like the other five senses except its function was to tell individuals, independent of reason, how they ought to act in certain situations. Here is Jefferson's explanation:

[27] *Portable Jefferson,* p. 538.
[28] C. B. Macpherson, *Democratic Theory: Essays in Retrieval* (Oxford: Clarendon Press, 1973), p. 135.

He who made us would have been a pitiful bungler if he had made the rules of our moral conduct a matter of science. For one man of science, there are thousands who are not. What would have become of them? Man was destined for society. His morality therefore was to be formed to this object. He was endowed with a sense of right and wrong merely relative to this. The sense is as much a part of his nature as the sense of hearing, seeing, feeling; it is the true foundation of morality and not the το χολον truth, & c., as fanciful writers have imagined. The moral sense, or conscience, is as much a part of man as his leg or arm.[29]

Like the other senses, a few individuals may not have a moral sense while others may have damaged ones; and, if this sense is not used, not exercised, it too will deteriorate. Consequently, if humans are not free to exercise this capacity, they will become incapable of self-government—yet another reason for ward-republics. A social creature destined to live with other humans, humans were given a moral sense, a sense of justice, which allowed them to rule themselves: "Man was created for social intercourse; but social intercourse cannot be maintained without a sense of justice; then man must have been created with a sense of justice," Jefferson wrote.[30]

It is noteworthy that Jefferson, the quintessential Enlightenment figure in America, saw the moral sense—not reason—as the critical capacity necessary for politics. In a captivating letter—composed in the style of a dialogue between his "Head" (reason) and his "Heart" (moral sense)—to a young woman he was romantically pursuing, Jefferson asserted that there exists a natural separation of power between the Head and the Heart. As the Heart recalls the Head "into the proper limits of your office," it explains the nature of the universe:

When nature assigned us the same habitation, she gave us over it a divided empire. To you she allotted the field of science; to me that of morals. When the circle is to be squared, or the orbit of a comet to be traced; when the arch of greatest strength, or the solid of least resistance is to be investigated, take up the problem; it is yours; nature has given me no cognizance of it. In like manner, in denying to you the feelings of sympathy, of benevolence, of gratitude, of justice, of life, of friendship, she has excluded you from their controul. To these she has adapted the mechanism of the heart. Morals were too essential to the happiness of man to be risked on the incertain combinations of the head.[31]

A radical democrat who nevertheless held his own prejudices on the intellectual differences among humans, Jefferson believed that in terms of the ability of making correct moral choices, all humans were indeed created equal. As the Heart stated it, since morality was so "essential to the happiness of man . . . she laid their foundation therefore in sentiment, not in science. That she gave to all, as necessary to all: this to a few only, as sufficing with a few."

In one of the most telling passages of the entire dialogue, the Heart retrieved the memories of two specific episodes in Jefferson's life when he behaved immorally. The first involved a soldier who "begged" Jefferson for a ride in his

---

[29] Jefferson, *Papers*, Vol. 12, pp. 14–15.
[30] Jefferson, *Writings*, Vol. 15, pp. 24–25.
[31] *Portable Jefferson*, pp. 408–9.

"chariot"; the Head, however, instantly "began to calculate that the road was full of soldiers, & that if all should be taken up our horses would fail in their journey." Jefferson left the individual stranded and continued safely on his way. But soon becoming sensible that the Head had made him do wrong, he returned to the spot in hopes of providing a ride for the man. Failing to locate him, Jefferson also lamented his inability "to ask his forgiveness." The second incident involved a "poor woman" who, when she asked him for "a charity," the Head whispered that "she looked like a drunkard, & that half a dollar was enough to give her for the ale-house." This time, after Jefferson regained his moral sense, he found his victim and was able to rectify the injustice. Jefferson understood that the Head, dominated by reason, had automatically calculated what would protect the self, save it from pain, and then attempted to rationalize the subsequent behavior in the name of either justice or morality. After all, if what is in our self-interest is always also what is moral, morality would not be a difficult matter. Nevertheless, the Heart would have none of it since it could peer through the Head's mental gymnastics. The Heart tells the Head: "In short, my friend, as far as my recollection serves me, I do not know I ever did a good thing on your suggestion, or a dirty one without it." Having said this, the Heart banished the Head from politics: "I do forever then disclaim your interference in my province."[32]

Jeffersonian Politics

As a scientist, Jefferson required empirical evidence to support his view of humankind. Observing the American Indian, it was as if Jefferson had discovered a state of nature that led him to his views on the human essence. He argued that the Indians could regulate themselves without the interference of traditional governments because they were moral agents who, in addition to using their moral sense, were receptive to community pressures; for example, loss of esteem, expulsion, and, in extreme cases, execution carried out by the person who was harmed.

Imperfect as these correctional devices may appear, Jefferson reported that crime among Indian tribes was low. This is not to say that the Indian communities were leaderless. Chiefs held "power" through their ability to earn continually the respect of fellow tribe members, thereby influencing their actions. Furthermore, tribal society lacked bourgeois property rights; consequently, it did not suffer from artificial class distinctions.

Confronted with the presence of a harmonious community without the presence of a Leviathan, Jefferson rhetorically queried "whether no law . . . or too much law . . . submits man to the greatest evil?" On the basis of his firsthand observations, he unreservedly concluded: "One who has seen both conditions of existence would pronounce it to be the last: and that the sheep are happier of themselves, than under care of the wolves."[33] In the same vein, he also wrote: "I am convinced that those societies (as the Indians) which live without government enjoy in their general mass an infinitely greater degree of happiness than those

---

[32] Ibid., pp. 409–10.
[33] *Portable Jefferson*, p. 134.

who live under European governments. Among the former, public opinion is in the place of law, and restrains morals as powerfully as laws ever did any where."[34] This preference for a sort of social anarchism, a community of "lawfulness without laws," is not just a passing whim. Shortly after news of Shays's Rebellion in Massachusetts reached Jefferson, he dispatched a letter to James Madison in hopes of allaying Madison's growing fears:

> Those characters wherein fear predominates over hope may apprehend too much from these instances of irregularity. They may conclude too hastily that nature has formed man insusceptible of any other government but that of force, a conclusion not founded in truth, nor experience. Societies exist under three forms sufficiently distinguishable. (1) Without government, as among our Indians. (2) Under governments wherein the will of every one has a just influence, as is the case in England in a slight degree, and in our states in a great one. (3) Under governments of force: as is the case in all other monarchies and in most of the other republics.[35]

Commenting on the forms, he easily characterized the last type as that of "wolves over sheep." Then, he candidly raised a question that he claimed plagued him: "It is a problem, not clear in my mind, that the first condition is not the best." Nevertheless, he admitted that, although anarchism is the optimal social arrangement, it may also be "inconsistent with any great degree of population."

As if hinting at the role of decentralization and community spirit of the ward-republics in his own theory (and responding in advance to the democratic elite theorists of the twentieth century), Jefferson carefully noted how the Indians handle the issue of size: "It will be said, that great societies cannot exist without government. The Savages therefore break them into small ones."[36] Jefferson viewed humans as social and evolutionary beings. Unlike both Hobbes and Locke, who began with arguments assuming an original sovereignty over oneself, Jefferson's theory began with sociability, not individuality. The Indians needed few positive laws because shared ideals, customs, and pasts could bind these untainted humans together with bonds of affection and friendship. Coercion under these circumstances would be superfluous. And since they as individuals were naturally both social and moral, as members of a community there was, to Jefferson's way of thinking, no reason why they should behave in a contrary manner. To Madison, author of *Federalist 10*, Jefferson wrote:

> I know but one code of morality for men whether acting singly or collectively. He who says I will be a rogue when I act in company with a hundred others but an honest man when I act alone will be believed in the former assertion, but not in the latter. . . . If the morality of one man produces a just line of conduct in him, acting individually, why should not the morality of one hundred men produce a just line of conduct in them, acting together?[37]

[34] Ibid., p. 415.

[35] Ibid., pp. 415–16.

[36] Ibid., p. 134.

[37] Thomas Jefferson, *The Works of Thomas Jefferson*, 12 Vols., Paul Leicester Ford, ed. (New York: Knickerbocker Press, 1904), Vol. 5, p. 92.

It is illuminating to compare this observation with Madison's assertion: "Had every Athenian citizen been a Socrates; every Athenian assembly would still have been a mob."

The writings of Thomas Jefferson provide an alternative view of liberal democracy for America. Since his political theory was designed to preclude the potential difficulties of capitalism from developing, he too argued for the dual sense of democracy as a way of life as well as a mechanism for constructing laws. Regarding the former, democracy required economic freedom and a view of people as developmental, social creatures; concerning the latter, democracy required political participation by all members of the population as a vital part of living a fully human life.

By way of summarizing before moving on, the following paradigms can serve to emphasize the similarities of Rousseau and Jefferson as well as highlight their differences from Hobbes, Locke, and Madison.

	Individualistic Liberalism	**Alternative Liberalism**
POLITICS	reason	commiseration or moral sense
EQUALITY	contentiousness	moral being
INDIVIDUALITY	a-partness	inherently social
RIGHTS	property as ends	property as means
CITIZENSHIP	minimal participation	maximum participation
GOVERNMENT	representative (trustee)	direct democracy
LIBERTY	secondary to authority	more important than authority
HUMANS	static	developmental
ECONOMICS	class-divided capitalism	one-class simple market

Once the level of discussion proceeds beyond the level that both individualistic liberalism and alternative liberalism believed in reason, both knew politics was inevitable, both thought property was valuable, and both embraced rights and valued liberty, it should become evident that on each of the above points of comparison, the two paradigms held rather divergent viewpoints. What each model saw as the role of reason, the scope and value of politics, the nature and hierarchy of rights, the essence of humanity, and the promise of the future was altogether different; it is almost as if these two branches of liberalism represent two distinct ideological universes.

Having described the alternative vision of a liberal democratic society, it should be emphasized, once again, that it was James Madison's liberalism that provided the philosophical framework for the institutions of the American political system. Jeffersonian liberalism existed, to a large extent, outside the mainstream of political discourse in the United States. It remained, however, a viable alternative to that mainstream, and provided inspiration to those who believed that Madisonianism was fundamentally flawed. One such person was John Dewey.

JOHN DEWEY AND THE LIBERAL TRADITION

John Dewey was a philosopher and educator who was quite influential in the United States in both of those areas during the first half of the twentieth century.

Although his political thinking was perhaps less well known than his other endeavors, for our purposes he can serve as an excellent example of twentieth-century attempts to modernize the alternative vision of Jeffersonian liberal democracy. Dewey may be particularly appropriate in this regard because his early speculations on political matters placed him squarely within the individualistic liberal tradition of Madison. However, he became disenchanted with that tradition largely because of its emphasis on competition, its ties to capitalist economics, and its lack of a meaningful conception of democratic community. Consciously seeking to "update" Jefferson's legacy for a new environment, he produced a conception of democracy that placed heavy emphasis on economic equality and the need for a participatory community—two of the major values of the alternative tradition of liberalism.

In the prior chapter we encountered several critiques of the mainstream liberal tradition—Utilitarianism, power-elite analysis, and, in spite of its similarities to the mainstream, rights-based liberalism. The alternative liberal critique as presented in this chapter raises more fundamental issues. Put in a graphic way, the question may be simply stated: Is liberal democracy, properly conceived, compatible with capitalism—even the adulterated forms of capitalism advocated by some Utilitarians and people such as John Rawls? We have seen that both Rousseau and Jefferson had their doubts, believing that the class-divided society that capitalism seemed inevitably to produce undercut the basic norms of their visions of a liberal democratic society.

In one sense, the thinking of John Dewey is the culmination of the Rousseau/Jefferson position in that his early doubts concerning the marriage of liberal democracy and capitalism eventually were to lead him to an advocacy of democratic socialism. In another sense, however, Dewey was far more radical. Both Rousseau and Jefferson had affirmed the necessity of a social dimension to humanity, arguing that participation, community, and self-realization in and through group activity were the only ways to achieve a truly human existence. And each, in his own way, thought he had "empirical" evidence to support his position: Rousseau had the noble savage and Jefferson Native Americans. Dewey, armed with the authority of twentieth century advances in knowledge—particularly experimental science—was to argue that the entire individualistic liberal enterprise was based upon faulty abstract concepts that were incompatible with the facts of human existence.

John Dewey was part of what, in Morton White's words, constituted a "revolt against formalism"—a revolution in which Dewey argued for a fundamental "reconstruction in philosophy." There were to be many dimensions to this reconstruction, but at a minimum it would require the recognition of certain empirically demonstrable facts concerning human existence that rendered any form of rights-based liberalism— that of Hobbes, Locke, Madison, or Rawls—simply obsolete.

Modern science had, to Dewey's mind, conclusively demonstrated that any search for fixed basic units—"atoms" in physical science or "discreet individuals" in political thought—was fruitless. Such searches had been the preoccupation of premodern thinking in an attempt to discover absolutes or eternal truths. Modern advances in scientific thinking had shown not only that such quests were

Quixotic but also that they had the result of placing a whole host of pseudo-problems at the heart of political discourse. People simply did not exist as discreet atomic units as the mainstream liberal tradition (most graphically, Thomas Hobbes) had thought. Rather, they were the ongoing product of a whole set of interrelationships, where numerous variables helped shape their character and behavior patterns. Both Jefferson and Rousseau seemed to have had a vague understanding of this, but neither of them had realized its full implications. Dewey argued not only that this had been conclusively demonstrated by modern advances in our knowledge but also that the acceptance of this fact necessitated a refocusing of the entire enterprise of liberal political thinking. The age-old preoccupations of the mainstream liberal tradition—individual rights versus community good, private versus public, freedom versus equality—were false dichotomies that were the result of the incorrect presuppositions of that form of liberalism. Such ideas and concepts were highly abstract human inventions and ultimately resulted in a distortion of our real experience.

In contrast, Dewey argued that our ideas and concepts should be viewed as working hypotheses—not abstract, *a*historical universals—which were to be constantly subjected to the test of their ability to solve the problems that arise from everyday human experience. Following the model of experimental science, ideas were to be judged better or worse in terms of their ability to solve "problematic situations," whether in thought or in practice. When an idea, a set of ideas, or even a well-established paradigm ceased to be able to explain experienced events, it should be creatively altered or, if need be, discarded in favor of a new, more satisfactory, way of thinking. From this perspective, a certain *pragmatism* can be seen to pervade all philosophic endeavors. In the context of political thought, the old mental "habit patterns" of Madisonianism—however appropriate they may have been at the time—were no longer capable of dealing with the problems of the modern world.

In his earliest writings on politics, Dewey operated well within the dominant tradition, referring, for example, to government as essentially an "umpire" supervising the competing groups generated from the private sector. By 1927, in *The Public and Its Problems*, however, he argued that the Madisonian solution had worked all too well—competition and checks and balances had virtually eliminated any conception of a truly *public* interest. "It is not that there is no public, no large body of persons having a common interest in the consequences of social transactions. There is too much public, a public too diffused and scattered and too intricate in composition," he wrote. In Dewey's mind this condition made the achievement of a democratic community impossible, and that fact undermined the essence of democracy. "The clear consciousness of a communal life, in all of its implications, constitutes the idea of democracy," he observed.[38] Finally, in the true legacy of Jefferson, Dewey argued for a fundamental reevaluation of the very idea of democracy, particularly as it related to modern times.

[38] John Dewey, *The Public and Its Problems* (Chicago: The Swallow Press, 1954), p. 149.

The initial step in that reevaluation process seemed quite clear to Dewey. We must begin by discarding individualistic politics and the ideology underlying it as not only outmoded but also simply incorrect. We must recognize the fact that natural and human events are based upon *interrelationships* and that this fact provides the basis for true human community. The recognition of the physical fact of associative behavior will provide the groundwork for developing a moral dimension of that association that will constitute a community. If human beings are heavily influenced by the interactive environment in which they participate, that environment should be structured in such a way as to ensure the development of "democratic habit patterns." We must create an arena—not unlike the one that Jefferson advocated in his ward-republics—where participation, interrelationships, and cooperative enterprise are encouraged. The entire social environment—the political system, communications, education, socialization processes—must be transformed to support a democratic community of actively participating adults.

Local communities, what Dewey deftly called "face-to-face" communities, could be structured in such a way as to teach values and ways of behaving that were conducive to a democratic way of life. People would learn that active participation, cooperation, and creative problem solving were appropriate and normal parts of their everyday existence. Armed with such values and empowered by feelings of efficacy gained through experiences in local communities, Dewey believed it would be possible for people to participate in a meaningful way in a truly national community. Obviously, the interaction, participation, and problem-solving activities would be "less vivid" at the national level than in the local face-to-face community. Nevertheless, Dewey believed that a nation wide community—in a meaningful sense of the term—could be created, in particular through the use of modern advances in communication. If face-to-face interaction were impossible on a national scale, people with the appropriate participatory democratic values developed in their rich experience at the local level could nevertheless engage in "symbolic interaction" through the use of mass-communications devices. Dewey did not live long enough to witness the full impact of television on modern culture, much less the interactive and participatory potential of "virtual realities" in this age of computers. Had he done so, one can confidently predict that his argument for the proper use of mass-communications devices as enhancing a democratic way of life would have been greatly strengthened.

Dewey attacked the fruits of Madison's labors in other areas as well, particularly with respect to the relationship between political and economic power. Recall that the individualistic liberal tradition had argued for a large private space in which human beings could pursue their essentially selfish interests. Recall also that the Madisonian tradition, following the lead of Hobbes and Locke, intimately tied its conception of democracy to capitalist culture. While this conception of democracy may have been desirable in Madison's time, by the twentieth century it had produced conditions of inequality that were incompatible with a democratic way of life.

Economics and the Common Man

Although he declared throughout his life that he was not a follower of Karl Marx (and certainly not the authoritarian tradition of Lenin), Dewey eventually came to advocate nationalization of the means of production as the only way to overcome the inequalities that capitalist economics had produced. Perhaps reflecting his early enthusiasm for the ideas of G. W. F. Hegel, whom we will meet shortly, Dewey believed that the political system must be used to provide not only political equality but also equality of economic opportunity. This was to be accomplished peacefully—through the ballot box. While Dewey was somewhat unclear as to the specifics of his proposal—indeed, the policies would alter as the society confronted ever-changing "problematic situations"—the goal was quite clear. The class bifurcations produced by capitalist economics had to be eliminated through national political control. Hence, it is appropriate to view John Dewey as a modern American representative of the position generally called *democratic socialism*. In a real sense, the Rousseau/Jefferson project to minimize the economic inequalities produced by capitalism reaches its fulfillment in Dewey's call for a single-class society based upon economic equality.

Whatever we may choose to label Dewey's views, there is no question that his ultimate commitment was to the ideal of a participatory democratic community. To his mind, democracy was the only way of life that permitted—even demanded—the constant examination of alternative courses of action, questioning of conventional wisdom, and individual and communal growth (he called it "creative intelligence") that was the essence of the human experience. Any other form of association—absolutism of any sort—is simply not compatible with human nature.

Finally, to those who would argue that the average person simply was incapable of, or not interested in, the type of active participation in decision making that he advocated, Dewey responded with a ringing defense of the capabilities of the "common man." He knew that masses of people were not inclined to participate in politics, were ignorant of political issues, and tended to support authoritarian rather than liberal democratic values. The reason for such behavior was not, in his view, some underlying "illiberal" human nature, but the result of undemocratic (even antiliberal democratic) environmental conditioning. In direct contrast to those who feared the "common man," Dewey argued that it was illiberal institutions and conditioning that resulted in illiberal behavior in people and that in the appropriate environment the average person was fully capable of the type of action required in a participatory democratic community.

While the political thought of John Dewey has served as our example of a modern manifestation of the alternative liberal tradition, we should note that a variety of other thinkers (and political activists) might well be regarded in the same fashion. Many of the so-called student radicals of the 1960s and 1970s articulated similar views in a less systematic way. Moreover, quite a few of the critics of "usual Madisonian politics" or the mainstream liberal tradition utilize arguments quite similar to those of Dewey in their efforts to reform liberal democracy. Nevertheless, we believe we are correct in using the term *alternative vision* to describe this tradition, for it has never achieved either the popularity or the stamp of legitimacy of the individualistic liberalism of Hobbes, Locke, Madison, and their contemporary followers.

FINAL THOUGHTS ON LIBERAL DEMOCRACY

What should be evident at this point in the discussion is that historically liberalism has meant something both more specific and more complex, if not altogether different, than its common American usage. Although in the United States the term *liberalism* is often erroneously associated with social reform movements, the welfare state, and "bleeding hearts" (whatever that means), in terms of the historical unfolding of the ideology it is the emphasis on the free individual and that individual's right to develop his or her full potential that is the center of liberal thought. We have argued that the broad liberal tradition can be separated into two general types—individualistic (capitalist) and alternative (noncapitalist). Each of those types has undergone numerous changes and alterations in the past four hundred years, but the two types remain, we think, clearly distinguishable.

Originally, the ideology of individualistic liberalism developed alongside of capitalism and the modern state. It was believed that in contrast to the feudal economic tradition, capitalism would free humanity from the past and put an end to economic scarcity, so both individual and aggregate material needs would be met in the most efficient manner. As class divisions became more apparent and increasingly unmanageable, individualistic liberal theorists extended the franchise. First, they included non-property-owning white males; eventually, all people were granted the vote. This extension of the franchise provided the precondition for the rise of majoritarian liberalism.

We have stated that the implementation of a more majoritarian form of the individualist tradition was more easily achieved in countries other than the United States, largely because of the impediments imposed by the Madisonian system. In America, the debate over how much majoritarianism does in fact exist or, for that matter, ought to exist goes on.

The second tradition of alternative liberalism sprang from different roots, but its ultimate goal was and is the same as that of individualistic liberalism—the freeing of the individual so as to ensure the full development of his or her potential. These liberals, however, differ in their view of what processes ought to be used to accomplish that purpose and what values a truly liberal society ought to pursue. Lacking ties to capitalist economics, espousing a more egalitarian society, and arguing for a full participatory community, alternative liberalism provides a legitimate alternative to the dominant individualist tradition.

Finally, we must emphasize once again the values of toleration and dialogue inside of the broad spectrum of perspectives contained in liberalism. Regardless of which liberal thinker one encounters, each values the necessity of an ongoing dialogue in the search for a democratic society. This position in favor of toleration is, at times, in marked contrast to the presentations that follow. If liberal democracy is a process in search of an unfolding and evolving truth, then Marxism, German National Socialism, Italian fascism, and Islamism seem far more certain that they have already found their path to the truth.

SUGGESTED READINGS

BERMAN, MARSHALL, *The Politics of Authenticity.* New York: Athenaeum, 1970.

DEWEY, JOHN, *Liberalism and Social Action.* New York: Capricorn Books, 1963.

HOROWITZ, ASHER, AND GAD HOROWITZ, *"Everywhere They Are in Chains."* Scarborough, Ontario: Nelson Canada, 1988.

MACPHERSON, C. B., *Life and Times of Liberal Democracy.* New York: Oxford University Press, 1979.

MATTHEWS, RICHARD K., *The Radical Politics of Thomas Jefferson.* Lawrence: University Press of Kansas, 1984.

WHITE, MORTON, *Social Thought in America: The Revolt Against Formalism.* Boston: Beacon Press, 1957.

5

Marxism

The philosophers have only interpreted *the world, in various ways;*
the point, however, is to change *it.*

Karl Marx

A strange phenomenon. At this moment, when many people in the United States are still celebrating the complete and final "victory" of capitalism over communism, Karl Marx's ideas may, nevertheless, be more relevant than ever! In some sense, this claim appears counterintuitive. After all, the "end of Marxism" was vividly marked by the demise of the Soviet Union and the rebirth of Russia, the collapse of the Berlin Wall and the tearing down of the "iron curtain," the "liberation" of the "Soviet bloc" and the "democratization" of Eastern Europe. The mass media, in its many forms, have broadcast countless images of capitalism as the apotheosis of economic wisdom, human freedom, and political democracy; and if its various stories are to be believed, even the most remote parts of the globe are awaiting anxiously to get "on-line," have a "Big Mac," and use their "American Express Card" to visit the closest "Disney World." But we believe, to paraphrase Mark Twain, that rumors of Marx's death have been greatly exaggerated.

As a student and critic of capitalism, Marx has few if any rivals. What he might have thought about the Soviet Union's experiment in building a socialist state, or its failure to do so, are interesting questions to ponder even if a definitive answer is impossible. However, what he would think about the vast, rapidly expanding global capitalist economic system that dominates life at the cusp of the second millennium is another issue altogether. For the moment, rather than attempt to summarize Marx's thoughts on that timely topic, it makes more sense to begin our discussion of communism by looking briefly at Marx's life and initiate the intriguing process of understanding his sophisticated analysis of alienation, capitalism, history, and the enormous possibilities he foresaw for human liberation and fulfillment.

MARX'S LIFE

Karl Marx was a revolutionary—it is said he even looked like one! His mature life was spent in never-ending attempts to transcend the capitalist system that he both admired and abhorred. History is filled with figures who rebelled against existing societies and failed, their careers being relegated to mere footnotes in scholarly works, but Karl Marx and his ideas comprise no footnote to history. If we were to speak of the number of people who have been influenced by his vision, to say nothing of those who have felt it necessary to condemn him, we would have a vast army indeed. On this scale, Karl Marx would rank among the great religious leaders of antiquity. Herein lies one of the major problems in speaking of Marx. As Robert Heilbroner has put it, Marx the symbol has come to obscure Marx the man, and Marx the revolutionary disguises Marx the thinker.[1] In more vivid terms, Michael Harrington makes a similar observation and passes along a valuable recommendation on how to begin a study of Marxism.

[1] Robert L. Heilbroner, *The Worldly Philosophers* (New York: Simon & Schuster, 1964), p. 115.

For most people the first step in grasping the new and future Marx is to forget everything they have heard or read about the familiar Marx. At the same time, they must
accept one of history's strangest ironies: that Marx and the Marxists made a major
contribution to the misunderstanding of Marxism.[2]

Marx's own view of this enigmatic circumstance may be surmised from his
comment when he learned of certain French "Marxists" who (mis)understood his
thought: "As for me, I am not a Marxist." It may be impossible to discover the real
man or to set forth a true picture of his ideas—getting inside another's skin is a
formidable task. Yet we can attempt to separate the man from the myth, Marx from
his interpreters. To begin on relatively safe ground, there is little controversy about
his life.

Karl Marx was born in 1818 in Trier, in the German Rhineland, the eldest
son of a rather prosperous Jewish lawyer. While appropriately described as bourgeois and secure, the Marx family was subjected to abuse from the periodic waves
of anti-Semitism that swept most of Europe. Shortly after Karl was born, his father
converted to Christianity and, despite the elder Marx's somewhat liberal ideas, the
family enjoyed a rather safe and comfortable existence.

Karl was a very intelligent, somewhat precocious student, entering the University of Bonn in 1835 at the age of 17 to pursue legal studies. With apparent
enthusiasm he entered into the life of a German university student, engaging in
his share of boisterous behavior. After transferring from Bonn to the University of
Berlin in 1836 he began a more intensive study of law, jurisprudence, and, eventually, philosophy. It was at Berlin that the young Marx was exposed to two major
influences of his early life—Hegelianism and materialism—ideas we shall explore
at greater length in the following discussion. In pursuit of an academic career,
Marx completed his doctorate in philosophy at Jena in 1841. However, the academic career never materialized. Marx took a job as a reporter and later editor for
the newspaper *Rheinische Zeitung*. Here, perhaps, was an early indication of Marx's
desire for action and change, a bent that throughout his life was to make him con-
temptuous of "armchair" philosophers and academicians. At any rate, his early
newspaper career ended abruptly in 1843 when the Prussian government suppressed the paper for being too radical (although thoroughly capitalist). Unre-
pentant, Marx moved to Paris to edit a newspaper for Prussian *emigres,* only to be
expelled at the request of the Prussian government in 1845.

His years in Paris proved extremely important, for it was here he met
Friedrich Engels, who was to be his lifelong collaborator and friend. Engels
brought to the relationship a firsthand knowledge of the barbarities of capitalism, garnered from his study of the conditions of the British working class, as well
as wit, charm, and a writing style in many ways superior to that of Marx. Their
collaboration was so close that for most people Marxism has since come to mean
the writings of both Marx and Engels; Marx himself referred to his work as "our
theory." Marx and Engels moved to Brussels where they attempted to organize

[2] Michael Harrington, *The Twilight of Capitalism* (New York: Simon & Schuster, 1976), p. 59.

workers and became associated with a group of radicals in an organization called the Communist League. It was for this group, in the fateful year of 1848, that they wrote what has become the creed of Marxism, *The Manifesto of the Communist Party.*

The year 1848 saw revolution sweeping Europe: uprisings occurred in Berlin, Paris, Rome, Vienna, and many other cities throughout the Continent. Although the publication of the *Communist Manifesto* certainly did not cause these revolutions, it did reflect the generally radical spirit of the times. Here, many people felt, was the long-predicted workers' revolution, and, while he played at best a small role in these activities, Marx was somewhat optimistic about the prospects. Without delving deeply into history, let us merely say that the great revolution substantially failed. Alfred Meyer has stated it nicely: "Altogether, few revolutions had been expected so openly and failed so miserably as that of 1848. The Marxist image of the proletariat had turned out to be a phantom."[3]

After 1848, Marx devoted more attention to the problems of developing class consciousness among members of the working class. He returned to Cologne late in 1848 and began publishing a revised version of his old newspaper, only to have it suppressed once again. Marx was banished from Prussia in July 1849. Not welcome in Paris, the safest place seemed to be England and, although intending to remain only a short time, he spent the rest of his life in exile there.

The early years in London were particularly harsh. Although he spent over a decade as a part-time correspondent for the *New York Tribune,* Marx and his family were plagued by poverty, chronic illness, and the death of several children; they became dependent largely on Engels's money to keep them from the streets. Nevertheless, with the death of his mother in 1864, and a bequest from a communist comrade, Marx was able to climb out from under poverty, but at this point his health deteriorated. Marx spent his days laboring at the British Museum where he sketched out, in seven lengthy notebooks called *The Grundrisse,* what appears to be the outline for his grand philosophic system. Out of this *Foundations [Grundrisse] of the Critique of Political Ecomony* grew his famous published work, *Das Kapital.*

Only the first volume of his *magnum opus* was published prior to Marx's death in 1883. The remaining two volumes were published posthumously under the editorship of Engels. What is important to note is that contrary to traditional opinion about *Das Kapital,* Marx's notebooks indicate that it was but one part of an even more ambitious project dealing with a multitude of topics, which concluded with a discussion of the timelessness of great art!

Even while engaged in these intellectual activities, Marx also devoted time and energy to the immediate tactical concerns of organizing the working class; in 1864 he participated in the founding of the International Workingmen's Association, and for the next seven years remained active in its General Council. Engels outlived Marx by some twelve years, interpreting and refining the basic Marxist ideas as well as continuing his engagement with international communist activities.

Even before his death, Marx's ideas were subject to a good deal of interpretation and alteration. After his death (particularly after Engels's demise in 1895)

---

[3] Alfred G. Meyer, *Marxism: The Unity of Theory and Practice* (Ann Arbor, Mich.: Ann Arbor Paperbacks, 1963), p. 108.

an entire band of followers sought to update, correct, or reinterpret Marxian teachings. This trend has, of course, continued to this day with *revisionists* and *orthodox Marxists,* to name but two schools, vying for the title of true interpreters. Thus we encounter another difficulty in trying to understand Marx. Is *Das Kapital* still to be considered his definitive work? Or has *The Grundrisse* changed that consideration? Are his earlier, more philosophic writings inconsistent with his later economic emphasis? Is there a young Marx and an old Marx or are his works all of one piece of cloth? The answers to these questions will significantly affect our presentation and discussion of Marx's ideas, so some of the scholarly controversy concerning the "true" Marx must be examined.

Marx's Writing and the "Real" Marx

One of the great difficulties in having a successful revolution proclaimed in your name is that the leaders of that revolution become self-appointed authoritative interpreters of your ideas. With the Bolshevik success in Russia in 1917 all future leaders of the Soviet Union found it necessary as well as expedient to interpret Marx's ideas to fit changing times. As we shall see in Chapter 6, Lenin began the process of *authoritative* interpretation and addition to Marxian thought. It was under Stalin's reign, however, that Soviet scholars began to treat Marx's works more as rigid dogma and placed greater emphasis on certain writings.

We have referred to the *Manifesto of the Communist Party* as Marxism's "creed"; for classical Marxist scholars *Das Kapital* is its "bible." The classical Marxist view tends to emphasize the concepts of (dialectical) materialism, the labor theory of value, and Marx's theory of the state as developed in *Das Kapital.* Some would say this view greatly neglects Marx's earlier writings; which are characterized as more philosophical and humanistic, emphasizing the Marxian concepts of humanity and human alienation. Coexisting with the orthodox interpretation of Marxian thought, a small group of scholars emphasized differences between a young and an old Marx, and placed greater weight on his earlier writings: Marx the humanist-philosopher as contrasted with Marx the scientist-economist.

With the decline in Stalinist orthodoxy in the latter part of the 1950s, this humanist interpretation of his work gained increasing acceptance, particularly in Eastern Europe. In terms of Marx's writings, the young period includes his doctoral disertation, *The Difference Between the Democritean and Epicurian Philosophies of Nature, Economic and Philosophical Manuscripts,* and the *German Ideology*—all of his works up to 1844–1845 (according to other scholars this period extends to 1847–1848). All later works, beginning with the *Communist Manifesto,* are then seen to be the product of the more mature scholar.

In contrast to the classical scholars' emphasis on materialism and economics, the revisionist scholars take as central the notion of alienation as developed in Marx's early works. This controversy still rages, though in a somewhat muted form today, especially since scholars in the West have turned their attention to Marx's recently translated *Grundrisse.* As discussed previously, *The Grundrisse* casts a considerable cloud over the futurity of these heated debates on the "real Marx" in that it makes clear Marx's constancy of thought on both the humanist-philosophic issues of his early work and the scientific-economic focus of the later years.

Our presentation assumes that, while undoubtedly there are differences of *emphasis* in the young and old Marx, all of his works can be seen as a whole. The concept of human alienation, while mentioned less frequently in the later works, still is a key element in Marx's analysis of the decline and fall of capitalist systems. This does not mean that the later economic arguments are to be discarded as outmoded or that dialectical materialism is not important in Marxism. If it is necessary to take a position in this ongoing debate, the attempt here is to present both sides in the belief that some sort of synthesis is possible. We have, however, been using concepts and ideas that have not been fully explored or even defined; it is time, then, to look at the main taproot of Marxism contained in the philosophy of Georg Wilhelm Friedrich Hegel.

HEGEL'S PHILOSOPHY AND POLITICS

> For it is not *what is* that makes us irascible and resentful, but the fact that it is not as it *ought to be.*[4]

The dominant philosophic system of nineteenth-century Europe was German Idealism, and its dominant philosopher was G. W. F. Hegel. Although Marx went to considerable lengths to spell out his objections to Hegel's political theory, it is important to note his acceptance of the core of Hegel's philosophy—dialectics. As Marx neatly put it a decade prior to his own death:

> The mystification which dialectic suffers in Hegel's hands, by no means prevents him from being the first to present its general form of working in a comprehensive and conscious manner. With him it is standing on its head. It must be turned right side up again, if you would discover the rational kernel within the mystical shell.[5]

Because of the significance of Hegel to Marxism, it is essential to understand Hegel on (1) dialectics, (2) labor, and (3) politics; Marx openly embraced much of the first two and vehemently rejected the third.

It was Hegel's contention that all prior philosophic thinking was incomplete, a limited form of understanding the world, due primarily to its reliance on formal Aristotelian logic. This logical form forced people to think about their environment in a particular, highly abstract fashion. One of the central rules of formal logic, known as the *principal of noncontradiction,* held that a concept could not be both itself and its opposite at one and the same time. That is, something could not be said to be both *A* and non-*A* and still convey any meaning. For example, think of red litmus paper. When red litmus paper turns blue

[4] G. W. F. Hegel, *Political Writings,* trans. T. M. Knox (Oxford: Clarendon Press, 1964) p. 145.

[5] Karl Marx, in *The Marx-Engels Reader,* 2nd ed., Robert C. Tucker, ed. (New York: W. W. Norton & Company, 1978), p. xxi.

its here-and-now existence as red litmus paper ceases, and its existence as blue lit-mus paper begins. Litmus paper is either red or blue; it cannot be both at the same moment in time.

The transition from childhood to adulthood is also illustrative. In order to make logically meaningful statements about this transformation, at some point during the maturation process the human creature stops being a child (possessing the properties of childhood) and becomes an adult, thereby replacing the earlier properties with those of adulthood. In these examples, however, it makes no sense, in terms of logic, to think of red litmus paper as being potentially blue litmus paper or a child containing within it the seeds of adulthood.

This type of formal logical rule led earlier philosophical thinkers to develop systems of categorization whereby objects in the real world were abstracted into categories of genus and species; something either existed or it did not; it was absurd to conceive of both "being" and "nonbeing" at the same time. Hegel believed that this formal logic resulted in a distortion of the true complexity of both the way human thinking occurred and the movement of the real world.

Hegel was influenced by the ancient Greek philosopher Heraclitus, who believed that there was no permanent reality, except the reality of change. The universe, and everything that comprised the universe, was constantly in the process of changing, altering, of transforming. Heraclitus's famous statement of not being able to step in the same river twice is illustrative of his conception of reality: The flow of the water makes it impossible to re-create precisely the same act of stepping in exactly the same river. He also believed that all things contained within them their opposites; for example, death was potential in life, being and nonbeing were part of the whole. The only reality, therefore, was the transitional one of *becoming*. Hegel accepted this Heraclitian view of the world, and he tried to discover a process by which people could come to know their constantly changing, continu-ally evolving world.

Hence, it was not at all absurd to think of something being both itself and its opposite; indeed the key to understanding reality was in seeing that everything in existence in some sense contained within itself its opposite or its negation. Imag-ine yourself *looking* at a salt crystal. As you perceive it, the salt appears white in color and cubical in shape. If you placed it in your mouth it would taste pungent; salt is neither black nor sweet. The properties of white, flat, and pungent seem to exclude their opposite of black, round, and sweet. And yet it would be impossible to *describe* salt if you could not *conceive* of the opposite properties. Without an idea of nonwhite (that is, black in this context), you could not know white. Without a conception of nonflat (roundness), you could not understand what is a plane. In order to understand any particular entity, therefore, one must be able to conceive of its negation.

It is equally important to point out the role of the thinking person in this process. For Hegel, it was the thought process between the object (salt) and the subject (you) that makes the world knowable. In a sense, you, the subject, make the salt "real" when you come to know it as a combination of a white (nonblack), cubical (nonspherical), pungent (nonsweet), et cetera, substance.

Transforming Logic

What Hegel was attempting was the transformation of the very meaning of the term *logic*. Formal or traditional logic consists of a system of rules by which we test the validity of one's own thinking. We say that a conclusion is valid if it has been reached from its premises by using the rules of logic. It was Hegel's contention that this involved a distortion of the complexity of events and that humans forced reality into an artificially contrived system. Rather than a set of rules devised to test the validity of thought processes, Hegelian logic purports to be both an actual description of those processes and an accurate reflection of events in the real world. Hegelian logic, hence, is not a logic at all, but an *ontology* or an explanation of existence. By using it we can accurately describe the true nature of reality. Since the world is constantly in transformation, the method of knowing this world of flux must also be based upon this conception of motion. Traditional logic presupposes a fixed, static world where time and motion do not operate. Hegel's dialectical method presupposes movement and change. The dialectical process is thus imbedded in the world of real events and can provide the only accurate explanation of that world. It was this belief that led Hegel to assert that he had discovered the only correct way of "explaining the world."

The dialectical process contains three basic elements, or stages, of development. Although the terms *thesis, antithesis,* and *synthesis* are often associated with his name, Hegel never used this empty schema to describe dialectics. Rather, he presented it as a dynamic unity of opposites. Hegel makes this difficult notion even more complex by using the German word *aufheben* to describe this process, for it has at least three meanings: to preserve, to eliminate, and to transcend. Hegel moreover, intends *aufheben* to mean all three at once! To illustrate, imagine a plant. It unfolds and develops itself. To Hegel, it is *not* now a bud, *then* a blossom, but a continuous movement from bud through blossom to decay. Even in the "final" stage of decay, the plant will break down into its organic components and begin the process anew, albeit in an altered form, or the plant will begin the process again in the spring.

If we change our example from a plant to a human being, an additional aspect of dialectics becomes present. That is, like any living organism, a human "unfolds" through its various stages of development, but unlike any other temporal entity, humans alone are capable of comprehending the dialectical process itself. Since people can comprehend this, they are also capable of consciously participating in it. Humans alone have the power of determining their own subjectivity in the process of becoming a human being.

Finally, dialectics is based on a theory of internal relations. For Hegel as for Marx, everything in the world is, ultimately, interrelated to every other part of the world. Nothing—neither objects nor ideas—exists independently of, or in isolation from, anything else. Although one begins to know the world by examining discrete parts of the whole, it is crucial always to be looking for the relationship to other parts. As the process continues, people gradually comprehend more and more about additional aspects and their interrelationships. Eventually, the whole is understood. At this point, the relationships among the parts, and the parts and the whole, are "complete" in that the human person has progressed beyond the abstract perspective of entities having meaning independent of other entities. At the same time, reality never can be comprehended—in a final, ultimate sense—because the Heraclitian universe is continually unfolding. Hence, our comprehension of reality must also continue to change. Our understanding of reality, then, is both complete and incomplete: Understanding is a *process* where each new discovery unfolds new relationships and a more complete comprehension of the world.

To give an example, think of this book. In order to understand the book in an appropriately dialectical fashion, it would be necessary to understand all the relationships, both past and present, involved in it. That would include (1) the relationships that created and produced the book, (2) the relationships that created and continue to re-create you, and (3) the relationship between you and the book. Looking at the first aspect, it is clear that the book uses words. This presupposes a society where words have common meanings and can be used to communicate ideas. The book is printed in ink and on paper. To understand this, it would be necessary to investigate every relationship involved from writing the book, setting the type (not to mention the invention by Gutenberg), to selling the book—for a profit. This further implies a market society, workers and owners, and alienation. Although this would by no means exhaust the first category, imagine the plethora of relationships involved in the second and third categories. Higher education? Tuition? Exams? The light that enables you to see the printed words? Questions—relationships—more questions—more relationships. Where would it end? It would "end" after you had discovered and understood the whole of reality up to that moment in history. And, by a theory of internal relations, both Hegel and Marx mean nothing less.

Hegel on Labor

This conception of human self-realization is central to the Hegelian system. What Marx also accepted in Hegel is the role of labor as the principal manner in which people realize themselves and their potential as true *human* beings. Through labor humans transform themselves from a pure, isolated subject into an object. That is, by interacting with the external world, by creating things, human beings put part of themselves in the object, thus obtaining objective status. The external world becomes a part of oneself; as people alter the external world, it is simultaneously altering them. The subject-object dichotomy apparently inherent in nature is thus transcended, or mediated—the subject (self) becomes objectified (object). In Hegel's rationalistic universe, this labor process was sufficient to provide for true self-consciousness and its corresponding freedom.

In Hegel's system, history consisted of an ongoing process of the embodiment of reason in the spatiotemporal world. Hegel used a number of words to capture a sense of the totality, the interrelated wholeness of this dynamic process: "Absolute Idea," "Spirit," "God," "Universal," "Truth." Regardless of the precise term used, for present purposes it is sufficient to say that Hegel's point is that both the world and the people who act in and on this world are becoming ever more

rational, ever more free; they are also continually approaching the ideal unifica
tion of all contradictions comprised in the "Absolute Idea," "God," "Spirit," and so
on. For Hegel, given the frugality of the material world, the final unification could
be achieved only in thought, in ideas. For Marx, however, it had to be fulfilled in
the material world: The point was not only to interpret but also to change the
world.

Within Hegel's broad historical process the individual human being is con
stantly trying to attain consciousness of self, and the process by which one achieves
this is interaction with the environment. Hegel called this interaction *labor*. When
interacting, however, humans perceive the rationality which is embodied in the
external world, hence becoming more rational themselves. The process of attain
ing self-realization is also the path toward increasing rationality. Further, human
freedom for Hegel could be achieved only when *all* people are capable of achiev
ing self-consciousness and rationality; hence, complete rationality would be the
same as "total" freedom and all people would achieve complete self-consciousness.
In this scheme humans are obviously limited in their ability to achieve personal
freedom by the temporal period in which they exist. If a person is living during a
historical period in which little rationality is present in the world, he or she is not
capable of finding true freedom. The important point here is that *all* persons must
be capable of achieving freedom and no one individual may possess it at the
expense of others. Thus there must be human institutions, particularly political
institutions, that permit all people to achieve self-consciousness and freedom.

Prior historical epochs were limited by the degree of rationality embodied in
the world and by corresponding human institutions that permitted only some to
achieve "freedom" (not true freedom, of course, for all must be free in order for
one to be free). Hegel spoke of an Oriental stage of human history where only one
person, the Oriental despot, could achieve freedom, and a Greco-Roman stage
where only a few were capable of freedom since the Greeks and Romans had
slaves. In Hegel's view, the rationality embodied in the world now provided for
another stage in human history, the German-Christian stage, during which, for the
first time, all people could achieve rationality and freedom. Hegel's description of
the French revolution, *the* watershed political event in humanity's movement
toward the creation of a free and rational political system, clearly conveys his sense
of excitement and expectation that this moment in history presented:

> Never since the sun had stood in the firmament and the planets revolved around
> him had it been perceived that man's existence centres in his head, i.e., in
> Thought, inspired by which he builds up the world of reality. Anaxagoras had been
> the first to say that *nous* [i.e., Rationality or Reason] governs the World; but not
> until now had man advanced to the recognition of the principle that Thought
> ought to govern spiritual reality. This was accordingly a glorious mental dawn. All
> thinking beings shared in the jubilation of this epoch. Emotions of a lofty charac
> ter stirred men's minds at that time: a spiritual enthusiasm thrilled through the
> world, as if the reconciliation between the Divine and the Secular was now first
> accomplished.[6]

[6] G. W. F. Hegel, *The Philosophy of History,* trans. J. B. Sibree (New York: The Colonial Press,
1956), p. 447.

From Hegel's perspective, once an Idea like Freedom is philosophically conceived—although initially in a restricted or limited form—it is but a matter of time, if it is a Real Idea, until it becomes universal; that is, until it is applied to all relevant things. So, through history, humanity slowly progresses from the Idea of Freedom in the material form of *one* human being free, to *some* humans, to *all* humans being free. If you recall our prior discussion of self-governance and the extension of suffrage in the United States, you can see how this works from an Hegelian perspective. First, America's elite applied this Idea of Freedom only to themselves, next it was extended to other white males, and eventually it had to be applied to everyone. It does not matter that the elite did this only in response to considerable political pressure; what matters is that it was rational for all to be free so it was impossible to stop this dynamic process once it had begun. The Hegelian reality emphasizes the power of the Idea itself. It is as if, once conceptualized, nothing can stop the ultimate realization of the Idea through history. Who knows, perhaps someday the Idea of Freedom will have to be extended beyond humans.

Hegel's Political Theory

Hegel's dialectical understanding of the German-Christian stage in history divides it into the three basic constitutional components of the Family, Civil Society, and the State. The *Family* stage is characterized by relationships of love and affection existing among members of the family unit; here is an entity in which all members are freely associated under communal norms—it is a cohesive unit. The family unit generates its own negation in a component called *Civil Society*. This is characterized by a more intense individualism and competition than the family stage; brother begins to compete with brother, largely in the economic realm. The cohesiveness and unity of the Family are lost and replaced by the particular wills of individuals in competition for self-development. These two stages are then mediated by the institution of the *State*, which takes the unity and general will aspect of the Family and combines it with the best of Civil Society, that is, the individual appropriation of the environment. We thus have a society that united both particular and general will, the individual and the society, humans with their fellow humans. This reconciliation in Hegel's ideal state is accomplished by the interaction of legally recognized classes called *estates*.

The estates were the peasantry (similar to the characterization of the Family); the middle class, comprised of burghers and businesspeople (reflecting the characteristics of Civil Society); and a well-educated, duty-bound bureaucracy. Individuals would have their interests represented through their estate association. Economic equality, universal education, and an open estate system with both upward and downward mobility were further guarantees of freedom and rationality. So well run and harmonious would Hegel's pluralist state be that the role of its sovereign would be to "dot the i's and cross the t's."

In our earlier discussion of Hegel, we saw that he believed the world was becoming increasingly endowed with the rationality of the Absolute Idea or Spirit or God. Hegel's system, then, is *teleological*. That is, it is movement upward toward some goal. However, it is important to note that for Hegel, there is *no permanent final goal:* As humans reach any particular level of rationality, the never-ending dialectical process will continue to unfold, providing people with the opportunit of achieving an even greater degree of rationality, freedom, and self-realization.

CRITICS OF HEGEL: FEUERBACH AND MARX

This notion of a rationally *becoming* universe had found many critics by the time Karl Marx came to study Hegel's ideas. Notable among those critics was Ludwig Feuerbach, whose criticisms of Hegel's abstractions were thoroughly assimilated by the young Marx, and whose ideas eventually led Marx to reject Hegelian ideal ism for something Western scholars have called *dialectical materialism.*

Feuerbach contended the entire Hegelian system was an unconsciou attempt to divert human attention from the real problems of existence. The notion of a rational "Absolute Idea" (or "God," or any of the other terms noted above gradually manifesting itself in history was seen by Feuerbach as nothing more than the invention of an abstract entity, which was then endowed with all of the attrib utes missing from real human existence. What people found lacking in their live was projected as part of something eternal, an attribute of the Absolute Idea. The difficulty with this form of reasoning was that it turned attention away from human beings and their predicament, and it made this highly abstract Absolute Idea the true subject of history. Humans were reduced to small elements in the overall pat tern of things, where to Feuerbach they were actually the central figure in all his tory. The entire Hegelian system focused on such abstractions and diverted attention from the true human condition. After all, if one can find intellectual sat isfaction in such a fashion why worry about the insufficiencies of everyday life Absolute Idea, rationality, and freedom became, to use Marx's word, *opiates* abstract ideas that falsely satisfy without attempting to solve problems.

Marx thoroughly accepted this criticism of Hegel and was determined to apply Feuerbach's critical insight to the realms of politics and economics. Recall that we spoke of Hegel's triad of Family, Civil Society, and the State, which medi ated the contradictions of the prior stages. It was Marx's contention that Hegel' notion of the State was exactly the same sort of abstract solution to real human problems as Feuerbach had found in Hegel's religious teaching. Civil Society in Hegel was the antipode of the cohesive Family unit in that it permitted individu als to appropriate freely objects in the environment. This process would inevitabl lead to conflicts among individuals desiring similar things and eventually, i unchecked, to much *inequality.*

The major source of this inequality, recognized as such by Hegel himself, was to be found in *private property.* Private property, while an essential part of human self-development that it permitted people to become closer to the environment would lead to inequality because some individuals would be able to accumulat more than others. Hegel realized all this and declared that the individual, ego dominated stage of Civil Society must be transcended in an ethical entity called the State, which would solve this inequality and provide for a truly cohesiv human community. The State would be a neutral agent that would express onl the general will of the entire state; it would be the personification of the will of all the members of the community.

In the eyes of Karl Marx, the Hegelian State was but another example of the insufficiencies of this abstract system. The State was a projection of all of the problems of Civil Society and provided only an intellectual solution, leaving untouched the real-world problem of inequality and lack of freedom. Further, anyone who took a clear look at the actions of existing states could readily see that they were anything but the neutral agents that Hegel envisioned. Indeed, a more appropriate description of state action would be that it served to perpetuate and enhance the existing inequalities. For these reasons Marx demanded a rejection of abstract philosophizing *à la* Hegel and a concentration on the real-world forces that produce the human condition. People must no longer be concerned with abstract *explanation* of the world; they must attempt to *change* it.

Rejecting Hegel's political theory and Hegel's overemphasis on ideas, Marx's concern turned to the real determining factor in all human experience; that is, he abandoned abstract philosophy to study economics. Hegel's dialectical process is thus no longer an abstract rational process, but is found to be embedded in the material world of economics and politics. Dialectics remain, but as a materialistic dialectical process, with human beings the true subjects of history. It is now time to return to the writings of Marx to uncover his view of humanity, capitalism, and, of course, communism.

Marx on the Human Condition

As individuals express their life, so they are. What they are, therefore, coincides with their production, both with *what* they produce and with *how* they produce.[7]

Marx and Engels lived and wrote during the period of European history generally called the Industrial Revolution. With the possible exception of Russia, all major European countries during the latter part of the eighteenth and throughout the nineteenth century experienced a rapid growth of industrial production, which involved the introduction of machinery, the establishment of factories, and the development of a specialization of labor. This period of industrialization is properly called a revolution in that it resulted in profound changes in the values and way of life of vast numbers of people.

The artisan who formerly produced objects by hand, to be consumed or exchanged, now toiled on a production line in a factory, placing bolts in a complex piece of machinery. The introduction of mass-production techniques forced individuals to become far more specialized in their work and to become part of a vast production process rather than fabricators of entire objects. Individuals who once fashioned a pair of fine shoes now found themselves operating a machine that stamped out the soles for thousands of shoes, to be assembled later by other workers in the factory. There is little doubt that the Industrial Revolution produced

---

[7] *Marx-Engels Reader,* p. 150.

tremendous hardships for members of the working class. History books are full of
examples: twelve- and fifteen-hour workdays, women and children forced to labor
under intolerable conditions, disease unchecked, and poverty everywhere. Even
today, one of the best descriptions of the excesses of the Industrial Revolution is
to be found in Friedrich Engels's *Condition of the Working Class in England in 1844*
an early pamphlet that greatly impressed Karl Marx.

Given these deplorable conditions it is easy to see how sensitive and sensible
people could condemn the results of industrialization and the capitalist economic
system that brought them about. Marx and Engels were by no means alone in their
violent reaction to these conditions. Such notable figures in the history of political philosophy as Thomas Jefferson, Jeremy Bentham, and James and John Stuart
Mill were openly critical of the conditions of the laboring poor. Yet, where others
fought for reform within the capitalist system and sought to bring about more
humane working conditions, Karl Marx believed that such conditions were an
inevitable part of capitalism. The condition of the working class led Marx to the
conclusion that the entire capitalist system was outdated and must be radically
changed. Marx's indictment of capitalism, while undoubtedly inspired to some
extent by the human suffering it produced, is far more profound. It was his contention that capitalism as an economic system denied people their own humanity—it literally dehumanized people. We can understand such a conclusion only
by examining the Marxian conception of the unique role that laboring plays in
human development.

Labor: Alienated versus Unalienated. Laboring, according to Marx, is not
merely a process whereby humans satisfy needs; rather, it is their existential activity. It is how people define themselves. It is the way in which they achieve their true
nature. It is the species-specific characteristic of humanity. People are seen as
actors capable of altering nature for their own human uses and, of course, are
altered by it as in the dialectical analysis. The individual confronts the external
world, enters it, and alters it by mixing his or her labor with it. In this process, the
individual (subject) comes to realize what he or she is and to appreciate his or her
potential as actor by discovering what one is not, that is, the external world, the
"object." Thus, humans in the process of mixing themselves with the environment
can be said to come to know, and to be themselves:

> But man is not merely a natural being; he is a *human* natural being. That is to say, he
> is a being for himself. Therefore he is a *species being,* and has to confirm and manifest
> himself as such both in his being and in his knowing.[8]

What Marx argued was that humans, whether they will it or not, actively participate in their own creation. Marx viewed people as beings comprised of a variety of "tendencies and abilities," who have certain "powers and needs." When they
labor (a human need), they interact with the external world (nature); they exercise and develop their tendencies, abilities, and powers. The more they interact
with nature the more refined their capacities and powers may become; if, however

[8] Ibid., p. 116.

the interaction is repetitive and boring, those same capacities and powers will deteriorate. Marx wrote: "That man's physical and spiritual life is linked to nature means simply that nature is linked to itself, for man is a part of nature."[9]

People are also unique creatures, what Marx termed the *species being,* in that they pass along their development to both the rest of society and to the entire species. In a sense, then, as one develops (the particular) so too may all people develop (the universal). Therefore, as people learn to understand and to interact with the world, they alter both the world and themselves; and, as they exercise and develop their unique human capacities, they absorb and transform the heritage of the species. As Marx put it:

> For not only the five senses but also the so-called mental senses—the practical senses (will, love, etc.)—in a word, *human* sense—the humanness of the senses—comes to be by virtue of its *humanized* nature. The *forming* of the five senses is a labour of the entire history of the world down to the present.[10]

Marx used the term *alienated* to describe the condition of human beings existing under a capitalist economic system. This word has become all too common in modern usage—we speak of alienated youth, voters, workers, artists, using the term to indicate some sort of vaguely perceived disenchantment with one's lot. Indeed, alienation can be and has been used to describe almost anything. For Marx, however, it had a specific meaning. As we have seen, the act of laboring is the process by which human beings attain self-realization, and the product of their labor is an integral part of that process. The sculptor who fashions a statue from a formless block of stone has endowed that stone with part of his or her person. Something of that person is there in the statue. The hallmark of a capitalist economic system is that one class of individuals (capitalists) possesses a monopoly of the means used to produce things; that is, the individuals own the machines and capital necessary for production. Under such circumstances the noncapitalists (the proletariat or workers) are forced to sell their power to labor—the only resource they possess—to the capitalists so they can survive. They then work for the capitalist to produce objects that the capitalist sells for profit, a portion of which is used to pay the wages of the workers and the rest is employed as investments and reinvestments in producing more capital. The relationship between capitalist and workers is necessarily exploitive.

As we shall see more fully in the later discussion of capitalist economics, the only way a capitalist can make a profit, that is, produce capital, is by exploiting the labor force. Thus, by laboring for the capitalist, workers give the capitalist additional power to be used against them and their fellow workers. Under the capitalist system, then, the product of labor (which, remember, is the only source of human development) is taken away from its fabricator (maker) and used to exploit that person because part of the profit is reinvested in the production process in order to extract ever-increasing amounts of surplus labor from the workers. Part of the worker's own being, embodied in the product, is now used against the

---

[9] Ibid., p. 75.
[10] Ibid., p. 89.

worker. Instead of recognizing the object of creation as a part of a process of self development, the worker sees it as an alien object, something that, under capital ism, is independent of its maker and is used to maintain the unequal and dehumanizing conditions of life activity. The relationship between workers and the product of their labor is one of the fourfold aspects of alienation. The other three are the act of production itself, the relations of production among persons and the relationship of people to their essence as the species being.

In a very real way, part of the laborer's self is being taken away and used to hurt that person. The product of one's creative power becomes a weapon in alien hands. Thus Marx concludes that humans are irrevocably alienated from them selves under a capitalist economic system. Further, under capitalism that joyous creative act of laboring, which is a uniquely human gift, becomes an activity to be dreaded. The act of laboring under capitalism increasingly becomes simplified and routinized so that mental fatigue gradually augments physical exhaustion. The labor process itself is alienating. Labor under capitalism becomes forced labor time spent away from the job is considered "free time" when it should be just the other way around.

> As a result, therefore, man (the worker) no longer feels himself to be freely active in any but his animal functions—eating, drinking, procreating, or at most in his dwelling and in dressing-up, etc.; and in his human functions he no longer feels himself to be anything but an animal. What is animal becomes human and what is human becomes animal.[11]

Under capitalism, an individual's humanizing activity, that which makes a person free, becomes the negation of humanity: It is wage-slave labor.

Capitalism produces still a third and fourth dimension of alienation, which completes the process of negating a truly human existence. People are alienated not only from themselves but also from their fellow human beings. This is because capitalism turns all human relationships into dollars and cents terms. People treat each other as commodities, as objects to be used and manipulated; their labor becomes something to be bought and sold. Under such a system they are related to one another only through the commodities they exchange; they treat each other as things, not as fellow humans. Human beings are forced into constant competi tion with one another; the things they produce come to take on an objective sta tus and prevent human interaction.

Even members of the exploiting class (capitalists) are not free because of the cutthroat competition among capitalists, and because of the wage-slave sta tus of the proletariat. Commodities become symbols and attain a status different from their production and use. Larger and more flashy cars, "keeping up with the Joneses," "clothes are the mark of the person"—these are the more simple modern examples of Marx's meaning. One relates to "Jones" not as a human being but as a competitor in the accumulation of status-laden products; one looks at the clothes of a person but not at the person. So all-inclusive is the apparent power of commodities, of people, and of things, that men and women

[11] Ibid., p. 74.

are reduced from multitalented individuals with numerous mental and physical senses to possessive creatures with the sole sense of "having." "In place of *all* these physical and mental senses there has therefore come the sheer estrangement of *all* these senses— the sense of *having,*"[12] Marx wrote.

Alienation as Estrangement. The final aspect of alienation is the estrangement of humans from their essence as the species being. Unlike animals that "produce" from instinct for immediate survival, humans can produce independently of instinct, in freedom. In addition, humans can produce the whole of nature (the human subject is the universal) and do so according to the laws of beauty, which are also a human creation. Humans, moreover, treat themselves as "The actual, living species."[13] As the individual refines and develops, so too does the species; as the species changes and adapts, so too the individual. Humans are *social individuals*. And yet, as Marx acutely pointed out, under capitalism all of these advantages of humans over animals are turned into disadvantages: Only humans can be alienated from their essence; only humans can help produce their own estrangement, for their alienation is, ultimately, a condition of *self*-alienation.

Marx, in an extended and rarely published passage on James Mill—taken from the notebooks he kept while working on his *Economic and Philosophic Manuscripts*—presented what can be taken as the obverse of his description of alienation contained in the *Manuscripts*. So important is this account of *un*alienated labor, that we quote the passage at length.

> Supposing that we had produced in a human manner; each of us would in his production have doubly affirmed himself and his fellow men. I would have: (1) objectified in my production my individuality and its peculiarity and thus both in my activity enjoyed an individual expression of my life and also in looking at the object have had the individual pleasure of realizing that my personality was objective, visible to the senses and thus a power raised beyond all doubt. (2) In your enjoyment or use of my product I would have had the direct enjoyment of realizing that I had both satisfied a human need by my work and also objectified the human essence and therefore fashioned for another human being the object that met his need. (3) I would have been for you the mediator between you and the species and thus been acknowledged and felt by you as a completion of your own essence and a necessary part of yourself and have thus realized that I am confirmed both in your thought and in your love. (4) In my expression of my life I would have fashioned your expression of your life, and thus in my own activity have realized my own essence, my human, my communal essence.[14]

Emphasizing both the essentiality and the communality of free, human labor, Marx closed this discussion with these words: "In that case our products would be like so many mirrors, out of which our essence shone. Thus, in this relationship what occurred on my side would also occur on yours. . . . My work would be a free expression of my life, and therefore a free enjoyment of my life."[15]

---

[12] Ibid., p. 87.

[13] Ibid., p. 75.

[14] Karl Marx, in *Karl Marx: Selected Writings,* David McLellan, ed. (Oxford: Oxford University Press, 1977), pp. 121–22.

[15] Ibid.

Marx drew a picture of capitalist society where people are prevented from becoming human—alienation is all encompassing. Every member of society is drawn into the never-ending web of alienation. Given the Marxian definition of freedom, no single class can ever attain that status: All must be free before any one can be. Having said all this, it must now be noted that in Marx's eyes the capitalist system is, in a limited sense, a good thing. It comprises an essential phase of an overall historical process that will eventually result in a society where all people can realize their true potential. Capitalism is the penultimate stage in the historical progression from a condition of impotence and limitation to one of power and freedom. In order to understand such statements, we must now explore Marx's view of this historical process and examine the role of dialectical materialism in his thinking.

HISTORY AND THE DEVELOPMENT OF CAPITALISM

Where Hegel sought to use the rationalistic Absolute Idea as the determining force in the historical process, Marx saw the central element to be ownership of the means of production and distribution of goods. He outlined five basic stages in human history: primitive community (primitive communism), slavery, feudalism, capitalism, and socialism. In each stage the determining factor is the control of the productive forces within the society, and when those means of production are owned by a particular group within the society, they will exploit some other segment of the population. Thus, slavery, feudalism, and capitalism are necessarily oppressive societies, for they ensure that one group will be able to control the means of production, thereby forcing the remaining individuals in the society to sell their labor in order to continue to exist.

In each instance there are two principal classes that exist in opposition to one another: Under slavery it is the masters versus the slaves, under feudalism the lords against the serfs, and under capitalism it is the capitalists against the workers. Both the primitive community and socialism are nonexploitive in that there is community control of the means of production and therefore no particular group can maximize its interests at the expense of others. Nevertheless, in the former epoch humans are not yet free in that they are still subject to the domination of nature; in the latter epoch due to the advance of science, technology, and productive forces, humans are finally free from both human and natural exploitation.

Marx was far too sophisticated to believe that this two-class analysis (oppressors versus oppressed) was a completely accurate description of the real world at any point in history. In all real-world situations there will be a mixture of different classes. Under capitalism there will still be groups within the society whose relationship is primarily feudal, and even master-slave, but the prevailing relationship in the society can be appropriately characterized in terms of the worker versus the capitalist. Without going into a detailed description of the development of each of these conditions, let us concentrate, as Marx did, on the situation under the capitalist mode (system) of production.

Marx was one of the earliest social scientists to place great weight on the conditioning effect that economics has on all phases of human activity. While today it is commonplace to assert that human thought and action are greatly conditioned by upbringing, socioeconomic status, and the values of a particular culture, in Marx's time the general tendency was to place far greater weight on the effect of ideas in shaping human behavior. This is especially evident in the thought of Hegel where ideas and rationality primarily determine the existence of the world. To Marx the fundamental—but not sole—conditioning factor in human action is essentially economic.

The class structure of a society is a direct reflection of its distribution of wealth, which is a result of past and present ownership of the means of production. Under the three antagonistic modes of ownership of the means of production (slavery, feudalism, and capitalism), all institutions, values, morality, and religion are conditioned, if not determined, by the class structure. These institutions and values occur as the result of the ruling class's desire for continued domination, and nothing more. Under capitalism, for example, the state, far from being the neutral agency seen by Hegel or the neutral judge envisioned by Locke, is a device used by the capitalist class to further its own interests. Religion is the "opiate of the masses" in that it is designed to provide comforting rationalizations for the oppressed classes so that they will become resigned to their lot. These institutions, part of what can be called the *superstructure,* are but reflections of the underlying *substructure* of economic relationships. Under capitalism, then, all morality is capitalist morality, religion is bourgeois religion, and the state is nothing more than an instrument of class oppression. It is in this context that Marx and Engels would later speak of the "withering away of the state" in a communist society, for the need for a state will cease to exist once the class antagonisms, which the state perpetuates, are abolished.

There remains some ambiguity as to the precise relationship between the substructure and the superstructure in Marxian thought. At times Marx and Engels speak as though the relationship is causal in nature; that is, the substructure can affect only the superstructure and not vice versa. This would deny the possibility, for example, of the political system in a capitalist country materially altering the process of allocating resources within the society. This position is commonly referred to as that of the "vulgar Marxist."

At other points Marx and Engels seemed to be saying that, while the economic substructure is the major determinant in all relationships, there is at least some interaction between substructure and superstructure and that superstructural institutions can alter the economic base. In an attempt to clarify this relationship, Engels noted:

> According to the materialist conception of history, the *ultimately* determining element in history is the production and reproduction of real life. More than this neither Marx nor I have ever asserted. Hence if somebody twists this into saying that the economic element is the *only* determining one, he transforms that proposition into a meaningless, abstract, senseless phrase.[16]

---

[16] *Marx-Engels Reader,* p. 760.

On other occasions, Engels used the word *codetermined* to emphasize the interdependent nature of the relationship. This notion is captured by Marx in his third thesis on Feuerbach:

> The materialist doctrine that men are products of circumstances and upbringing, and that, therefore, changed men are products of other circumstances and changed upbringing, forgets that it is men who change circumstances and that it is essential to educate the educator himself. Hence, this doctrine necessarily arrives at dividing society into two parts, one of which is superior to society.
>
> The coincidence of the changing of circumstances and of human activity can be conceived and rationally understood only as revolutionizing practice.[17]

Although it appears from these sources that the relationships are clearly codetermined, for our purposes it is sufficient to emphasize the tremendous weight Marx placed on economic factors as determinants of all human activity. Many people assert that Marx's major contribution to social science was his recognition of this preponderant role that economic matters play in human affairs. However, it makes sense to follow Engels on this point:

> Marx and I are ourselves partly to blame for the fact that the younger people sometimes lay more stress on the economic side than is due to it. We had to emphasize the main principle vis-à-vis our adversaries, who denied it, and we had not always the time, the place or the opportunity to allow the other elements involved in the interaction to come into their rights.[18]

The relationship between the forces of production and the relations of production has also been the source of considerable confusion in Marx. The mode, or system, of production is the basis of every society since it determines how that society will produce the material needs of life. Marx discovered four historic modes: Asiatic (primitive communist, tribal societies), ancient (slave societies of Egypt, Greece, Rome), feudal, and capitalist. Each of these systems implies a different relationship of human dependence or independence, a relationship of domination and subordination. Each mode consists of particular *forces of production* and *relations of production*. The *relations* of production are the extratechnical relationships between people in the production process; for example, the particular division of labor in society (hunters versus gatherers, or slaves versus masters) or the means of exchange (barter or money). The *relations* of production *correspond*, Marx said, to a definite stage in the development of the forces of production.

The *forces* of production are comprised of the techniques (including labor skill), technology (including tools), and the natural resources made workable by them. Another way of explaining this is that the forces of production consist of the matter and energy, both human and natural, which people have and know how to use. By using the word *correspond*, Marx again made clear the interrelatedness of the relationship between the forces and the relations of production. Marx offered no simple, unicausal explanation of history. Historical change takes place when

---

[17] Ibid., p. 144.
[18] Ibid., p. 762.

the *forces* of production are impeded by the *relations* of production. The latter become "fetters" on the former. When this develops, class antagonisms crystalize, producing a revolution into a new mode of production. As capitalism continues to overproduce due to technological innovation, there develops a tendency for both opulence (in terms of commodities) and impoverishment (workers without the money to buy goods because the workers have been rendered superfluous). At this point, change will occur.

One final point. Although the *mode* of production is the base of Marx's analysis, and although it is comprised of both the *forces* and the *relations* of production, it must be remembered that both are creations of human beings.

The Progress of Humanity

Although Marx substantially altered Hegel's dialectical process by embedding it in the material world, he did not forsake the general notion of gradual progress in world history. Thus, each of the stages in history mentioned earlier is appropriately seen as part of a dialectical process moving toward the goal of a communist society. In another more important sense these societal stages can be viewed as part of the process of humans achieving greater and greater control over their environment. We have seen that the fundamental fact of human development is people's ability to mix themselves with the environment, to interact with it, and to change it. Indeed, it is not inappropriate to view Marx's conception of human development as involving an ever-increasing control over the natural world.

Humanity moves through varying historical stages, from a condition of scarcity to one of abundance; from a state of lack of control to one of power. Herein we can see the major difficulty Marx envisioned in his nonantagonistic stage of the primitive community. While it was a classless society in that the means of production (however primitive) were possessed by all, individuals could not labor freely because they were totally preoccupied with satisfying the basic needs of subsistence. Humans had not achieved sufficient control over their environment to enable them to develop their nature without being constrained by the simple need to survive.

If the laborer under capitalism can be said to be forced to work because of the exploitive class structure, in the primitive community human beings were in a similar sense forced to labor for their very existence. In the primitive community, despite its lack of class antagonisms, people could not achieve true self-consciousness or freedom because they were hampered by the natural environment. The dialectical process thus moved on to other stages whereby humans achieve the potential of greater and greater control over their lives. It is for this reason that the capitalist stage is particularly important and the capitalist or bourgeois class is crucial for eventual human freedom. Capitalism was particularly effective in unleashing individual human wills to exploit the environment for their own personal benefit. In so doing it provided the technology that would permit future generations to achieve a new society.

It is important to remember, however, that this discussion of the liberating tendencies of technology is, in many ways, relegated to the future, to potential freedom, since under capitalism the same technology that can liberate is being used to exploit the workers even more.

Marx's View of the Bourgeois Class

There is little doubt that Marx had tremendous admiration for the bourgeois class even while he was predicting its eventual overthrow. Under the capitalist mode of production and its corresponding ideology of liberalism, the bourgeoisie had succeeded in throwing off most of the values of traditional cultures and had further developed a technological base hitherto unknown in human history. Although this technology was based in the end on the exploitation of others (proletarians), this does not alter the fact that the capitalist system provided people with the tools at last to control their environment. Expressing sentiments worthy of a John Locke or an Adam Smith, Marx observed:

> The bourgeoisie during its rule of scarce one hundred years, has created more massive and more colossal productive forces than have all preceding generations together. Subjugation of Nature's forces to man, machinery, application of chemistry to industry and agriculture, steam-navigation, railways, electric telegraphs, clearing of whole continents for cultivation, canalisation of rivers, whole populations conjured out of the ground—what earlier century had even a presentiment that such productive forces slumbered in the lap of social labour?[19]

Using England as his model, Marx believed that eventually capitalism would spread throughout the world and provide the economic preconditions for a truly human existence. The internal dynamics of the system itself would force it to gradually spread around the world in search of new markets and new sources of raw materials. In doing this the capitalist system would destroy all of the traditional values and morals and provide the preconditions for a new society for all people.

> The bourgeoisie, by the rapid improvement of all instruments of production, by the immensely facilitated means of communication, draws all, even the most barbarian, nations into civilization. The cheap prices of its commodities are the heavy artillery with which it batters down all Chinese walls, with which it forces the barbarians, intensely obstinate hatred of foreigners to capitulate. It compels all nations, on pain of extinction, to adopt the bourgeois mode of production; it compels them to introduce what it calls civilization into their midst, i.e., to become bourgeois themselves. In one word, it creates a world after its own image.[20]

Yet, by unleashing individual egos in cutthroat competition and exploitation (the very thing which made it so successful), capitalism ensured its own demise. As Marx stated, "What the bourgeoisie, therefore, produces, above all, is its own grave-diggers."[21]

In pitting person against person in economic competition, capitalism denies the fundamental equality of all humans, making some superior to others

[19] Ibid., p. 477.
[20] Ibid., p. 477.
[21] Ibid., p. 483

while prohibiting vast numbers of others from achieving their true nature. Capitalism must therefore be transcended in a pure communist stage, which will utilize the technological expertise of the capitalist epoch to provide a "postscarcity" economic situation. Here humans for the first time in history will engage in the free conscious activity of labor for its own sake. No longer will it be necessary for human beings to struggle at a mere subsistence level as was the case in the primitive community. No longer will they be buffeted about by the forces of nature, for they now can control these forces. The inequalities and sufferings that capitalism produced will vanish once the ownership of the means of production is, in a sense, given to the entire community. Human relationships will once again be harmonious as people consciously move beyond their "prehistoric" forms of social organization. They will freely interact with the environment and each other in harmonious accord.

Such is the broad outline of the Marxian vision of a communist society. We shall speak at greater length of this at another point, but first it is essential to describe in detail Marx's analysis of the contradictions inherent within capitalist society, contradictions which lead to its eventual downfall.

THE CAPITALIST ECONOMIC SYSTEM: ITS DECLINE AND FALL

We have seen how the young Marx described the dehumanizing and alienating effects of a capitalist economic system. The system itself inevitably produces a vast class of nonhuman wage slaves. This philosophical analysis is by no means Marx's only method of attacking capitalism; after all, anyone who asserts that the economic substructure of any society is the prime determining factor in its development must deal at length with the economic structure of that system. Marx's analysis of the decline and fall of capitalism is to be found primarily in *Das Kapital* a work both brilliant and boring, insightful and repetitious.

The two key concepts in Marxian economics, concepts which are the building blocks for his entire analysis, are the *labor theory of value* and the *theory of surplus value*. Given what we know of Marx's regard for humans as "laboring animals," it is not surprising that he, along with John Locke and most of the classical economists (Adam Smith, David Ricardo), regarded the amount of human labor involved in producing an object to be the sole source of any value that product might have. Simply, the quantity of labor *socially necessary* to produce any object determines its exchange value. By "socially necessary," Marx means the quantity of labor necessary to produce the object given the average level of labor productivity and skills existing in a country at a specific historic time. In addition, the word *quantity* incorporates within it the difference between skilled and unskilled labor: An hour of labor by a skilled worker is considered as compound labor to be measured as a multiple of an hour of unskilled labor; the coefficient of multiplication cannot be arbitrary but rather is based on the cost of acquiring the given skill.

Thus, if it takes three hours of human labor to produce a pair of shoes, and labor is priced at one dollar an hour, the shoes have a true value of three dollars; if a suit takes six hours to produce, it will be valued at six dollars. In a purely competitive capitalist system, the market value of a product is determined by the amount of human labor it took to produce it. Marx was by no means unaware of the effect of supply and demand in establishing the market price of an object, but he asserted that in the long run, for the capitalist system as a whole, that price is ultimately reducible to the true value of the product, that is, the amount of human labor in it.

Furthermore, the labor involved in a product need not be merely the direct physical labor of an individual. It can be indirect labor, such as conceiving of a more efficient design for the product or a better way of packaging it. Despite these qualifications, all value is in the end reduced to what Marx called "simple average labor," which, it seems, is somehow determined by convention.

The labor theory of value was an attempt by economists to find some common element that would provide a measure of value for products that was more objective than the fluctuations of supply and demand. The demand for a particular product is, after all, a subjective thing, subject to the taste and preferences of the individual. While most non-Marxian economists today would declare that the labor theory of value is at best an awkward way of explaining capitalist economics, Marx did succeed in using it to point out some basic facts about capitalism. Grounded in the labor theory of value, Marx's analysis led him to an amazingly acute understanding of the dynamics of capitalism and to a host of farsighted predictions.

If everything is ultimately reducible to the amount of labor necessary to produce it, and the prices of objects in the long run reflect the amount of labor in the object, Marx then asked where the capitalist's profit came from. If the price of a product is equal to its actual value, there can be no such thing as profit, at least for the system as a whole. Granted, one individual capitalist might benefit from a temporary variation between the actual value of a product and its current market price, but this is not sufficient to explain the existence of profit in the entire capitalist system. The only explanation of profit in capitalism is to be found in the monopoly of the means of production that the capitalists possess. Because they control the means of production the capitalists can force the working class to produce a profit for them by paying them an amount of money less than the value of the product they produce.

The analysis goes like this. Labor power, like anything else, has a certain exchange value, defined in terms of the amount of labor necessary to sustain and reproduce it. The true value of an individual laborer, since he or she too is a commodity, can be seen as the amount of human labor necessary to keep that worker alive and to reproduce the worker; hence, to support a family. If it takes five hours of human labor to produce the goods necessary to keep one laborer alive (food, clothing, and so forth), then the value of the laborer is five. This is what Marx called *necessary labor,* the amount of labor time necessary to sustain one worker. Since capitalism needs an ever new supply of workers, the role of the family is to produce workers. As real wages decrease due to competition and technological innovation, the nuclear family, as the core of the *reproduction* process, must find additional sources of wages to survive. Similarly, as the rate of profit falls, the capitalist must find additional sources of workers to exploit. As if providentially planned by some invisible hand, the needs of the family and the capitalist are met as women are forced into the market to help keep their families afloat and to provide another source of exploitation for the capitalist.

The Surplus Value of Labor

Why do the workers tolerate this condition? How does it develop? Because the capitalist class possesses a monopoly of the means of production, it can force the workers to labor longer than is necessary for their own existence as the price extracted for using the means of production. For example, let us say the laborer signs a contract with the capitalist to work ten hours a day; five of these ten hours are involved in necessary labor. The rest of the time is spent, in effect, working to produce a profit for the capitalist because the worker receives wages only for his necessary labor. The worker is producing five hours of extra value for the capitalist, five hours of *surplus labor,* which is the source of the capitalist's profit. Workers have no choice but to do this. If they refuse to work for the capitalist this additional period of time they have no livelihood, for the means of production are controlled by the capitalist class. From this perspective, then, it is the workers who are ultimately paying the owners for the access to the means to live.

Surplus value, the difference between the actual value produced by a worker in a laboring day and the worker's necessary labor, is the source of profit in a capitalist system. It is money extracted from the worker solely by virtue of the fact that the capitalist class—backed by the power of the state—can force the worker to either accept this inherently exploitative situation or fail to survive. To be sure, the worker can choose by whom he or she will be exploited, but workers cannot choose to be unexploited. Small wonder that Marx declared all labor under capitalism to be forced labor!

The most pervasive aspect of capitalism is its emphasis on competition. Members of the bourgeois class are in constant competition with one another to maximize profit. We have seen how the only means of acquiring profit is through the exploitation of the laborer; the capitalist, then, increases profits by driving workers harder and harder, still paying them a subsistence wage. If we can say that the hallmark of capitalism is the acquisition of profit and capital by private individuals, it is now evident why Marx saw this type of system as necessarily exploitative. If the laboring class were to receive the true value in wages for their labor, capitalism would literally cease to exist for there could then be no private profit. Capitalism must have a class of "wage slaves" in order to exist. One cannot overemphasize the necessity of constant competition that capitalism generates. Individual capitalists are constantly seeking ways in which they can increase profits, and this leads them to behave in ways that will eventually ensure the demise of the entire system.

Increasing Profits at Worker Expense

Let us assume we have a capitalist operating within one industry producing a single product. While the price that product can command on the open market may fluctuate slightly from day to day, the long-range price is determined on an industrywide basis. Our individual capitalist then can attempt to increase his or her profit margin by driving workers harder to achieve greater productivity from them during the time they are at work. Marx gives several examples of how this can be done, including such things as shortening the time allowed for eating and rest periods. In doing this our capitalist makes his or her position with respect to the whole industry more attractive, producing a greater number of products at the industrywide price, thereby increasing profits. Or our capitalist can lower the price of his or her products and attempt to undersell competitors, thus capturing a larger share of the market.

Although our hard-driving capitalist now seems to be in a favorable position vis-à-vis the rest of the industry, it is really only a temporary solution. Initially, by the very nature of capitalist economics the other firms in the industry will respond to this initiative by driving their workers equally hard thereby reducing our capitalist's competitive advantage. In effect, the industrywide price is lowered so that our capitalist is no longer able to produce at a lower than industry cost.

Moreover, this process of extracting more and more from one's laborers has physical limitations; a person can be driven just so far. Still, the internal dynamics of capitalism demand that our owner increase profits so our capitalist looks for other means of doing so. This is accomplished through the introduction of labor-saving devices (machines), which make it possible to produce more products than the industrywide norm. Once, again, our capitalist is in a favorable position with respect to the industry as a whole.

In addition, insofar as machinery is capable of performing the more complex tasks involved in the production process, the capitalist can reduce the number of people employed, particularly skilled workers. The skilled technician who was essential before the advent of the machine can now be replaced by an unskilled laborer or even by children for that matter. As the necessary labor required for sustenance is based upon the family unit as a whole, the wages paid to such workers can be further reduced, thus adding even more to the owner's profit. A final consequence is that work becomes increasingly boring and repetitious and the laborer loses all interest in what he or she is doing; the worker becomes a mere appendage of the machine he or she operates.

Although the introduction of machinery does give the innovating capitalist a temporary advantage with respect to the rest of the industry, eventually the same forces we noted earlier will come into play and negate that advantage. In order to remain competitive other owners will have to follow the lead and replace their workers with machines, thus ensuring the increasing mechanization of the industry and a growing pool of unemployed laborers. While machines may well bring increased profit to the innovating capitalist (and even this is not certain because of the high costs of invention), it is only a temporary thing, for competition will inevitably drive the industrywide price downward.

There are, however, further consequences for the industry as a whole that result from increasing mechanization. Machinery (Marx called it *constant capital*), like any other product, has a value equal to the amount of human labor necessary to produce it. A machine is appropriately seen as stored-up human labor and is capable of producing only as much value as human labor put into it. The "life" of a piece of machinery can be seen as a gradual process of spinning out the amount of labor in it. A machine cannot be exploited in the same way workers (*variable capital*) can. Further, the use of machines produces a great flood of products on the market and there is no one to buy them. As more and more machines are introduced, the number of unemployed workers greatly increases and even those who have jobs find their wages at the subsistence level. Thus they are unable to consume the machine produced products. The system experiences ever more serious crises of overproduction and begins a frantic worldwide search for new markets for its products.

In addition, the ever-increasing cost of machinery makes the competitive situation of many capitalists untenable. Because of the dramatically increasing costs of constant capital, many of the smaller capitalists are simply unable to continue the struggle; they are bought out by the more affluent ones. There is an ever-increasing concentration of capital in fewer and fewer hands, and the marginal capitalists are forced into the ranks of the proletariat. Here is a second major Marxian prediction of capitalist development: It will tend inevitably toward *monopoly*.

Finally, the system has succeeded in producing a vast army of unemployed workers who are living barely at the subsistence level and have little or no hope for a better future (Marx's *Law of Increasing Misery*). It is this vast, alienated, proletarian class which is to provide the negation of the capitalist system; capitalism has sown the seeds of its own destruction. Metaphorically, Marx captured the dynamics of this process:

> Let us sum up: *The more productive capital grows, the more the division of labour and the application of machinery expands, the more competition among the workers expands and the more their wages contract.*
>
> In addition, the working class gains recruits from the *higher strata of society* also; a mass of petty industrialists and small rentiers are hurled down into its ranks and have nothing better to do than urgently stretch out their arms alongside those of the workers. Thus the forest of uplifted arms demanding work becomes ever thicker, while the arms themselves become ever thinner.[22]

Thus, the condition of the individual worker continually deteriorates while the number of people suffering continually increases.

Beyond Capitalism

It is now evident why Marx saw the great proletarian revolution occurring in highly developed capitalist countries. Highly developed capitalist economies would inevitably produce this radical cleavage between the few remaining capitalists and the vast industrial proletariat, and the latter would gradually become aware of the fact that the only way they could improve their lot was through the overthrow of the entire system. Marx expected this revolution to be both spontaneous and violent. Although he did concede the possibility of a nonviolent revolution, perhaps

[22] Ibid., p. 216.

in England or the United States, in general, his expectation was that the bourgeois class would fight for the existing system with all the weapons at its command. And, as long as the working class was without the vote, the likelihood of peaceful transition seemed remote. As the capitalists used more and more repressive measures to keep the proletariat in line, the workers, heretofore unorganized and impotent, would begin to see that their real enemies were the bourgeoisie and would begin to realize their collective power. In the Marxian language, they would develop *class consciousness,* a realization of their power as a unit and the firm conviction that their emancipation from slavery lay in the abolition of capitalism. Consequently, the workers must realize not only that they have the real power but also that a more human system of production is necessary so that there are no longer classes. Once they achieved class consciousness, the revolution would simply occur, a spontaneous uprising of the alienated.

Although Marx became somewhat disenchanted with the revolutionary potential of the proletariat after the abortive revolutions of 1848, he retained throughout his life this belief in spontaneous revolution. This is particularly important in that Marx consequently had only a somewhat vague conception of a revolutionary Communist party dedicated to producing a revolution. The idea of a group of dedicated revolutionaries constantly attempting to foment revolution, to light the "spark," is not Marxian in origin but a Leninist idea that produced many changes in the classical Marxian analysis.

Finally, it must be noted that from Marx's perspective there is very little that the bourgeois class can do about all this. Its members may attempt to placate the proletariat in a variety of ways, but ultimately the very nature of the capitalist system will, in proper dialectical fashion, ensure its own destruction. It is this "scientific," inevitable aspect of the analysis that gives Marxism much of its revolutionary appeal. Capitalism is doomed; it is merely a question of time and volition.

Neither a clairvoyant, a soothsayer, nor a prophet, Marx was necessarily vague as to the specifics of the society that would follow capitalism. Still, the broad outlines should now be rather clear. The abolition of private property and the establishment of community control of the means of production will ensure a society where classes and exploitation cease to exist. Marx, and later Engels, talked specifically of universal suffrage and direct responsibility of leadership elements to the people through a process of referendum and recall. Any hierarchical power structure, whether based on class or expertise, was rejected. The technological base provided by the capitalist stage in history will provide humans with the means to control their environment and make scarcity and poverty a thing of the past. Marx metaphorically captured this image when he wrote:

> . . . in communist society, where nobody has one exclusive sphere of activity but each can become accomplished in any branch he wishes, society regulates the general production and thus makes it possible for me to do one thing today and another tomorrow, to hunt in the morning, fish in the afternoon, rear cattle in the evening, criticize after dinner, just as I have a mind, without ever becoming hunter, fisherman, shepherd or critic.[23]

---

[23] Ibid., p. 160.

Marx's passage emphasizes the point that humans will be able to exercise and develop all of their talents, powers, and abilities rather than becoming accomplished in only one area. Humans will become active verbs, rather than static nouns. People will interact with their environment freely, treating each other as fellow humans all engaged in the common task of self-realization. Marx wrote:

> In a higher phase of communist society, after the enslaving subordination of the individual to the division of labour, and therewith also the antithesis between mental and physical labour, has vanished; after labour has become not only a means of life but life's prime want; after the productive forces have also increased with the all-round development of the individual, and all the springs of cooperative wealth flow more abundantly—only then can the narrow horizon of bourgeois right be crossed in its entirety and society inscribe on its banner: From each according to his ability, to each according to his need.[24]

The oppressive superstructural state of capitalism will vanish, bourgeois morality will be replaced by a truly human morality, people will labor according to their ability and be rewarded according to their needs. Simply put, Marx envisioned a community of peace, tranquility, and power over nature that would ensure true freedom for all humanity.

Marx wrote:

> Assume *man* to be *man* and his relationship to the world to be a human one: then you can exchange love only for love, trust for trust, etc. If you want to enjoy art, you must be an artistically cultivated person; if you want to exercise influence over other people, you must be a person with a stimulating and encouraging effect on other people. Everyone of your relations to man and to nature must be a *specific expression*, corresponding to the object of your will, of your *real individual life.*[25]

It is now almost a cliche to say that Marxism possesses great appeal for masses of people because it promises the equivalent of a heaven on earth. Combine this ethical vision with a doctrine that promises "scientific" inevitability and one has a most powerful ideology. We shall not attempt specific criticisms of Marxism at this point largely because the other ideologies discussed provide us with a highly critical perspective of Marxism. In the final analysis, criticisms of Marxism—and all ideologies—must deal with views of people, society, history. Only then is it possible either to evaluate it or to determine whether a world built upon such promises is possible or, for that matter, desirable.

Marxism did not, of course, die with Karl Marx. While his ideas to this day provide the building blocks for socialist and communist thought, one may now speak of Marxism-Leninism or perhaps Marxism-Leninism *and* the Thought of Mao Zedong. Marx's ideas undergo changes in the hands of his dedicated followers, changes that often make the current doctrine quite different even while it retains the broad outlines of classical Marxism. We must now look at some of those changes, in particular those made by the leader of the first successful revolution proclaimed in Marx's name—Vladimir Ilich Ulyanov, better known as V. I. Lenin.

[24] Ibid., p. 531.
[25] Ibid., p. 105; Marx's emphasis.

SUGGESTED READINGS

ALTHUSSER, LOUIS, *For Marx.* New York: Vintage Press, 1970.

AVINERI, SHLOMO, *Hegel's Theory of the Modern State.* Cambridge: Cambridge University Press, 1972.

COHEN, G. A. *Karl Marx's Theory of History: A Defense.* Princeton, N.J.: Princeton University Press, 1980.

HEILBRONER, ROBERT L., *Marxism: For and Against.* New York: W. W. Norton & Company, 1980.

KAUFMANN, WALTER, *Hegel: A Reinterpretation.* Garden City, N.Y.: Doubleday and Company, 1966.

MANDEL, ERNEST, *Marxist Economic Theory,* 2 Vols. New York: Monthly Review Press, 1971.

MARCUSE, HERBERT, *Reason and Revolution: Hegel and the Rise of Social Theory.* Boston: Beacon Press, 1960.

McMURTRY, JOHN, *The Structure of Marx's World-View.* Princeton, N.J.: Princeton University Press, 1978.

MILIBAND, RALPH, *The State in Capitalist Society.* London: Weidenfeld and Nicolson, 1969.

OLLMAN, BERTELL, *Alienation,* 2nd ed. Cambridge: Cambridge University Press, 1976.

TUCKER, ROBERT C., ed., *The Marx-Engels Reader,* 2nd ed. New York: W. W. Norton & Company, 1978.

6

Marxism and Leninism

Without revolutionary theory there can be no revolutionary movement.

Lenin

By the time of Karl Marx's death in 1883, his ideas had become a recognized school of thought among European radicals; there was an established international communist movement, a quite strong socialist party in Germany, and potentially serious stirrings elsewhere on the Continent. Behind the facade of a united, monolithic international movement, however, there were many debates and arguments about the real meaning of Marx's thought. Until Engel's death in 1895, he, because of his status as a founding father of the movement, was able to maintain some cohesiveness to the interpretations of Marxism, yet even during this period warring factions were beginning to arise. This intellectual ferment about the true meaning of Marx's teachings was to continue even after the imposed Stalinist orthodoxy of the 1930s.

Nevertheless, the period between Marx's death and the Bolshevik success in Russia in 1917 shows, in ways not unlike that of early Christianity following the death of Christ, the varying controversies in all of their richness. Indeed, so multifaceted, vociferous, and polemical were these ongoing debates that one noted scholar of Marxism, Leszek Kolakowski, has called this era the "Golden Age" of Marxism.[1] While it is impossible to go into great detail regarding these arguments and their effects on the international communist movement, we must have some basic understanding of the contending positions if only to set the stage for Lenin's contributions.

THE DIVISIONS WITHIN MARXISM—PEACEFUL OR VIOLENT REVOLUTION?

Two major subjects dominated the Marxist debate of this period: (1) the question of violent or peaceful revolution and (2) the question of the readiness of the industrial proletariat for the revolution. With regard to the first question, Marx's response depended upon specific historic context. Although Marx always noted the *possibility* of a peaceful revolution, his 1872 speech in Amsterdam perhaps best captured Marx's view on revolution:

> We are aware of the importance that must be accorded to the institutions, customs, and traditions of different countries; and we do not deny that there are countries like America, England (and, if I knew your institutions better, I would add Holland), where the workers can achieve their aims by peaceful means. However true that may be, we ought also to recognize that, in most of the countries on the Continent, it is force that must be the lever of our revolutions.[2]

Given the class antagonisms that capitalism produced and the fact that many workers had not been given the vote, Marx did not expect the bourgeois class to

---

[1] Leszek Kolakowski, *Main Currents in Marxism*, 3 Vols. (Oxford: Oxford University Press, 1978), Vol. 2, passim.

[2] Karl Marx, in *Karl Marx: Selected Writings*, David McLellen, ed. (Oxford: Oxford University Press, 1977), pp. 594–95.

sit back calmly and preside over its own demise. Hence, Marx argued that force would probably be necessary.

The years between Marx's death and World War I produced a growing belief in the political power the working classes could achieve, especially now that they had the vote, through democratic processes. Even Engels, although hardly renouncing the right of the proletariat to take up arms to ensure revolutionary success, believed that significant changes were occurring via the ballot box. On this specific issue of the vehicle for revolution, violence versus voting, three divisions within Marxism developed: *orthodox Marxism, revisionism,* and *Marxism of the left.*

Marxism of the Center

The first position, that violence still might be necessary but that significant progress toward socialist goals was being made through legal means, is generally called Marxism of the center, or *orthodox Marxism.* The major spokesman for this position was Karl Kautsky (1854–1938), the intellectual leader of the powerful German Social-Democratic party (SPD) and a major theoretician of the time. While emphasizing the fact that Marxian political parties were indeed revolutionary in nature, Kautsky made a rather clear distinction between a party that tries to foment a revolution and one that reflects the inevitable historical progress being made toward the achievement of a socialist society. It was Kautsky's unwavering commitment to the inevitability of the revolution that led to the orthodoxy label. According to Kautsky's interpretation, Marxism was a theory and a method of historical investigation that provided people with the *only* system that was valid for understanding social phenomena. Believing Marxism theoretically complete in itself, Kautsky opposed attempts to supplement it with other philosophic doctrines—the exception being his support of the addition of Darwinism. In his efforts to popularize Marxism and to establish it as a mirror image of the natural sciences, Kautsky was chiefly responsible for creating the stereotype of "scientific socialism"; that is, Kautsky's erroneous view that Marx had uncovered the universal, inevitable, objective laws of human development that, by necessity, would culminate in communism. Tied to this notion of scientific socialism is the (mis)understanding that moral questions are irrelevant to Marxism: Given the deterministic, inevitability of the future, it is silly to discuss the question of how humans *ought* to live—they will be socialist.

Placing great weight on Marx's doctrine of the historical inevitability of a socialist society, Kautsky cautioned against trying to speed up the process of history by reckless and clandestine revolutionary activity. He advocated open and active participation in the political processes of capitalist states, fully confident that the revolution would, in time, occur. If Marx was somewhat ambiguous regarding the violence necessary for the transition into socialism, the orthodox Marxist position seems much more so. Violence, its adherents seem to say, may be necessary in order to achieve their goals, but only when dictated by history, when conditions are "ripe"; we are revolutionary, but not actively engaged in the starting of revolutions. Perhaps the orthodox position may be explained by the general optimism concerning democratic processes that existed prior to World War I. Unwilling to renounce the Marxian prediction of violent revolution, the orthodox wing of the movement nevertheless stands very much in the position of not rocking the boat. Its adherents are appropriately called Marxists of the center, and perhaps their position will become clearer through an examination of the two extreme positions prevalent at the time.

Marxism of the Right

Marxism of the *right* or more commonly *revisionism* does not share the ambiguity of the centrists or, for that matter, of Karl Marx. With Eduard Bernstein (1850–1932), a somewhat heretical member of the German Social-Democratic party as their principal spokesman, revisionists simply abandoned the Marxian doctrine of violent revolution. While acknowledging that this was a significant revision of Marx's teaching, Bernstein asserted that the political power of the newly enfranchised proletariat made it possible to achieve most of the socialist goals by lawful means. Bernstein called for *Evolutionary Socialism*, the English title of his book, rather than revolutionary socialism. He also rejected Marx's predictions of the increasing concentration of capital and the theory of the polarization of the classes leading to a single, worldwide revolution. He further argued that the ultimate goal of socialism was not as important as the movement involved in achieving it—the process was everything. Instead of expending all their energy theorizing about a communist society or dreaming of the violent overthrow of capitalism, true socialists should be working to improve the lot of the proletariat through trade unions and political parties. Bernstein and his allies—principally Jean Jaurès, a French socialist, and the leaders of Britain's Fabian Society—thus laid the theoretical ground work for many social democratic parties and trade union movements throughout Europe.

Still, Bernstein considered himself a dedicated follower of Marx, thinking only that he was making the doctrine compatible with changing times. Given the revisionist position, Marxism of the center perhaps makes more sense. Both the revisionists and the centrists were forced to deal with increasing evidence that the demands of the proletariat were being realized within the capitalist system. Nowhere was this more evident than in Germany under the leadership of its arch-conservative chancellor, Otto Edward Leopold von Bismarck. While Bismarck's initial attempts to thwart socialism by outlawing socialist political activities failed miserably, his introduction of state-sponsored health, accident, and old-age insurance successfully drew workers to the support of the government. It seems somewhat ironic, then, that the push for the creation of a welfare state came from conservatives who understood both Marx's analysis of capitalism and how best to combat socialism by taking the sting out of some of the crueler dimensions to unmodified capitalism. The revisionist position acknowledged that fact and went on to assert that most of the goals of socialism could be satisfied in this way, and further that a significant improvement in the lot of the workers was more important than the achievement of some abstract and far-off goal. Centrists attempted to combat the revisionist position by declaring that some, but not all, demands could be achieved in this fashion, and they affirmed the revolutionary nature of the struggle.

Marxism of the Left

As might be expected, *Marxism of the left* completes the spectrum of positions on the role of violence in producing revolution. With V. I. Lenin and, to a certain extent, German Socialist Rosa Luxemburg as its leading advocates, Marxism of the left places great weight on the antagonistic nature of the class struggle under capitalism, advocates mass strikes as the workers' most valuable weapon, and declares violent revolution to be absolutely necessary in the realization of socialism. The revisionist and centrist positions can be seen from this perspective as denying the true Marxian vision of a socialist society and as distorting Marx's teachings on the relationship between substructure and superstructure. The supposed gains made by the trade union movement and by social-democratic political parties working through parliament—itself a bourgeois sham—are nothing but sops given by the capitalists to keep the workers in line. A fundamental change in the system can come about only through a true revolution.

Instead of allowing themselves to be used by the capitalists through participating in politics, true Marxists should be engaging in general strikes to paralyze the system, using violent activities to reveal the true repressive nature of capitalism, and constantly agitating for revolution. Left Marxism is, then, the position of the uncompromising revolutionary who is dedicated to the overthrow of the system and refuses to believe that reformist measures of any sort will benefit the movement. Indeed, those so-called Marxians who believe in progress within a capitalist system are really helping the capitalists retain their superior position, for they lead the working class to renounce the necessity for radical action and inhibit the growth of class-consciousness. Action, agitation, and revolution are the cries of the left. Their position on the second of our two major questions of this period—the readiness of the proletariat for revolution—exhibits the same traits, and it is to that question we must now turn.

The Readiness of the Proletariat

A considerable period of time had passed since Marx predicted the spontaneous mass uprising of the proletariat in highly developed capitalist states. While he attached no specific timetable to this prediction, there was a general expectation that revolution was imminent. The abortive revolutions of 1848 forced Marx to think about the problem of working toward a revolution rather than just waiting for it to happen, but his confidence in the proletariat as the class chosen by history for this task never seriously wavered. It is important to note that the entire "scientific" interpretation of Marxian thought is at stake here. A large, alienated, class-conscious proletariat was the necessary outgrowth of highly developed capitalism, and the fact that no uprising of major consequence had occurred cast Marxism's entire set of scientific propositions in doubt. As we shall see later in this chapter, Lenin and other Marxists developed an ingenious explanation for this lack of proletarian activity in developed capitalist states. However, for the moment it is sufficient to note that the entire question of the readiness of the proletariat for revolution was widely debated in the period leading up to World War I.

As might be inferred from their position on the question of violence in the revolution, orthodox Marxists retained Karl Marx's basic belief in the spontaneous uprising of the proletarian class in highly developed capitalist countries. Because of this there was no need for a revolutionary activist party; class-consciousness would naturally develop because of the inherent contradictions of capitalism, and no amount of "adventurism" or revolutionary agitation on the part of dedicated Marxists would help.

Here again we see the reliance of the orthodox Marxists on the doctrine of historical inevitability and their faith in the scientific nature of Marx's predictions. They believed that Marxian political parties should be mass-based organizations that would provide some help in increasing the consciousness of the working class, but their prime function was to work by legal means for the betterment of the proletariat. In sum, the orthodox position was that the proletariat would become ready for revolution sometime in the future as a result of the internal contradictions of capitalism, and the task of dedicated Marxians was to work through mass-based political parties to gradually increase the proletariat's consciousness and improve its lot.

The revisionist position on this question should be quite evident. Disavowing the violent nature of revolution, revisionist Marxists advocated the recruitment of the entire working class in individual countries so that workers' political power would be enhanced. By developing a strong working-class movement, workers could force the capitalists to change the very nature of the system and implement most of the goals of socialism. The question of whether the working class was ready for revolution was rather irrelevant to the revisionist. What was necessary, and immediately realizable, was the development of class solidarity in order to maximize the achievement of the workers' goals. It was in left Marxism, particularly in the thought of Lenin, that this question of proletarian readiness became particularly important and eventually led to profound alterations in classical Marxian teaching.

TWENTIETH-CENTURY RUSSIA

To explain Lenin's beliefs on the revolutionary potential of the proletariat we must introduce, for the first of many times, the subject of the peculiar position of Russian Marxists. Most of the major figures in the international communist movement prior to World War I resided in developed capitalist countries that possessed a significant urban proletariat. In their eyes Russia was generally viewed as an anachronism: a country half-Asian, half-European, backward in industrial development, and possessing only a small working class—hardly fitting Marx's model of a well-developed capitalist state. This is not to say that Marx was ignored in Russia. The Russian intelligentsia, a class of well-educated individuals cut off from participation in political affairs by the autocratic rule of the czars, had a long tradition of radicalism, even anarchism.

The first major Russian Marxist group was formed in Switzerland by Georgi V. Plekhanov in 1883, and Marx found a ready ear among the highly alienated Russian intelligentsia. Despite this, the notion of a proletarian revolution in Russia remained problematic: Out of a population of 129 million, approximately 3 million could be called proletarians, while 80 percent were peasants. This fact forced Lenin and his followers to make many alterations in Marxian doctrine so that it fit the Russian experience, but for present purposes it also led Lenin to question the revolutionary potential of the working class.

In contrast to the orthodox Marxist position of waiting for the development of class-consciousness and the spontaneous uprising of the urban proletariat, Lenin came to believe that the proletariat in alliance with other disaffected groups in the society would require strong leadership to accomplish its revolutionary mission. Probably because of his Russian background, Lenin was not optimistic about the possibilities of a spontaneous proletarian revolution. Even in a highly developed capitalist country such as Germany it seemed that the proletariat, under the influence of revisionists and orthodox Marxists, was losing its revolutionary potential and tending to adopt bourgeois values.

However, for Lenin this did not preclude the possibility of revolution. These facts dictated a new strategy for committed Marxists—they required a new conception of the role of a party structure in the movement as well as an analysis of the place of other dissatisfied groups in the revolution. In formulating a new strategy, Lenin began the process of materially altering classical Marxism to fit the new circumstances of the twentieth century. We will treat these Leninist contributions to the doctrine under three headings: the Communist party and its roles, state socialism and a socialist transfer culture, and the theory of imperialism. First, however, let us meet Lenin, the individual and the revolutionary.

LENIN'S LIFE

Vladimir Ilich Ulyanov (1870–1924), who later adopted the "party" name Lenin, was born in Simbirsk (later renamed Ulyanovsky in his honor) on the Volga River, the son of a moderately prosperous director of provincial education for the Russian state. Vladimir was the third child in a family of seven and the second eldest son. He and his brother, Alexander, were rather close, the younger Vladimir always trying to emulate the intellectual and athletic feats of Alexander. Both were excellent in school, earning the highest marks throughout their academic careers. During this period, Russia was undergoing a severe political reaction to the assassination of the reformist Czar Alexander II in 1881. His successor, Alexander III, proceeded systematically to repress dissent, discourage education, and make even more absolute the famed absolutism of Russian rulers.

The intelligentsia was understandably unhappy with this turn of events and prepared to make use of their favorite political weapon—another assassination. The Ulyanov family became intimately involved in these political affairs when Alexander, in St. Petersburg to continue his studies, was arrested by the police for plotting to bomb Alexander III. Because of his knowledge of chemistry he had been assigned to make the bomb. Following an eloquent defense at his trial of revolutionary action, Alexander was convicted. Refusing on principle to ask the czar for clemency, Alexander was executed. It was then that young Vladimir began, according to his sister, to think seriously about revolution.

The next several years saw the Ulyanov family move to the larger city of Kazan and then to the city of Samara on the Volga. The young Lenin completed his gymnasium (high school) education and briefly attended the University of Kazan only to be dismissed for being involved in protest activities. There is still a good deal of disagreement as to when Lenin began to study Marxism seriously. We have his sister Anna's statement that, while the ill-fated Alexander was reading Marx in 1886, the younger Vladimir was preoccupied with the works of Turgenev and had no real political views. The period in Kazan and in Samara undoubtedly provided him with the opportunity to read extensively and to think about his future since he did not have to work to maintain himself. He did, however, pursue a degree in law during this time and was admitted to the bar in 1892. Although he was permitted to practice law, Lenin spent much of his time at various radical meetings where he eventually developed a reputation for debating skills in defense of Marxist ideas.

Although we cannot pinpoint the exact time when he came to accept the Marxian credo fully, by 1893 Lenin was an identifiable advocate of its doctrines. In 1895, he took what had by now become a customary trip for Russian radicals—a journey through Western Europe, meeting most of the leading Marxists of the time. Returning to St. Petersburg, he joined several other young radicals in the formation of a revolutionary action group designed to put some of the ideas of the radical "debating societies" into practice. The experience was short-lived: They were arrested by the police in December 1895. Lenin spent more than a year in prison in St. Petersburg, using the time to begin a major book, *The Development of Capitalism in Russia,* until the authorities decided he should spend three years in exile; in Siberia. Ironically, the years of exile, near the river Lena from which he took the name Lenin, provided a rather pleasant interlude for the budding revolutionary. He had a good deal of freedom of movement, time to read and write as well as to plan strategy for his return.

His situation was further enhanced when he was joined by a young comrade, Nadezhda Krupskaya, whom he had met earlier in radical circles in St. Petersburg. She became his wife and lifelong collaborator. By the time he left Siberia in February 1900, Lenin was a dedicated revolutionary with a rather clear plan of how to accomplish his goals. This well-formulated strategy distinguished him from most other radicals, who tended to be vague regarding the methods of achieving their ideals.

Lenin's Years in Exile

With the exception of a brief return to Russia in the revolutionary period of 1905–1907, Lenin spent the entire time prior to 1917 in political exile. For a man of action, this must have been a particularly trying period: Cut off from events in Russia, he could only spend his time in forming a group of dedicated followers who would be ready to seize opportunities as they arose. It is a testament to Lenin's dedication to the cause of Russian Marxism that during all of this time, spent in a great number of European cities, he thought of nothing but the coming struggle. Lenin had by now become one of the major figures in the movement and the leading spokesman for its left wing.

At the Second Party Congress of Russian Marxists in 1903, Lenin led a fight to establish the party as a close-knit organization of dedicated revolutionaries, and he succeeded, after several splinter factions had withdrawn from the congress, in achieving a majority for his position. Because of this, Lenin was thereafter able to refer to his group as representing the majority *(bolshinstvo* in Russian) position even though it was actually just one of many splinter factions warring for domination of the Russian Marxist movement. Such was the condition of Russian Marxism when, in reaction to an extremely unpopular and unsuccessful war with Japan, revolution broke out in St. Petersburg in 1905. Beginning with the massacre of peaceful demonstrators in February ("Bloody Sunday"), the revolt spread to most of European Russia, with councils ("soviets") of workers attaining a great deal of power in the major cities. During this time, Lenin and his followers attempted to turn the general discontent of the population toward Marxian ends, only to see the revolution brutally crushed by troops still loyal to the czar and by the granting of numerous concessions, notably the October Manifesto of 1905, which established a parliament. Alternately impressed by the potential power of the discontented Russian masses and convinced that only through his tightly organized party could any revolution be a success, Lenin withdrew once again into exile.

The years after the abortive revolution of 1905 saw Lenin and his Bolshevik faction increasingly split off from the other, more moderate Marxists in Russia. They held their own conferences, published their own newspaper (with the name of *Pravda* or "truth" in Russian), and in general took a standoffish attitude toward the international Marxist movement. Lenin's final break with the more moderate socialists of the international movement came with the start of World War I. Confirming his worst fears of the moderates and revisionists, he found most European socialists supporting their respective national governments in the war effort. Instead, Lenin advocated "turn the imperialist war into an international civil war" between classes. Castigating others for supporting a bourgeois war, Lenin, now in Switzerland, could only consolidate his Bolshevik faction even further and hope that the strain of a major war would finally topple the czarist regime. That hope (perhaps dream is a better word) was fulfilled in March 1917 when, with Russia completely out of control, the czar—the final vestige of Europe's *ancien regime*—at long last abdicated.

For Lenin, however, this was but the beginning. Learning of the Romanov abdication, he immediately made arrangements to leave Switzerland to return to Russia. The Germans, only too eager to have a revolutionary like Lenin causing further trouble in Russia, arranged the famous trip by sealed train through Germany and Finland. The exile returned to a triumphant celebration at the Finland Station in St. Petersburg in April 1917.

The remaining events of that fateful year are far too complex to summarize here. Our intention has been to understand something of Lenin the person and to describe briefly the society with which he was dealing, rather than to attempt a history of the Russian revolution. Our prime interest is in Lenin the contributor to Marxist ideology; thus it is to his ideas that we must now turn.

THREE THEMES FROM LENINISM

Revolutionary Leadership and the Party

The history of all countries shows that the working class, exclusively by its own effort, is able to develop only trade union consciousness, i.e., the conviction that it is necessary to combine in unions, fight the employers, and strive to compel the government to pass necessary labour legislation, etc. The theory of socialism, however, grew out of the philosophic, historical, and economic theories elaborated by educated representatives of the propertied classes, by intellectuals.[3]

If there was one thing that made Lenin stand apart from his Marxist colleagues prior to 1917, it was his unique conception of a Communist party. Most commentators would rate the notion of the party as Lenin's foremost contribution to Marxist thought, if only because it turns highly abstract doctrine into a revolutionary movement. In another sense, Lenin's party provides an excellent example of the direction of all of his thought, which was to make Marxist doctrine compatible with the facts of the twentieth century and with the particular conditions in Russia.

Lenin's need to make Marxism applicable to specific situations makes it important *not* to treat the theme of any one era as if it were a timeless position; he, indeed, did alter the revolutionary theory to fit the constantly changing revolutionary context. Nevertheless, on the role of the party, his thought remained unchanging.

As we have seen, Karl Marx had at best a rather vague notion of a revolutionary party because of his belief that the contradictions of capitalism would produce a spontaneous revolution of the proletariat. His orthodox followers, still retaining the belief in spontaneity, believed that a workers' party operating within the bourgeois political system could provide material gains for the working class and develop in the proletariat a sense of its potential power. Although Lenin in his early days accepted this notion, he gradually came to the belief that such mass-based workers' organizations were ineffective and tended to impede the goal of revolution. Partially owing to the lack of a large proletariat in Russia and partially because the proletariat in more highly developed countries tended to adopt bourgeois values as it gained even limited political power, Lenin called for the establishment of a small, tightly organized band of dedicated Marxists whose task was to lead the alienated classes within a country to revolution. Here Lenin argues the need for a secret group of *professional revolutionaries* to bring about the revolution:

I mean *professional revolutionaries*, irrespective of whether they have developed from among students or working men. I assert: (1) that no revolutionary movement can endure without a stable organization of leaders maintaining continuity; (2) that the broader the popular mass drawn spontaneously into the struggle, which forms the

[3] V. I. Lenin, in *The Lenin Anthology*, Robert C. Tucker, ed. (New York: W.W. Norton & Company, 1975), p. 24.

basis of the movement and participates in it, the more urgent the need for such an organization, and the more solid this organization must be (for it is much easier for all sorts of demagogues to side-track the more backward sections of the masses); (3) that such an organization must consist chiefly of people professionally engaged in revolutionary activity; (4) that in an autocratic state, the more we *confine* the membership of such an organization to people who are professionally engaged in revolutionary activity and who have been professionally trained in the art of combating the political police, the more difficult will it be to unearth the organization; and (5) the *greater* will be the number of people from the working class and from the other social classes who will be able to join the movement and perform active work in it.[4]

In adopting this position Lenin more or less stood alone. Rosa Luxemburg, who shared many of his radical tendencies in interpreting Marx's thought, retained her belief in a spontaneous revolution and, therefore, did not see the need for a militant party. Even Leon Trotsky, a trusted lieutenant of Lenin's during the revolution, did not come to share Lenin's view until 1917. The reason for this lack of acceptance was that Lenin, at least implicitly, was advocating a substantial alteration in Marxian thought. Simply, he was saying that since it was impossible for the proletariat to achieve class-consciousness by their own efforts, it was also impossible to have a leaderless revolution.

However, in a country where there was a considerable amount of discontent with the existing regime, it would be possible for a dedicated band of revolutionaries to seize upon the people's "alienation" and direct their energies toward Marxist ends. This is not to say that Lenin believed in the possibility of a palace revolution engineered by a few people in strategic places. He was firm in the belief that a revolutionary movement had to have mass support, and he argued at great length with those who advocated such a coup d'état strategy. Even so, the important point here is that class-consciousness on the part of the proletariat is not a prerequisite for revolution, provided that class-consciousness exists in the revolutionary leadership. Given this addition to Marxian thought, one can see all sorts of opportunities for revolutionary agitation opening up. If class-consciousness among the proletariat is not necessary, the party could attempt to use any dissatisfied group within society to further its ends. All kinds of alliances with different groups would be possible, depending upon the degree of capitalistic development in a particular country. If an alienated proletarian class, conscious of its own plight and potential power, is no longer a prerequisite for a Marxian revolution, then it is quite appropriate to advocate a revolution in countries that do not possess the modern, industrialized characteristics of the classical Marxian model.

We have earlier spoken of Russia as a most unlikely place for a classical Marxist revolution because of its lack of economic development. While this remains true it must be noted that Russia had made very rapid strides toward industrialization during the latter part of the nineteenth century. The success of the workers' soviets in the revolution of 1905 indicated the presence of a growing proletariat in major Russian cities. Still, the country was primarily rural and the population mostly comprised of peasants. Most Marxians considered Russia a feudal society,

[4] Ibid., pp. 76–77.

where the economic substructure was beginning a rapid movement into industrial capitalism while the state superstructure lagged behind, retraining its feudal elements. In such a situation it would be necessary to have not one but two revolutions: first, the bourgeois, and then the proletarian.

The Doctrine of Permanent Revolution

Leon Trotsky had earlier advanced the doctrine of *permanent revolution*, which argued that in Russia the two revolutions could take place within a very short period of time. Even while the bourgeois revolution was occurring, Marxists should be organizing and agitating for the proletarian revolution—the two revolutions could be "telescoped." In such a situation, the task of Marxist revolutionaries was to speed the success of the bourgeois revolution and then attempt to foment a proletarian one. Consistent with this principle, Lenin, prior to 1905, advocated an alliance between the proletariat and the liberal bourgeoisie, so that the aims of the bourgeois revolution might be accomplished. The proletariat's role was temporarily that of assisting the bourgeoisie in the overthrow of the autocracy of the czar. However, the revolution of 1905 changed all that.

The bourgeoisie, by accepting the czar's liberal October Manifesto, had, in Lenin's eyes, sold out to the forces of oppression; they had denied their own revolution. Moreover, the events of 1905 had produced a situation which must have wet the lips of a true revolutionary such as Lenin; there had been a temporary alliance between the small urban proletariat and the vast Russian peasantry. These events led Lenin to abandon the Russian bourgeois class and to rely increasingly upon an alliance between the peasants and the proletariat. Once again, we observe Lenin altering Marxian doctrine to suit the conditions of semifeudal Russia.

Karl Marx, who based his observations on the already developed capitalism of Western Europe, had concluded that the peasant class was one of the most conservative forces in society. However, the situation of the Russian peasantry was quite different, and Marx was aware of this fact. Achieving emancipation from serfdom only in 1861, the Russian peasants found their lot was unbearable and, from Lenin's perspective, not at all dissimilar in revolutionary potential to that of Marx's alienated urban proletariat. After 1905 Lenin spoke with increasing frequency of a revolution of the *masses* allying the proletariat with all dissatisfied classes in the society. It must be remembered, however, that Lenin retained a clear conception in his mind of the role of these groups: They were subservient to the class-conscious proletariat.

The task of Lenin's small, tightly disciplined party is now quite clear. Its function was to coordinate the actions of these various groups, always keeping control of the situation. When the revolution occurred, the party, because of its discipline and organization, would be in a position to assume overall leadership. To Lenin's thinking, one of the fundamental failures of the 1905 revolution was the lack of effective leadership and coordination, and he was determined not to let that happen again. To provide that leadership Lenin set up the decision-making process of the party to conform to the principles of a doctrine called *democratic centralism*. This doctrine presupposes that all the people involved in the process of making decisions for the party are committed to the Marxian goal culture. Given this, decisions still will have to be made regarding party tactics and there will undoubtedly be disagreements as to the right way of proceeding.

As the term implies, democratic centralism theoretically allows for a full democratic discussion of alternatives, but once a decision is made all members of the party must agree to abide by it. There are no minority reports in the party. This doctrine provided Lenin with precisely the tool he needed for revolutionary action: It is democratic by taking into account all positions, but it also provides for the unswerving allegiance necessary for swift action. Many people justifiably contend that the adoption of this decision-making process marks the beginning of a totalitarian party in communist thought, for the "democratic" part of democratic centralism is so easily forgotten in the presence of a strong leader such as Lenin. Whatever the case, Lenin's Communist party, organized in this fashion, provided him with the means of taking control in the more chaotic days of the Russian revolution. While others debated, the Bolsheviks acted.

Despite all of Lenin's attempts to alter Marxian doctrine to suit the special situation in Russia, the fact remains that he succeeded in presiding over a revolution that appeared distinctly un-Marxian in nature. The first communist revolution in the world occurred in a country which, on a substructural level, was singularly unprepared for communism and was a revolution via the political, or superstructure. As a dedicated Marxist, Lenin was aware of this. With his success in Russia he was now faced with the task of using the political structure of the society to develop the economic conditions that Marxism decreed necessary for a pure communist society. To revert to jargon, Lenin had to develop a "transfer culture" that would lead toward the "goal culture" of pure communism. The Communist party was to play a crucial role in this transfer period, but its activities after the revolution are best treated under the heading of the second of our "three themes of Leninism," namely, state socialism and the socialist transfer culture.

THE STATE AND REVOLUTION

Marx had taught that the workers' revolution, once begun, would eventually spread around the entire world until all capitalist regimes were overthrown. Therefore the immediate problem facing the Bolsheviks after their takeover in November 1917 concerned the relationship between the worldwide communist movement and the revolutionary regime in the Soviet Union. Many dedicated Bolsheviks wanted to carry the red flag of Marxism westward into the heart of Europe and at least partially fulfill Marx's prophecy. Initially Lenin agreed with this analysis, contending that the spark of the Bolshevik revolution could ignite the flames of revolution throughout Europe. The beachhead that had been established in Russia would be secured through the overthrow of other capitalist regimes.

In the euphoric days immediately following the Russian revolution, Lenin apparently saw the possibility of the rise of the proletariat throughout Europe, making the Soviet experience a sort of trigger for the revolt in more highly developed capitalist countries. However, such events did not occur, and it became increasingly obvious that some new analysis of the situation was needed.

Characteristically, Lenin shifted ground and began to theorize that even though the Russian revolution was inextricably linked to the international movement there would probably be a lag in time between the initial success of the Bolsheviks and the revolution in other countries. Although he continued to believe that this lag would be of short duration, possibly a few years, admitting of its existence forced the young Soviet regime to develop policy for the interim period and to address itself at least tentatively to the question of the existence of a Soviet state surrounded by capitalism.

On a more practical level, the Bolsheviks were surrounded by chaos; the years of war and revolution had reduced the army to a disorganized mass, a civil war was raging, and the regime was in real danger of losing control completely. And if that were not enough to contend with, over a dozen nations—including Great Britain and the United States—had thousands of troops on Soviet soil. The optimism of the immediate postrevolutionary period, which envisioned a quick transition to economic socialism at home and the rapid spread of revolution abroad, was replaced by a grim struggle for existence. Whatever the ideological costs, the situation required that Russia get out of World War I, and after a good deal of argument this was accomplished through the Treaty of Brest-Litovsk (1918), which ceded large portions of European Russia to the conquering Germans.

Lenin was simply unwilling to sacrifice the Bolshevik success for the sake of a *potential* worldwide revolution. Still, consistent with the broad Marxian analysis he similarly refused to abandon the international struggle for the sake of an independent Soviet nation-state. Confronted with the potentially conflicting goals of the Russian revolution and international Marxism, Lenin opted for both. The long-range goals of the international movement were not inconsistent with the idea of a Soviet state, for the latter would serve as an inspiration to proletarians the world over. Since the time lag between the Russian revolution and the world uprising would be of short duration, the Soviet Union could exist as an entity even though it was surrounded by hostile capitalist states. Marx's prophecy of an international movement was never in doubt; it was simply a question of time. While the international movement was by no means ignored, the Soviet leadership could now expend some energy in securing the gains of the revolution within Russia.

Dictatorship of the Proletariat

As we have said, the Russian revolution was of a political nature, accomplished by a small band of revolutionaries supported by a variety of discontented groups in the society. From the viewpoint of classical Marxism, the two things most conspicuously lacking in Russia were economic development and the presence of large-scale class-consciousness. Until these two goals were achieved it would be impossible to think of a truly communist society. Lenin's task inside the Soviet Union was to develop institutions and a value structure that would achieve these two goals; he had to develop a *transfer culture*. Because the people at large lacked true class-consciousness and had lived for so many years under the false value structures of feudalism and emerging capitalism, it would be necessary to have a group of leaders to direct the economic development of the society and lead the people as a whole toward proletarianization. The Communist party would provide such leadership after the revolution in its role of vanguard of the proletariat by establishing a *proletarian dictatorship*. If the society as a whole was lacking in class-consciousness, it would be absurd, from the Leninist perspective, to give all people an equal say in the running of the country. Thus, it would be temporarily necessary for the party to act as the spearhead of the revolution and to assume a dictatorial role until the time when the last vestiges of capitalism and feudalism were removed.

In this type of environment Lenin argued for the temporary use of dictatorial state power to continue the class conflict; this time, however, it would be the instrument of the proletariat to be employed against all counterrevolutionary forces, especially the bourgeoisie. Lenin captured these ideas in his book *The State and Revolution:*

> The proletariat needs state power, a centralised organisation of force, an organisation of violence, both to crush the resistance of the exploiters and to *lead* the enormous mass of the population—the peasants, the petty bourgeoisie, and semi-proletarians—in the work of organising a socialist economy.
>
> By educating the workers' party, Marxism educates the vanguard of the proletariat, capable of assuming power and *leading the whole people* to socialism, of directing and organising the new system, of being the teacher, the guide, the leader of all the working and exploited people in organising their social life without the bourgeoisie and against the bourgeoisie.[5]

We must pause and note the enormity of the task confronting the Bolshevik leaders. If they were to remain true to their Marxian commitment they had to attempt to wipe out all of the institutions, values, and habit patterns acquired under generations of bourgeois and feudal rule. Consciously, they had to attempt to reeducate an entire people. This same task was accomplished in industrialized Europe through the influence of liberalism—over the course of centuries! The Bolsheviks' situation was completely different. They had to use education, propaganda, even coercion, to achieve their goals in the short run.

The same situation obtained in the economic realm. Despite the rapid growth of capitalism in Russia in the three decades before the revolution, Russia was appropriately called an underdeveloped country. Further, the revolution and civil war that followed it had destroyed much of the small industrial base which had existed in 1917. If extensive economic development was necessary to achieve the Marxian vision, the Soviet Union would have to go through a quasi-capitalistic phase, which would give to the society the technological expertise achieved elsewhere under capitalism. Recall Marx's observation in the *Communist Manifesto*:

> The bourgeoisie, during its rule of scarce one hundred years, has created more massive and more colossal productive forces than have all preceding generations together. Subjection of Nature's forces to man, machinery, application of chemistry to industry and agriculture, steam-navigation, railways, electric telegraphs, clearing of

[5]Ibid., p. 328.

whole continents for cultivation, canalisation of rivers, whole populations conjured out of the ground—what earlier century had even a presentiment that such productive forces slumbered in the lap of social labour?[6]

The country, under the leadership of the party and the state apparatus, must develop itself, but without the excesses of capitalism. To do this Lenin developed the notion generally called *state socialism*. Initially, this concept involved the appropriation of the means of production by the state as a whole so that the capital generated in the economy could be directed to ensure maximum economic growth. The word *capital* is appropriate here in that there was still exploitation of a sort under state socialism. Workers still labored longer than necessary to support themselves, and therefore generated a profit. Under socialism, however, this profit went to the state, which, acting as a trustee, used it for the benefit of the entire society, not for one particular class; similarly Lenin hoped the society would acquire the technological expertise of capitalism without its class structure.

Thus, it is not surprising that there was very little by way of radical change in the economic structure in the immediate postrevolutionary period. Nor is it surprising to see policies promulgated that encouraged some individual competition, such as the New Economic Policy (NEP) of 1921. Under Lenin's *transfer culture*, he argued that "The socialist principle, 'He who does not work shall not eat,' *is already* realised; the other socialist principle, 'An equal amount of products for an equal amount of labour,' is also *already* realised."[7] Nevertheless, he knew this was not communism. The original Marxian principle—from each according to his ability, to each according to his needs—still remained the unfulfilled goal; and, until this was achieved, it was premature to expect the proletarian state to "wither away."

In summary, the objective of the Soviet transfer culture was the attainment of a highly developed economy similar to that in the West, which would provide the technology and expertise necessary for communism. In addition, because of the nature of the Bolshevik revolution, the entire value structure of the people must be changed so that they would possess the consciousness necessary for communism. It may well be that these two goals produced through Lenin's means become antithetical, that the achievement of one of them makes the other impossible. After all Marx long ago recognized that the thing that made capitalism so successful was its emphasis on individual reward for increased effort, which eventually leads to some sort of class structure. Leninism requires the individual initiative of capitalism, yet must avoid its class divisions—a difficult thing indeed. We shall meet this problem again in our discussions of Mao Zedong (Mao Tse-tung) and Mikhail Gorbachev but for the moment it is necessary to move to a discussion of the theory of imperialism, Lenin's third major contribution to Marxian doctrine.

---

[6] Karl Marx, in *The Marx-Engels Reader,* 2nd ed., Robert C. Tucker, ed. (New York: W. W. Norton and Company, 1978), p. 477.

[7] *Lenin Anthology,* p. 378.

THE THEORY OF IMPERIALISM

We have seen how Lenin and numerous other followers of Karl Marx attempted to make Marxist teaching more relevant to the twentieth century. In many respects this was not a difficult activity, for Marx had made some amazingly accurate predictions about the development of capitalism. His assertion that capitalism would spread around the world seemed confirmed in 1917; in accordance with his second law of capitalist development, the monopolistic nature of modern capitalism was increasing; various business crises with worldwide implications seemed to be occurring more frequently; and World War I seemed to confirm the hypothesis that capitalists would struggle mightily with each other for economic advantage.

Despite the apparent correctness of these predictions, a key hypothesis of Marx's entire analysis—that the material condition of the proletariat would become increasingly worse and inevitably lead to revolution—simply was not happening. Indeed, proletarians in highly developed capitalist countries seemed every year to grow more content with their lot as they shared in the benefits of the expanding economies. This fact led some Marxists to adopt the revisionist position of working within the system, and others such as Lenin to foment revolution in an underdeveloped country. But the fundamental question remained—why was the proletariat in developed capitalist systems becoming increasingly passive? Addressing himself to this question in 1916 Lenin published a book titled *Imperialism, the Highest Stage of Capitalism*, which set out the basic ideas of the theory of imperialism.

Before exploring these ideas it must be noted that the theory of imperialism was by no means original with Lenin. Many other Marxists, and some non-Marxists, had earlier advanced similar explanations for the decline in revolutionary activity by the proletariat, and Lenin borrowed freely from them. Still, Lenin's position as head of the only Marxist state in the world probably made it inevitable that his explanation would become *the* theory of imperialism.

At its broadest, the theory asserts that, despite the accuracy of his predictions concerning *unmodified* capitalism, Marx never fully developed his own theory of imperialism contained in the third volume of *Das Kapital*. Although he clearly saw the worldwide spread of capitalism, Marx did not foresee some of the implications this would have, particularly on the working class of the industrialized countries. As Marx noted, the dwindling number of capitalists would be forced into a mad scramble for new markets because of overproduction and diminishing profits at home. Lenin observed that given the level of competition, production would become increasingly concentrated and capitalists would have to attempt to absorb each other, creating huge monopolies that would play *the* central role in economics. Saddled with great quantities of both nonexploitable *constant capital* (machinery) and *finance capital* (bank and industrial investment money), monopoly capitalists and investment bankers would be forced to seek out new sources of cheap raw materials and labor. In short, it was incumbent upon them to find and develop new markets, new sources of exploitation. Remember, like the small capitalist, the monopoly capitalist exploits out of necessity; not to expand and exploit would mean to be taken over by some other monopoly capitalist. So too *imperialism*, as a governmental policy is not a mat ter of free choice. Imperialist nations must expand and control markets in order to survive in a capitalist world. The underdeveloped countries of the world become absolutely essential to sustaining monopoly capitalism and must therefore be brough under their economic control. In an attempt to show the incontrovertibility of this description of imperialism on these points, Lenin quoted the wealthy British indus trialist Cecil Rhodes:

> I was in the East End of London [a working-class quarter] yesterday and attended a meeting of the unemployed. I listened to the wild speeches, which were just a cry for "bread! bread!" and on my way home I pondered over the scene and I became more than ever convinced of the importance of imperialism. . . . My cherished idea is a solu tion for the social problem, i.e., in order to save the 40,000,000 inhabitants of the United Kingdom from a bloody civil war, we colonial statesmen must acquire new lands to settle the surplus population, to provide new markets for the goods produce in the factories and mines. The Empire, as I have always said, is a bread and butter question. If you want to avoid civil war, you must become imperialists.[8]

The worldwide competition among capitalists had also led to the creation of international, monopoly-capitalist associations that were starting to dominate the world economy in ways analogous to the domestic monopolies. Lenin, writing in the early part of this century, called these associations combines, trusts, and cartels; if he were writing today, he would have used the better-known terms *multinational corpora tions* and *transnational corporations*. (The latter term hints at what may well be the nex phase in imperialism; contemporary political analysts have introduced new concept like "virtual corporations" and "postnational" corporations now that a few of the mos massive of these economic entities have become more powerful than many nation states.) Be that as it may, Lenin described how, with the armies of the capitalist state leading the way, capitalism would carve out specific spheres of influence and proceed to exploit the resources of these areas, both material and human, for all they were worth. With this seemingly inexhaustible labor supply, monopoly capitalists could force the native population to work under deplorable conditions for tiny wages and extract tremendous profits. Some of the *superprofit* derived in this manner could then be used to bribe their own internal proletariat with higher wages and better working conditions, thereby increasing consumption of the capitalists' products. Lenin wrote

> Obviously, out of such enormous *superprofits* (since they are obtained over and above the profits which capitalists squeeze out of the workers of their "own" country) it i *possible to bribe* the labour leaders and the upper stratum of the labour aristocracy. And that is just what the capitalists of the "advanced" countries are doing: they are brib ing them in a thousand different ways, direct and indirect, overt and covert.[9]

Therefore, the domestic proletariat of highly developed capitalist countrie was bought off with the profit from the exploitation of the underdeveloped countries. Instead of the vast army of unemployed workers that Marx predicted what resulted was an increasingly affluent middle class largely content with its lo and a firm defender of the bourgeois status quo. In addition, those workers who

---

[8] Ibid., p. 236.
[9] Ibid., p. 209.

do suffer economic hardship can be aided by an emerging welfare state that could, in part, also be paid for by the superprofits. Here we see the major reasons for the lack of revolutionary activity on the part of the proletariat in industrialized countries. Their condition was not growing worse but actually improving because of the material exploitation of underdeveloped countries. This results in a new exploiter-exploited relationship: It is no longer the bourgeois class versus the proletariat but highly developed capitalist *countries* pitted against underdeveloped ones. Marx's class analysis had changed under the imperialistic stage of capitalism to a situation in which "prenation" confronts nation.

This change to a nation-state orientation under the theory of imperialism cannot be overemphasized. Lenin had long ago recognized the revolutionary potential of nationalist slogans, and he had utilized all classes within Russia to achieve the revolution. Still, classical Marxism was avowedly internationalistic, and all good Marxists thought of nationalist ideology as nothing but another capitalist ploy to keep the workers in one country from allying with those in another.

Furthermore, the nation-state was a uniquely capitalist invention whose major purpose was to enhance the power position of the bourgeosie; it would, after all, vanish under pure communism. The theory of imperialism united these seemingly contradictory goals of nationalism and internationalistic communism and in the process provided a completely new revolutionary strategy for modern communism.

Wars of National Liberation

With the internal proletariat in industrialized countries bribed by superprofits, Marxists now looked elsewhere for revolutionary groups. Under imperialism, revolutionary potential lay not with a particular class or alienated group within a society, but with entire exploited countries. Revolutionary activity would take place in the form of *wars of national liberation,* which would unite nationalistic groups and communists with underdeveloped countries to throw off the capitalist yoke. Once successful, these nationalist movements should be controlled by communists who would then lead the country into a socialist transfer culture, following the pattern of the Soviet Union. It is easy to read too many things into the theory of imperialism; the revolutions in China, Cuba, and Vietnam, for example, fit perhaps too neatly. Nevertheless, contained within this theory are all the implications of most of the communist revolutions that have since occurred. Lenin had turned economic backwardness into a virtue; underdevelopment was now almost a prerequisite for revolution.

What, we might now ask, of the old Marxian prophecy of an international class-based revolution? Obviously Marx's predictions had been greatly changed under imperialism; class revolt had become national revolution, and underdevelopment was a virtue. Despite these changes Lenin, once again, remained true to the theoretical outlines of Marx's analysis. As we saw in our discussion of socialism in one country, Lenin both altered the time sequence of Marx's predictions and used somewhat different means. But this is the *method of Marxism:* As history changes, so must the theory. Ultimately, however, the overall Marxian analysis remained unchanged; capitalism will collapse.

Similarly, the wars of national liberation in underdeveloped countries were but the initial events that would eventually lead to worldwide communism. As these nationalist revolutions met with increasing success, they would cut off the source of cheap labor and raw materials from the capitalists. The superprofits that the capitalists formerly reaped from these countries would no longer be available to them, and in order to continue to make a profit, they would have to go back to exploiting their own internal proletariat. Once this occurred, all of Marx's predictions concerning highly developed capitalism would come to pass: overproduction, a vast army of unemployed, crises, and revolution. The worldwide revolution would occur, although in a way not envisioned by Marx; even so, his overall analysis would be vindicated.

The changes wrought in classical Marxism by Lenin's revolutionary experience are significant, so significant that it is appropriate now to speak of Marxism-Leninism. It should be emphasized that we have only skimmed the surface of Lenin's contributions and neglected many aspects of his thought that others might deem crucial. He was, for example, most interested in the concept of dialectical materialism and wrote a goodly amount on that subject. Yet in his thoughts on the party, a socialist transfer culture, and the theory of imperialism, we clearly see the tremendous impact this person had upon the development of the doctrine. In a sense, V. I. Lenin was a perfect Marxian man: a thinker and a revolutionary, a dedicated (almost doctrinaire) Marxist and an opportunist, unscrupulous yet idealistic. If, as Karl Marx said so many years ago, the point of philosophy was not to explain the world but to change it, Lenin surely was a success, for the world has not been the same since November 1917.

SUGGESTED READINGS

BERNSTEIN, EDUARD, *Evolutionary Socialism: A Criticism and Affirmation.* New York: Schocken Books, 1961.

DEUTSCHER, ISAAC, *The Prophet Armed, Trotsky, 1879–1921.* New York: Oxford University Press, 1954.

———, *The Prophet Unarmed: Trotsky, 1921–1929.* New York: Oxford University Press, 1959.

———, *The Prophet Outcast: Trotsky, 1929–1940.* New York: Oxford University Press, 1963.

FISCHER, LOUIS, *The Life of Lenin.* New York: Harper & Row Publishers, 1964.

GAY, PETER, *The Dilemma of Democratic Socialism: Eduard Bernstein's Challenge to Marx.* New York: Collier Books, 1962.

HOOK, SIDNEY, *Marx and the Marxists: The Ambiguous Legacy.* Princeton, N.J.: Van Nostrand Company, 1955.

KAUTSKY, KARL, *The Dictatorship of the Proletariat.* Ann Arbor: University of Michigan Press, 1964.

MAGDOFF, HARRY, *The Age of Imperialism.* New York: Monthly Review Press, 1969.

MEYER, ALFRED B., *Leninism.* New York: Frederick A. Praeger, 1963.

TUCKER, ROBERT C., ed. *The Lenin Anthology.* New York: W. W. Norton & Company, 1975.

WILSON, EDMUND, *To the Finland Station: A Study in the Writing and Acting of History.* Garden City, N.Y.: Doubleday and Company, 1953.

WOLFE, BERTRAM D., *Three Who Made a Revolution: Lenin, Trotsky, and Stalin.* New York: Dell Publishing Co., 1948.

7

Marxian *Praxis*:
The Soviet Experiment

I stress once again: perestroika *is not some kind of illumination or revelation. To restructure our life means to understand the objective necessity for renovation and acceleration. And that necessity emerged in the heart of our society. The* essence of perestroika *lies in the fact that it* unites socialism with democracy *and revives the Leninist concept of socialist construction both in theory and practice. Such is the essence of* perestroika, *which accounts for its genuine revolutionary spirit and its all-embracing scope.*

Mikhail Gorbachev

STALIN'S RISE TO POWER

After the successes of 1917, Lenin's position as the leader of Russian Marxism was virtually unchallenged. He was, after all, the "father" of the revolution and, in spite of the many difficulties which confronted the Bolshevik regime during its early days, Lenin's stature could only be enhanced. His preeminence was such, particularly after the successful conclusion of the civil war in 1920, that the dictatorship of the proletariat became virtually the "dictatorship" of Lenin. While it is perfectly understandable that this would be the case, it provided a dangerous model for the development of Soviet Marxism; this precedent, when combined with Lenin's tightly knit, highly centralized Bolshevik party, provided many of the preconditions for the Stalinist totalitarianism that was to dominate and, once entrenched in his bureaucratic legacy, ultimately haunted the Soviet Union throughout its existence. Indeed, legacies of the past have had a significant influence thoughout Russian and Soviet history, often creating, as everywhere else, powerful constraints on choices their leaders think they can make.

To understand Stalin and his place in Soviet history, then, it is helpful to remember all of Russian history and the role played by strong leaders throughout its past. Few nations have been invaded as often and as devastatingly as Russia. Recall that not the least destructive of these invasions was conducted by troops from over a dozen foreign countries, including the United States and Great Britain, during the early revolutionary months of the Soviet Union. At this as well as other crucial moments in its history, the presence of a strong, often ruthless leader—the *vozhd*—seemed required. Ivan the Terrible, Peter as well as Catherine the Great, and certainly Lenin, each was the *vozhd*. This concept has been translated as "Leader," "Duce" or "Führer," carrying with it notions of infallibility and extraordinary power. Given this tradition, it is understandable that during the initial months after the death of Lenin and during the bleaker months of the Great Patriotic War (how Russians still refer to the Second World War), the Soviet people looked to a *vozhd* to succeed him.

It may seem strange that Stalin, in spite of the indelible imprint he left on Soviet life and despite his long tenure as supreme leader, made at most minor contributions to the development of Marxist-Leninist ideology. Yet from a Stalinist perspective such a situation makes a good deal of sense. The broad, theoretical outlines of the Soviet transfer culture had been described by Lenin, and it can be argued that what was now required was a practitioner to transform those outlines into reality. Whether a Lenin would have had the determination, patience, or, for that matter, the stomach to pursue the type of policies that characterized Stalin's reign is, of course, a moot point. Whether Lenin would have pursued alternative more democratic policies and thereby reached alternative ends is also moot. In fact, there is some evidence, which we shall explore later, that indicates Lenin had real misgivings about the direction the regime was taking. Be that as it may, *if a* total transformation of the Soviet economy and a radical alteration of the belief of an entire people are the stated prerequisites of socialism, an argument can be made that some sort of Stalin-like era was *a*—if not *the* (only)—logical outgrowth of the Bolshevik revolution. If Lenin had provided the theoretical tools for the future development of Soviet Marxism, Stalin interpreted them to suit his purposes and used them with a vengeance.

This raises the crucial Marxist issue of *praxis*. As you may recall, Marx was highly critical of all thinkers who constructed abstract idea systems that seemed to have no direct connection to material reality. He stated his position succinctly in his second "Thesis on Feuerbach":

> The question whether objective truth can be attributed to human thinking is not a question of theory but a *practical* question. Man must prove the truth, that is, the reality and power, the this-sideness of his thinking in practice. This dispute over the reality or non-reality of thinking which is isolated from practice is a purely *scholastic* question.[1]

Marxian *praxis* is the unity of theory and practice. To Marx, theory without practice is just as "scholastic" as practice without theory. But when practice involves the use of political power, the word "scholastic" does not begin to convey the importance of this issue in terms of human costs. Friedrich Engels makes an additional significant point when he notes:

> In every epoch, and therefore also in ours, theoretical thought is a historical product, which at different times assumes very different forms and, therewith, very different contents. The science of thought is, therefore, like every other, a historical development of human thought. And this is important also for the practical application of thought in empirical fields. Because in the first place the theory of the laws of thought is by no means an "eternal truth" established once and for all, as philistine reasoning imagines to be the case. . . .[2]

What this means in terms of Marx's complex worldview—of an even more complex world—is that there may well be a few, perhaps several, equally valid Marxist ideologies at any historic moment—variations on a Marxian theme if you will. The Soviet experiment in trying to build a socialist base was one such variation, the Chinese yet another. But confronted with the reality of a kind of pluralism, a central evaluative question of the soundness of these differing approaches would be this: Given the historic and cultural context of the ideology, will the means x, y, and/or z bring about the corresponding (and appropriate) Marxian ends? This also raises the fascinating, and hopefully not "scholastic," question: Can an experiment in building socialism fail and yet be considered legitimate Marxism? Or, is the final success of an experiment the sole criterion of legitimacy? You may want to return to these questions at the end of the subsequent chapter on Chinese *praxis*. For the moment, we will continue our extended discussion of the Soviet experience and the role of Stalin.

[1] Karl Marx, in *The Marx-Engels Reader*, 2nd ed., Robert C. Tucker, ed. (New York: W. W. Norton & Company, 1978), p. 144.

[2] Karl Marx and Friedrich Engels, *Selected Works, 3 Vols.* (Moscow: Progress Publishers, 1966), Vol. 3, p. 60.

Stalin's Life

Stalin's rise to the pinnacle of power in the Soviet Union is an extremely complex tale, one largely outside the confines of our concern. However, during his early life and his rise to power, he exhibited most of the personal traits that were to constitute his major contributions to the doctrine. For approximately twenty-five years Stalin was the Soviet Union; his personal whims governed the state, making it impossible to ignore Stalin, the man of steel.

Joseph Stalin was born to poor artisan parents in 1879 in a small village in the Caucasus Mountains of Georgia. His father, Vissarion Dzhugashvili, was apparently a rather bitter man who, it is sometimes said, took much of his frustration out on young Joseph (the pseudonym "Stalin" was adopted later in his life). His father died when Joseph was quite young, leaving his upbringing and schooling to his illiterate mother. Through tremendous personal sacrifice she was able to provide the means for her young son to study in Tiflis (now Tbilisi), the capitol of Georgia, where he received his education in a seminary. Whatever the quality of this education, Stalin was to be plagued throughout his life by his Georgian background, notably by his difficulties with the Russian language and by the generally "provincial" nature of his upbringing. In spite of its provincial setting, the seminary apparently was a center for the dissemination of liberal if not radical ideas and the young Stalin gradually came under the sway of them. He got into increasing trouble with the school authorities and was finally dismissed for reading banned books.

By 1899, the year he was expelled from the seminary, he considered himself a committed Marxist and was to spend much of the time between 1900 and 1917 in prison, mostly in Siberia, a fact which surely indicates his dedication to the cause. With the split between Lenin's Bolsheviks and the Mensheviks occurring at the Second Party Congress in 1903, Stalin was increasingly drawn to the Leninist notion of a tightly organized, revolutionary action party. Some observers have noted that this was a perfectly natural development in that Stalin was always a man of action, a practitioner, and Lenin's call for agitation instead of discussion must have greatly appealed to him.

When he was not in prison Stalin was a major Bolshevik figure in the Caucasus, organizing strikes and leading raids against the czarist establishment. His relationship with Lenin during this period was apparently that of a trusted functionary who could be counted on to carry out party directions to the letter. Certainly he was not well known, even in Russian Marxist circles. At that time, writing theoretical treatises was the means by which young Marxists enhanced their reputations within the movement, and although Stalin had done some writing it was not of the sort to attract much attention. Leon Trotsky, while not the most objective of observers, later asserted that he hardly remembered Stalin's name in May 1917. Stalin was, however, exactly the type of person that Lenin needed. He was tough, efficient, brave, and above all, loyal. It was not a coincidence that this was precisely the sort of person that Stalin himself found useful in his later rise to personal power.

Stalin's part in the revolution remains the subject of a good deal of interpretation. Later Bolshevik accounts, written under the watchful eye of Stalin himself place him at Lenin's side throughout the events of 1917. While this seems to be an obvious fabrication, Stalin was a member of the Central Committee during the revolutionary year and later played an important role during the civil war. Throughout this period he accumulated a variety of titles and posts, the most important being that of general secretary of the party in 1922. Most of these positions added to the personal power of Stalin, but as long as Lenin was alive it was he who dominated the revolution and its aftermath. When Lenin's health deteriorated further in 1922, however, these offices proved quite useful in Stalin's bid to be Lenin's successor.

Lenin's Distrust of Stalin

During the last years of his life, Lenin's relationship with Stalin began to sour. Lenin became increasingly distressed with the problems of overbureaucratization and the arbitrary use of power by some of his subordinates. Stalin, in particular, seemed guilty of these offenses. In an early indication of what was to become a persistent theme of Stalinism, he had rather ruthlessly removed some Georgian Bolsheviks who favored more local autonomy for Stalin's native land. Stalin, who one might think was ill suited at least by birth for the role, had become an advocate of *Russification,* that is, the spreading of Russian culture and language throughout the ethnically diverse country controlled by the Bolsheviks. Some commentators believe that the motivation behind such action was Stalin's mania for centralized bureaucratic control rather than any love of the Russian culture, but the results were the same. Stalin was accused of "Great Russian Chauvinism" and castigated by Lenin for his high-handed tactics. These events in Georgia coupled with several others led Lenin to a growing distrust of Stalin, which culminated in his famous last testament to the party in which he criticized Stalin's actions and recommended that he be removed from his position as general secretary.

> Stalin is too excessively rude and this defect, although quite tolerable in our midst and in dealings among us Communists, becomes intolerable in a secretary-general. That is why I suggest that the comrades think about a way of removing Stalin from that post.[3]

This recommendation was never carried out. Stalin's position as general secretary had given him sufficient power to prevent widespread circulation of Lenin's views and the ailing leader could not summon the strength to implement them. With Lenin's death in January 1924 Stalin was very much in position to contend for power.

The period between 1924, and 1930, when Stalin achieved complete control, is marked by a tremendously complicated series of maneuvers by various aspirants to Lenin's mantle. While we cannot discuss these events in any detail, some mention of them is necessary if only to indicate how different Stalin was from the other

---

[3] Nikita S. Khrushchev, "Special Report to the Twentieth Congress of the CPSU," in *The Betrayal of Marx,* Frederick L.Bender, ed. (New York: Harper & Row, Publishers, 1975), p. 414.

major Bolshevik figures, for example, Leon Trotsky and Nikolai Bukharin. Stalin' primary rival, particularly during the early years, was Leon Trotsky, who probabl had the best credentials to succeed Lenin. Although a late convert to Bolshevism Trotsky had served admirably during the revolution and was everything Stalin wa not: a highly respected Marxist intellectual, well known for his contributions to th doctrine, and steeped in the Western liberal traditions of the movement. Indeed Stalin was easily distinguished from most of his Bolshevik colleagues: He was les educated, apparently dull witted, always somewhat provincial in his outlook, and above all, untouched by the Western liberalism that was an important part of th Marxist heritage.

Despite the fact that Lenin had mentioned Stalin and Trotsky as his mos likely successors, few people in leadership positions in the Bolshevik regime fel Stalin to be a genuine contender. In a sense this was a real asset for him since any one else with aspirations for power saw Leon Trotsky as his main obstacle, which led to numerous coalitions within the major decision-making organs designed to "stop Trotsky." This was not simply a matter of personal rivalry. Being schooled in history, the leadership feared *Bonapartism*—that Trotsky might be to the Russian revolution what Napoleon Bonaparte had been to the French revolution. Con sequently, the period between 1924 and 1930 saw a constant shifting of alliance among the major figures of the party. Stalin's role in this maneuvering appar ently was largely that of playing the moderate, all the while using his position a general secretary of the party to advance the careers of younger Bolsheviks who were loyal to him. By 1927 Stalin had amassed sufficient power to have Trotsk and his followers dismissed from the Politbureau, by then the central decision making organ of the party, and by 1929 that group passed a resolution expelling Trotsky from the USSR. In the same year, Stalin began the process of collec tivization and relocation of the Russian peasantry, a series of events that resulted in enormous loss of life and property. Thus began the Stalinist reign of terror which, with varying intensity, was to last for almost twenty-five years. Stalin died at age 73, in March 1953.

After successfully orchestrating Trotsky's demise, Stalin set his sights on the next most powerful figure in the party, Nikolai Ivanovich Bukharin. An intellec tual who wrote on a wide range of topics from economic theory to literary criticism and who was universally acknowledged as the party's leading theoretician Bukharin served as editor of *Pravda* and *Izvestia* and was the author of numerou books and pamphlets, including *The ABC of Communism, The Economic Theory of th Leisure Class,* and *Imperialism and the World Economy.* Among his numerous theo retical contributions were his theory of imperialism, which Lenin drew upon and "socialism in one country," which Stalin in time would skillfully employ; he was also the chief supporter and principal architect of the New Economic Policy Recall that the NEP was initiated by Lenin in 1921 as a reaction to the socia unrest generated by the centralized state planning and forced collectivization o War Communism.

The NEP legalized private *"profit"* among the peasants and other worker as incentives to stimulate production. It created a somewhat mixed economy; i divided industry in two broad categories, private and socialist, but the stat enterprises remained the most significant sector, employing over four-fifths of the workers and continuing to control all heavy industry and banking. In addition, the NEP reinstituted market relationships into the economy, with the state no longer enjoying a privileged position in terms of contracts, and it decentralized the administrative direction of state enterprises. The initial results from NEP were impressive; Bukharin argued that NEP must be allowed to continue for at least a generation as part of the long transition to socialism. This liberalization of the economy had inevitable, corresponding consequences in the political and social arenas: Intraparty democracy and open debate existed among the party elite while artistic freedom flourished as intellectuals like Stanislavsky, Eisenstein, Shostakovich, Prokofiev, Chagall, Blok, and others enjoyed the false dawn which lasted from Lenin's final years until Stalin had gained a firm grip on the machinery of power. Nevertheless, the NEP was short lived, becoming but one of the victims of the power struggles that followed Lenin's death.

Labeled "soft wax" by Lenin, Bukharin shifted positions inside the party throughout his career. He was both ally and antagonist of Lenin, Trotsky, and Stalin at different historic moments. With Lenin's death, Bukharin initially sided with Stalin against Trotsky over the direction and control of the party. In 1928 Stalin destroyed the NEP with the implementation of his first five-year plan: It called for a command economy with centralized planning and drastic measures to ensure the rapid collectivization of agriculture and the creation of the heavy industrial base prerequisite to socialism. The following year Stalin also implemented the unanimity principle, altering the concept of democratic centralism, wherein now even members of the Politburo were forbidden to voice dissent inside the party. Thus Lenin's idea of democratic centralism became Stalin's notion of bureaucratic authoritarianism, providing all the advantages of centralization without the "inefficiencies" of democracy. In 1936, after less than a decade of Stalin's economic policies, he declared that the foundations of socialism had been built. Ironically, if unsurprisingly, Bukharin eventually suffered a fate similar to Trotsky's. In one of the great show trials of Soviet history, in the spring of 1938, Bukharin along with over a dozen other party officials was charged with treason, acts of diversion, terrorism, and numerous violations of the criminal code. Among the charges against Bukharin was that he attempted to assassinate Lenin. On the ides of March after a trial of approximately two weeks, the Soviet state announced that his execution had taken place. But the news of this event received scant international attention as it was overshadowed by Hitler's march into Austria three days earlier.

MARXISM-LENINISM-STALINISM

We have already noted that Stalin's theoretical contributions to the development of Marxism-Leninism were rather meager; indeed, it was Stalin who first used the term *Marxism-Leninism,* rather than Marxism *and* Leninism. The compound expression signifies the apparent unity of the two theories, while the latter wording implies two separate theories with separate views. Moreover, Marxism-Leninism symbolizes the correctness of this theory, implying that it would be impossible to have another Marxism coeval with Marxism-Leninism. As early as 1924, in *The*

Foundations of Leninism, Stalin began the process of canonizing Marxism-Leninism. He, or writers using his name, authoritatively established what was, and what was not, Marxism-Leninism. At the height of Stalin's power in 1938, *History of the Communist Party of the Soviet Union (Bolsheviks): A Short Course* was published with Stalin identified simply as the author of Chapter Four. After World War II, Stalin was reported to be the author of the entire work, which was now to be taught to the whole nation.

The *Short Course* reiterates the notion of socialism in one country and introduces the idea that class struggle will become fiercer as the building of socialism progresses. But the real addition to the history of Marxism was Stalin's attempt at the institutionalization of theory: Stalin wanted to codify Marxism-Leninism into a single authoritative and legitimate worldview that would simultaneously provide him, as sole interpreter of the doctrine, with a potent instrument of power. Indeed, given the paucity of Stalin's contributions to theory, Stalinism is not so much a system of independent thought as it is a particular mechanistic, and pedestrian interpretation of Marxism and Leninism.

At some risk of oversimplification, it could be said that all of Stalin's ideological contributions revolved around the intensification of the doctrine of *socialism in one country* and the resultant enhancement of the Soviet nation-state. Stalin had exhibited his penchant for Russification and centralized control in his dealings with Georgia in 1923, acts which evoked Lenin's displeasure. Now he was in a position to apply the same types of devices throughout the entire Soviet state. From Stalin's ideological point of view it was essential that the young Soviet state develop the industrial base necessary for socialism, as well as provide for the proletarianization of the people. Whether his motivation was born of a desire for a powerful Russian nation-state or from a commitment to Marxist ideas, Stalin was determined to industrialize the nation rapidly and was willing to inflict the costs that this action might entail upon the Russian people.

With a planned economy directed from Moscow, it was possible to reinvest the capital generated throughout the country in heavy industry at the expense of consumer goods and general creature comforts for the people. Those who dissented from such policies were easily dealt with through slave-labor camps and the secret police. Whether such policies were necessary given the hostile, anticommunism of the West and whether the industrialization of the country would have occurred rapidly with other economic measures are questions we cannot answer here. It is enough to say that, while the cost in human lives was tremendous, with Stalin's death in 1953 the Soviet Union had emerged as a major industrial and military power.

The World's First Totalitarian State

Industrialization was, however, only one of the two goals of the Leninist transfer culture. Stalin was equally interested in proletarianizing the people. To establish a Soviet socialist state, it would be necessary to eradicate all bourgeois values, to remove those people who continued to hold them, and to develop a new "Soviet man," loyal to the regime and dedicated to the advancement of the Soviet state.

Utilizing the same sort of centralized control, with the Communist party and the secret police as the primary tools, Stalin produced what is generally recognized as arguably the first truly totalitarian state the world had seen. At least as early as the presidency of Harry Truman—when Stalin's image of "Uncle Joe," trusted ally against the Axis powers, was being altered to that of anticapitalist, totalitarian dictator—the image much of the world had of the Soviet Union under Stalin was one in which everything became a political matter; the heretofore private affairs of individuals were now matters of state concern. An essential instrument for the destruction of social bonds was the universal system of spying on one's neighbors. Every citizen was under moral and legal obligation to do so. As a result, millions were arrested, and uncounted numbers executed. A gigantic propaganda machine, youth organizations, art, music—all were used to impose "proletarian" consciousness from above.

With the party as the vanguard of the proletariat leading the way, every aspect of human experience was examined for its political import. Schoolbooks were rewritten to reflect proletarian values and to correct bourgeois falsifications; socialist realism in art became the only permissible form; a rigorous system of censorship was instituted to ensure there was no deviation from the party line; and, after suppressing all university chairs in philosophy, Stalin expelled all non-Marxist philosophers from the country. Capping this gigantic system of state control was Stalin himself, a kind of giant puppeteer, pulling the strings to manipulate every aspect of Soviet life. The worship of Stalin as a great man became an integral part of the ideology. Indeed, there is evidence to indicate that Stalin believed that this sort of dictator worship was to become a permanent part of the ideology, even after his death.

It is almost impossible to describe the impact of these policies on the Soviet citizenry, peasants and high-ranking party members alike. The policy of forced collectivization in agriculture radically altered the lives of millions of peasants, while purges, capped by obviously staged trials, attempted systematically to remove any potential dissenters from the society. By 1939 Stalin had achieved a true cultural revolution, forcing thousands of old Bolsheviks into slave-labor camps, retirement, or death. The effect of all this was to develop a mass of people conditioned to respond to Stalin's personal notion of the correct path to socialism and to endure any hardships that this journey might entail. At this time one was a Marxist not because of a commitment to any particular set of ideas or values as being true, but because one was prepared to accept whatever Stalin might proclaim. All of the horrors of Stalin's domestic policies were rationalized as being necessary to the development of a strong Soviet state. This enhancement of the Soviet nation-state dominated the Stalinist ideology in other ways as well, notably in the area of foreign affairs.

Interests of the Soviet State Come First

We earlier noted some of the difficulties that Lenin faced in reconciling the goals of the Soviet nation-state with those of the international communist movement. After some equivocation, he opted for strengthening the socialist-safe area of the USSR while temporarily suspending the worldwide revolution. Stalin, faced with the same set of problems, adopted a similar solution and expanded it to the extent that he is justifiably famed for his emphasis on the doctrine of socialism in one country. The implications of such a position in terms of both international communism and Soviet foreign policy were so vast that they constituted a genuine Stalinist contribution to the ideology.

Given what we know of Stalin's nationalist proclivities stemming from the early days of "great Russian chauvinism," it is perhaps not surprising to find that Stalin placed the interests of the Soviet nation-state above those of the international communist movement. Some of his earliest battles with Trotsky had resulted from Stalin's reluctance to involve the Soviet Union in "international adventurism." This does not mean that he doubted the eventual triumph of communism on a worldwide scale, but that he regarded the Soviet nation-state as being the prime vehicle for ensuring that eventual victory.

In its simplest terms, Stalin's policy was that the interests of the Soviet Union came first. When the base in the USSR was reasonably secure, more aggressive action in the international area was in order: But if Soviet national interests were threatened, the international activity was suspended. This policy, in effect, made the international movement (the formal body of which was called the Comintern a tool of Soviet foreign policy and made Communist parties in other states agent of the Soviet Union. Stalin's penchant for centralized control, which was manifested in so many ways within the USSR, was applied to the international movement. Everything was directed from Moscow. While other Communist parties throughout the world were theoretically equal, Stalin made it quite clear that the Communist Party of the Soviet Union (CPSU) was first among equals. This situation posed some very interesting problems for the parties in other countries; they were accused not only of advocating the overthrow of legitimate capitalist regimes but also of being the active agents of a foreign power dedicated to that goal. Further, they were constantly subjected to rapid shifts in the party line when it suited Stalin's plans for Soviet foreign policy. The most notable of these shifts occurred in 1939 when, after years of active opposition to Adolf Hitler's regime in Germany Stalin signed the Nazi-Soviet Pact making the USSR and, consequently, the international movement, a temporary ally of a doctrine dedicated to the destruction of Marxism. Strange bedfellows indeed, but a quite logical manifestation of Stalin's "Soviet Union First" foreign policy.

The Problems of Directing World Revolution

Even more interesting were the consequences of this policy in countries where indigenous communist movements were in open rebellion against existing regimes. We shall explore the somewhat special case of China more fully later, but a brief mention of Chinese difficulties will illustrate the problems of directing a world revolution from an apartment in the Kremlin. Following the current Moscow line of collaboration with other dissident groups within a society, the young Chinese communist movement had allied itself with the bourgeoi nationalists of Jiang Jieshi (Chiang Kai-shek), only to have Jiang turn and slaughter thousands of communists. When the Chinese communists, led by Mao Zedong finally succeeded in 1949, it was largely without Soviet help and as the result of a strategy far removed from the model of the Bolshevik revolution. Owing little to the Soviet Union, it was perhaps inevitable that the Chinese would begin to think for themselves in matters of both doctrine and strategy.

Further evidence of cracks in the monolithic facade of the Moscow controlled international movement was apparent during the 1940s. Joseph Broz Tito had succeeded in establishing a socialist regime in Yugoslavia through the use of a partisan army formed to combat the Nazi enemy. Tito simply refused to follow Moscow at every turn or to become a satellite of the USSR, and this led to his expulsion from the international movement by Stalin. Nevertheless, from the Stalinist perspective, the ideal situation was the general condition of Eastern Europe after the war, which was a fortuitous blend of expanding the international movement and serving Soviet national interests. The satellite states were creations of the Red Army and were clearly subservient to the USSR both materially and ideologically. They provided a buffer for the Soviet nation, ever fearful of German and eventually American military might, while partially serving the ideological goal of spreading communism throughout the world.

From the ideological perspective perhaps the best word to use in summing up the career of Joseph Stalin is consistency. From his earliest days his vision of the path to pure communism required a Soviet nation state, economically and militarily powerful, and he was prepared to sacrifice anything to achieve that goal. Internally, this resulted in the slaughter of thousands, perhaps millions, of people, many of them dedicated Bolsheviks. Externally, this vision reduced the once potent international communist movement to a puppet of the Soviet Union, a mere caricature of the movement of Lenin's time. It is quite tempting to see the mass horrors of the Stalinist era as a tragic mistake, the product of an unstable mind bent on achieving tremendous personal power. Yet from an ideological perspective there was a cruel logic to Stalin's actions, a method to his "madness." The "unity of theory and practice" ironically had been accomplished by Stalin, who effectively concentrated all doctrinal, political, and police power in his own person. It is imperative to remember that the USSR, symbol of the communist movement, was surrounded by openly hostile forces from fascism and capitalism—armies from both ideological systems had invaded its territory and almost destroyed the revolution. Stalin's task, therefore, was to drag the young Soviet state into the twentieth century, to develop a strong economy, to eradicate any vestiges of bourgeois life, and to establish a military power which could guarantee the autonomy of communism. By the time of his death in 1953, he had in many respects succeeded.

SOVIET MARXISM AFTER STALIN

Common sense tells us that when a dictator dies the country he had ruled might fall into mass confusion. When the identifiable center of power ceases to exist, one could expect the people to feel a sense of great liberation and usher in an immediate and bloody struggle for power. While there was some of this type of reaction among the elite in the USSR at the death of Stalin, the most general response was a feeling of grief, coupled with disbelief and disorientation. In a sense, the fact that there was no uprising and little chaos following his death is a tribute to the success of Stalin's policies, especially those that allowed the party to control virtually all information received by the people. Understandably, large numbers of people admired Stalin: He had, after all, successfully brought them through the Great Patriotic War. The rest of the populace, if not happy with the Soviet regime, was conditioned to accept its rule, and even the demise of the "master conditioner" was not enough to produce even the hint of outright rebellion. It is also a tribute to the rapid action and common sense of the remaining members of the ruling elite. The word *members* is appropriate, for Stalin had left no heir to his throne, and there was no one person with sufficient power to establish authority.

In many ways the situation was similar to that which occurred after Lenin's death, and the solution of the leadership elements within the state and party was much the same, with one major exception—at the top levels of the bureaucracies there existed an unspoken acceptance of the idea that a Stalin-like dictatorship could never again be allowed to develop. They reestablished the principle of collective leadership of the state and began an involved struggle for power that was to last ultimately until 1957. This leadership group realized that both their collective safety and any personal aspirations they might harbor depended on having Stalin quickly forgotten. Thus a process of "silent de-Stalinization" began almost immediately. A new purge, which was begun by Stalin in his final years, was halted and the principal figures in this so-called doctors' plot were declared innocent. The number of members of the collective leadership was reduced by one when Lavrenti Beria, long hated as chief of Stalin's secret police, was declared an enemy of the state, removed from power, and executed.

These events are indicative of the general relaxation of totalitarian control that followed Stalin's death. It can be argued that such a process was inevitable in order to secure support of party members and the people for the new regime. Nevertheless, few people in the Soviet Union or, for that matter, in the world were prepared for the wholesale rejection of the Stalinist years, which was to become the dominant theme of the latter 1950s. In pointing to these events and in marking their effect on Soviet ideology we have, for once, a rather clear benchmark—the Twentieth Party Congress of the CPSU held in February 1956.

If the period prior to the Twentieth Party Congress can be called the time of silent de-Stalinization, the congress marks the beginning of overt and vociferous de-Stalinization. The dominating theme of the entire congress was the errors of the former dictator. Beginning with speeches decrying Stalin's economic policies and censorship control, it culminated with Khrushchev's famous "secret speech" denouncing Stalin's cult in all of its manifestations. This congress has been called the most important one held since the time of Lenin, and from an ideological point of view that is correct. In the process of a wholesale renunciation of the Stalinist era, the collective leadership, dominated more and more by the figure of Nikita Khrushchev, adopted a series of policies which were, at least temporarily, to alter the face of Soviet communism. More important, Khrushchev's return to the principles of Leninism would establish a precedent for Mikhail Gorbachev's more contemporary attempts of defining the appropriate paths to achieving socialism. For our purposes we can once again summarize these changes using the categories of domestic and international reforms.

Denunciation of Stalin

The most far-reaching alteration in internal policy was the rejection of the one-person leadership, which had been the cornerstone of Stalin's personal dictatorship. Khrushchev portrayed Stalin to the party elite as a man with a mania for absolute control who presided over the slaughter of millions of loyal citizens only to gratify his desire for personal power.

> Lenin's traits—patient work with people; stubborn and painstaking education of them; the ability to induce people to follow him without compulsion, . . . were entirely foreign to Stalin. He [Stalin] discarded the Leninist method of convincing and educating; he abandoned the method of ideological struggle for that of administrative violence, mass repressions, and terror.[4]

Stalin was painted as the perverter of the Soviet state, an incompetent military strategist who refused to take seriously evidence of Hitler's plans to invade the Soviet Union, a butcher who forced the Soviet people to conform to his personal whims in matters as far ranging as architecture and economics. Quoting from Lenin's last testament, Khrushchev contrasted the democratic party of Lenin's day with the autocratic rule of Stalin, declaring the latter to have betrayed the goals of Bolshevism. One could go on, but it is enough to note here that this remarkable speech constituted a renunciation of the Stalinist regime and demanded a return to the true principles of Leninism. This ostracism of Stalin was symbolically represented some five years later when the party voted to remove Stalin's body from its hallowed burial place alongside the still godlike Lenin in the Red Square mausoleum.

All leaders of the Soviet Union were under considerable ideological pressure to demonstrate how their regime is progressing toward the goal of socialism. To this end the Soviet Union published Lenin's official works in fifty-five volumes, Stalin's in thirteen, Khrushchev's in eight and Leonid Brezhnev's in nine. In the 1930s Stalin declared that "the dictatorship of the proletariat," introduced by Lenin, had been surpassed. Following this example, both Khrushchev and then Brezhnev felt the need to show their contribution to what Khrushchev called the "comprehensive building of communism." In the early 1960s Khrushchev declared exuberantly that "the present generation will live under communism!" With Khrushchev's political demise in 1964, the new leadership carefully retreated from this wildly ambitious claim to a more modest one of achieving "developed socialism"—a "stage on the road to communism." The Brezhnev leadership emphasized the prolonged and gradual nature of the transition process: The goal was the same as Khrushchev's, only the pace of implementation was slowed considerably.

---

[4] English translation of Khrushchev speech to the Twentieth Party Congress on February 25, 1956, released by the U.S. State Department on June 4, 1956.

Khrushchev also helped initiate the process of the gradual *democratization* of the political system by expanding the degree of participation in the state. From the late 1950s the Soviet councils were revitalized in order to elevate their role in economic and cultural development. This, it was believed, would further demonstrate the progress toward communism, by beginning the process of the "withering away" of the state: The Soviets would eventually cease to be organs of state power and would become organs of self-administration. Further attempts at reform on the domestic front saw the cautious institution of some additional types of decentralization in decision making and a gradual movement away from Stalin's emphasis on heavy industry in the economy. Once the Stalinist censorship system was loosened, all types of criticisms of his regime began to appear in print. All of these measures contributed to the period that is generally called the "thaw," a gradual movement away from the total political control of the previous era. We must note, however, that the type of criticism that emerged in the party after Stalin's death has to be taken in context. Stalin was condemned for denying the principles of Leninism and perverting the role of the party in building a socialist society. There was never any public doubt about those principles, or more important, about the ultimate control of the party as the carrier of revolutionary consciousness. Krushchev's rule, then, helped establish a liberalization of considerable magnitude when contrasted with the previous twenty-five years, and in a groping, limited way it was a return to some of the principles of Leninism.

Changes in the International Movement

In the international sphere the same general relaxation of control occurred, but here it had much more far-reaching consequences for Marxist-Leninist theory. Almost immediately after Stalin's death the collective leadership began making overtures to Yugoslavia's Marshal Tito in an effort to bring his country back into the international movement. Tito had been expelled from that movement in 1948 for refusing to follow Moscow's line in international affairs and for numerous heresies on the economic front. Even during the last years of Stalin's reign it had become obvious that Tito was not going to knuckle under to Moscow, and that the only way the monolithic facade of international communism might be preserved would be by invading Yugoslavia. Short of this, Tito's brand of socialism might be seen as an attempt to apply the principles of Marx and Lenin under circumstances different from those in the Soviet Union and his experiment applauded as another way to build a socialist society.

Stalin could not possibly have taken such a position for at least two reasons. First, it would have denied Stalin's control of the international movement. Second, and perhaps more important, it would have challenged the Stalinist interpretation of Marxism-Leninism, which, as we saw earlier, held that while there could be a Marxist-Leninist-*Stalinist* view of the world there could not be—at the same point in history—an equally valid Marxist-Leninist-*Titoist* theory. Since Stalin could not control Tito, the latter must be declared illegitimate! Stalin's successors had no such qualms and saw a rapprochement with Yugoslavia as one method of establishing their legitimacy as rulers of the international movement.

Thus, in May 1955, a high-level delegation headed by Khrushchev went to Belgrade in an attempt to patch over grievances between the two countries and discovered that Tito was as adamant as ever about pursuing his own course. All that could be done was to recognize Tito and the Yugoslavian Communist Party as legitimate socialists and declare that their regime was striving for the same basic goals as the USSR. Once it was admitted that there might be ways to achieve socialism that were different from the Soviet pattern, a host of possibilities presented themselves. At the Twentieth Party Congress, Khrushchev and several other speakers formally proclaimed the doctrine of *different paths to socialism,* which struck the final blow to Stalin's monolithic facade. Appealing with justification to the writings of Marx and Lenin, the speakers declared that there were numerous ways a socialist society might be achieved. At least three different paths were recognized: (1) the traditional Soviet revolution model (which, by this point, had been idealized into an urban proletarian revolution), (2) a nationalist-oriented partisan army type (like Tito's and to some degree Mao Zedong's), and (3) a peaceful, electoral revolution. While the last might seem to be a vast departure from the Leninist approach to the doctrine, we must recall that Marx himself admitted of the possibility of a parliamentary revolution in a country like England. Since it appeared that Moscow had given up its monolithic control of the international movement, reactions to this new policy were almost immediate.

The combination of de-Stalinization and the rehabilitation of Marshal Tito's brand of socialism triggered revolutionary changes throughout the communist world. This was particularly the case in Stalinist satellite countries of Eastern Europe where reformist groups began clamoring for radical changes. The agitation culminated in the summer of 1956 when workers' strikes erupted in Poland and, with ominous overtones, a new government in Hungary proclaimed itself in favor of a whole series of reforms including free speech and a type of multiparty system. The new leadership in Moscow was losing control: Prepared to make mild reforms in Stalin's policies, its actions had produced a revolutionary situation. Faced with the crumbling of empire in Eastern Europe and growing liberalization at home, it acted swiftly and decisively. The Hungarian regime was crushed by an invading Red Army, many Stalinist control devices were reinstituted, and reaction set in within the USSR itself.

The announcement of different paths to socialism and the renunciation of complete control of the international movement had beset the Soviet leadership with a dilemma. If complete control from Moscow was no longer possible, or perhaps even desirable, did that mean that the Soviet Union was giving up its role as the leader of world socialism? Obviously it did not, and the question at the moment was *how much* deviation from Moscow's wishes was possible? How much independence could be tolerated? This remained one of the central problems for the USSR and resulted in a pendulum-like movement with respect to international communism—at one time the hard line, as in Hungary in 1956 or Czechoslovakia in 1968, at other times a toleration of experimentation or deviance within the movement, as in Eastern Europe in 1989. Of course, with 20/20 hindsight, it is possible to see this complex series of political actions and reactions to the loosening of centralized, dictatorial power after the death of Stalin as an intriguing prelude to the watershed events that unfolded in and around the Soviet Union after Leonid Brezhnev's death in 1982 and culminated with the relatively peaceful dismantling of the Soviet state on December 25, 1991—not exactly the "withering away" that Marx envisioned.

While we will return to this topic, for now a final ideological change that emerged from the Twentieth Party Congress and produced additional problems for modern Soviet communism needs to be discussed. This is the doctrine of *peaceful coexistence*.

The Doctrine of Peaceful Coexistence

It was a long-established Marxist tenet that communism was inevitably locked in an unceasing battle with the capitalist forces of oppression throughout the world. While the doctrine of socialism in one country and the alliance with Western capitalist powers during World War II can be seen as deviations from this general policy, on the ideological level the doctrine remained firm: constant struggle and the eventual triumph of worldwide communism. Although many of the other ideological changes of the Twentieth Party Congress could be justified as a return to Leninism, any change in this doctrine would be counter to the words of both Lenin and Marx, who foresaw unceasing wars during the capitalist phase. Still, the reality of Soviet foreign policy for many years had been the tacit acceptance of coexistence, and at times cooperation with the enemy.

To justify these actions, the leadership group now proclaimed that socialism had achieved sufficient power that it was no longer threatened with annihilation by the capitalist powers or, if it were, the outcome would be mutual annihilation. Modern weaponry, particularly the development of nuclear devices, made the prospect of all-out war between the two camps less than desirable. Thus, cooperation with the enemy was seen as necessary in the second half of the twentieth century. This did not, however, alter the basic premise of Marxism-Leninism that communism would eventually triumph. Peaceful coexistence was described as a change in tactics in that competition with the capitalists would be carried on in other ways. Later Khrushchev would declare that socialism would beat capitalism at its own game by outproducing it and achieving world economic domination. Further, the Leninist doctrine of imperialism was given greater emphasis, and small wars of national liberation in the Third World were seen as sapping the strength of the major capitalist powers. Given these alterations in tactics, it became perfectly consistent for Khrushchev to proclaim coexistence and cooperation on the one hand and to declare that socialism would bury capitalism on the other.

Nonetheless, the elevation of peaceful coexistence to the level of dogma displeased many loyal Marxists throughout the world. Indeed, as we shall see in the following chapter, it constituted one of the main ideological arguments between the Soviet Union and China. Many Western observers saw the doctrine of peaceful coexistence as the major symbol of a general deradicalization of Soviet Marxism, and there is some basis for this view. As a large and powerful nation-state, the USSR was bound to have a stake in preserving the status quo, irrespective of its ideology. Moreover, with the ouster of Khrushchev in 1964, the pace of ideological change came to a near halt during the next regime only to return to the fast track under the last of the Soviet premiers.

PERESTROIKA

If Khrushchev represented a liberalization of policy, the years of Leonid Brezhnev's leadership (1964–1982) were a conservative, bordering on reactionary, return to the slow-paced stability of the final Stalin years. Under Brezhnev a movement to rehabilitate Stalin made some progress, although it was blocked by many anti-Stalinists in power. Brezhnev returned the bureaucracy to its powerful position and attempted to transfer the concept of *vozhd* from the general secretary to the party itself. During his regime those individuals with *nomenklatura* status, that is, those holding important positions in the party or the state, or securing high-level party clearance for significant posts, comprised an elite who had access to special privileges and powers, including exclusive stores and spacious apartments. The daily lives of those with *nomenklatura* were so fundamentally different from the average Soviet citizen that it could be said that it was as if they lived in a different country. Toward the end of Brezhnev's life, corruption and lethargy seemed to pervade many facets of society.

It has been well said that during the Stalin years the "state swelled up, the people grew lean." This was certainly true in the Brezhnev years as well: And on the ideological level Brezhnev's achievements are even more lean than Stalin's. Ironically, Brezhnev nevertheless did create a political situation that seemed to both demand and permit the emergence of a dynamic, almost puritanical leader whose first task became awakening the Soviet Union from its slumber in cynicism, corruption, alcoholism, and moral decay.

Following the death of Brezhnev in November 1982, the Soviet Union underwent two rapid changes in party leadership with the deaths of Yuri Andropov in February 1984, and thirteen months later, Konstantin Chernenko. In March of 1985, Mikhail Sergeyevich Gorbachev, a lawyer and agronomist, became the youngest general secretary of the party since Stalin. More significantly, he ushered in a new phase in Soviet ideology with his demands for *perestroika*.

Perestroika, usually translated simply as restructuring, was both the central theme in Gorbachev's plans for the necessary economic, political, and psychological changes in the Soviet Union and the title of his widely read book. "*Perestroika* is a revolution," Gorbachev wrote, "and the most peaceful and democratic one at that."[5] In fact, it was a call for a total, cultural revolution that was to affect not only the economic and political structures but also the very individuals who comprised the Soviet Union; it was to affect not only the elites of the State and the party but also the entire population down to the lowest individual. Gorbachev explained that "The greatest difficulty in our restructuring effort lies in our thinking, which has been molded over the past years. Everyone, from general secretary to worker, has

[5] Mikhail Gorbachev, *Perestroika: New Thinking for Our Country and the World* (New York: Harper & Row, Publishers, 1987), p. 74.

to alter this thinking. . . . We have to overcome our own conservatism." Clearly, this change in attitudes, in consciousness, would have to be total, starting with *perestroika* of oneself. Economic and political structures must be restructured; so too must individuals: "I can see from my own experience that all of us are changing in the course of *perestroika*. It would be unfair to deny someone the right to experience their own *perestroika*."[6]

Gorbachev skillfully returned to the glorious moments in Soviet history, especially the NEP days of Bukharin and Lenin, to gain legitimacy for his own ideas. Initially the need for *perestroika*, seen and developed by the party elite, took on the attributes of a "revolution from above," a troubling image from Stalin's early days. However, *perestroika's* success, Gorbachev explained, depended upon it ultimately becoming a "revolution from below." As *perestroika* gained energy from the "grass-roots" activities, it would take on a dynamic of its own. He believed that if he could gain the support of the masses by drawing them into the decision-making processes of both production and politics, what he called the "democratization of all aspects of society," he would succeed in "guarantee[ing] that the current processes are irreversible."[7] In a very real sense, then, one of Gorbachev's tasks as the leader of *perestroika* was to ensure that he, as leader, "withered away." Unintentionally, he succeeded in bringing about this end but not by the means he desired—a point to be returned to later.

While the subtitle of Gorbachev's treatise on *Perestroika—New Thinking for Our Country and the World*—emphasized the human subjective dimension to *perestroika*, there is little doubt that Gorbachev failed to appreciate the monumental objective factors standing in his way. While the Soviet Union's economic achievements since the end of its civil war were, in quantitative terms, impressive, the quality, variety, and distribution of consumer goods were notoriously poor. The problem of goods and services was twofold: First, the average citizen lacked the money to purchase desired goods and when they had the money, the goods were simply not available for purchase.

Shortly after assuming the position of general secretary, Gorbachev addressed a large audience of local party officials in Leningrad. While criticizing the waste and inefficiency of the economy, he paused and told his audience, "You know what the trouble is? You don't feel it here [as he tapped his pockets and jangled his coins]. . . . And it's about time you did!"[8] Returning to many of the ideas behind the NEP programs of the now fully rehabilitated Bukharin, Gorbachev repealed many of the state regulations which prohibited individual economic initiative, created an enormous black market, and like prohibition in the United States turned millions of citizens into lawbreakers. Scores of different kinds of small, private enterprises were legalized: Of the two lawful categories, one was based on individuals, the other on cooperatives. While neither category was permitted to hire labor, they could employ family members, retired persons,

---

[6] Ibid., p. 65.

[7] Ibid., p. 32.

[8] Martin Walker, *The Waking Giant: Gorbachev's Russia* (New York: Pantheon Books, 1986), p. xvi.

housewives, students, and other citizens. The cooperatives involved groups of individuals who shared in the proceeds from the services provided, for example, restaurants and taxi services.

This utilization of positive incentives and market mechanisms led some in the West to argue that the Soviets were finally recognizing capitalism as a more efficient and dynamic mode of production and one that they too must adopt. This assessment was premature. It confused using economic incentives and limited markets with capitalism. While Gorbachev had promised an end to the authoritarian, bureaucratic system of strict planning through administrative edicts, this was not synonymous with establishing capitalism. In *Perestroika* the historic goals of the USSR were reaffirmed: The Soviets were continuing the process of building a society based on the communist principle "From each according to his or her ability, to each according to his or her needs." Yet Gorbachev finally acknowledged that the USSR was generations away from realizing that goal. In the transition period, he hoped that the distribution principle of socialism, "From each according to his or her ability, to each according to his or her work," would become firmly established, thereby allowing individuals to earn the extra income they desired as well as help build the economic base needed for the ultimate transition to communism.

To further ensure the opening, or liberalization, of society Gorbachev advocated an emphasis on the "rule of law," extending its protection of the individual against the state. To this end, he initiated a discussion of the desirability of implementing into the criminal code the Western idea of "presumed innocent until proven guilty" and pushed for the even more sweeping legal notion that "everything which is not prohibited by the law is allowed."[9] (These two concepts comprise Articles 49 and 34 of the present [1993] *Constitution of the Russian Federation.*) Under both Stalin and to a lesser degree Brezhnev, the obverse of this notion was the norm; that is, unless the law specifically permitted a particular behavior, the legality of the behavior was questionable. Obviously, this led to self-censorship and stifled individual creativity. Moreover, it was precisely individualism, the "liberal" individualism of Marx and Engels, which Gorbachev argued had been one of the casualties of a misconceived collectivism. Gorbachev's position of valuing both individualism and freedom encouraged widespread and divergent approaches to all facets of life. (This approach, we shall momentarily see, spilled over into the international arena.) It is no small wonder that the intellectual, professional, and artistic sectors of society enthusiastically supported his programs, hoping that this return to the ethos of Lenin's final weeks would this time become permanently entrenched into the nation's consciousness.

To Gorbachev, the success of *perestroika* was dependent upon the idea of *glasnost,* or openness. Consequently, he quickly adopted the concept of *glasnost* into his own policies: "We need *glasnost* as we need air." Like *perestroika, glasnost* is an attitude, a cultural norm, which had to become internalized by the bureaucracy and the population if it were to succeed. Not only would this further encourage individual initiative, but it would also encourage "criticism and self-criticism" of

[9] Grobachev, *Perestroika,* p. 108.

individuals, history, and the entire social system.[10] Even Lenin's thought, once considered sacred ground beyond questioning, became the object of reinterpretation by Gorbachev. On several occasions, Gorbachev maintained that in spite of a common misunderstanding, Lenin never possessed a concrete, detailed, specific program of action designed to lead the Soviet Union from feudalism to socialism. Consequently, it was important to look to Lenin's writings as a guide, not a blueprint, to future action; it was the spirit, not the letter, of Lenin's ideas that provided fruitful insights to individuals and the party.

In this spirit of *glasnost,* Gorbachev ordered the publication, without commentary, of the proceedings of the "Central Committee" of the party. Gorbachev also exposed, for the first time to the average Soviet citizen, Stalin's crimes and criticized actions of some of the more recent Soviet leaders, among them Leonid Brezhnev and the once powerful Andre Gromyko, the last of the Soviet elite to have direct connections to Stalin's regime. In an economic and political milieu where corruption had come dangerously close to being considered "standard operating procedure," encouraging the truth and exposing criminal corruption certainly aided in weakening the bureaucracy and increasing the public perception that massive change was sweeping into all segments of the society, even into the party itself. Although Gorbachev believed that the party itself had to undergo *perestroika,* he initially made it clear that he envisioned the revitalized party remaining as the sole "political vanguard" of the newly liberated society. But this was not to be.

The multiple electoral processes—in the workplace, the party, and the state—opened up politics by including choices among candidates in contested elections. In the first elections to the newly created Congress of People's Deputies, several high-ranking party officials were defeated by alternative candidates. Among the most publicized of these defeats centered around former Moscow party boss Boris Yeltsin who ran on a platform calling for a more rapid pace to *perestroika,* an end to corruption, and the elimination of the *nomenklatura* system. But not all party candidates were defeated by rival candidates; some were simply rejected by the voters who chose to strike the unopposed candidate's name off the ballot. This legal action on the part of Soviet voters constituted an interesting, and potentially very powerful, political option, one which even liberal democratic governments do not normally provide for their citizens. When Soviet citizens crossed off the ballot the name of a candidate for office, they were in effect voting for "none of the above"; if a significant number of voters—under the appropriate circumstances—exercised this option, it could call into question the legitimacy of any political system.

Gorbachev also called for a two-term limit on all offices, including the general secretary of the party and the then newly created office of "president." Along these innovative lines, he argued for a clearer division between the party and the State and attempted to create a strong, independent judiciary. Significantly, after preliminary discussions among some of the party elite had taken place on the possibility of an official multiparty system, Gorbachev specifically rejected this idea and continued to endorse the necessity of remaining a single-party state. However,

---

[10] Ibid., pp. 78–79.

given the logic and dynamics of *perestroika*, the degree of pluralism and openness that had already developed inside the Soviet Union and throughout much of Eastern Europe, it was but a matter of time until multiparty politics became a *de facto* reality that would turn into a legal reality. Some ideas, after all, take on a power of their own. In March of 1990, under his leadership, the Congress of Peoples' Deputies abolished the party's constitutionally guaranteed monopoly of political power and thereby paved the way for legalizing alternative parties.

Glasnost also improved the Soviets' standing in the international arena. Here, too, Gorbachev revived some old themes and initiated a few new ones. He returned to Khrushchev's doctrine of peaceful coexistence and to Lenin's position that there exists a "priority of interests common to all humanity over class interests," which, in a nuclear age, took on new meaning. "With the emergence of weapons of mass, that is, universal destruction," wrote Gorbachev, "there appeared an objective limit for class confrontation in the international arena: the threat of universal destruction."[11] Chemical, biological, and nuclear technologies of death made it clear to him that humanity was at a turning point: For the first time in history "mankind had lost its immortality."[12] To this end, Gorbachev initiated substantial cuts in the Soviet military as, in part, a good-faith gesture on the need for universal arms reduction and his commitment to peaceful coexistence.

Furthermore, the Soviets acknowledged that there were different paths to "development," and "a nation may choose either capitalism or socialism. This is its sovereign right."[13] The theme of national self-determination runs throughout Gorbachev's thought. Given recent past events in Afghanistan, Poland, and Czechoslovakia under Brezhnev, it took considerable courage for some of the so-called Soviet bloc nations to test the limits of this possibility even if Gorbachev appeared to be inviting it. Indeed, Gorbachev linked himself with the famous "Prague Spring" of 1968 by condemning the Soviet reaction to it and calling for "socialism with a human face" for his own Soviet Union. Major political changes throughout Europe developed—at first, slowly, but then gaining unstoppable momentum. Gorbachev encouraged and endorsed these changes in the international arena and became the central figure in ending the Cold War. He seized every opportunity to support communist reform movements in Eastern European countries. When the communist regimes there collapsed, he both accepted their demise and agreed to a phased withdrawal of Soviet troops from those countries. He agreed to the reunification of East and West Germany and even assented to the new Germany joining NATO. For his monumental efforts, Gorbachev was awarded the 1990 Nobel Peace Prize.

Nevertheless, in terms of ideology with regard to the West, Gorbachev's position, "that we respect the right of the people of the U.S., as well as that of any other people, to live according to their own rules and laws, customs and tastes," must be appropriately understood.[14] Like any Marxist-Leninist, Gorbachev still believed in

[11] Ibid., pp. 145–46.
[12] Ibid., p. 138.
[13] Ibid., p. 143.
[14] Ibid., p. 12.

Lenin's theory of imperialism. "Western states continue to collect neocolonialist 'tribute.' Over the past decade alone, the profits U.S. corporations have siphoned off from the developing countries have quadrupled investments."[15] But confronted by the reality of the nuclear age, tragically felt by the Soviets at Chernobyl, where in Europe alone there exists hundreds of nuclear power plants and countless chemical manufacturers, the option of war—conventional or nuclear—was ruled out of the question by Gorbachev. While the Soviets would continue to support the liberation struggles of colonial peoples, these "wars of national liberation" would now be fought on the economic, political, and cultural levels. Moreover, Gorbachev's confidence in the scientific basis of socialism remained unshaken: In the long run, "if we adhere to its basic principles, if we take fully into consideration human interests and the use of benefits of a planned economy, socialism can achieve much more than capitalism."[16] And ultimately, capitalism would fall. Still, a class war between these two systems could be fought out only in nonmilitary ways: Nuclear war would truly be the "end of history." Gorbachev furthermore understood that the potential for ecological disaster also linked humanity in its common threat to total extinction: "We are all passengers aboard one ship, the Earth, and we must not allow it to be wrecked. There will be no second Noah's Ark."[17]

Gorbachev inherited not only the lethargy and corruption of the Brezhnev era, but all the political problems confronting the leader of a vast country which spans five time zones and is comprised of different nationalities and ethnic groups, each with its own history and culture. In fact, *glasnost*—an ideal most Americans assume all individuals want—remained a foreign notion to some of these groups who found it threatening to their very being; hence, Gorbachev encountered strong resistance to *perestroika* among ethnic and national groups inside his own country. Gorbachev tried to draw a distinction—which in theory if not practice was perfectly consistent with the notion of different paths to socialism—between what was appropriate behavior for foreign governments in their own territory and what was permissible action inside the Soviet Union. Gorbachev was willing to permit complete autonomy outside, but not inside, the USSR. Domestically, he willingly dismantled the totalitarian political dimensions to the Soviet state in his movement toward a more representative democratic system, but refused to move as quickly in giving up state control of the economic system. In vain, he struggled to find an economic middle ground that had attributes of both a (nonexploitive) free enterprise system and a command economy. Nevertheless, the Soviet economy deteriorated rapidly and so too did Gorbachev's political power and influence.

On August 18, 1991, members of the famous Soviet KGB entered Gorbachev's summer dacha and placed him under house arrest; simultaneously and characteristically, the KGB announced that Gorbachev had to resign for health reasons and that a self-appointed group called the Extraordinary Commission (composed of communist hard-liners) would be running the country. This coup was short lived, crumbling just days after it started. Although the reasons for its failure

---

[15] Ibid., p.171.

[16] Ibid., p. 86.

[17] Ibid., p. 12.

are numerous and beyond the scope of this discussion, two must be singled out. First, the coup's backers failed to realize the genuinely radical political and social transformation that had already occurred under Gorbachev. While Gorbachev had run out of history before he could reach any substantive economic reforms, it was no small measure of the success of *perestroika* and *glasnost* that the return to old-style, Soviet politics-by-coup failed miserably. Bureaucratic authoritarianism had already been delegimized to a significant degree. Second, while the coup's leaders vacillated, Boris Yeltsin seized the day. Yeltsin, who had been handpicked in 1985 by Gorbachev to help him clean out corruption in the Moscow party, had become an open critic of Gorbachev and called for a market economy and multiparty politics. He quit the Communist party in 1990 and, over Gorbachev's opposition, was the first directly elected president of the Russian republic. Nevertheless, when word of the coup reached Yeltsin, he defied the Extraordinary Committee by organizing resistance in Moscow and demanding the return of Gorbachev to power.

From the beginning of Gorbachev's rule, there appeared to be a split in the Soviet system between the center, where *glasnost* and *perestroika* were widely embraced, and the periphery, where they failed to penetrate beneath the surface and where conservatives controlled the local machines. While a majority of the provinces may have supported the coup, its fate was determined in the cities, where it was defeated. Gorbachev was returned to office, but his power had all but evaporated. He too quit the Communist party, helped strip it of control over the military and secret police, and moved to shift political power to the constituent republics of the union. The Russian government under Yeltsin, the *vozhd* apparent, assumed the power of the collapsing Soviet state as the various republics agreed to form a new commonwealth under Yeltsin's leadership. It is not without irony that Gorbachev elected to resign his presidency and at the same moment mark the end of the Union of Soviet Socialist Republics on December 25, 1991.

Perestroika was a profound revolution. Its significance has already far surpassed that of 1917 in terms of importance for not only the former Soviet Union but the entire world as well. Whatever the final verdict on Mikhail Sergeyevich Gorbachev, as a direct result of his ideas, the world again shook.

Boris Yeltsin and Post-Soviet Marxism

With Gorbachev out of the political picture—free to write books, give lectures, and receive honors from the West while fate ensured he also had to endure the disdain, disgust, and animosity of his homeland—all eyes turned to the new leader. Yeltsin grabbed the international spotlight and assumed leadership of Russia and the crumbling Soviet Union from the moment when he dramatically stood atop a tank in front of the Russian White House and defied the leaders of the August coup. Perhaps it was the euphoria of this enormous success that led him to believe that as *vozhd* he could accomplish anything. With what seems to have been astonishing naiveté, he took sweeping steps designed not simply to continue the transition to democracy but to create instant capitalism. To this specific end, he adopted Western counsel and introduced an economic program known as "shock therapy." It called for the freeing of all prices, the stabilization of the currency, and the privatization of most of the state property. The consequences for many Russians were catastrophic. Hyperinflation wiped out the life savings of most citizens, the currency remained destabilized, and a handful of Russians (now called the Oligarchs) made a financial killing on privatization while most never knew what had happened. The Russian economy continued its downward spiral. By 1993, Russia seemed on the verge of civil war. In September, Yeltsin dismissed the Congress of People's Deputies who then retaliated by declaring Yeltsin's presidency null and void, one of several attempts to oust him. On October 3, in response to an attempted takeover of the main television station and mayor's office in Moscow, Yeltsin returned again to the Russian White House, but this time he ordered a military assault on it that left more than 150 people dead—a chilling example of Marx's observation on historic events repeating themselves, sometimes as tragedy, other times as farce.

While Yeltsin was able to solidify his power and succeeded in implementing the new (1993) constitution that gave the presidency considerable power, his personal power was waning as shock therapy seemed to be a cure far worse than the disease. On New Year's Eve 1999, in a startling move reminiscent of Gorbachev's Christmas *dénouement* less than a decade earlier, Yeltsin humbly addressed the nation on television. He announced his immediate resignation of the presidency, turned over all presidential power to Vladimir Putin, the person he handpicked to be Prime Minister less than six months earlier, and asked Russians to forgive him for failing to fulfill their dreams. In spite of this peaceful transition of power, it may well be temporary as acting-president Putin faces an impending election.

At the beginning of the twenty-first century, then, Russia continues to flounder in an ocean of political uncertainty, economic decay, and social unrest. Putin's immediate popularity will be helpful, but if he is to succeed he too must deal with the many groups contending for power: The Russian Communist Party, made up of pre-Gorbachev people, is the most organized group, but viable nationalist and fascist parties of the extreme right are also contending for power along with the Liberals, the Oligarchs, and the military. Meanwhile, as the economic situation deteriorates, social unrest rises, resentment of the West increases, and all too many observers have noted the eerie parallels with Germany after the First World War. Perhaps the only lesson that can be drawn at this moment is that whatever the virtues of capitalism as a social system, it cannot be adopted in a non-liberal, political culture overnight. Capitalism, over the span of many generations, slowly developed in the West, causing massive, often painful changes in that way of life wherever it embedded itself; capitalism can neither be simply legislated nor imposed on a culture to which it is foreign.

We have made only a small attempt to spell out the more recent twists and turns of Soviet-*cum*-Russian politics, largely in the belief that without the perspective afforded by history it is extraordinarily difficult to know when such alterations are merely temporary. But for more than sixty years, Soviet Marxism produced numerous and far-reaching changes in Marxist-Leninist ideology. All Soviet leaders felt the necessity of showing their personal allegiance to the ideological demands of progress toward the Marxian goal culture: Lenin introduced the "dictatorship of proletariat"; Stalin the "building of socialism"; Khrushchev the "comprehensive building of communism"; Brezhnev the more elegant "developed socialism"; and finally, Gorbachev's *perestroika*. Still, one could argue that prior to Gorbachev the broad outlines of Marxism-Leninism remained fairly intact and that the alterations made by the other leaders of the USSR had been merely tactical adaptations to fit changing political circumstances. But *perestroika* changed that forever.

Many Western leaders proclaimed the failure of the Soviet experiment as the end of Marxism. We think not. That the Soviet Union did not reach its goals could be attributed to many factors, some of which had little to do with Marxism. Whatever that case, many Western Marxists and post-Marxists believe that the collapse of the Soviet Union was anything but a disaster, indeed, it may well be the best thing to have ever happened to Marxism! Now that the Soviet experiment is over, Marxism can be liberated from its immediate, albeit inappropriate, exclusive association with Stalinism and economic disaster; this would make it possible for new generations to approach Marx's analysis of alienation and class struggle under capitalism without the negative associations of this experiment. And, as our contemporary, interdependent global marketplace continues to mirror a Marxian analysis, who knows what effect Marxist ideas may have this time.

We have now completed the discussion of the Soviet experiment of attempting to put into practice its understanding of Marxism-Leninism, but other leaders, other countries, have seen fit to interpret the doctrines differently. Thus, we will now turn our attention to a discussion of a central issue in modern communism—the existence of another major interpreter of Marxism-Leninism who claimed that much of the history of Soviet Marxism involved a perversion of the original doctrine. We will now examine the political thought of Mao Zedong.

SUGGESTED READINGS

COHEN, STEPHEN, *Bukharin and the Bolshevik Revolution.* New York: Vintage Books, 1975.

———, *Rethinking the Soviet Experience.* New York: Oxford University Press, 1985.

DEUTSCHER, ISAAC, *Stalin: A Political Biography.* New York: Random House, 1960.

GORBACHEV, MIKHAIL, *Perestroika: New Thinking for Our Country and the World.* New York: Harper & Row, Publishers, 1987.

HOUGH, JERRY, *The Soviet Prefects: The Local Party Organs in Industrial Decision-Making.* Cambridge, Mass.: Harvard University Press, 1969.

MARCUSE, HERBERT, *Soviet Marxism.* New York: Random House, 1961.

MERLEAU-PONTY, MAURICE, *Humanism and Terror: An Essay on the Communist Problem,* trans. John O'Neill. Boston: Beacon Press, 1969.

STALIN, JOSIF, "The Foundations of Leninism," in *Essential Works of Marxism*, Arthur P. Mendel, ed. New York: Bantam Books, 1961.

TROTSKY, LEON, *The Revolution Betrayed.* New York: Merit Publications, 1937.

TUCKER, ROBERT, *Political Culture and Leadership in Soviet Russia.* New York: W. W. Norton & Company, 1987.

WALKER, MARTIN, *The Waking Giant: Gorbachev's Russia.* New York: Pantheon Books, 1986.

8

Chinese *Praxis:* The Political Thought of Mao Zedong

. . . a revolution is not a dinner party, or writing an essay, or painting a picture, or doing embroidery; it cannot be so refined, so leisurely and gentle, so temperate, kind, courteous, restrained and magnanimous. A revolution is an insurrection, an act of violence.

Mao Zedong

CHINESE MARXISM

Although Lenin's theory of imperialism prepared us for the phenomenon of a Marxist revolution in a Third World country, the notions of either Chinese Marxism or "socialism with Chinese characteristics" still seem a bit strange from a European perspective. Indeed, the transplanting of a technologically based Western European ideology in an agrarian-based Asian culture has produced some interesting and unique results, as should be expected. Certainly, if either the United States or Canada would become socialist, each nation would bring to socialism its own, *sui generis,* national characteristics. Having said this, one must still admit that the total impression of Chinese Marxism, at least while Mao lived, is quite consistent with the basic doctrine of classical Marxism-Leninism, and the political thought of Mao Zedong can be seen as a logical outgrowth of those doctrines. Indeed, even the recent reforms inside China have been carried out in the name of Marxism-Leninism and Mao Zedong Thought. Of course, China is not the only example of Marxism in an Asian setting—or for that matter—in a lesser developed country. It is, however, an early example of Marxism in a non-European culture. Moreover, in the figure and Thought of Mao Zedong we encounter a major contributor to the evolution of Marxism. In general, Mao's contribution to theory has come in the form of tactical application. Yet, given the Marxist notion of *praxis,* the unity of theory and action, it is easy to understand how Mao's innovations have had a profound effect on expanding the applicability of Marxism-Leninism.

The mere presence of a figure like Mao Zedong presents a host of difficulties. Much as in the case of Stalin, Mao's writings have been edited and changed at various times in order to establish his credentials as a major Marxist theoretician. As recently as 1977 the Chinese Communist Party (CCP) published the fifth, and perhaps final, volume of the *Selected Works of Mao;* this volume included only articles and speeches from 1949 to 1959, thus ignoring his more radical and politically threatening thoughts which led up to the now officially infamous Cultural Revolution. Nevertheless, his thoughts on even the most prosaic matters at times were treated by the Chinese as absolute dogma and elevated to the position of commands of God. To Western minds some of his thoughts seem silly, if not simply absurd. Still, there is little doubt that the figure of Mao Zedong loomed large not only in China but also on the international scene. During a time when the rising aspirations of the so-called Third World produced widespread instability and revolution, the Mao-led Chinese revolution became a major symbol of success.

To communists troubled by the apathy of the proletariat in highly developed capitalist countries, Mao's model of a successful revolution in an underdeveloped country was a source of hope for the future of international communism. To Western capitalists, the spread of Chinese influence under Mao appeared to be one of the major obstacles to world peace. Consequently, it is understandable that Westerners have found the new, post-Mao Chinese leadership's more open-door policy toward capitalism to be a welcome change. Still, if assessments of Mao differ, all groups could agree on his importance and on the details of his colorful life.

The Life of Mao Zedong

Born December 26, 1893, in Shaoshan, a village in the south China province of Hunan, Mao was the eldest child of a peasant family. He spent most of the first twenty-five years of his life in this area. Although his father was reported to be a demanding, authoritarian figure, his industriousness allowed Mao the freedom to pursue a classical education in a local village. From 1901 to 1906 Mao attended primary school in his district. At the age of 14, the family arranged Mao's marriage to a local girl; never living together, Mao repudiated the marriage. At the age of 17, Mao entered the Tungshan Higher Primary School. There he became interested in politics while participating in the Chinese Revolution of 1911. The revolution ended the Manchu dynasty, established the Republic of China under the short-lived, provisional government of Sun Zhongshan (Sun Yat-sen, 1866–1925), and initiated a prolonged period of political instability and warlordism. Following this initial brush with revolution, Mao returned to his studies, spending the next five years in the equivalent of a local college. In 1919 Mao took part in the May 4 Movement—an intellectually led reaction to the provisions of the Versailles Treaty, which left Japan in control of the former German concessions in Shandong; this developed into a boycott of Japanese goods when industrial and craft workers joined the scholarly community in political action. Shortly thereafter Mao embraced Marxism and participated in the First Congress of the CCP in 1921.

It was during the 1920s that Mao, on his own initiative, discovered, investigated, and helped develop the revolutionary potential of the peasants. The revolutionary potential of the peasants was so great that it is not too much to claim that, from Mao's perspective, they became the single most important force in altering China. As Mao put it in his famous 1927 *Report on Investigation of the Peasant Movement in Hunan:*

> In a very short time, in China's central, southern and northern provinces, several hundred million peasants will rise like a mighty storm, like a hurricane, a force so swift and violent that no power, however great, will be able to hold it back.[1]

The year 1927 witnessed two other crucial events in Mao's life. The disastrous Autumn Harvest Uprising in Hunan made Mao a wanted fugitive who was forced to seek refuge in the countryside. There he successfully established a revolutionary base in the Chingkang Mountains. These early years of struggle culminated in 1934–1935 when Mao, his movement facing imminent destruction, led the remaining 100,000 adherents of the Chinese Communist Party on the famous Long March some 6,000 miles north from Jiangxi to Yanan. Many of the leadership but less than 20,000 of the rank and file survived the arduous ordeal of the march. The

---

[1] Mao Zedong, *Selected Works of Mao Tse-tung.* 4 Vols. (Peking: People's Publishing House, 1960), Vol. 1, p. 23.

Long March became a symbol of Mao's and the party's commitment to struggle against tremendous odds, and, as we shall see, that concept of struggle was to become one of the most important parts of Mao's later teachings.

Throughout China's war with Japan (1937–1945), Mao continued to struggle and build a support base in north China, this time fighting against both the Kuomintang (KMT), under the leadership of the American-supported Jiang Jieshi (Chiang Kai-shek), and the invading Japanese—even though the KMT was supposed to be in an alliance (called the United Front) with the CCP. Near the conclusion of the war, the Seventh Party Congress of the CCP in 1945 adopted the Thought of Mao Zedong as the official guide in all party work. The decade symbolically ended on October 1, 1949, when Mao, standing high atop Tiananmen, the Gate of Heavenly Peace in Beijing (Peking), proclaimed the founding of the People's Republic of China, which he would serve as the first chairman. Thus, like Lenin, Mao can be considered the father of the revolution as well as the founder of his nation's first united modern state. Until his death in 1976, Mao continued to act as a crucial force in the evolution of China. Indeed, few individuals have had as profound an impact, in both thought and deed, on the modern world. Mao's continuing influence on China's development will depend, as in the past, on the role played by his ideas—the Thought of Mao Zedong.

Imperialism and Mao's Rural Strategy

China's 600 million people have two remarkable peculiarities; they are, first of all, poor, and secondly, blank. That may seem like a bad thing, but it is really a good thing. Poor people want change, want to do things, want revolution. A clean sheet of paper has no blotches, and so the newest and most beautiful words can be written on it, the newest and most beautiful pictures can be painted on it.[2]

It has often been said that China provided a nearly perfect test case for the Leninist theory of imperialism. Here was a country that had long dominated its neighbors, both militarily and culturally, only to succumb to the superior technology and military strength of colonial European powers. The beginning of the twentieth century saw China subservient in every sense of the word; the country had been carved up into spheres of interest by Western imperialists and subjected to the machinations of great-power politics. Faced with this condition of impotence, some Chinese saw a solution in the wholesale importation of Western technology and culture, others in the return to the basic strength of a superior Chinese culture. Given what we know of the process of cultural transformation and rejuvenation, it was perhaps inevitable that certain Western values were imported and altered to fit traditional Chinese patterns. Prime among those Western idea systems was Marxism.

Throughout its early days, the Chinese Communist Party operated as if the classical proletariat model of a Marxian revolution had a direct application to

---

[2] Quoted in Stuart R. Schram, ed., *The Political Thought of Mao Tse-tung*, rev. ed. (New York: Praeger Publishers, 1969), p. 352.

China. Efforts were largely concentrated on recruiting members of the working class, and organizational work was primarily in the larger cities. While Lenin's example in the Soviet revolution made the establishment of *peasant cadres* possible as well, there was no question in Lenin's mind that the proletariat retained its role as the leading element in revolutionary activity. Mao Zedong, although he was of peasant background, originally adhered rather strictly to the classical line advocating an urban-based, essentially proletarian revolution. Indeed, his peasant background initially made him quite skeptical of revolutionary action on the part of the Chinese peasantry, a position closer to Marx than Lenin. Further than that, the urban-based activities of the Chinese Communist Party were at odds with the revolutionary advice emanating from Moscow—advice which emphasized the central role of the peasant class in underdeveloped countries. Lenin and later Stalin both declared the peasantry to be a prime asset in revolutionary activity in China. Although it is difficult to date precisely, Mao's position on this matter apparently began to change during 1925, and the change became decisive in 1927 with his report on peasant activities in Hunan Province.

In his report on the Hunan peasants, Mao emphasized that most of the revolutionary activity in the province was being carried out by the poor peasants and that in the future they would play the major role in the Chinese revolution. So vast and mighty did Mao find the peasants as a revolutionary force, that he described to his party only three alternatives: The party could march at the head of the peasants and lead them, trail behind them, gesticulating and criticizing, or stand in their way and oppose them. Unequivocally, Mao advised his party, in the mold of a classical Marxist-Leninist, to organize them!

Although Mao may have been somewhat slow in initially discovering the peasants as a revolutionary vehicle, once that occurred he never abandoned them as the source of revolutionary power and theory. Indeed, Mao began to speak of the increasingly important role that the Chinese peasantry would play in *leading* the revolution, eventually coming to the position that some of the leadership elements of the party could be drawn from the peasantry. Whether or not such a position constitutes a genuine contribution to Marxism-Leninism, Mao had definitely altered the tactics of revolutionary activity. Even Lenin, who used the Russian peasantry extensively and emphasized their role in revolutionary activity, never granted them leadership status. To Lenin's mind the peasantry constituted an allied force that was always to be subservient to the control of the class-conscious proletariat. Given the leading role of the Chinese peasants, and Lenin's theory of imperialism, it was a natural step for Mao to declare that the focus of revolutionary activity ought to be carried out on the peasant's home ground—in the countryside, rather than the cities. Here, then, are the three major elements of the rural strategy: (1) a revolution in which poor peasants could participate in leadership roles, (2) a base in the inaccessible countryside, and (3) the advocacy of guerilla warfare. These constitute genuine Maoist contributions to the doctrine.

It can be argued that Mao's entire rural strategy is an ingenious, culturally appropriate extension of the doctrine of imperialism. Under imperialism, the stronghold of the foreign capitalists is bound to be in urban areas where their monopoly on the use of force is most effective. If this is the case, the urban area

is the least likely place for revolutionary activity to occur since the small urban proletariat, whatever the extent of its consciousness, is easily suppressed. In much the
same fashion as Lenin's imperialism, Mao advocated gradually gaining control of
the countryside where the capitalist armies were most vulnerable, assaulting the
capitalist citadels in the cities only at the end of the revolution, when success was
guaranteed. Just as Lenin would have revolution in underdeveloped countries cut
off the mother country's source of superprofit, depriving them of resources, so
Mao would encircle the urban areas effecting the same result and thus ensuring
the eventual capitulation of the imperialist-dominated, bureaucratic, *compradore*
regime in the cities.

Similarly, Mao looked on the backwardness of the peasants in the rural areas
as a virtue. Since they lived in the countryside, removed from the destructive economic and cultural impact of imperialism, the peasants represented an unadul-
terated class, a class that had not been exposed to the embourgeoisement of
capitalism. "Poor" and "blank," the countryside of China was the ideal area for bas-
ing a revolution. Mao summarized these tactics in four principles: When the
enemy advances, we retreat; when the enemy camps, we harass; when the enemy
tires, we attack; when the enemy retreats, we pursue. In support of this strategy,
Mao urged the development of rural "safe areas," where peasant support was
assured and supplies were plentiful, to which the revolutionary army could retreat
in the face of concentrated opposition. The essential element in guerrilla warfare
is the ability of the armed forces to live with the people and to be able to fade back
into the mass of peasants when required. From this rural safe area, the guerrilla
forces would launch periodic attacks on the enemy, avoiding major confrontations
where the enemy's superior firepower would prevail, all the while expanding the
area under their control.

From an international viewpoint, this meant that the underdeveloped
countries of the world were like the countryside in China, and the imperialist
nations were like China's cities; the international strategy, then, was for the
international "countryside" to *encircle* the "cities" of the world. Naturally, China
would serve as model and supporter of guerrilla wars around the globe. Guerrilla warfare against major Western powers has become common practice during the past several decades and, while there have been numerous refinements
in the tactics of this type of military action, the basic strategy for this kind of
communist revolution originated with Mao. From the theoretical perspective
the entire rural strategy can be seen as an adaptation of the basic teachings of
Marx and Lenin to Chinese circumstances. The leading role of the peasantry
was undoubtedly dictated by the large number of peasants in China whose support was necessary for a successful revolution. In a sense, Mao was altering the
doctrine to maximize his support, but the alteration in Marxist-Leninist theory
nevertheless remains. Similarly, in an effort to gain further support from the
Chinese people, Mao developed a concept of the advancement to and through
socialism, which differs from the Soviet model and which may be seen as yet
another contribution to the doctrine.

CHINA'S PATH TO SOCIALISM

Owing to the extremely backward state of the Chinese economic base, it was generally conceded that the country could not immediately move into a socialist phase after a successful political revolution. Further, Mao realized that it would be necessary to retain the technical skills and the general support of many classes in order to develop the industrial base necessary for the march to socialism. We have seen that Lenin had similar problems in the USSR and tolerated a degree of bourgeois capitalism, particularly under the New Economic Policy. Still, Lenin was never very happy with the existence of a small bourgeois class, however weak, for he was sure that they would eventually try to subvert revolutionary goals; Stalin later solved this problem by eradicating most bourgeois elements in the society. Because of the semifeudal nature of China, Mao contended that it would be necessary to adopt a somewhat different solution. He proclaimed the existence of a People's Democratic Dictatorship, which would unite all anti-imperialist elements within the country in support of the revolutionary regime. Particularly noteworthy was his treatment of the bourgeoisie in Chinese society. He made a distinction between the *national bourgeoisie,* who were anti-imperialist, and the *compradore bourgeoisie* (also known as the *international bourgeoisie),* who were deemed lackeys of the imperialist powers. The latter were intractable "enemies of the people," while the former were considered to be part of the four-class bloc called "the people." At that time, the four classes were the *proletariat,* the *peasantry,* the *petite bourgeoisie* (which included "rich peasants"), and the *national bourgeoisie.* Given the Marxist perspective, Mao emphasized the point that even the term *the people* had different meanings in different countries and in different historical periods within each country. Consequently, nearly any group—if its thinking is correct—can belong to the people. As Mao put it in 1957:

> At this stage of building socialism, all classes, strata, and social groups that approve, support, and work for the cause of a socialist construction belong to the category of the people, while those social forces and groups that resist the socialist revolution and are hostile to and try to wreck socialist construction are enemies of the people.[3]

Anyone, then, could be considered a legitimate member of the People's Democratic Dictatorship provided that person was willing to help China become autonomous and move through the presocialist phase into the establishment of a socialist society. Here we see another attempt by a Marxist to integrate the values of nationalism and communism for the purposes of revolution. Mao was willing to tolerate the existence of bourgeois elements within the society, even to declare them an integral part of the process of developing socialism, if the historic conditions deemed it necessary. This is not unlike the ideological logic employed by Deng Xiaoping in his economic reform program initiated after Mao's death.

[3] Ibid., p. 305.

Although this is a significant departure from earlier thought, it must not be overemphasized, for the national bourgeoisie must be *nationalist* and ultimately assimilated into a single-class society, which turns itself into a classless community. Indeed, the economic developments within China from 1953 until Mao's death can be seen as a continuing process in reducing the power of these bourgeois elements. The significant fact is that this will be accomplished through the reeducation of the bourgeois group within the society. Articulating what seems to be a recurring theme of Chinese communism, Mao declared that the bourgeoisie would be gradually reeducated so that they would gain the *people's perspective,* thus becoming full-fledged members of the socialist regime. In discussing this matter of the reeducation of the population, Mao gave great emphasis to the process of proletarianization. Recall that the two major difficulties for any modern communist regime are the establishment of an industrial base and the development of a class-conscious proletariat. While Stalin's totalitarian state attempted to propagandize the entire population and was somewhat successful in that endeavor, there is little doubt that the Soviet Union had expended most of its effort on the development of an industrial base. On the contrary, throughout his writings Mao placed heavy emphasis on the human consciousness side of the coin. People of all classes were called upon to struggle with themselves to cast off old bourgeois values and to approach their everyday problems from the perspective of the new morality.

Emphasizing what Mao called the "red" side of the *red/expert* problem (that is, proletarianization/industrialization) does not mean that industrialization is to be ignored—no good Marxist could infer that. On the economic front the Chinese Communist regime engaged in numerous experiments in an attempt to advance industrialization. Indeed, as we have already seen, Mao advanced the imaginative thesis that because China was so backward it could leap forward economically at a faster rate than even the Soviet Union, with the use of vast peasant communes and backyard industries. Still, Mao seemed above all concerned that the population should become, and remain, red; and if the industrialization of the country had to suffer slightly in order to ensure that goal, so be it. Nevertheless, proletarianization—properly united with consciousness—always remained Mao's goal. As we shall see in the forthcoming discussion of the Sino-Soviet rift, one of Mao's persistent criticisms of the leadership of the Soviet Union was that it had lost its touch with the people, becoming a bureaucratic class which advanced its own interests at the expense of the ongoing revolution. Such themes, somewhat ironically, were to become central in Gorbachev's drive to "open" the USSR. This general theme of struggle, self-criticism, and interaction with the environment can also be seen as manifesting itself in another of Mao's developments in Marxism-Leninism: the notion of contradiction.

Mao on Contradiction

While Mao is generally given credit for his contribution on the question of a rural strategy for revolution in underdeveloped countries, the Chinese communists, apparently stung by the charge that this was merely a tactical adaptation of Leninism, attempted to emphasize other more theoretical contributions of their famous leader. Following a long and distinguished line of Marxist thinkers, Mao is said to have made genuine theoretical breakthroughs in the study of dialectical materialism, notably through his ideas on contradiction in socialist societies.

In a 1937 essay on dialectical materialism, Mao explained the ubiquitous nature of contradiction, contending that everything contains contradiction and that without contradiction nothing would exist. Everything in the universe contains contradictions; from ideas, to matter, to social relationships, contradiction is the nature of reality. Given this position, Mao asserted that certain contradictions will continue to exist, even in communism.

In the discussion of the Chinese path to socialism, we examined Mao's argument that there would be different classes and groups in society who would unite, primarily through their opposition to imperialism. Naturally, Mao asserted that there would be conflict and struggle between these groups as they pursued their goal. This raised no real difficulty as long as these groups were united in moving toward a socialist society. However, Mao also argued that not all contradictions are the same. There are *antagonistic* and *nonantagonistic contradictions.* This doctrine of nonantagonistic contradictions constitutes a specific denial of the then-existing Soviet ideology and, despite some Leninist precedents, seems to be a genuine addition to the doctrine.

In classical Marxism the major source of conflict in the world was the struggle that was constantly occurring between classes. A basic Marxist teaching was that once the source of such conflict was eliminated through the institution of a classless society, peace and harmony would prevail throughout the world. In the final analysis, Mao reaffirmed the basically antagonistic nature of class conflict, or antagonistic contradictions; he asserted that this type of conflict can be resolved only through complete victory of the proletariat. There must be no compromise in the unending battle with capitalist powers.

There are, however, other types of contradictions present among the people that are nonantagonistic and that may be peacefully resolved. Perhaps we can characterize this type of conflict, as opposed to conflicts between the people and the enemies of the people, as resulting from a disagreement of the means to be pursued in achieving socialism. All agree on the goal but differ, and are in conflict, on how to get there. In a 1957 speech, Mao gave an example of contradictions worth examining:

> The contradiction between exploiter and exploited that exists between the national bourgeoisie and the working class is in itself an antagonistic one. But, in the concrete conditions existing in China, such an antagonistic contradiction, if properly handled, can be transformed into a nonantagonistic one and resolved in a peaceful way. But if it is not properly handled, if, say, we do not follow a policy of uniting with, criticizing, and educating the national bourgeoisie, or if the national bourgeoisie does not accept this policy, then the contradiction between the working class and the national bourgeoisie can turn into an antagonistic contradiction as between ourselves and the enemy.[4]

This illustrates two important aspects to the issue of class antagonism. First, the antagonistic/nonantagonistic nature of a relationship varies with historic

---

[4] Ibid., p. 306.

circumstances. Second, although violence may be necessary to halt counterrevolutionary forces, peaceful methods of criticism and education are preferable. As Mao explained, "A man's head is not like a scallion, which will grow again if you cut it off; if you cut it off wrongly, then even if you want to correct your error there is no way of doing it."[5]

Mao's theories on class conflict, then, put him at odds with the Soviet ideology of the time. The Soviets, adhering to the official line, had long ago asserted that conflict and contradiction had ceased to exist in their territory, and the Maoist notion of the necessity of nonantagonistic contradictions during the building of socialism was a direct refutation of that assertion. Further, Mao seemed to be saying that this contradiction was a rather desirable thing for it would produce, in proper dialectical fashion, a series of *qualitative changes* in the society, since the tension of the conflict would produce a synthesis that was notably better than that which preceded it. Thus a socialist society would be in a state of *permanent revolution,* with the results of these contradictions constituting changes or revolutions.

Even after the establishment of a communist society, the conflict between the forces of production and the relations of production will generate conflict and that, in turn, will produce conflict and resolution among the people. Echoing Heraclitus and Hegel, Mao emphasized the permanence of change through contradiction. To do otherwise would have denied one of the fundamentals of Marxism. Unsurprisingly, Mao believed Marxism also subject to these forces of change: "Marxism also has its birth, its development, and its death. . . . To say that it won't die is metaphysics. Naturally, the death of Marxism means that something higher than Marxism will come to replace it."[6]

What Mao had done was to reemphasize the dialectical basis of Marxism. Contradictions exist throughout reality. Although class conflict is still important, Mao believed other conflicts in a person's relationship to the world were also crucial. Mao's differences with the more dogmatic, Soviet view of dialectics at that time was characteristic of the relationship between the two nations, at least from the late 1950s until the 1980s. We have mentioned several points of ongoing disagreement between these two major socialist powers; now we must look more systematically at the Sino-Soviet split.

THE PRC AND THE USSR

The Sino-Soviet split must be called one of the most important events in the history of international communism. In spite of their historic, geopolitical relationship, the prospect of the world's two major socialist powers, supposedly friendly allies in the fight against capitalism, lashing out at one another on ideological grounds, even engaging in warfare on their common border, is rather difficult to understand. Marx or Lenin, to say nothing of Stalin, would have been horrified by this apparent breakup in the international communist movement. Mikhail Gorbachev'

---

[5] Ibid., p. 92.

[6] Quoted in John B. Starr, *Continuing the Revolution: The Political Thought of Mao* (Princeton, N.J.: Princeton University Press, 1979), p. 43.

historic visit to China in the spring of 1989, was a step to end the ideological and great-power difficulties between these two countries. We can say, however, that during Mao's reign, despite numerous attempts at accommodation, the disputes raged on with little hope for complete resolution. For the student of political ideologies this era presents a fascinating area for study because the battle for ideological supremacy brings out numerous contradictions and variations in the doctrine that might otherwise be papered over in the name of a united front. Once again, we shall emphasize the ideological nature of the conflict, largely ignoring the very real interests of the two nation-states in competition for territorial and economic domination. Although there are commentators who will defend the proposition that differences between China and the Soviet Union began as early as 1949, with the success of the Chinese Communist Party, a far more concrete benchmark appears to be the death of Stalin and the emergence of de-Stalinization in the Soviet Union.

The Chinese response to the de-Stalinization policies of the Soviet's Twentieth Party Congress was ambivalent. Reacting to the wholesale denunciation of the Stalinist era by Stalin's successors, Mao agreed that the Soviet leader had made some errors; in particular he denounced the Stalinist cult of the hero. Still, the tone of Chinese de-Stalinization was far more muted than the same process within the USSR. Despite Stalin's errors, Mao asserted that Stalin was a great leader of Marxism-Leninism and had performed a most valuable role in developing the Soviet Union economically. In retrospect it is obvious that the tone of the Chinese response to Stalin's death was far more laudatory than that of the USSR, undoubtedly presaging the much more acrimonious ideological splits that were to follow.

In a sense, however, one could argue that some sort of contest for ideological supremacy was inevitable from the beginning. As far back as 1936, Mao declared that he was not fighting a revolution in China only to turn the country over to Moscow. Moreover, the Chinese revolution was successful without a great deal of Soviet support and it evolved a strategy for revolution far different from the classic Soviet model. This being the case, it was perhaps only natural for Mao to declare that his revolutionary model was more appropriate for Marxists in the less developed world, and that the winds of revolution would blow much more strongly from the East during the imperialist phase of capitalism.

Implicitly, then, merely by existing as an alternative to the Soviet model, the Chinese revolution offered a different way. It is, of course, a long way from the establishment of an alternative revolutionary model to the acrimonious exchanges that marked relations between the two socialist powers in the 1960s and 1970s, but in a sense it all revolves around Stalin's figure and his policies.

Faced with increasing denunciation of Stalin by the USSR, Mao found himself in a difficult position. He believed that strong party leadership was necessary in order to achieve the goals of a socialist state, and he knew that a good deal of suffering on the part of the Chinese people would be part of that process. One can argue that under such circumstances it was necessary to invent an almost superhuman leader who could act as a unifying symbol for the struggle of all the people and serve as a source of inspiration. Briefly, Mao created a different "cult of the hero" in order to speed the development of China, yet he was faced with constant denunciation of that very concept from the Soviet Union. This, as much as anything, seems to be the reason for the Chinese emphasis on Stalin as a hero of Marxism-Leninism. They were going through a process similar to that of the Soviet Union in the period from 1930 to 1953, a period which necessitated tremendous sacrifice and iron-handed control.

Thus, although Stalin could be condemned for certain excesses, a wholesale denunciation of his type of regime might lead to an undermining of Mao's position. Much of this is, of course, in the realm of speculation, and there are other ideological points where the split between the two powers was more obvious. Using one of the nastiest words in Marxist-Leninist jargon, the Chinese accused the Soviet Union of a general policy of *revisionism.*

Revisionists and "Paper Tigers"

There are many facets to this particular charge, but the most general statement that can be made is that the USSR was seen as pursuing a policy of conciliation with capitalism and denying the goals of Marxism-Leninism. Specifically, the Chinese simply refused to accept the Soviet doctrine of peaceful coexistence with capitalism. In response, the CCP issued their own "five principles of peaceful coexistence" emphasizing that, unlike the Soviets, they would not *capitulate* to capitalism. We have seen that Khrushchev's (and more recently Gorbachev's) notion of peaceful coexistence did not deny the ongoing struggle with capitalism but affirmed that all-out war would be mutually destructive and must be avoided. Adopting a pugnacious stance, at least ideologically, Mao declared that Khrushchev was selling out to capitalism, denounced the West as a "paper tiger," and asserted that China with her vast population would survive a nuclear war if the imperialists elected to employ their nuclear superiority to attempt to save their decaying system. This is a particularly difficult notion to understand when we compare public statements with actual practice.

Despite his denunciation of the capitalist powers as "paper tigers" and however often he called for an all-out, protracted war hitting the imperialists powers at the weakest link in the system, Mao's actions were not much more bellicose than those of the USSR. We cannot go into the various armed conflicts that the Chinese have had with the West, nor can we examine the Chinese role in fomenting revolutionary movements in other underdeveloped countries. What Mao seemed to be trying to achieve by denouncing peaceful coexistence and adopting this belligerent stance was the unification of the Chinese people in the face of outside enemies. Furthermore, such a position placed Mao in the forefront of revolutionary ideology in modern times and permitted him to call the Chinese the true bearers of the revolutionary idealism of Marx and Lenin. Perhaps he was only scoring some ideological points at the expense of the Soviet Union, but the image of Mao, the eternal revolutionary, has had great attraction for dissatisfied people throughout the world, and continues after his death.

Peaceful coexistence/capitulation was not the only manifestation of Soviet revisionism condemned by the Chinese. They saw the USSR illicitly experimenting with various economic reforms at home and attempting to advance Soviet national interests abroad at the expense of world revolution. Most important from the ideological perspective, they accused the leadership elements of the USSR of divorcing themselves from their own people and of constituting a leadership elite that advanced its interests at the expense of the Soviet people.

We noted earlier that Mao viewed classes and nonantagonistic class conflict as part of the process of building socialism in China. From his point of view, the Soviet Union, while declaring that it had achieved a single-class society, was actually covering over the existence of a vast bureaucratic class that was so eager to preserve its position of privilege that it had become counterrevolutionary. This is, of course, a most serious charge. Ironically, as we noted earlier, it is similar to one of the charges made by General Secretary Gorbachev, justifying his demands for *perestroika.* But, if the Soviet Union after more than fifty years of building socialism had succeeded only in producing a society based upon a different class relationship, there must have been something wrong with the Soviet model. Put differently, the Soviet experiment was failed *praxis:* The theory and practice of the USSR was not genuine Marxism. In criticizing the class-based nature of the Soviet Union, Mao exhibited two additional traits that seem to be persistent in his thought: dislike for formal education that leads to elitism and emphasis on the innate wisdom of the common people.

In summary, let us stray briefly from the ideological plane to say that much of the Sino-Soviet conflict seemed to be the result of the differing perspectives of an almost developed nation-state and one that is still in the early stages of economic development. From the Chinese perspective the Soviet Union had become antirevolutionary because it was basically satisfied with its position in the world. As a major power, the USSR seemed to support the maintenance of the status quo, both by accommodating competing capitalist powers and by supporting existing regimes irrespective of their ideology. Insofar as support of the status quo meant keeping China in a relatively powerless position, the USSR was bound to be condemned by Mao as reactionary. It is in this sense that Mao could speak, as he did, of the possibility of an alliance between the USSR and the United States designed to keep China in a condition of relative impotence.

From their "have-not" perspective, the Chinese under Mao demanded change and revolution throughout the world and condemned their fraternal socialists in the Soviet Union for collaborating with reactionary capitalists. Here, for the final time, we observe the difficulty of reconciling the aspirations of nation-states with the internationalism of Marxism-Leninism. This is a persistent problem of modern communism, one that shows no signs of being resolved in the near future.

MAO ZEDONG AS A SYMBOL

Throughout Mao's life many endearing labels were associated with him: Great Leader, Great Supreme Commander, Great Teacher, and Great Helmsman, to name a few. Nevertheless, Mao considered these titles to be a nuisance; he claimed that his desire was to be remembered simply as "teacher." This, it seems, is consistent with Mao's thoughts. Although he played the roles of leader, commander, and helmsman, they were not what he considered to be his greatest contribution to the revolution. At times he even seemed to disdain his exalted position, as in 1966 when he denounced the "superhuman power" attributed to his writings: "When tigers are absent from the mountain the monkey then becomes king. I have become such a king."[7] Still, his role as teacher is of tremendous importance not only to the Chinese experience, but also—as Paulo Freire has made evident in his influential *Pedagogy of the Oppressed*—to the exploited throughout the Third and Fourth Worlds; therefore, it should be discussed in some detail.

Despite repeated exhortations to the Chinese people to reeducate themselves, Mao had considerable dislike for formal education. Numerous references abound in his writings to the basic wisdom of the uneducated masses. In a discussion of education, Mao articulated his basic epistemological position: "You know I've proclaimed for a long time: we must teach the masses clearly what we have received from them confusedly."[8] Here Mao demonstrates that if it is appropriate to conceive of "truth" residing anywhere, it is with the people, not with an educated elite. He consequently warned against producing a technologically sophisticated elite that is divorced from that wisdom. Related to this was his fear of producing a Soviet-like managerial class that advanced the economy at the expense of proletarianization, or redness. Evidence now shows that the Cultural Revolution of 1966–1969 was in part instituted in an effort to break down what Mao perceived as growing class stratification in China. By sending the most radical elements in the population—the students—out to destroy pockets of embourgeoisement throughout the country, Mao was giving an object lesson to those who might stray from his model. Furthermore, by insisting that these student groups then retire to rural areas to work with their hands among the peasants, he was again emphasizing the innate wisdom of the masses.

During the Cultural Revolution, countless copies of the then famous "little Red Book"—*Quotations from Chairman Mao Zedong*—were distributed by the People's Liberation Army (PLA) to help in the reeducation of China. Coming on the heels of the Vietnam War, the Cultural Revolution was yet another attempt by Mao to bring about what can be called a spiritual transformation of humanity. It was designed to shake China to its very core in hope of creating the consciousness needed for the years of struggle ahead: a China that appeared increasingly isolated and a China that soon would be without the example of Mao. Thus Mao returned to his essential belief in the desirability of struggling through contradictions, and he produced his final revolution.

Quotations from Chairman Mao Zedong was to be used as a personal guide to achieve *correct thinking*. Although the book contains numerous "inspirational" thoughts, it does not contain one practical, operational prescription. Hence, individuals are forced, by reading Mao, to struggle with, and incorporate into their own existence, the appropriate manner of life. During the more hectic, final months of the Cultural Revolution, it was reported that roving army medical teams were on rare occasion able, by thinking and correctly applying the chairman's

[7] Ibid., p. 96.
[8] Cited in Paulo Freire, *Pedagogy of the Oppressed* (New York: Continuum, 1970), p. 82.

thoughts, to raise the dead. Clearly, blind obedience was not the goal. Rather, the creation of hundreds of thousands of "Mao-like," dedicated revolutionaries is what was desired. The Cultural Revolution also reflected Mao's faith in the human (existential or subjective) element in history. Mao told the following story:

> There is an ancient Chinese fable called "The Foolish Old Man Who Removed the Mountains." It tells of an old man who lived in northern China long, long ago and was known as the Foolish Old Man of North Mountain. His house faced south and beyond his doorway stood the two great peaks, Taihang and Wangwu, obstructing the way. With great determination, he led his sons in digging up these mountains hoe in hand. Another graybeard, known as the Wise Old Man, saw them and said derisively, "How silly of you to do this! It is quite impossible for you few to dig up these two huge mountains." The Foolish Old Man replied, "When I die, my sons will carry on; when they die, there will be my grandsons, and then their sons and grandsons, and so to infinity. High as they are, the mountains cannot grow any higher and with every bit we dig, they will be that much lower. Why can't we clear them away?" Having refuted the Wise Old Man's wrong view, he went on digging every day, unshaken in his conviction. God was moved by this, and he sent down two angels, who carried the mountains away on their backs. Today, two big mountains lie like a dead weight on the Chinese people. One is imperialism, the other is feudalism. The Chinese Communist Party has long made up its mind to dig them up. We must persevere and work unceasingly, and we, too, will touch God's heart. Our God is none other than the masses of the Chinese people. If they stand up and dig together with us, why can't these two mountains be cleared away?[9]

If the necessary will and consciousness could be created and sustained, nothing could stand in the way of the revolution. And, from the perspective of a man who rose from the ranks of the peasantry, who spent over two decades in armed conflict, including a 6,000-mile forced march, who saw his country emerge from the crippling effects of abject poverty to the status of a strong, economically self-reliant nation, this was understandable indeed.

Thus Mao's thought could become a perpetual, ongoing guide for revolutionary action. And Mao, even after his death, could continue his cherished role as teacher.

CHINA AFTER MAO

With the death of Mao in 1976, China began the process of continuing the revolution without his physical presence. After the initial power vacuum was filled by the silencing of Mao's widow as part of the "gang of four" and the eventual emergence of Deng Xiaoping as undisputed leader of the party, Deng astutely moved to solidify his position by coming to terms with Mao's legacy, carefully using his name and memory to legitimize efforts at reform. The term *de-Maoification* is used by some Western scholars to describe the process employed by the new leadership of slowly separaring itself from Mao. To be sure, it was important for the new leaders to establish their own credibility as they emphasized the industrial/technological side of the red/expert debate; however, to claim that they wanted to disassociate themselves totally from Mao seems excessive.

[9] Mao Zedong, *Selected Works,* Vol. 3, p. 272.

De-sacralization, rather than de-Maoification, seems the more appropriate term to explain Deng's usage of the image of Mao. Deng openly criticized errors made by Mao, calling the Cultural Revolution an "appalling mistake." He also silently rebuked Mao by rehabilitating the good name of, and if possible reappointing to positions of power, many of Mao's former enemies. Deng himself was twice purged, first during the Cultural Revolution and then immediately following Mao's demise. Perhaps the most significant change, at least symbolically, was the omission of the reverential title "Chairman" before invoking Mao's name; indeed even the head of the CCP is no longer called chairman but simply general secretary to emphasize further the point that no person should ever again have as much power as Mao. Since Deng's third coming to power, Mao's humanity and revolutionary vision was to be celebrated, but his godlike, infallible status was to be destroyed. All of this being said, Deng willingly and skillfully invoked the specific language and images of Mao most supportive of Deng's position, especially those reflecting Mao's undogmatic and realistic approach known as the "Yanan Heritage." Mao thus became a legitimizing tool for Deng's own policies and programs. And in point of fact, none of the new vocabulary and symbols employed to implement China's economic reform programs were antithetical to Mao Zedong Thought. It appears, then, that Deng preferred to use Mao as a symbol of the revolutionary past to assist in the dual policies of reaching out to the West and initiating economic development at home. In terms of both of these policies, Deng adroitly shifted Mao's notion of "self-reliance" to fit China's new needs: China must take technological and scientific advancements from the West in order to become self-reliant; at the same time China must remain independent of, not isolated from, capitalism. Nevertheless, this ongoing attachment to Mao is inherently risky: Like the angels in "The Foolish Old Man Who Removed the Mountains," the spirit of Mao the revolutionary instigator of the Cultural Revolution remains present, albeit officially repudiated, for the more red, existentially oriented of China's leaders. Before attempting to assess both Deng's ability to carve his own path with Mao's image and his handling of the Pro-Democracy movement, it is necessary to examine briefly the significant changes in China since Deng's reemergence.

The Rise of Deng Xiaoping

Deng Xiaoping represented the expert/bureaucratic side in the red/expert debate. A rugged survivor of the Long March and years of struggle inside the CCP, his rise to leadership after Mao's death represented a clear signal that a majority of the elite inside the party recognized the need for a substantive change in the direction of China. While Deng was critical of the "whatever faction"—those who argued that *whatever* policies and directives Chairman Mao articulated before his death should be carried out—he also wanted to have the prestige of Mao's legacy on his side. His strategy seemed to be one of declaring the Mao of the Cultural Revolution *persona non grata,* except to criticize and humanize him. Mao's thought and writings independent of the Cultural Revolution, especially the early Mao, were to be read, analyzed, and applied as a guide to current practice. While not a theoretician, Deng had a talent for standing Marxism-Leninism-Mao Zedong Thought on its head so it could be used to support his programs.

Almost a decade before Gorbachev's calls for *perestroika* in the Soviet Union, China launched its own program for rational, systematic development under the "four modernizations" campaign and the "new open-door" policy: The former was to modernize agriculture, industry, national defense, and science and technology; the latter to open China to Western ideas and markets. Proclaiming itself in the "primary," or underdeveloped, stage of socialism, China recognized the need for major economic reform. Even with massive reform, China could not "leap" over this primary stage and would remain in it until sometime around the middle of the next century, and the attainment of communism remained many generations away. Unlike Mao who emphasized the subjective over the economic element, Deng argued for vast substructural changes. With a population of over 1 billion, 800 million of whom lived in rural areas and used hand tools to scratch out an existence, Deng proclaimed the urgent need to both establish rigorous family planning and modernize China while remaining consistent with the goals and values of socialism. Material, not spiritual, incentives were deemed essential to developing socialism. Consequently, China's economic policies were to be redesigned to achieve industrialization and to commercialize, socialize, and modernize production. A kind of "commodity socialism" or market socialism was needed at that historic moment to modernize China. The party attempted to blend planning with market mechanisms, where the state regulates the markets and the markets guide enterprises. This did not mean that China must go through a period of capitalism in order to develop the economic base to sustain developed socialism: This type of argument was labeled "mechanistic" by the CCP, who believed, in Mao-like fashion, that subjective forces remain crucial to history. While supporting the development of the forces of production, Deng adamantly opposed the *"bourgeois liberalization"* of China. To assist in the guidance and limitation of this modernization process, Deng proclaimed allegiance to "Four Cardinal Principles": (1) keeping to the socialist road, (2) upholding the people's democratic dictatorship, (3) following the leadership of the Communist party, and (4) applying Marxism-Leninism and Mao Zedong Thought as the defining and limiting factor in the reform programs.

While Deng strove to revitalize China by opening up its economic and political system to new and younger voices, a clear notion of *continuity* with its revolutionary past was also apparent. He instituted a Central Advisory Committee as part of the upper levels of the CCP. Formally only a consultative body, membership on this prestigious committee required at least forty years of service in the party. Its role was to provide an institutionalized memory of China's past as a generation was coming to power who had no firsthand experience with the party's founding era. The committee's first chair, Deng Xiaoping helped establish the committee's position inside the party structure where it could shape and mold party programs.

Deng's economic policies included NEP style programs which linked financial rewards to profits earned. The term *entrepreneurship* was now officially used in English language publications. And intellectuals and experts who assist in the development of science and technology were to be materially rewarded. Of course, agriculture remained a, perhaps *the,* major economic problem facing China. Again, NEP-like programs were developed, emphasizing decentralization and individual initiative. "Peasants who get rich first" were no longer proclaimed enemies of the people, but rather were held out as role models in an attempt to encourage productivity. The rationale behind the peasants getting rich *first* campaign was that once China had developed economically, became "rich," then—but only then— could questions of socialist distribution be dealt with. "Chinese socialism" or "socialism with Chinese characteristics" became the hallmark of Deng's economic reforms.

On the political front, Deng was far more reserved in carrying out widespread reforms in spite of calling for "democratization" of the system. Personal freedoms were tolerated, provided they did not extend to the political realm where only minor political reforms were instituted. For example, at the lower levels of the political system, the electoral machinery mandated secret ballots, open nominations, more candidates than positions, and direct elections up to the county level. Deng also took some measures to create an independent judiciary and a new legal code, to separate along functional lines the party from the state, and to improve the oversight role of legislative bodies. Finally, the party itself was to undergo reform; while still playing the leadership role, it was to be subject to the law. Nevertheless, corruption and nepotism continued to be major problems throughout the political system. The net result of the economic and political alterations remained the creation of de facto pluralism in the economic arena combined with deepening, widespread resentment over both the rampant political corruption and the failure to institutionalize the promised liberalization of the political arena.

Deng's advanced age made it imperative that he move swiftly if he were to make a lasting impression. He solidified his own power base by replacing reds with experts in positions of power. This alteration in economics had given China a decade of its most rapid economic progress ever; yet tied to this development came a nearly 30 percent rate of inflation, rampant and open corruption, and all the problems associated with the rising expectations of the masses. He opened China to Western ideas and culture, scholars and tourists, inviting cultural exchange programs varying in diversity—rock groups, the Boston Symphony, Western literature, philosophy, and films. Reciprocally, large numbers of Chinese students were permitted to study abroad. While Deng was anxious to open China to Western science, technology, and economic innovation, he failed to realize that liberal political ideals would also penetrate the system and take on a life of their own. There can be little doubt that China experienced a relatively significant degree of liberalization during this period. But this served only to whet the appetite of the students and intellectuals; for some, the pace of liberalization was too slow, and for others, it appeared to be coming to a stop. Although Deng, the expert, was willing to tolerate economic reform, he was opposed to the necessary corresponding political alterations. The consequences were predictable: As Marx had discovered, when the substructure and superstructure fall out of harmony, conflict results. In what has been called "four days that shook the world," in the spring of 1989, forty years after Mao first seized control over China, the world watched in disbelief as the People's Liberation Army openly fired upon students and workers in Tiananmen (which ironically means Gate of Heavenly Peace) Square.

The Fall of Deng Xiaoping

Since 1949, every decade has witnessed a major, dramatic "revolution" inside of China: the Hundred Flowers campaign and Great Leap Forward (1957–1958), the Cultural Revolution (1966–1969); the Democratic Wall campaign (1979–1980) and the 1989 Pro-Democracy movement. The last events were sparked by the death of Hu Yaobang, the once hand-picked successor of Deng. Hu, one of the remaining survivors of the Long March, was credited with opening China to the West and as the first of the old guard elite to adopt Western dress. In fact, he was buried in a Western-style suit and tie while Deng, dressed in the traditional Zhongshan ("Mao") jacket, looked on at the man he had sacked from head of the party months earlier. Shortly after Hu's funeral, Mikhail Gorbachev visited China: As if following Mao's advice to "Seize the day, seize the hour!" thousands of students, later joined by more students and workers, the combined forces numbering in the hundreds of thousands, jammed central Beijing and occupied Tiananmen Square; they embarrassed the party and caused Deng the loss of face by making it impossible for the party to meet Gorbachev in the Great Hall of the People. Gorbachev's reforms, especially *glasnost,* had captured the imagination and support of the students. The students chanted "Dialogue, Dialogue, We must have Dialogue!" and demanded a free press, publication of the finances of state leaders to help end corruption and nepotism, self-criticism for mistakes in education policy, and a fair assessment of Hu's career. Students and workers called for an end to corruption and nepotism, a chilling reminder to Deng of strikingly similar demands made during the high point of the Cultural Revolution.

Events between the party and the Pro-Democracy movement quickly escalated. Zhao Ziyang, second of Deng's hand-picked successors, refused to carry out orders to suppress the demonstrators. Instead, he elected to visit the hunger strikers among them and was reported to have said: "We have come too late. We are sorry. And it is right for you to criticize us." While this helped solidify his position of champion of the students, it also signaled that his reign as general secretary of the CCP was over: Deng did not want a replay of the Cultural Revolution. Deng, who had maintained his position as head of the Central Military Commission, ordered the PLA to restore order and control over the capital. Realizing the fragility of their position as troops encircled the city, the students rapidly constructed the famous Goddess of Democracy statue. The students sang the *Internationale* as they assembled the statue and finally placed it facing a giant portrait of Mao—all three of these symbols representing what the students ultimately wanted. The rest of the events are well known. After some initial reluctance, the PLA stormed the protestors killing hundreds, and perhaps thousands; workers and students by the hundreds who participated in the demonstrations were rounded up, put on trial, and punished—a few losing their lives. The crackdown was swift, brutal, and very public, to make sure all Chinese received the unambiguous, official message: "Counterrevolutionary activities" and *"bourgeois* liberalization" would not be tolerated. Although this was the official party line, creating the face-saving illusion that Deng's desperate actions saved the revolution, the students had a different response. Rhetorically they asked: "What color is Deng now?" And sarcastically they answered, "Red, with the blood of Tiananmen."

After Tiananmen, Deng's power began to slip away but not before he successfully replaced Zhao with Jiang Zemin, an expert who fully supported the suppression of the students. Deng maintained his figurehead status while his health slowly deteriorated until February 19, 1997, when he finally died at age 92. Later in the year, the CCP paid homage to him by officially acknowledging "Deng Xiaoping Theory" to mark his contribution to Marxism-Leninism-Mao Zedong Thought. Now that the last vestige of leadership from the Long March is gone, two questions arise: one about China's future, the other about its past.

Concluding Thoughts

As China continues its Long March toward communism using "market socialism" to construct the prerequisite substructure, it must deal with the inevitable difficulties associated with trying to "liberalize" a command economy, permit personal freedoms, and yet maintain an authoritarian political system. This is exceptionally hard to do, as the final days of the Soviet Union make clear. For the present, the party appears to be trying to steer away from the possibility of another powerful, long-term leader in the form of either Mao or Deng. To that end, it has instituted and exercised term limits on many political offices. Still, Jiang Zemin has established himself as a strong leader, in part because he has successfully followed the path established by Deng after Mao's death. Jiang has praised Deng's economic policies even while he has permitted criticism of the handling of Tiananmen Square and exposed widespread corruption in the army. Like Deng, he seems willing to permit considerable personal freedom and allow increasing amounts of autonomy into the lower levels of economic activity but unwilling to budge on the party's exclusive control over the Forbidden City of politics. Greater market incentives have resulted in agricultural productivity, although the farmers, who still do not have Western property rights, seem reluctant to engage in anything more than short-term endeavors. Jiang has been able to accommodate a "shareholding system" and a strong stock market with China's ideology by keeping these Western notions separated from any of the powerful state-owned enterprises. In fact, the party seems anxious to increase its control over the "pillar" economic entities like the army, steel, and energy. Even simple talk of "privatization" among party members remains out of the question—at least for the moment.

As long as the economy continues to develop, China in all likelihood will remain stable. It is questionable, however, how long the CCP can maintain its monopoly on political power while it slowly permits greater economic freedom. If the Soviet experience is applicable, it has been virtually impossible to stop liberal ideas introduced in one realm from seeping into the other. And if the economy turns sour, charges of widespread corruption and criticism of China's nomenclature system are sure to resurface. It is also questionable how far market freedoms and "entrepreneurship" will be permitted to develop in the economy before they run into challenging the critical issue of state-owned enterprises. It is one thing for the party to permit peasants to get rich first and quite another for it to give up control of major industries. All of these difficulties may be exacerbated by Western capitalists who are anxious to export their surplus capital and develop this potentially enormous consumer market. Finally, the West continues to assume that liberalization of the economy must translate into peaceful liberalization of international relations. To assume that China will forget about its years of domination by colonial powers, at the moment when it is finally approaching the level of superpower status, belies historic experience.

What then, will become of Mao? What will become of Deng? The Western world seems anxious to bury most of Mao, except those negative images of him lifted from the Cultural Revolution; in contrast, it wants to maintain most of Deng Xiaoping Theory and gloss over his involvement with events surrounding Tiananmen. In spite of much of the American press's coverage of the events in Tiananmen Square, the students were *not* calling for either capitalism or liberal-style democracy. Rather, they wanted to begin to create a socialism that tolerated free expression but not corruption. As for Mao, even if it is appropriate to collapse Mao Zedong Thought to nothing more than his ideas during the Cultural Revolution, then obviously many of the elite in the CCP have turned their backs, at least for the present, on China's Maoist heritage. But the student protestors of the spring of 1989 must have found something of value in even this narrow slice of Mao, as some of their demands clearly rekindled memories of the earliest months of the Cultural Revolution. On the other, more realistic, hand, when Mao Zedong Thought represents the entire corpus of his work, spanning well over half a century, then Mao lives—continuing to color China's future red. Indeed, given Mao's writings "On Contradiction," it seems dialectically appropriate that an expert like Deng should have failed to appreciate the subjective side to reform movements. There can be little doubt that Deng's own, harsh judgment on the Cultural Revolution as an "appalling mistake" will be history's judgment of his handling of Tiananmen.

This is no place for a summary of the teachings of Marx and Engels as they have been developed and applied over the past century. In a very real way the four previous chapters provide only the bare outlines of the development of Marxist-Leninist ideology, thereby in themselves constituting a summary. Neither is this the place for an attempt at an extended critique of those doctrines. As we stated in the introductory discussion, the major aim is an understanding of the ideology as a prelude to evaluation. Still, there are numerous problems of communism that have entered the discussion, ranging from the lack of a truly classical communist revolution anywhere in the world to the difficulties of integrating nationalist values with Marxist internationalism. These problems surely are the beginning of a critique for anyone who feels the need to attempt one. Indeed, if there is one thing we possess in abundance in the West it is authoritative and, in many instances, well-reasoned criticisms of communist thought.

SUGGESTED READINGS

FREIRE, PAULO, *Pedagogy of the Oppressed.* New York: Continuum, 1970.

LIFTON, ROBERT J., *Thought Reform and the Psychology of Totalism.* New York: W
W. Norton & Company, 1961.

————, *Revolutionary Immortality: Mao Tse-tung and the Chinese Cultural Revolution*
New York: W. W. Norton & Company, 1976.

MOODY, PETER R., *Chinese Politics After Mao.* New York: Praeger Publishers, 1983

SCHRAM, STUART R., ed., *The Political Thought of Mao Tse-tung.* New York: Fred
erick A. Praeger, 1963.

————, *Chairman Mao Talks to the People.* New York: Pantheon Books, 1974.

SCHURMANN, FRANZ, *Ideology and Organization in Communist China.* Berkeley
University of California Press, 1966.

SNOW, EDGAR, *Red Star Over China.* New York: Modern Library, 1944.

STARR, JOHN BRYANN, *Continuing the Revolution: The Political Thought of Mao*
Princeton, N.J.: Princeton University Press, 1979.

TOWNSEND, JAMES R., and BRANTLY WOMACK, *Politics in China,* 3rd ed
Boston: Little, Brown and Co., 1986.

WAKEMAN, FREDERIC, JR., *History and Will.* Berkeley: University of California
Press, 1973.

9

Fascism

Fascism is therefore opposed to that form of democracy which equates a nation to the majority, lowering it to the level of the largest number; but it is the purest form of democracy if the nation be considered—as it should be—from the point of view of quality rather than quantity, as an idea, the mightiest because the most ethical, the most coherent, the truest, expressing itself in a people as the conscience and will of the few, if not, indeed, of one, and tending to express itself in the conscience and the will of the mass, of the whole group ethnically moulded by natural and historical conditions into a nation, advancing, as one conscience and one will, along the self-same line of development and spiritual formation. Not a race, nor a geographically defined region; but a people, historically perpetuating itself a multitude unified by an idea and imbued with the will to live, the will to power, self-consciousness personality.

Mussolini

How does one begin to write about a set of ideas as apparently varied as fascism? To people who lived through World War II, the term itself is almost a synonym for evil, for the "war to defeat fascism" contains many bitter memories. Even those who had no firsthand experience with the fascist regimes of Italy and Germany invariably use the word with a bad connotation. When the police are thought to be overzealous in performing their duty they are called fascist; sometimes people who deem themselves to be good conservatives are referred to as fascists by other ideologists; and we speak darkly of fascist tendencies in the modern nation-state. It is probably inevitable that any word which is frequently used in common language will lose some of its initial meaning and be employed in a vague or general way, but that phenomenon seems compounded in the case of fascism. Sometimes it seems that almost anything a person dislikes is arbitrarily labeled "fascist." There are some reasons for such a situation.

Fascism as a set of ideas was never as clearly formulated as Marxism-Leninism or liberalism, although we believe that there is more coherence among the ideas than is frequently supposed. Further, people speak of fascism as a rather peculiar phenomenon, existing only during a particular period in history and largely confined to the nation-states of Italy, Germany, and Japan. Because of this identification with historical nation-states there is a tendency to refer to all of the actions of those states as somehow expressive of the phenomenon of fascism. It is as though every action of the former Soviet Union or of China were to be seen as expressive of the doctrine of Marxism-Leninism or every American policy a manifestation of the liberal tradition when we know that the actions of these countries are best seen as attempts to apply certain ideas that exist independently of their application. There is a relatively coherent set of ideas called Marxism-Leninism and there have been numerous attempts to apply those ideas, but that is not to say that the ideas are to be equated with every practical policy of a particular nation. The same thing obtains with liberalism and, we believe, with fascism. Fascism can be viewed as a set of ideas that attempts to say something about human beings, their society, and their future development, and that set of ideas can be analyzed separately from attempts to apply it to particular nations.

The difficulty of understanding fascism is compounded by the fact that we have surprisingly little scholarship that has concerned itself with fascism as a set of ideas. There are numerous books on Mussolini's Italy or biographical studies of Hitler, or discussions of fascism in other countries, but there have been few attempts to look at the ideology per se. As A. James Gregor has noted, "We have been studying fascism for half a century and the number of competent works devoted to the ideology of Mussolini's Fascism could be counted on one hand."[1] While recent scholarship has remedied the situation somewhat, the contrast between the number of studies of fascist ideology and liberalism or Marxism-Leninism remains quite striking.

[1] A. James Gregor, *Interpretations of Fascism* (Morristown, N.J.: General Learning Press, 1974), p. 244–45.

Again, there are reasons for this. Drawing support from the statements of promi-nent fascists, many commentators have concluded that there is no ideology of fas-cism, that it is a doctrine lacking in established principles, that it celebrates violent, irrational action for its own sake, and that to look at it as though it were a relatively coherent set of ideas is simply to distort it. Such interpretations of fascism see it as a highly pragmatic form of extreme nationalism and view any attempt to examine it through intellectual categories as doomed to failure. Other interpretations place great emphasis on the leadership element in fascist doctrine and assert that lead-ership is so fundamental to the phenomenon that a study of fascism ought to con-sist of a series of political biographies.

There is a degree of truth in both of these positions. The role of the leader in fascist regimes is crucial, so much so that Mussolini could declare late in life, "What would Fascism be, if I had not been." Furthermore, there is little doubt that fascism appeared to celebrate a form of irrationalism and that its doctrines changed considerably with the passage of time, making it difficult to apply tests of traditional logic to the doctrines. Despite these difficulties we contend that it is possible both to discover among fascist ideologists certain shared characteristics and values, and to develop an ideology of fascism that is appropriately coherent, given the premises of it. Stanley G. Payne, summarizing the more recent view of Italian fascism, has noted: "Though an exact and elaborate codification of doctrine was never achieved, it is now becoming recognized that Italian Fascism did func-tion on the basis of a reasonably coherent set of ideas."[2]

A glance at the table of contents of this book reveals an additional point con-cerning our treatment of fascism: The discussion is confined to only two, relatively short chapters. Such a structure indicates that fascism will be viewed largely in the reflected light of communism and liberalism; that is, fascism will provide us with a critical perspective of the other two idea systems. This relatively brief treatment should not, however, be taken as an indication that we regard fascism as less impor-tant than the other two ideologies, or that we view it as a "dead" phenomenon. As Mussolini put it:

> Given that the nineteenth century was the century of Socialism, of Liberalism, and of Democracy, it does not necessarily follow that the twentieth century must also be a century of Socialism, Liberalism, and Democracy: political doctrines pass, but human-ity remains; and it may rather be expected that this will be a century of authority, a century of the Right, a century of Fascism.[3]

An excellent although controversial case can be made for the position that fascism, in its various manifestations, has had at least as much impact—perhaps more—during the twentieth century as either of the other two ideologies. A. James Gregor, for example, argues, "However one chooses to characterize 'fas-cism,' it is clear that modern revolutions share more affinities with the fascism

---

[2] Stanley G. Payne, *Fascism: Comparison and Definition* (Madison: University of Wisconsin Press, 1980), p. 42.
[3] Benito Mussolini, "The Political and Social Doctrine of Fascism," in *Fascism: An Anthology*, Nathanael Greene, ed. (New York: Thomas Y. Crowell, 1968), p. 43.

of Benito Mussolini than they do with the Marxism of Karl Marx or Friedric
Engels."[4] Mussolini's observation may be as accurate today as it was in 1932 whe
he stated that every age has its own characteristic doctrine and that there were
thousand signs that point to fascism as the characteristic doctrine of his time. I
addition, as to fascism being a dead phenomenon, Anthony Joes argues: "The fa
cist solution to the problem of economic frustration and political instability seem
to 'fit' in many cases. A formula of nationalism, corporatism, and elitism, original
concocted in a European 'great power' environment, has been adapted at variou
times from Lima to Accra, and from Cairo to Tokyo."[5]

As a final introductory point, mention must be made of the rather strict sep
aration herein made between fascism and National-Socialism. In common lan
guage, fascism is often used to refer to the particular political structures in bot
Italy and Germany. As previously noted, such use is inappropriate in that a set o
fascist ideas can be seen as existing independent of those two particular natior
states, something that could be called *generic fascism*. Further complicating this mat
ter is that the founding father of the movement, Benito Mussolini, served as th
leader of Italy during its fascist period. Hence, it becomes quite difficult to sepa
rate the doctrine from its applications in Italy. While we should not see ever
action of Mussolini as head of the Italian state as an expression of fascist doctrine
in many ways Mussolini's Italy can provide us with an ideal model of a fascis
regime. If this is the case, the actions and doctrines of other so-called fascist lead
ers can be evaluated in terms of the degree to which they conform or deviate from
the Italian archetype. From this perspective, Adolf Hitler cannot appropriately b
called a fascist even though his regime expressed many fascist traits. We shoul
note that taking such a position is somewhat controversial. As Anthony Joe
explains:

> In any case, it is not legitimate to equate all fascism with Nazism. Some scholars . .
> deny that Nazism is an example of fascism at all. Others argue that fascism include
> regimes remarkably different from Hitler's Germany in many important ways. It is ou
> position [Joes] that the Nazis were one manifestation, and not a typical one, of a ger
> eral fascist phenomenon.[6]

We concur with Joes: In our view, at best, National-Socialist Germany can b
seen as an extreme form of fascism, but it can more appropriately be characte
ized as the worst form of biological racism the modern world has ever seen.

We conclude our attempt to deal with this difficult phenomenon with a dis
cussion of "continuing issues" in fascism. There, through an extended presenta
tion of Islamic thought, we attempt to provide the reader not only with som
understanding of that very important contemporary movement, but also t
determine whether, as is often contended, contemporary fundamentalist Islami
thought can appropriately be considered a type of fascism. These definitiona

---

[4] A. James Gregor, in *Fascism in the Contemporary World,* by Anthony Joes (Boulder, Colo.
Westview Press, 1978), p. xii.

[5] Joes, *Fascism in the Contemporary World,* p. 199.

[6] Ibid., p. 4.

distinctions will become clearer as we pursue the subject matter, but for the moment the term *fascism* is restricted to the ideas of Benito Mussolini and their application in Italy.

EVOLUTION OF THE DOCTRINE

While it is certainly true that Marxism did not emerge full blown from the pen of Karl Marx at any particular date, we have argued that the development of Marxist doctrine followed a rather consistent pattern at least from 1844. Such is not the case with fascism. There is a parallel between the two doctrines in that they were both articulated largely by one person; thus we can speak of a founding father or at least a group of founding fathers—in many ways, this distinguishes them from the liberal tradition. At first glance, however, Mussolini's ideas seem to have undergone a considerable change during his lifetime. He began his political career as a confirmed Marxist socialist, added some rather vague voluntarist and elitist elements at an early date, took a seemingly abrupt turn from international socialism to Italian nationalism during World War I and emerged from that war proclaiming the existence of something called fascism—an Italian word referring to a tightly knit political group. Even then the doctrine was only beginning.

Further developments included the emergence of an ethical dimension to the conception of the state, the creation of the idea of corporativism, and the insertion of social Darwinism, which can take the form of racism. What, then, are we to do with such a grab bag of ideas? To most commentators the critical change in Mussolini's intellectual development occurred in 1914 when, as editor of the major socialist paper *Avanti!,* he abandoned the socialist line of international class war and called for the intervention of Italy in the "bourgeois" world war. Whatever the reasons for this change, or however great a change it actually was, it provides us with an excellent vantage point for viewing the evolution of his ideas. Let us, then, look at the socialism of Mussolini prior to 1914 and then attempt to determine how orthodox a Marxist he was with an eye toward partially explaining his radical change during World War I. First, however, a brief look at the man and his historic age.

Benito Mussolini

Benito Mussolini was born in 1883 in the Italian town of Predappio. His father, who the young Benito much admired, was a blacksmith whose political views can best be described as radical: socialist, anticlerical, republican. Most scholars of Mussolini believe that Benito's early home environment, coupled with local customs and traditions, had a profound and lasting effect on him. Whatever his basic character, the young Mussolini's early life was beset with rebellion. His formal education was interrupted several times because of acts against authority figures; nevertheless, he did graduate in 1902 certified as an elementary school teacher. He pursued that career off and on, but it seemed to be somewhat of a sidelight to his growing political involvement. The first decade of the twentieth century saw Mussolini becoming more and more prominent in socialist circles,

culminating—after several terms in prison for revolutionary agitation—in his 191
election as editor of the socialist paper *Avanti!* This brief sketch of the man give
an indication of some of his personality traits. But what of Mussolini's ideas?

Even today, after years of scholarship on the man, one still can evoke cries o
surprise or at least raised eyebrows by calling Mussolini a *Marxist,* yet of this ther
is no doubt. Indeed, it can be argued that his early Marxism was in many ways sim
ilar to that of Lenin. The intellectual battle against the revisionist tendencie
within the international communist movement found Mussolini and Lenin on th
same side. They were uncompromising in their advocacy of the necessity of violen
class warfare. Both were disgusted by the nationalist sentiments that seemed to b
undermining the internationalism of classical Marxism, and both thought th
adventurism of capitalist armies to be but a device for delaying the revolution. On
could go on, but the significant point is that during the period between 1902 an
1914 Mussolini constantly used Marxist terms, cited Marx as an authority for hi
actions, and thought in categories that can only be called Marxist. Having said thi
however, we must recall that there were many different schools of Marxism exis
ing during the first decade of the twentieth century. Ranging from the outrigh
revisionism of Bernstein to the radical revolutionary position of Lenin, Marxisn
was many things to many people. Where did Mussolini fit in this ideological spec
trum? As mentioned earlier, his position was rather close to that of Lenin; he to
opposed revisionism and called for revolutionary agitation but, most importan
he also shared Lenin's distrust of a mass spontaneous revolution.

Recall that Lenin advanced the conception of a small, tightly knit revolu
tionary party as a solution to proletarian apathy and as a device for fomenting re
olution in a largely underdeveloped country. While we have not emphasized th
term *elitist* in the prior discussion, there is little doubt that Lenin's party was a
explicitly elitist organization. Its purpose was to utilize the latent energy of th
masses of people and direct it toward appropriate Marxian ends. Mussolini share
this skepticism concerning the revolutionary potential of the masses, and h
argued with increasing frequency for the need for a force to guide the supposed
spontaneous revolution. Numerous times during this early period of developmer
Mussolini spoke with a good deal of contempt for the apathetic masses and h
emphasized the need for *elite leadership.* In doing this he was reflecting the curren
thinking in Italian intellectual circles.

Two of the most prominent advocates of elitist theories of the state, Gaetan
Mosca and Vilfredo Pareto, had advanced theories of political participation tha
denied any important role for the masses in politics and thought government wa
best seen as the rule of successive elite groups. Pareto, in particular, had a direc
influence on Mussolini, for the latter enrolled in two of his courses at the Univer
sity of Lausanne and later called Pareto's theory of elites "the most ingenious soc
ological conception of modern times." Although this reliance on elite leadershi
was by no means uncommon with Marxists of this period, it does provide us wit
an early indication of a doctrine that later became central in fascist thought. I
mass participation in political life was to become a fact of the twentieth century
there must be an elite leadership group to mobilize and guide. Here, then, is a
initial deviation from classical Marxism in Mussolini's thought.

Another facet of Mussolini's early thought, which was to have important consequences in the development of fascism, was his emphasis on *human will*. This is a difficult concept to describe in that it is more of a way of approaching reality and an affirmation of action rather than an intellectual category. Mussolini was desperately concerned with creative action and firm in his belief that it was well within the power of properly directed human beings to create their own history. Rather than being mere pawns in the hands of some superhuman Hegelian historical process or limited in their power by an economic system, human beings were capable of reshaping the world to fit their image of what it ought to be. Looked at from a Marxist-Leninist perspective, this can be seen as a major deviation from the doctrine. By asserting that human will is capable of altering the environment by sheer determination to change it, Mussolini was implicitly undermining Marx's "scientific" laws of development. After all, for Marxism-Leninism, human consciousness and will are largely determined by the objective economic conditions obtained at any time; the individual human being is generally limited by the class circumstances in a particular period in history. In implying that the creative actions of human beings could radically alter history, Mussolini was saying that human will was independent of economic conditions. There is then an extreme emphasis on *voluntarism* in the young Mussolini, which is distinctly un-Marxian and emerges full blown in later fascism. Perhaps this reliance on will can be attributed to Mussolini's interest in the writings of Friedrich Nietzsche, who believed that a truly human person could transcend his or her environment, throw off one's chains, and reconstruct the world according to that person's own image of what it should be.

Whatever the case, this voluntarism led Mussolini to an interest in the role of myth in human affairs, and specifically to the question of how myths could be used to mobilize masses to engage in acts of change and creation. Here Mussolini could rely on the authority of the French philosopher Georges Sorel, who in investigating human motivation came to the conclusion that myths were the prime force in human affairs and that violent activity in pursuit of the fulfillment of a myth is not to be feared. Whether Sorel had any direct influence on the development of Mussolini's ideas is a matter of conjecture, but we do know that Mussolini claimed he was influenced by him. These difficult notions of will and myth are more fully explored later in this chapter; for the moment it is sufficient to note their presence in Mussolini's early thinking.

CHARACTERISTICS OF FASCISM: THE NATION-STATE, ANTI-LIBERALISM, ANTI-BOLSHEVISM, CORPORATIVISM

Despite being bound by treaty to Germany, Italy remained neutral during the early stages of World War I. Socialists in Italy were in many ways more consistent than their counterparts in other countries, for they agitated in behalf of neutrality and continued to proclaim the international solidarity of the working class. While the German proletariat and many of its leaders were rallying around the banner of nationalism, Italian socialists remained firmly neutralist. Given this, imagine the surprise when *Avanti!* under Mussolini's editorship, appeared in October 1914 and called for the abandonment of neutralism and the entry of Italy in the war on the side of the Allies. It was to be Mussolini's last editorial: He was forced from his position as managing editor and eventually drummed out of the party.

How can we explain such an action—the public flouting of a basic tenet of Marxism by a dedicated Marxist? Before leaping to the conclusion that Mussolini was simply jumping aboard the bandwagon of growing nationalist sentiment in Italy, we must recall the dilemma that World War I caused dedicated socialists throughout Europe. The war provided the first real test of Marxism's internationalism, and in general the subjective component of the doctrine failed to pass the test. There were exceptions such as Rosa Luxemberg and Lenin, but for the most part European socialists supported their respective countries in the "bourgeois" war. In a sense, then, Mussolini was in the mainstream of socialist action. Further, we have already noted some early tendencies toward voluntarism and violence in Mussolini's thinking, where the human will is seen capable of performing tremendously heroic actions, even remaking history. Given this, it must have been extremely difficult for a man of Mussolini's temperament to sit back calmly and assume a neutralist posture while the world-shaking events of the war were occurring all around him. Listen, for example, to the tone of that famous editorial in *Avanti!*:

> We enjoy the extraordinary privilege of living at the most tragic hour of the world's history. Do we wish to be—as men and Socialists—inert spectators of this grandiose drama? Or would we prefer to be, in some way, its protagonists?[7]

The Nation-State

Whatever the reasons for this change, the idea that forms the keystone of fascist ideology was gradually being established, and this concept of the nation-state was to dominate Italian political thinking for the next thirty years.

We must now leave the historical development of Mussolini's intellectual and political career to concentrate on the major doctrines that comprise the ideology of fascism, remembering that these doctrines emerged only gradually. It is also important to remember the political context of Italy in the first quarter of the twentieth century. World War I was an exceptionally bitter experience for most Italians. In addition to the economic problems of acute inflation and high unemployment there was considerable social dislocation as a result of the war. As if this was not enough, the Versailles Treaty failed to grant Italy her share—as co-victor—of the spoils of war. Years of strikes and violence along with an ineffective parliamentary system created a general mood of disillusionment and discontent. When the government failed to act on the social problems, Mussolini emerged with promises and plans for a glorious Italian future. If there is one single authoritative statement of fascist ideology it in all probability is Mussolini's *The Doctrine of Fascism,* published in 1932, and that document appropriately emphasizes the notion of the *nation-state.*

[7] Benito Mussolini, in *Fascist Italy,* by Alan Cassels (New York: Thomas Y. Crowell, 1968), p. 19.

The change from the concept of class to the concept of nation involves a major change in conceptual framework. In Marxism, the fundamental unit of analysis is class. Everything is defined in terms of its class base: With the qualifications noted earlier, one is either proletarian or bourgeois; institutions are bourgeois; consciousness is defined largely by class. In fascism the fundamental unit of analysis is the nation: One is either a member of it or one is not; values are national values; one achieves realization of human potential only in and through the nation. Moreover, the nation is not simply the numerical summation of the individuals comprising it, but it possesses a history, a cohesiveness, and a destiny of its own. The nation is thus an entity that is both real and ideal; it can be physically defined in terms of national boundaries and size of population, but it is more than these two features. It has a past that differentiates it from other nations and a future potential that may or may not be achieved.

Fascist speakers constantly used an organic metaphor in referring to the relationship of the nation to the individuals who comprise it. The nation was seen as a biological organism that lives, breathes, grows, and, presumably dies, while individuals are seen as cells that perform their function and achieve fulfillment only insofar as the entire organism is healthy. The individual simply does not exist without the nation, for humans are by nature social animals and can realize themselves as individuals only as members of a collectivity. If the nation thus constitutes the highest ethical entity, the state becomes its political manifestation, the expression of its will and power. Here is how Mussolini explained it:

> The State, as conceived of and as created by Fascism, is a spiritual and moral fact in itself, since its political, juridical, and economic organization of the nation is a concrete thing; and such an organization must be in its origins and development a manifestation of the spirit. The State is the guarantor of security both internal and external, but it is also the custodian and transmitter of the spirit of the people, as it has grown up through the centuries in language, in customs, and in faith. And the State is not only a living reality of the present, it is also linked with the past and above all with the future, and thus transcending the brief limits of individual life, it represents the immanent spirit of the nation.[8]

Perhaps this conception of the nation-state can be more completely explained by briefly examining fascist arguments against liberal democratic thinking.

Anti-Liberalism

We have discussed the intellectual origins of liberal democratic thought at length in the earlier chapters, but we must briefly restate some of its basic assumptions at this point so that we may understand fascist opposition to it, for *anti-liberalism* is an important fascist value. In general, as we have seen, the liberal democratic tradition saw people existing as individuals prior to the establishment of political institutions. Further, they possessed certain rights—as

[8] Benito Mussolini, "The Doctrine of Fascism," in *Social and Political Philosophy,* John Somerville and Ronald E. Santoni, eds. (Garden City, N.Y.: Doubleday and Company, 1963), p. 44.

individuals—granted to them by God or nature. Because of certain inconvenience
of this presocial, prepolitical situation (recall the state of nature), individual
banded together and gave up certain of their natural rights to a collectivity s
that they could, as individuals, live a more comfortable existence. State and soc
ety are thus established for specific purposes, have limited powers and function:
and may be abolished if they exceed their granted powers. The state and societ
are, in short, artificial creations of sovereign individuals. Democratic represer
tative institutions (parliaments, congresses, and so forth) are generally designe
to translate the desires of individuals in the society, normally on a majority rul
basis, into public policy. Representative institutions are, by their very nature
intended to express the *particular wills* of individuals within the society. The pre:
erences of a majority of individuals on any issue are simply that—a summatio
of individual preferences totaling more than 50 percent. Finally, liberal demc
cratic thought is quite clear about the locus of sovereignty in the society: Ult
mately it lies with each individual, and the actions of the state must be with th
consent of those individuals.

To the fascist this is all simply absurd. The mainstream liberal tradition
defines freedom as an absence of restraint on individual action, yet it require
humans to give up some freedom (for example, relinquish natural rights) in orde
to attain freedom. How, fascism asks, does one become free by giving up freedom
Indeed, a fascist would argue, in talking about giving up natural rights so as to
achieve a more convenient situation, the individualistic liberal exposed the fallac
of the entire enterprise. As fascists view it, liberal democrats are saying that free
dom cannot exist without a stable body of laws and political institutions, and th
only way true freedom can exist is through obedience to those laws. It is *law* and
framework of *order* that ensures freedom. The myth of the isolated sovereign ind:
vidual is thus destroyed and we come to understand that the individual can exis
only in and through the state.

As Mussolini stated:

> Anti-individualistic, the Fascist conception of life stresses the importance of the Stat
> and accepts the individual only insofar as his interests coincide with those of the State
> which stands for the conscience and the universal will of man as a historic entity. It i
> opposed to classical liberalism which arose as a reaction to absolutism and exhauste
> its historical functions when the State became the expression of the conscience an
> will of the people. Liberalism denied the State in the name of the individual; Fascisr
> reasserts the rights of the State as expressing the real essence of the individual. An
> if Liberty is to be the attribute of living men and not of abstract dummies invented b
> individualistic liberalism, then Fascism stands for liberty, and for the only libert
> worth having, the liberty of the State and of the individual within the State.[9]

Any rights that individuals may possess are granted and may be removed b
the state; similarly, the private interests of individuals must be subordinated to th
general interests of the collectivity. Insofar as representative institutions, politica
parties, and all of the other trappings of parliamentary democracy are designe
to reflect the interests of individuals (particular wills), they must be discarde

---

[9] Ibid., p. 426.

and replaced by institutions that will determine the *general will* of the nation. The properly constituted state thus becomes the articulator of the general will of the nation.

One of the more commonly used modern attempts to describe the function of political institutions refers to them as authoritative allocators of value for the society as a whole, meaning that states can, within certain limits, control what is done by other institutions and individuals within the society. Fascist ideology takes this type of descriptive statement, expands it, and adds an ethical dimension. The nation is the source of ultimate values for all members of the community and the political arm of the nation—the state—gives articulation to those values. There is, simply, no higher ethical authority. If this is the case, individual human beings fulfill themselves by assuring that the goals of the collectivity are achieved. Indeed, the terms *individual* and *state* are incorrect abstractions insofar as they indicate separate entities—in fascism they are but two sides of the same coin. The nation is struggling to achieve actuality, to fulfill its potential; individuals are human when they contribute to that quest. Given this, it is obvious why fascism was opposed to liberal democratic thought: The latter's assumption is that the state is ultimately the creation of and subservient to the individual. Fascism contended that such thinking had led to conflict, disunity, even chaos in society and afforded no notion of national cohesiveness. Liberal democratic thought was in the end predicated upon assumptions of selfishness and conflict and as such prevented human beings from living in moral association with one another. As Mussolini declared in 1929, "When the conception of the State declines, and disunifying and centrifugal tendencies prevail, whether of individuals or particular groups, the nations where such phenomena appear are in their decline."[10]

Anti-Bolshevism

If the basic fascist premise is that the nation-state is the ultimate authority in all matters, it must, of necessity, be in direct opposition to Marxism-Leninism, providing us with another basic fascist value—*anti-Bolshevism*. To the Marxist, nationalism is but another capitalist trick designed to prevent the formation of an international proletarian movement. From the fascist point of view, communism is one of the prime sources of disunity in the state for it preaches unending class conflict and therefore divides the people. Further, communism is particularly dangerous in that it asserts that nation-states are but passing phenomena on the path toward a world society. It was thus almost inevitable that fascism would adopt a radically anti-Marxist stance, whatever the intellectual origins of its founder. Indeed, the anti-Bolshevism of fascism was so vehement that it has been seen by some as the central trait of the ideology.

While fascism had little use for the excessive individualism of liberal democratic theory, it was especially polemical about Bolshevism. Indeed, at many points fascists thought of themselves, or at least let it be thought, that they were improving on the liberal democratic form of governance in order to combat more

---

[10] Benito Mussolini, in *Anthology*, Greene, ed., p. 44.

effectively the Bolshevik menace. This is one of the reasons why many people continue to believe that fascism was a conservative or reactionary movement. If Marxism is on the radical left of the political spectrum, it is assumed that any movement violently opposed to it must be on the right wing. As we shall see, however, fascism was in many ways as revolutionary as Marxism ever hoped to be, and to dismiss it as simply a right-wing reaction to communism is to deny its complexity and power as an ideology.

Any attempt at comparison between fascism and the state socialism of a Lenin or a Stalin reveals a tangled web, but also may afford some insights into fascist ideas. At the same time Mussolini was calling for national strength to resist the "red menace" of Bolshevism and his fascist squads were violently attacking Italian socialist groups, he was adopting many policies in the economic realm that can clearly be called socialist. From his early appeals for the destruction of the monarchy and his battles with the Catholic Church, to the nationalization of many sectors of the economy, there was a definite socialist thread in his thought. But to call the mature Mussolini a socialist would certainly be a mistake, for he was quite tolerant of particular aspects of capitalism as an economic system, and the fascist movement received considerable support from big industry. Indeed, it is still quite common to hear that it was Mussolini who not only "made the trains run on time" (no doubt a major accomplishment in strike-prone Italy) but also saved Italian capitalism from the Bolsheviks. Moreover, Mussolini eventually reached accommodation with both the Catholic Church and the monarchy. On the other hand, frequent references were made to a "national-socialist" state. The fascist regime often intervened in economic affairs, and the authority of the state to totally control all aspects of life was constantly emphasized. How, then, is one to understand fascist economics?

We can, it seems, make sense of this only by reemphasizing the prime goal of fascism—*autarky:* the creation of a more productive, powerful, and autonomous nation. Private property and the accumulation of capital were certainly acceptable—sometimes highly desirable—insofar as they contributed to that goal. Similarly, socialist economic policies (planning, collectivization, and nationalization) were to be utilized where they seemed best suited for the pursuit of economic productivity. It is here that the comparison with the state socialism of Soviet Marxism, particularly that of Lenin, may prove useful.

Corporativism

We have seen that in the transfer culture of Soviet Marxism the state and party are viewed as temporarily assuming control of all facets of national life for the purpose of building a strong socialist state. When Mussolini stated that the goal of fascism was to create a greater and more powerful nation and that the state must have total power to pursue that end, he was articulating a not dissimilar doctrine. Indeed, in 1925 Mussolini and the Italian philosopher Giovanni Gentile began describing the state as a totalitarian entity, which in Stanley G. Payne's words was "aspiring to an organic unity of Italian society, economic activity, and government

. . . [exercising] total guidance of national goals."[11] Of course, for a Marxist-Leninist such a concept of the nation-state was to be a temporary measure, necessitated by the special circumstances of the Russian revolution and an exceptionally hostile, capitalist world—the goal remained international communism. For Mussolini's fascism the powerful nation was the ultimate goal, and in pursuit of it a policy of *corporativism,* or corporatism, was adopted. In Mussolini's words:

> The Corporation is established to develop the wealth, political power and welfare of the Italian people. Corporativism means a disciplined and therefore a controlled, economy, since there can be no discipline which is not controlled. Corporativism overcomes Socialism as well as it does Liberalism: it creates a new synthesis.[12]

How does the corporate state work? What kind of "synthesis" does it provide? Herman Finer, writing in 1935, concluded that there was "considerable mystification" about these ideas of ". . . the Corporation, and State tonics for private enterprise," not only abroad but in Italy itself.[13] Much of that "mystification" remains. But insofar as Mussolini declared the notion of the corporate state to be the "keystone of fascist doctrine," we must try to understand at least what it was designed to accomplish.

The idea is relatively simple. If liberal capitalism produces class conflict and uncontrolled competition in the economy because of its excessive individualism, and if Marxism supports class warfare between workers and owners, corporativism is designed to remove all conflict in the economic sector. Labor and management, rather than attempting to win gains for their respective groups, are to achieve a unity of purpose in pursuit of the goal of greater productivity. To this end the state will set up various corporations representative of different segments of the economy (for example, the steel industry, the transportation industry) which will contain representatives from both workers and management. These will be organized vertically; that is, representing the whole industry, rather than the more familiar horizontal organization wherein a group or class of workers confronts a group or class of owners. These corporations will be empowered to make decisions on wages and production quotas on an industrywide basis. All of this, of course, will be under the watchful eye of the party and the state. A corporative chamber, designed to replace parliament, would contain representatives from the various corporations, and this chamber would aid in making economic decisions for the entire nation. We cannot go into the institutional details of this conception of the corporate state—indeed, they were never really very clear; for our purposes it is primarily important as a device to eradicate the influence of selfish interests, whether expressed by a single capitalist or by an entire working class.

Finally, one must note two things with respect to fascist economic policies. It must be emphasized that corporativism is not necessarily synonymous with fascism, although many people tend to think so. There are numerous examples of the

[11] Payne, *Fascism: Comparison,* p. 73.

[12] Herman Finer, *Mussolini's Italy* (New York: Grosset & Dunlop, 1935, 1965), p. 502.

[13] Ibid., p. 492.

operation of aspects of corporativism in nonfascist societies. In Great Britain, Sweden, Japan, and even to a lesser extent the United States, industrywide decision concerning wages and profits are made in many sectors of the economy—all under state supervision.

Looked at from another perspective, the corporate state was Mussolini' answer to the five-year plans in the Soviet Union, which attempted to set production goals, centralized economic decisions, and rationalized the allocation of resources for the entire country. Second, it must be emphasized that the goal of all this is increased productivity, social unity, and collective strength, not necessarily greater redistribution to the people. But, given the logic of fascism, as the productivity of the nation rises through cooperative action, all Italians, whatever their status, will benefit. Given this argument, the "socialist" in Mussolini could accommodate his support of Italian capitalist elements in the name of making things better for everyone. From the ideological perspective one thing stands out institutional arrangements are carefully constructed by the state and the party to achieve the goals of national unity and strength. Those aspects of capitalism and socialism that support these goals are maintained; those that detract are discarded In clear control of all aspects of the economy, the state and the party construct a "third way," an alternative economic system that utilizes the best components of the other two economic systems. Still, it seems Stanley Payne is correct when he states, "No point remained less clear in the doctrines of most fascist movement than economic structure and goals."[14]

NATIONAL GOALS, ELITISM, AND LEADERSHIP

We have seen that one of the major goals of fascism is to supplant the selfish individualism of liberal democracy with national solidarity expressed in the form of the will of all of the people. We must now inquire as to the source of that will, what it is and how it is to be found. Asking such questions immediately involves us in *voluntarism, anti-intellectualism,* and *elite leadership,* three additional doctrines in the constellation of fascist ideas.

If the nation is to be seen as a type of organism, it must possess certain functions, a purpose, and have goals which it is to accomplish. While it is true that Italian fascists constantly spoke of the spirit of the nation and invoked the concept of a will that was general in nature, there was little in the way of systematic articulation of the goals of the Italian nation. Vague references abounded to the glories of ancient Rome and the potential greatness of the Italian people, as well as aspirations to Empire, but nothing as specific as the goal culture which we shall find in Nazi Germany. Perhaps it was inevitable that the concrete form of these vague references to Italian power resulted in various attempts to expand the influence of the nation-state in foreign affairs. Italian adventurism in Ethiopia and, for that matter, in World War II can be seen as an attempt to provide the material resources and physical boundaries necessary for national greatness. We should not, however, be surprised by the lack of specificity of goals to be reached

[14] Payne, *Fascism: Comparison,* p. 9.

by a great Italy, for Mussolini's celebration of action for its own sake is an important element here.

> Fascism was not the nursling of a doctrine worked out beforehand with detailed elaboration; it was born of the need for action and it was itself from the beginning practical rather than theoretical; it was not merely another political party but, even in the first two years, in opposition to all political parties as such, and itself a living movement.[15]

He later declared that the fascist movement of the early 1920s had no specific goals, and surely did not possess a well-formulated program for political action. *Social Darwinism,* a general name given to describe social theories that view life as a struggle for survival between groups, is also very much part of fascism. In an almost Hegelian fashion, the nation and its people come to know what they can be only by constantly testing themselves through ceaseless action. The exercise of national will is as important, perhaps more important, than the fulfillment of any set of goals; action and violence are celebrated almost for their own sake. Emphasizing what we might today call a "macho syndrome," fascism viewed forceful and violent actions as indicators of a strong and healthy movement. Only by continually testing itself through struggle with other countries can the nation find its limits. The advocacy of what Mussolini called "controlled violence" and the seemingly unnecessarily violent actions of fascist groups against perceived enemies seem to support this conclusion. However, in attempting to describe this, there is no substitute for Mussolini's own words:

> The years which preceded the march on Rome were years of great difficulty, during which the necessity for action did not permit of research or any complete elaboration of doctrine. There was much discussion, but what was more important and more sacred—men died. They knew how to die. Doctrine, beautifully defined and carefully elucidated, with headlines and paragraphs, might be lacking; but there was to take its place something more decisive—faith.[16]

It should be apparent from the above that fascism has little use for the "rational" quibbling of intellectuals. If action is what is desired there is little point in spending a great amount of time debating or spelling out logical systems of ideas. There is a very distinct and deep strand of anti-intellectualism in fascism, accompanied by the belief that human emotions provide the true seat of wisdom and truth. Human beings, while they are thinking animals, find true wisdom in their emotional responses to words and actions and show that wisdom through committing their collective will to further activity. As such, speeches and written statements are not used to communicate information so much as to induce certain emotional responses in the audience, to stir them to action.

To a cynical observer, this means that the speaker or writer is merely using symbols for their propaganda effect. There is, however, evidence to indicate that

---

[15] Benito Mussolini, in *Anthology,* Greene, ed., p. 40.

[16] Benito Mussolini, in *Sources in Twentieth Century Political Thought,* Henry S. Kariel, ed., (Glencoe, Ill.: The Free Press of Glencoe, 1964), p. 89.

both Mussolini and Hitler believed that the interchange of emotion that occurred during their speeches and at mass rallies was actually a fundamental method of communicating with the people. Here again we encounter the elitist element in fascist doctrine, for if the spoken word is seen as a device for inducing emotional response and is a fundamental method of communication between people, the person who is speaking those words becomes most important indeed. Hence, to appreciate fully the notions of emotionalism, will, and mass action we must look at the person who is to be the source of all these—*the leader.*

The fascist leader is the person who discovers the general will of the nation, interprets it, and communicates it to the people in a way that will lead them to fulfill its commands. As such, the leader is in many ways the key to all fascism. To return to the organic analogy, the leader is literally the personification of the nation; the leader's body and will express the will of all of the people. We must emphasize that fascist doctrine asserts that the leader does not act out of personal interest; that is, all of the leader's words and actions are supposedly dictated by the general will. In a sense the leader is a captive of that will and could not act arbitrarily or on the basis of personal whim. Benito Mussolini is unimportant; *Il Duce* is everything.

We have already noted that the spirit of the people exists throughout time independent of any person, so the leader is really discovering and being led by a national will which already exists. Thus, we must ask how a particular person such as the leader comes to know what that will is. Fascist doctrine provides us little in the way of an explanation of this discovery process. The leader's communication with the general will is shrouded in mystery; the leader simply knows it and is chosen by history to be the one person who gives verbal form to the national spirit. That will always existed in potential, but it required a great person to know it, translate it for the rest of the nation, and mobilize the people to ensure that the potential is fulfilled.

How do people know when a particular person such as Mussolini or Hitler is the authentic manifestation of the general will? Fascists assert that the true greatness of the people and the leader is manifested when the people simply recognize the leader when the leader emerges from the struggle for political power and they agree to follow all of the leader's commands. Again we see the emotional, irrational, social Darwinist base of fascism. How does the leader know that he (or she) is chosen to articulate the will of the people? The leader simply knows it! How do the people recognize the leader when he (or she) appears? They simply do and thereafter follow the leader's commands! There just is no rational explanation for these phenomena for they arise from the will and emotions of the people or, as Mussolini said in the passage just quoted, the process is based on faith.

From another vantage point one can see the tremendous power that fascism gives to the leader, particularly when this concept is combined with other doctrines. If, as we stated earlier, the nation is the final authority in all matters and the leader is the personification of the nation, that person's commands are by definition law. Ultimately, the leader is accountable only to the will of the nation. The masses show both their wisdom and demonstrate their greatness by acknowledging and following the leader. Here we can see with greater clarity the elite-mass distinction observed in the thought of the young Mussolini. The leader possesses the truth, and it is the leader's historical duty to communicate that truth to the masses and to ensure that the nation fulfills its destiny. Fascism sees the masses as possessed of great potential energy, the problem is to mobilize them toward the proper goals. Thus, the question of the method of communication between the leader and the masses is of great importance. Here the elite finds the use of myth and propaganda extremely useful. Much as the "noble lie" of Plato, myths are used to communicate to the people a simplified version of the general will, and propaganda is used to direct their energies. Note that according to the doctrine this does not mean that the leader is manipulating the masses for the leader's own personal power. Rather, what the leader is doing is leading them on the proper path to personal and national fulfillment. If successful, the entire nation will be mobilized in pursuit of national glory, and the will of the people, however vaguely defined, will be achieved. What could be more democratic?

Here, then, are some of the central traits of Mussolini's fascism: corporativism, irrationalism, emotionalism, will, leadership, action for its own sake—all within the confines of that supreme value of national greatness. Before moving to a more explicit summary of the ideas of Benito Mussolini, we must talk briefly about the role of racial doctrines in Italian fascism, for it provides one of the major distinctions between fascism and National Socialism.

Fascism and Race

It is difficult to encapsulate the racial doctrines of Fascist Italy, for the issue is clouded by confusion, lack of consistency, and most important, the alliance with Nazi Germany. Even after 1936, when Italy officially referred to itself as a racist society, there was a good deal of confusion as to what the term meant. Further, several of the major theoreticians of the fascist movement, notably Giovanni Gentile, explicitly denounced German national-socialist racial doctrines as simplistic and unproved. Finally, despite the eventual existence of anti-Semitic legislation in Italy, there is a good deal of evidence to indicate that its application was halfhearted and that many major fascist figures gave covert assistance to Jews escaping the expanding German empire.

The confusion surrounding these doctrines revolves around the concepts of *race* and *nation*. Early in the 1920s, Mussolini had spoken of the superiority of the Italian race and its potential for greatness. Yet it is quite clear from the context of his speeches that he used the word almost as a synonym for nation. The notion of an Italian race was simply impossible, for Italy was a country made up of individuals of myriad racial backgrounds—more of a cosmopolitan melting pot than a homogeneous body. Furthermore, while Hitler and the Nazis were proclaiming the existence of one particular race (variously referred to as Aryan, Nordic, and sometimes even German) as physically and culturally superior to all others, Italy was in the position of having very few so-called Nordics in its population. How can one refer to Italy as a superior nation if superiority is defined in terms of the prevalence of Nordics? This is but a more complex way of saying that Italian racism was constantly associated with Italian nationalism and that references to an Italian race generally included all Italians irrespective of their racial background. "There were few epithets used by Western liberals against Nazis that were not applied by Fascists, who also coined special slurs of their own, denouncing the Nazis, for example, as a 'political movement of pederasts.'"[17] Even after the alliance with Germany was concluded and a policy of racism was officially announced, Mussolini, speaking in defense of that policy, could say:

> Jews possessing Italian citizenship who have unquestionable military or civil merit in the eyes of Italy and the regime will find understanding and justice.[18]

This is not to deny that there are theoretical bases in fascist doctrine for some sort of racial and cultural separatism. The concept of a people, or a *Volk*, immediately asserts that there is something distinctive and usually superior about a particular group of people. If that group can be seen as "chosen," as separate and superior, it is but a short step to assert that they should somehow dominate other groups who are less fortunate. Further, fascism contained a distinct strain of anti-Zionism, opposing it largely on grounds similar to its opposition to Marxism; Zionism preached a doctrine which placed the values of international Jewry higher than those of the nation-state. Given fascism's opposition to any doctrine challenging the ultimate authority of the nation, it is obvious why such sentiments had to be countered. Having said all that, what is apparent, once again, is that the central conceptual category of Italian fascism was the nation, and that any racism involved was usually defined in terms of the nation. Such, as we shall see, was not the case with German National Socialism.

Perhaps the single most correct statement one can make concerning racism in Mussolini's doctrine is that it was part of an attempt to cement relations between Fascist Italy and Nazi Germany. How else can one interpret Mussolini's early attempts to dissuade Hitler from his racial policies? How else can one explain the prominence of people like Giovanni Gentile in the fascist state, whose opposition to Hitler's racial policies was well documented? On balance, racism in Italy is best seen as an ad hoc addition to the doctrine, instituted for strategic purposes and never made fully compatible with the far more basic value of Italian nationalism.

Fascist Traits

Before moving to a discussion of German National Socialism, it seems worth attempting a summary of the major themes of Italian fascism, if only to serve as a source of comparison and contrast for further discussion. Little more need be said of the doctrine of the nation-state, for it has dominated our discussion throughout the chapter. Much like the notion of "class" in Marxism-Leninism, the "nation" forms the fundamental unit of analysis in fascist doctrine. One is tempted to dismiss fascism by simply asserting that anything that is good for the nation-state is, by definition, part of the doctrine. Yet we have seen that there

---

[17] Payne, *Fascism: Comparison*, p. 79.

[18] Benito Mussolini, in *Mussolini and Italian Fascism*, by S. William Halperin (New York: Van Nostrand Reinhold, 1964), p. 175.

were several general themes used to enhance that goal of national greatness, certain traits and values that are appropriately associated with the term "fascism," even if they do not constitute a precise definition. Let us attempt to summarize and clarify those themes and traits by looking at some attempts at systematic definition of the fascist phenomenon. For example, a dictionary definition reads:

> Any authoritarian, anti-democratic, anti-socialistic system of government in which economic control by the state, militaristic nationalism, propaganda, and the crushing of opposition by means of secret police, emphasize the supremacy of the state over the individual.[19]

This definition is accurate in many respects, containing many of the themes we have associated with fascism, but it suffers, perhaps inevitably, from superficiality. Moreover, it is in the complex interrelation of traits that fascism achieves its power as an ideology. For example, fascism is "antidemocratic" if by that we mean that it opposes the excessive individualism of classical liberalism and the representative institutions associated with it. But we know that fascism was fully willing to borrow from that tradition, or leave it undisturbed, when it suited its purpose, as in the case of capitalism.

Further, fascism is indeed "antisocialistic" if that means violent opposition to the internationalism and class analysis of socialism. However, it did rely on many socialist measures in the economic realm and had its intellectual origins in the mind of a confirmed Marxist. What about "the supremacy of the state over the individual"? Is this good fascism? Yes, if by that phrase we mean the nation-state defines the norms for action for all people and admits of no higher authority. Still, a good fascist would declare that the implied opposition of the terms *state* and *individual* in the definition is but another example of excessive democratic individualism. Being social animals, humans can fulfill themselves as individuals only in and through the nation; to imply that there is some sort of opposition between the two is to distort human nature. Finally, the dictionary definition suffers by ignoring other aspects that seem central to fascism: Where, for example, are elitism, leadership, activism, and corporativism?

Another attempt at a "first definition" of fascism is offered by Ernst Nolte in his *Three Faces of Fascism:*

> Fascism is anti-Marxism which seeks to destroy the enemy by the evolvement of a radically opposed and yet related ideology and by the use of almost identical and yet typically modified methods, always, however, within the unyielding framework of national self-assertion and autonomy.[20]

The major virtue of this definition is that it correctly points out the centrality of anti-Marxism and nationalism while attempting to show the complexity of the doctrine through the use of qualifying phrases. Still, it seems incomplete and

---

[19] Charles Earle Funk, ed., *New Practical Standard Dictionary of the English Language,* Vol. 1 (New York: Funk & Wagnalls Company, 1954), p. 481.

[20] Ernst Nolte, *Three Faces of Fascism,* (New York: Holt, Rinehart and Winston, 1966), pp. 20–21.

surely suffers from vagueness. More helpful, it would seem, is the summary of fas cist concepts offered by Anthony Joes: nationalism, explicit repudiation of parlia mentary liberalism, statism, productionism, corporativism, authoritarianism, and elitism. Perhaps this, or something like it, is the best we can hope for in trying to come to grips with the phenomenon of fascism—a list of traits, tendencies, and values. As A. James Gregor has stated:

> There is little prospect that the near future will deliver a fully competent theory of Fascism. We will have to be content with plausibilities and detailed historical accounts The best efforts will be "eclectic," attempting to weave together the most defensible of plausibilities into a narrative in which we can invest some confidence.[21]

All this is but to underscore the emotionalism and anti-intellectualism of the fascist movement, for its repudiation of rational argument makes systematic expo sition of the doctrine most difficult. Such is not the case, however, with our next subject for discussion: Adolf Hitler was all too explicit about what he intended. The problem was both too few and too many people believed him.

SUGGESTED READINGS

FINER, HERMAN, *Mussolini's Italy*. New York: Grosset & Dunlap, 1965.

GREENE, NATHANAEL, ed. *Fascism: An Anthology*. New York: Thomas Y. Crowell 1968.

GREGOR, A. JAMES, *The Ideology of Fascism*. New York: The Free Press, 1969.

LAQUER, WALTER, ed., *Fascism: A Reader's Guide*. Berkeley: University of Califor nia Press, 1976.

LEWIS, SINCLAIR, *It Can't Happen Here*. New York: New American Library, 1963.

MUSSOLINI, B., "The Doctrine of Fascism," in *Social and Political Philosophy*. John Somerville and Ronald E. Santoni, eds. Garden City, N.Y.: Doubleday and Company, 1963.

NOLTE, ERNST, *Three Faces of Fascism*. New York: Holt, Rinehart and Winston 1966.

O'SULLIVAN, NOËL, *Fascism*. London: J. M. Dent & Sons Ltd., 1983.

PAYNE, STANLEY G., *Fascism: Comparison and Definition*. Madison: University of Wisconsin Press, 1980.

SCHNEIDER, HERBERT W., *Making the Fascist State*. New York: Oxford University Press, 1928.

WEBER, EUGEN, ed., *Varieties of Fascism*. Princeton, N.J.: Van Nostrand Company 1964.

WOOLF, S. J., ed., *The Nature of Fascism*. New York: Random House, 1969.

---

[21] A. James Gregor, in Joes, *Fascism in the Contemporary World*, p. 261.

10

National Socialism

All who are not of good race in this world are chaff.
Adolf Hitler

With the foregoing words in *Mein Kampf (My Struggle)*, Adolf Hitler pointed at once to the prime difference between Italian fascism and German National Socialism as well as to the major category of national-socialist thought. We have stated in the preceding chapter that the idea of the nation provided the fundamental building block in Italian fascist thinking and that despite some rather awkward attempts to speak of an Italian race, Mussolini's doctrines remained fundamentally nationalist. While it is a subject by no means free from controversy, almost the opposite situation existed in Hitler's doctrines of National Socialism. Despite his appeals to German nationalism and his constant references to German history and greatness, Hitler was primarily the champion of a particular racial group, and the fruition of his plans would have eventually led to the supersession of the German nation-state. To support such a conclusion we must once again enter into that murky area of the relationship between nation and race, or better, between the *Volk* (people) and the racial group.

In discussing these ideas with respect to Italian fascism, we found that Mussolini was rather obscure as to the history and composition of the Italian people, preferring to make vague references to the glories of ancient Rome and the future potential of the nation. In the case of Germany we are dealing with a different situation, for the celebration of uniquely Germanic myths, culture, and history was very much part of both popular and intellectual traditions. Tracing their roots back to the Germanic tribes who conquered mighty Rome, an entire line of writers was able to refer to an idealized German *Volk* that was unique insofar as it possessed characteristics which separated it from—and made it superior to—all other peoples.

In our discussion of Italian fascism we emphasized that the concept of a people does not merely refer to the individuals populating a given geographic area at a particular period of time. Rather, the *Volk* consists of an entire tradition, possesses a will of its own, and has a destiny which is unique to it. In Germany of the nineteenth and early twentieth centuries, these vague and essentially mystical ideas were given specific content through reference to a whole host of events in the history of the region. As such, the notion of a German *Volk* received a far more concrete manifestation and provides us with a much better example of this type of *volkish* thinking than does its Italian counterpart.

GERMAN ROMANTICISM

The *volkish* or romantic tradition as it is sometimes called was in many respects a reaction to the complexities produced by a rapidly developing industrial economy. The relative security and stability of the feudal era were being replaced by rapid change and apparent instability. The urban areas that grew up around varying industrial complexes attracted uncounted numbers of people with promises of greater rewards and a new life. While the opportunity to "better themselves" undoubtedly existed, in many cases people encountered the type of conditions that so repelled Karl Marx. Torn by impersonal forces from the familiar surroundings of the rural village and performing the seemingly meaningless tasks of modern industry, the alienation of which the young Marx spoke was a very real thing in Germany, even for those who did not share his specific definition of the term or his vision of the future. This condition of perceived alienation or "rootlessness" was, as we have noted, a general phenomenon throughout industrializing Europe, and a common response was a desire to revert to an idealized past. In Germanic areas, this response was advocated most vociferously by a diverse group of social critics, artists, and intellectuals generally placed under a rather large umbrella called German *romanticism*. One of their responses to this situation was an attempt to construct an idealized past, where life was simple and a person had historic and cultural roots. If there was one central idea in the diversity of notions that characterized German romanticism, it was that humans had somehow lost their bearings in modern civilization and had to return to a more natural, simple setting in order to cure their sickness. Romantics of all stripes stressed the necessity of restoring a harmonious interrelationship between the human animal and the forces of nature. As George Mosse described it:

> The genuineness of the natural environment was held up to praise and credited with engendering in the population such qualities as sincerity, integrity, and simplicity. The culture of a Volk rooted in nature was posited as the very opposite of a mechanical and materialistic civilization. . . . Only nature was genuine, since it was infused with both the life force and historical meaning for the Volk.[1]

Moreover, this was seen as particularly true for the German *Volk*, whose strength and wisdom lay in natural settings and whose grandeur could be achieved only by remaining true to those origins. The *volkish* spirit was believed manifesting itself in the physical environment—indeed, in the very landscape populated by Germans. In particular, the Germany of mists, hills, and dark forests was seen as being something uniquely German and an appropriate manifestation of the *volkish* spirit. Despite its veneer of Christianity, there was a good deal of pagan pantheism in much of the romantic tradition. The spirit of the Germanic people was to be found in the forests and streams which made up its ancestral home, and it communicated with members of the *Volk* through those natural objects. The image of the sun, for example, played a very important role in popular *volkish* literature as the symbol of the strength and power of the German spirit. Germans were seen as looking up from their dark and mysterious forests to the sun for guidance and strength in achieving their unique goals as a people. This contrasted with the experience of other peoples whose existence was arid and devoid of mystery because of their origins in flat, treeless regions. The development of this form of stereotype and determinism by the natural environment was to play an equally important role in later racist literature, but it is

---

[1] George L. Mosse, *The Crisis of German Ideology: Intellectual Origins of the Third Reich* (New York: Grosset & Dunlap, 1964), p. 19.

important to note that it already was an essential part of the *volkish* tradition prior to the development of the racial doctrine.

Such an image of the true German provided a stark contrast with the modern rootless laborer whose spirit had been corrupted by the supposed sophistication of civilization. The modern German was a sick animal whose life was devoid of meaning. If the greatness of the German spirit lay in the mystery and simplicity of the natural setting, the metropolis could be viewed as only an artificial thing—a corruptor of nature, culture, and the *Volk*. This juxtaposition of urban-dominated *civilization* with true *volkish culture* produced a bevy of interesting contrasts as well as some real problems for the romanticists. Civilized people were seen as preoccupied with the superficialities of life such as clothing styles, whereas the true German was content with simple functional dress—protection from the elements and little more.

Typical of this desire for simplicity was the advocacy by one Father Jahn—an early romantic spokesman—of a sort of "cult of the body," which included a celebration of the virtues of nude bathing. Urban dwellers were caught up in the marketplace, necessitating the constant pursuit of material objects and the money necessary for their purchase, whereas true members of the *Volk* worked the soil for their everyday necessities and harmoniously interacted with nature.

Many writers contrasted their stereotyped German with an equally fictionalized French citizen, the latter being materialistic, shallow, and lacking in the virtues of true humanity. A good expression of the antimodern stance of German romanticism can be seen in some of the proposals that were made for economic reform, for, as we have noted, a major cause of all of the difficulties of modernity was to be found in economic growth. There were numerous proposals to return to the equivalent of the guild system of the Middle Ages and to break up industrial complexes and move them to rural areas. Here again we can observe both the desire for simple solutions to complex problems that was characteristic of romanticism as well as a willingness to renounce the materialistic rewards of economic progress in the name of reuniting humans with their natural environment. Some of the later literature of this tradition managed to accommodate itself to the necessity of large-scale industry and modernization in order to produce a strong nation-state, but the deepest roots of German romanticism rejected the notion.

Emotionalism versus Rationalism

It should not be surprising that a movement that placed tremendous emphasis on reuniting humans with nature also tended to celebrate human emotions and to deprecate rationality. Indeed, the mystical communication that occurs between the individual will and the *volkish* spirit cannot really be described with words; it is something that must be felt. Many of the problems of modernity could be directly attributed to the overdevelopment of human rational capacities. As such, there was a need to return to the soil (mother earth), thereby resurrecting the emotional side of the human animal so that it might once again become whole. Much as in the case of Mussolini's fascism, a person's immediate emotional responses were considered more correct guides to truth and action than lengthy deliberation and intellectualizing. Or as Hitler, echoing this romantic theme, was to put it in 1923: "The Movement must not rust away in Parliament, it must not spend itself in superfluous battles of words, but the banner with the white circle and the black Swastika will be hoisted over the whole of Germany on the day which shall mark the liberation of our whole people."[2] In the process of denying validity to the trappings of rationality, some of the writers in the romantic tradition went so far as to celebrate violence for its own sake, seeing the desire to inflict punishment on others as a natural expression of human emotion. Thus, if intellect and excessive rationality were the cause of most human problems, the simple solution was to resurrect the will as the prime vehicle for directing thought and action.

A final example of the romantic effort to place myth and mystery at the center of human nature can be found in the attempts that were made to transform Christianity in such a manner as to make it more compatible with *volkish* ideas. From the romantic perspective, Christianity through its long history had become institutionalized to such an extent that it was dominated by sterile dogma—mere form with little substance. Living doctrines had been rationalized, intellectualized, drained of their spiritual and mystical origins. In the view of romanticists, Christ was as much a symbol of the divine spirit as an originator of a body of doctrine; furthermore, his religious experience exemplified precisely the sort of mystical communication that German romanticists envisioned existing between the *volkish* spirit and the people. To put it all too simply, the tradition placed a great emphasis on the irrational and mystical side of Christianity, thereby making it quite compatible with their *volkish* themes. Finally, in a manner later to be copied by Nazism, several efforts were made to "Germanize" Christianity, to make it a national religion by deemphasizing the more internationalistic aspects of the Christian tradition.

Here, then, is the romantic view of the human condition as well as an ideal type to which all members of the *Volk* ought to aspire. There is a great danger in reading too much into this tradition, despite the apparently widespread dissemination of *volkish* ideas in both popular literature and in intellectual circles. To imply that the romantic tradition was the only strain of thought present in nineteenth- and early twentieth-century Germany and that somehow its existence caused the later developments of National Socialism would be to distort reality. After all, the same region that produced *volkish* thinkers also generated the highly rationalistic G. W. F. Hegel as well as the scientific and materialistic Karl Marx.

Having dismissed the notion that romanticism and *volkishness* were somehow uniquely characteristic of a monolithic German mind, we must note, however, that the existence of this type of tradition provided fertile soil for the growth of National Socialism. With such ideas as part of the popular and intellectual marketplace, it was possible for national-socialists to pick and choose ideas from the tradition to suit their purposes and build their own mythology. On the other side of the coin, then, it would also be a distortion of reality to deny that romanticism

[2] Adolf Hitler, *My New Order*, Raoul de Roussy de Sales, ed. (New York: Reynal & Hitchcock, 1941), p. 49.

and *volkish* thinking contributed significantly to German National Socialism. But one crucial element was necessary before this volatile mixture of ideas that characterized Nazism was possible—the factor of racism.

RACISM

The notion that a particular racial group is somehow culturally and spiritually superior to all others is surely not German in origin. Minimally, the distinction is as old as that between Greeks and barbarians, the latter being regarded in ancient times as literally subhuman. One is tempted to say that some form of racism is as old as humanity. Similarly, the singling out of a particular racial group for censure, or as a scapegoat for all human ills, was not unique to Germany, whether that group was designated as Jews or nonwhites. Indeed, a rather convincing argument can be made that during the nineteenth and early twentieth centuries, France and Russia, rather than Germany, were the real hotbeds of anti-Semitism; and prior to and throughout this same time period, the United States had its own racism to confront. Racism, it seems, knows no national boundaries nor is it new in human affairs. Yet it was in Nazi Germany that ideas of racial superiority and anti-Semitism became the official policies of the state and resulted in the slaughter of uncounted numbers of innocent people.

Why in Germany? Obviously that question cannot be answered within the brief confines of this discussion; perhaps the final answer can only be found in the mind of Adolf Hitler. Nevertheless, that would be too easy an answer: There already existed a distinct tradition of racist ideas of which Hitler was an adherent, and Nazi policies, however horrible, cannot simply be dismissed as manifestations of a disturbed mind. Nor can one, as some have suggested, simply be silent in the face of the Holocaust, somehow allowing the horror to speak for itself. It demands explanation, or at least the attempt at explanation.

One might consider it ironic—if irony is possible in this discussion—that the person whose racist ideas had the greatest impact on late nineteenth-century German thought was French, the people so derided by the romantic tradition. Despite the existence of numerous racial theories throughout Europe, it was the publication of Count Joseph Arthur de Gobineau's *Essay on the Inequality* of *Human Races* in 1854 that gave the "scientific" study of race its most coherent form. While Gobineau's work achieved fame in Germany only at a somewhat later date, it is generally recognized that his theories had a great influence on most of the Nazi racial theorists and that his ideas provided much of the framework for later racist thought. Gobineau asserted that race was the only significant variable that could be used to explain human progress and decline. Ideas, institutions, culture, and freedom were, to borrow the Marxian phrase, mere superstructural elements that were reflections of the more basic category of race. Gobineau divided the human species into three basic racial groups—white, yellow, and black—and gave each certain dominant characteristics. The black race possessed little intelligence but was endowed with a very powerful type of primitive sensuality; the yellow race was stereotyped as lacking in imagination and creativity, being prone toward excessive materialism. It was the white race that was endowed with all of the virtues of humanity—nobility, freedom, honor, and spirituality. Once understood, these basic racial characteristics provided the key to the understanding of all of human history. As Gobineau put it, "The basic organization and character of all civilizations are equal to the traits and spirit of the dominant race."[3] All too simply, where the white race (increasingly coming to be called *Aryan*) dominated, people and culture flourished; where other races were in ascendancy, degeneration occurred.

Gobineau was, however, generally pessimistic about the future of humanity, for he saw that the Aryan race (which, by the way, was seen to have its origins in India) tended to "intermingle" with inferior races, thus diluting its superior characteristics. Europe, for example was initially populated by the "yellow" race, its greatness as a region only occurring when the Aryan strain of blood was superimposed as the result of migration. But Aryans intermarried with their inferiors, thus diluting the pure strain and ensuring decline.

What are we to make of this? While it is difficult to regard such thinking seriously, it must be emphasized that Gobineau was laying the groundwork for a body of ideas that in varying forms would be accepted by untold numbers of people as fundamental truth. Again, in terms of emphasis, Gobineau and other racial thinkers asserted that this is not merely one way of looking at human history, but the only way—it was scientifically provable. However crude or simplistic this may appear it must be regarded seriously. Finally, it must be noted that Gobineau was no anti-Semite. He viewed Jews as a strong and intelligent people. Their fate, moreover, was the same as that of Aryans, for they too tended to mix their blood with the lesser races. It is only with the importation of Gobineau's basic ideas into Germany that his view of Jews was altered to produce anti-Semitism.

Influence of Richard Wagner

As mentioned earlier, Gobineau's work lay dormant in Germany for a period of time but eventually came to be accepted and popularized by a group of intellectuals and artists who formed a group centered in the small Bavarian town of Bayreuth. During the last decades of the nineteenth century, Bayreuth became the principal center for the dissemination and popularization of racist doctrines for the entire region. Most of the individuals who later served as intellectual apologists for Hitler's regime had some connection with the Bayreuth Circle, so much so that the town became a religious shrine for the Nazi movement. The originator and major light of Bayreuth until his death in 1883 was the composer Richard Wagner, who gathered around him a cluster of people whose purpose was the celebration of the *volkish* tradition. Wagner's influence is somewhat difficult to assess and his works, both musically and politically, remain even today the subject of a good deal of controversy. His operas served as vehicles for popularizing German mythology; the image of a Teutonic Siegfried—a primitive German beyond the petty conventions of good and evil—became a central symbol of the Third Reich.

---

[3] Joseph Arthur de Gobineau, quoted in George Mosse, *Toward the Final Solution* (New York: Howard Fertig, 1978), p. 52.

There is little doubt of Wagner's influence on Hitler; Wagner was his favorite composer, and Hitler himself asserted that his early life was greatly influenced by the composer's operas.

Thus, it was from Bayreuth that the clearest popular formulation of racial doctrines emanated, particularly after Wagner's death. Toward the end of his life the composer had befriended Gobineau and that relationship apparently solidified some of the racist themes that were present in Wagner's earlier political writings. It was, however, his widow, Cosima, son Siegfried, and son-in-law Houston Stewart Chamberlain who expanded on those themes and made Bayreuth a magnet for anyone with racist inclinations.

It is in the work of the Bayreuth Circle that we can see the blending of German romanticism with doctrines of racial purity in their clearest fashion. Wagner himself asserted that the source of German woes was race mingling and that the sole hope for the future was the resurrection of the pure Aryan strain. To accomplish this a leader would emerge, dedicated to German greatness and determined to purify the race—in particular to eradicate French and Jewish elements. That Wagner himself would have approved of Hitler's final solution to the "Jewish problem" is doubtful in light of the many liberal themes in both his writings and his music. Still, he did lend his famous name to the anti-Semitism that culminated in the Holocaust.

It is extremely difficult, if not impossible, to assess the influence of the Bayreuth Circle either in the popularizing of racist doctrines or in the thinking of the young Hitler. We know, for instance, that Hitler met and talked with Houston Stewart Chamberlain shortly before the latter's death, but many of the racial doctrines Hitler adopted were at odds with Chamberlain's teaching. Some commentators assert that Hitler's ideas crystallized in conversations with Dietrich Eckhart while others contend that his ideas about race derived from Ludwig Woltmann and Hans F. K. Guenther. While we can make no attempt to show a causal relationship between the ideas of any of these men and later Nazi doctrines, we can spell out several additional aspects of the amorphous body of racist ideas that later influenced Nazi policies.

Emphasis on Aryan Leadership

The Aryan race, however it was defined, was seen as the sole source of all of the positive achievements of humanity. The existence of sophisticated civilizations in other parts of the world was explained by the aforementioned migration of Aryan elements to those areas. Using the argument familiar to racists of all stripes, its theorists explained the existence of superior achievements in non-Aryan regions by attempting to prove that Aryan blood flowed through the veins of their leaders. Italy, Spain, and France were, as nations, capable of greatness only because of the existence of Aryan leadership. The worldwide spread of Aryans, while providing truly human values for other less fortunate races, did, however, tend to produce the blood-mingling that caused Gobineau to despair. The pure Aryan strain was gradually being lost.

In modern times, one of the remaining groups of Aryans was found in north- ern Europe, particularly in Germany; here the destiny of the German nation and all humanity resided. These Aryans had to be identified and elevated to positions of leadership so that they could lead humanity to further glories. The problem, then, became the identification of those persons possessing the purest quality and largest quantities of Aryan blood—surely all Germans did not possess it!

To aid in this identification process a list of typically Aryan traits was drawn up; these physical characteristics gave evidence of an indwelling Aryan spirit. These characteristics included a general lightness of skin color (further indication of the tendency to identify Aryanism with the "white" race), blonde hair, blue eyes, a long narrow skull, and a perfect proportion between head size and body length. Com- mon to these attempts was a reliance on the authority of a crude "science" of anthropology, later, as we shall see, to be buttressed by a similarly superficial reliance on the theories of Charles Darwin. This attempt to determine traits of Aryanism scientifically through external observation was later to cause the Nazis some minor difficulty because of the obvious fact that many of their leaders, including the Fuhrer himself, did not seem to have such bodily attributes. This was circumvented by saying that physical traits were not the only way of identifying an indwelling Aryan spirit, but simply a good rule of thumb. The introduction of this type of "scientific" facade to racial doctrine provided additional means by which the "chosen people" could be identified, and it lent a form of scientific credibility to the doctrine.

We must emphasize here how the traditions of German romanticism and nationalism were rapidly becoming merged with racial doctrines. The Siegfried of the German romantic tradition had become the blonde, blue-eyed bearer of the Aryan strain of blood. Germany, although long dormant as a nation-state, was des- tined for glory because the fatherland possessed people with a significant amount of the primal strain of Aryan blood. Indeed, Germany would fulfill its destiny as a nation through the leadership of the master race. Typical of this blending of Ger- man romanticism, nationalism, and Aryan racism was a speech by Hitler in 1922:

> They [conservative politicians] ought day by day to din into the ears of the masses: "We want to bury all the petty differences and to bring out into the light the big things, the things we have in common which bind us to one another." That should weld and fuse together those who still have a German heart and a love for their peo- ple in the fight against the common heredity foe of all Aryans.[4]

In much the same fashion, several other elements of the romantic tradition were amalgamated with racial dogma and transformed to produce a more dynamic synthesis. The traditional romantic fear of industrialization and the evils inherent in it was overcome by noting that non-Aryans had presided over past economic development. Industrialization, by itself, was not an evil as some romantics had argued; it had resulted in alienating conditions only because inferior people were in positions of power. Rapid economic growth and the development of an

---

[4] Hitler, *Order*, p. 20.

industrial base could now be seen as positive benefits in the assertion of German greatness, provided, of course, that Aryans were supreme in the economic sphere.

Similarly, the pessimism that had pervaded much of the earlier racial literature was circumvented. It was argued that although blood mixing had led to a decline in the human condition, this did not necessarily have to continue. Rather than pointing to a glorious but long-lost past, people of will and energy could work to resurrect the Aryan strain, which would provide the precondition of an era of even greater human progress. In buttressing this argument, racial theorists appealed to the authority of a crude social Darwinism, which held that the human race was in a constant struggle in which only the fittest survived. If this were the case, Aryans, who were by definition the most fit, needed only to assert their natural superiority and the future of humanity would be assured. This lent a type of scientific credibility and historical inevitability to the doctrine. In effect, it became a crude syllogism: Aryans are most fit; the fittest will survive; therefore, Aryan culture will triumph over the forces of evil!

The Struggle Between Aryans and Jews

One final aspect of this general grab bag of ideas of racism in the early twentieth century must be emphasized before we move on to a discussion of the young Hitler. This was a change in the stereotype of the Jew. Anti-Semitism, of course, existed in the world for a long period prior to the nineteenth century; it varied in intensity, one could argue, with the perceived power Jews possessed in particular countries. Despite the Jewish people's ability to attain political and economic power, most early anti-Semitic doctrines pictured Jews as inferior beings who through some mysterious craft and cunning were able to succeed in spite of their innate failings. As we have noted, there were exceptions to this general picture—Gobineau is an example—but the general view, particularly in popular literature, was that Jews were inferior. However, the difficult question of how a supposedly inferior race could achieve power at the expense of a superior race was seldom directly addressed in racist literature. A rather ambivalent attitude developed toward Jews whereby, on the one hand, they were viewed as inferior objects of ridicule and, on the other, as a potent force to be feared and demolished. Indeed, it was noted that Jews seemed to possess the solidarity as a racial group that the supposedly superior Aryans lacked. Viewed in this fashion, history could be seen as a perpetual struggle between Aryans and Jews: one group representing culture and progress, the other evil and decay. Jews were seen not merely as parasites and debasers of culture but as a formidable foe to be treated most seriously. In Hitler's words:

> The Jew is not only a foreign element differing in his essential character, which is utterly harmful to the nature of the Aryan, but the Jewish people in itself stands against us as our deadly foe and so will stand against us always and for all time.[5]

[5] Ibid., p. 32.

It is in this context that we meet full blown the notion of a Jewish conspiracy against mankind, whereby Jews, through cunning and treachery, seek to control the world. The infamous *The Protocols of the Elders of Zion,* which was purportedly the outline of the Jewish plan for world domination, was a clear forgery, yet it fed popular belief in the myth of a Jewish conspiracy. Inferior though they be, Jews represented a threat to all that is truly human, so the doctrine preached.

It was from this inconsistent mixing of racial ideas that the Nazis fashioned their racial *myths.* The fact that such doctrines were common currency around the turn of the twentieth century is surely more important than the writings of any one racist thinker. Whether the young Hitler ever read Houston Chamberlain or Ludwig Woltmann or any other treatise on the subject is somewhat immaterial. These thinkers provided a respectable, pseudoscientific overlay for very deep-seated human prejudices, and they permitted a person like Hitler an appeal to authority in support of his own emotional prejudices. In Nazi hands these myths became reality, with genocidal consequences.

ADOLF HITLER: RACE, LEADERSHIP, AND THE NATIONAL-SOCIALIST STATE

The life and personality of Adolf Hitler have in all probability been subjected to more detailed analysis than any other figure in the twentieth century. Confronted with the enormity of the evil committed by Nazi Germany under his leadership, untold numbers of scholars and laypersons have attempted to find an explanation for—and too often to explain away—Nazism in Hitler's personality. We make no attempt to summarize that scholarship or to add to it, but brief mention of Hitler's life and the circumstances in Germany that permitted his rise to power seem necessary to any understanding of Nazi ideology.

Adolf Hitler was born in 1889 in the small town of Braunau on the border between Austria and Bavaria. Hitler was later to describe his early life as one of poverty and suffering, although the evidence indicates that his father, who was a minor civil servant, provided adequately for the family. The young Hitler was not a success in formal education; his grades were poor, he was a disruptive influence, and he seemed to lack the discipline necessary for concentrated study. Some have argued that these early experiences led to Hitler's lifelong contempt for formal education and those who possessed it. In any case, his dream was to be an artist or an architect. After his father's death, his mother moved to Linz, in Upper Austria, where the young Hitler pursued that dream doing sketches and drawings in an effort to sustain himself. In 1907, after two years in Linz, Hitler journeyed to Vienna to further his artistic ambitions by attempting to enroll in the Academy of Fine Arts. He was denied admission on the grounds that he lacked artistic talent. In spite of this, he remained in Vienna until 1913. By his own account, these years were crucial to the development of both his personality and his ideas.

He lived an essentially solitary existence, barely sustaining himself through sketching and architectural drawing. He was described by contemporaries as moody, incapable of finding a job, and possessing a passion for politics and opera (particularly Wagner). Alan Bullock characterized the young Hitler as possessing the artist's temperament without talent, training, or creative energy.[6] In 1913 Hitler left Vienna for Munich, where he led basically the same type of existence, until the outbreak of World War I.

There is little doubt that the war gave direction to Hitler's life and provided an outlet for his energies. He volunteered for and was accepted into a Bavarian regiment that saw considerable action throughout the war. Although he was decorated several times for his actions, he was able to achieve only the rank of corporal, whether through lack of ability or lack of ambition. He was gassed, temporarily blinded, and in the hospital recovering from his wound when the war ended.

We cannot attempt to chronicle the events that led to Hitler's rise in 1933 to the position of Chancellor of Germany. Our concern must remain with Hitler's ideas. Before exploring them, however, we need to sketch briefly the social and political environment within Germany after the war, particularly since many commentators believe that these circumstances were crucial to the eventual success of Nazism.

Germany at that time presented a general picture of political and economic chaos, interrupted only briefly by periods of relative stability. The nation had been defeated on the battlefield, although the myth that the German army had been "stabbed in the back" by leftist politicians rather than defeated militarily was to grow in strength in the coming years. The country was saddled with an economy in shambles and a large debt for war reparations imposed by the Treaty of Versailles. Further, the economic depressions that swept all of Europe throughout the 1920s had particularly severe effects in Germany, producing rapid inflation and dislocations throughout the economy.

On the political front, there existed very strong socialist and communist parties, paralleled on the right by an established conservative movement as well as a new grouping of "radical rightists" from which the Nazi party was eventually to emerge dominant. Street violence and political assassination, particularly in the early 1920s and 1930s, were common occurrences. As economic conditions worsened in the early 1930s, the Nazi party, heretofore a somewhat obscure regional group, rose to a position of national prominence, winning, for example, 107 seats in the Reichstag elections of 1930. By early 1932, the Nazis controlled 230 seats out of 608 in the Reichstag as nearly 14 million Germans voted for Hitler and his Nazi party. Taking into account the fact that Germany had many political parties, this represented an unprecedented success accomplished in a very short period of time. It should also be noted, however, that the parties of the left remained quite strong even as the Nazis grew in power. The German political arena was polarizing on the left and right. Finally, on January 30, 1933, Hitler was appointed chancellor and the Nazi era began.

With this brief background completed, let us return to our major concern and summarize the ideas of the young Hitler to see how they incorporated the various intellectual traditions we have been describing, and to provide points of comparison with Italian fascism. It is appropriate to speak of the *young* Hitler because

[6] Alan Bullock, *Hitler: A Study in Tyranny* (New York: Bantam Books, 1961), p. 8.

in large measure the ideology of National Socialism was firmly set in his mind by the time he was 24. Ernst Nolte in a deft phrase refers to National Socialism as "practice as fulfillment," asserting that the ideology was "preformed" in Hitler's mind and that all that was necessary was its "fulfillment." As such, the ideas of Hitler's youth can be used as keys to understanding not only the ideology of National Socialism but also the entire Nazi movement. Once again, we must point to the centrality of racist ideas, for in Hitler's mind race explained everything.

Hitler's own description in *Mein Kampf* of his conversion to anti-Semitism perhaps will help us to understand this point:

> Once, when I was walking through the inner city, I suddenly came across a being in a long caftan with black sidelocks. My first thought was: Is that a Jew? In Linz, they did not look like that. I watched the man stealthily and cautiously, but the longer I stared at the strange countenance and studied it feature by feature, the more the question in a different form turned in my brain: Is that a German?[7]

From this early experience on the streets of Vienna, Hitler moved to the position of finding race at the core of all human affairs. In particular, it was the existence and widespread influence of Jews that served both as an explanation for the sorry condition of Germany and a rationalization for Hitler's personal lack of early success in life.

It is true that Hitler went on in *Mein Kampf* to spell out most of the major themes that we have associated with Italian fascism. He condemned Bolshevism, class, democratic institutions, the liberal press, and spoke in glowing terms of national unity, organicism, duty, and a vaguely socialistic economy. What differentiated Hitler from Mussolini, however, was that blood mixing and Jews were seen as the basic cause of all of the problems of modern life contained in the fascist litany. Marxism, for example, was viewed by both men as a dire threat to national unity and as a revolutionary doctrine that competed with fascism for recruits. But for Hitler, Marxism was a doctrine invented by a Jew (Marx's father was a convert to Christianity) and used by international Jewry to prevent the German working class from realizing its prime allegiance to *Volk* and state. "And so the Jewish leaders succeeded in hammering into the minds of the masses the Marxist propaganda: 'Your deadly foe is the bourgeoisie; if he were not there, you would be free!'[8] Similarly, liberal democracy, and all of the so-called freedoms associated with it, was a doctrine designed and dominated by Jews. By asserting that political equality was a basic presupposition in governing, Jews had tricked people into believing that they were equal to legitimate members of the *Volk*. Thus, democracy as a political form ensured the debasement of the *Volk* while at the same time permitting Jews to rise to positions of power.

Finally, free speech and press, two of the cornerstones of a liberal democratic society, were seen as vehicles of international Jewry in that they spread egalitarian falsehoods or, at the least, prevented a united *Volk* by fostering differences among

---

[7] Adolf Hitler, *My Battle*, abridged ed., trans. E. T. S. Dugdale (Boston: Houghton Mifflin Company, 1933), p. 19.

[8] Hitler, *Order*, p. 57.

the people. Behind all of these evils of modernity was the Jew, a member of a lesser race, a parasite living off the body politic, yet a clever and dangerous adversary. Perhaps one can fully appreciate the depth of Hitler's racism by reading his own words—presented here at length—from a 1922 speech in Munich:

> The Jews are a people of robbers. He has never founded any civilization, though he has destroyed civilizations by the hundred. He possesses nothing of his own creation to which he can point. Everything that he has is stolen. . . . He has no art of his own: bit by bit he has stolen it all from the other peoples or has watched them at work and then made his copy. He does not even know how merely to preserve the precious things which others have created: as he turns the treasures over in his hand they are transformed into dirt and dung. He knows that he cannot maintain any state for long. This is one of the differences between him and the Aryan. True, the Aryan also has dominated other peoples. But how? He entered on the land, he cleared the forests; out of wilderness he created civilizations, and he has not used the others for his own interests, he has, so far as their capacities permitted, incorporated them into his State and through him art and science were brought to flower. In the last resort it was the Aryan and the Aryan alone who could form States and could set them on their path to future greatness.[9]

Having discovered his truth—that is, that Jews *destroy* and Aryans *create* civilization—it became Hitler's self-appointed task to communicate it to the German masses so that the evils of Jewish control could be eradicated and a new Aryan culture established. Sure of his truth, Hitler's main difficulty was in conveying it to masses conditioned by false values; nevertheless, it was in this area, perhaps more than anywhere else, that his particular genius lay. While we have discussed the notions of leadership, emotion, and mass psychology in connection with Italian fascism, Hitler's development of these doctrines are of such proportion that they merit additional attention.

Mystical Exchange of Spiritual Energy

He, at one with Mussolini, had considerable contempt for masses of people; at the same time he believed that they possessed tremendous potential energy. They needed, therefore, leadership by an elite. This leadership was to be achieved largely through emotional communications between elite and mass and, in particular, through the spoken word. Mass rallies and emotion-laden speeches designed to achieve a religious-like catharsis for both speaker and audience were Hitler's major devices for ensuring the success of the Nazi movement. In his words: "if a people is to become free it needs pride and will power, defiance, hate, hate, and once again hate."[10]

There is a good deal of evidence that shows Hitler regarded his speeches as the fundamental means of communication between the leader and the followers. They were designed not primarily to communicate ideas or to convey information but to provide for a mystical exchange of spiritual energy. As Alan Bullock observed:

[9] Ibid., p. 35.
[10] Ibid., p. 49.

Speech was the essential medium of his power, not only over his audiences but over his own temperament. Hitler talked incessantly, often using words less to communicate his thoughts than to release the hidden spring of his own and others' emotions, whipping himself and his audience into anger or exaltation by the sound of his voice.[11]

In even bolder terms, Joachim C. Fest describes a speech by Hitler at Hamburg:

There, amid the cheers of thousands, he delivered one of his passionate speeches that whipped the audience into a kind of collective orgy, all waiting tensely for the moment of release, the orgasm that manifested itself in a wild outcry. . . . No doubt there was a deeper meaning to Hitler's frequent comparison of the masses to "woman." And we need only look at the corresponding pages in *Mein Kampf* at the wholly erotic fervor that the idea and the image of the masses aroused in him, to see what he sought and found as he stood on the platform high above the masses filling the arena—his masses. Solitary, unable to make contact, he more and more craved such collective unions. In a revealing turn of phrase (if we may believe the source) he once called the masses his "only bride." His oratorical discharges were largely instinctual, and his audience, unnerved by prolonged distress and reduced to a few elemental needs, reacted on the same instinctual wave length. The sound recordings of the period clearly convey the peculiarly obscene, copulatory character of mass meetings: the silence at the beginning, as of a whole multitude holding its breath; the short, shrill yappings; the minor climaxes and first sounds of liberation on the part of the crowd; finally the frenzy, more climaxes, and then the ecstasies released by the finally unblocked oratorical orgasms.[12]

This is, of course, thoroughly consistent with the antirationalism and emphasis on mystery and emotion that we have noted before. Hitler saw himself as the reincarnation of ancient German rulers, returned by history to lead the people in fulfilling their destiny. In asserting these ties to historical Germany, Hitler was able to draw on large portions of the romantic tradition that had become so much a part of everyday culture. Ancient symbols were resurrected to assert these historical ties; the simple strong man of the soil became an ideal German; even architectural styles copying the designs of the Middle Ages were in vogue. These symbols of the romantic tradition were, as we have noted earlier, combined with those of racism to produce a view of the forthcoming Third Reich that was simultaneously German and Aryan. All this is but another way of saying that Hitler was an instinctive master of the new art (science?) of propaganda and mass psychology.

Use of Propaganda

Early in life he was greatly impressed with British efforts at propaganda during World War I, and he realized the potential of mass communication. All of the media were used to emphasize the Aryan ideal and to condemn the Jewish influence in German life. The motion picture art form was perfected by the Nazis even

[11] Bullock, *Hitler*, pp. 323–324.
[12] Joachim C. Fest, *Hitler*, (New York: Harcourt Brace Jovanovich, 1973), pp. 323–24.

though the use of films for political purposes had only been recently recognized. Hitler's personal taste in art and architecture dictated aesthetic values for the entire society, while the whole cultural and educational structure was revamped to wipe out liberal values and Jewish influences.

> This cleansing of our culture must be extended to nearly all fields. Theater, art, literature, cinema, press, posters, and window displays must be cleansed of all manifestations of our rotting world and placed in the service of a moral, political and cultural idea. . . . The right of personal freedom recedes before the duty to preserve the race.[13]

Typical of such movements, particular emphasis was placed upon ensuring that the *youth* of Germany—the next generation—would grow up uncontaminated by foreign influences. Führer worship became an integral part of the socialization of the youth of Germany. For example, the following is a prayer that was to be said before meals by children in Cologne:

> Führer, my Führer, bequeathed to me by the Lord, Protect and preserve me as long as I live! Thou hast rescued Germany from deepest distress, I thank thee for my daily bread. Abideth thou long with me, forsaketh me not, Führer, my Führer, my faith and my light!
>
> *Heil, mein Führer![14]*

Similarly, Christianity was "Germanized" and "Aryanized" to lend the weight of religion to the movement:

> As with every people, the eternal God also created a Law for our people especially suited to its racial character. It acquired form in the Führer Adolf Hitler and in the National-Socialist state that he formed. . . . One People!—One Reich!—One Church![15]

Such examples could be duplicated endlessly.

Racist Internationalism

It is in this attempt to develop what George Mosse has called a "Nazi culture" that we can see the genuinely revolutionary nature of Hitler's enterprise. He was attempting to change the values of an entire population and point them toward a new society composed partially of elements of an idealized historical Germany but dominated by a vision of a new Reich. Finally, we must underscore the fact that such an attempt at producing a total culture was only possible because of the existence of a modern bureaucratic state. The rise of a rationalized *bureaucratic class* whose purpose was the effective implementation of orders given to it provided a mechanism for putting Nazi culture in place. The bureaucrat's purpose was not to

[13] Adolf Hitler, *The Speeches of Adolf Hitler, 1922–1939*, Norman H. Baynes, ed. (London: Oxford University Press, 1942), p. 568.

[14] George L. Mosse, ed., *Nazi Culture* (New York: Grosset & Dunlap, 1966), p. 241.

[15] Ibid., p. 242.

question the orders given, but to implement them efficiently, without bias or scorn, regardless of how absurd or inhuman they appeared to be.

We cannot enter into a detailed discussion of the economic policies of Nazi Germany. It can be argued that none is necessary, for Nazi economic policies in general exhibited the same type of eclectic accommodation to varying groups in the society that we have observed in Mussolini's Italy. At an early date, Hitler had proclaimed socialism to be a doctrine only possible within the confines of the nation-state; international socialism, particularly Marxism, was declared to be a perversion of the fundamental doctrine—a central element in the "international Jewish conspiracy."

After their assumption of power the Nazis were able to blend this vague socialism with the existing corporate interests in Germany to produce economic policies whose goals were easily stated—power and greatness. Such practical accommodation was not, however, a distinguishing trait of National Socialism, nor was it characteristic of Hitler. We noted earlier the fascism of Benito Mussolini possessed no clear conception of a goal culture and tended to emphasize action and involvement almost for its own sake. Such was not the case with Hitler; he had an all too clear conception of his new society and the actions that would be necessary to achieve it.

At the beginning of this discussion of National Socialism, it was asserted that Hitler was fundamentally an Aryan racist and that the fruition of his plans would have led to the destruction of the German nation-state. By now we believe we have established the importance that race played in Hitler's mind, but the full import of those doctrines can be seen only by examining his plans for the future society. Once again, perhaps it is better to let Hitler speak for himself:

> The main principle which we must observe is that the State is not an end, but a means. It is the foundation on which higher human culture is to rest, but it does not originate it. It is rather the presence of a race endowed with the capabilities for civilization which is able to do this.[16]

Hitler asserted clearly that the state serves as a vehicle for the elevation of the Aryan race to a position of power where the race can create higher human culture and civilization. That is the state's prime purpose. Surely, one might ask: But doesn't that mean greater power and glory for all Germans? By no means. It must be remembered that the existing German nation had been corrupted by blood mixing and therefore contained impurities that had to be eradicated.

> In its capacity as a State, the German Reich must gather all Germans to itself; it must not only select out of the German nation *only the best of the original racial elements* and conserve them, but must slowly and surely raise them to a position of dominance.[17]

Not merely the state, but the existing German *Volk* itself is a device for resurrecting the pure Aryan strain. In effect, a German whose blood is not pure is at best a culture sustainer, at worst a destroyer of culture and civilization. The

[16] Hitler, *My Battle*, p. 158.
[17] Ibid., p. 161 (emphasis added).

only true human is an Aryan, and anyone existing within the state who has mixed blood must either be a slave to the Aryan or be eliminated. While Jews are both the most obvious and dangerous of culture destroyers, they are not alone.

Here we see Hitler's racism in full bloom. The thousand-year Reich will not be a German nation-state, but an Aryan state in which any non-Aryans exist only to serve the interests of the culture creator. Extermination became Hitler's final solution to the Jewish menace, but it must be remembered that Auschwitz and Buchenwald were also slave-labor camps whose bureaucratically calculated goal was working "people" to death—a world, in Richard Rubenstein's words, "of the living dead." In addition, the expansionist military policies of Nazi Germany against other non-Aryan nations were not simply designed to provide "living space" for the German nation as Hitler frequently stated. Their ultimate objective was the subjugation of all non-Aryan peoples to the master race. And all destroyers of culture would have to be themselves destroyed.

This, then, is not German nationalism but *racist internationalism*. Given that, many of Hitler's actions and Nazi policies fall into a pattern. The "scientific" efforts to determine Aryan blood, and programs formulated literally to breed people possessing Aryan characteristics, can be seen as direct means for achieving the goal culture. Further, during the latter days of World War II, Hitler could declare that Germany had failed him without destroying the basic premise of his racism. That is, the fact that Germany was losing the war had nothing to do with the innate superiority of Aryans but showed that Germans of mixed blood had not been strong enough to fulfill their task of achieving Aryan supremacy. Finally, with retreating armies on all sides, Hitler could declare that he had been successful, because his extermination camps and breeding policies would ensure that from the ashes of a defeated Germany would inevitably arise a new Aryan-dominated society, one free of Jews. His racial doctrines, with all of their horrifying consequences, remained with him to the end.

The results of Hitler's racist policies defy comprehension. One searches in vain for words to describe the horror of Auschwitz and the other concentration camps. In a fundamental way, Nazism denies the basic purpose of this entire book, which is an attempt to understand—rationally—competing ideologies, as alien as they may seem to be. But if comprehension is beyond our reach, silence is not the answer. We must continue to try to understand, for like Marxism, fascism, Islamism, and liberal democracy, racism is not a dead doctrine.

SUGGESTED READINGS

ADORNO, THEODOR W., et al., *The Authoritarian Personality*. New York: Harper & Row, Publishers, 1960.

BULLOCK, ALAN, *Hitler: A Study in Tyranny*. New York: Bantam Books, 1961.

HITLER, ADOLF, *Mein Kampf*, trans. Ralph Manheim. Boston: Houghton Mifflin Company, 1971.

———, *The Speeches of Adolf Hitler, 1922–1939*, Norman H. Baynes, ed., 2 Vols. Oxford: Oxford University Press, 1942.

MOSSE, GEORGE L., ed., *Nazi Culture.* New York: Grosset & Dunlap, 1966.

————, *The Crisis of German Ideology: Intellectual Origins of the Third Reich.* New York: Grosset & Dunlap, 1964.

————, *Nazism: A History and Comparative Analysis of National Socialism.* New Brunswick, N.J.: Rutgers University Press, 1978.

RUBENSTEIN, RICHARD L., *The Cunning of History.* New York: Harper & Row Publishers, 1978.

SHIRER, WILLIAM L., *The Rise and Fall of the Third Reich.* New York: Crest Books, 1962.

11

Theopolitics and Islamism

[Islam] is a religion that provides guidance for conducting the affairs of state and a guide to the straight path, which is neither Eastern nor Western. It is a religion where worship is joined to politics and practical activity is a form of worship.

Imam Ayatollah Khomeini

The recent revival of religiously centered—or *theopolitical*—ideologies has become the subject of renewed scrutiny in political studies and considerable concern for the world's policy makers. The causes for the resurgence of theopolitics are complex and their manifestations are various. Theopolitics reemerges in different cultural, economic, and political circumstances, both in periods of decline and alienation as well as in periods of growth and optimism. It emerges from within different religious traditions throughout the world, including North America. Contrary to common impressions, theopolitical movements are often more than merely reactions against perceived threats to sacrosanct ways of a traditional order. They also have progressive tendencies and are interested in creatively accommodating the constantly changing circumstances of modern life. It is important to note that some theopolitical actors have aimed as much for greater democracy and social justice as others have for turning the clock back by restoring ancient practices of patriarchal subordination. At times, they not only wield the instruments of violence—with which, as we have seen, other ideological traditions are comfortable—they also stand strongly for peace and reconciliation, and not merely for pragmatic reasons, but because, in some cases, God has commanded them to do so.

Every religious tradition has diverse ideological possibilities. We cannot, however, review every theopolitical ideology that has captured attention in recent years. Our focus, rather, will be on the revivalism associated with Islam, something we shall refer to as *Islamism*. This focus is appropriate for several reasons. Initially, in terms of sheer numbers, Islam in various forms claims the allegiance of fully one-fifth of the world's population and ranks third, after Christianity and atheism, in the number of adherents. While usually associated exclusively with the Middle East, most Muslims live outside of that region in South and Southeast Asia. In the countries of the former Soviet Union, after Slavic groups, Muslims comprise the largest grouping, consisting of approximately 20 percent of the population. In part, because Islam is and has been a belief system containing a built-in command to spread its truth, it is one of the world's fastest-growing religions. At various points in its long history, that command has produced events of history-altering proportions, and, in the minds of many, we have been experiencing such a period today.

THE ISLAMIC REVIVAL

Since the end of the Cold War, Islam has often been portrayed in the West as the next global foe of liberal democratic capitalism. We hasten to add, however, that neither is Islam necessarily opposed to private property nor have Western liberal states been reluctant to forge deep economic and geostrategic relations with very conservative Islamic regimes. In the 1980s, for example, Western capitalist states supported the radical Islamist *mujahideen* (strugglers) in Afghanistan in their fight against Soviet forces. Similarly, immense political, economic, military, and strategic relations have been built during the twentieth century between the Western states and the petroleum-rich Islamic monarchies of the Arabian peninsula. Such relations, including the 1990s military operations to either restore these regimes (Kuwait) or defend them (Saudi Arabia), have led the Western powers to clarify their position: The enemy is not "Islam" as such, but what they have termed the "rogue states and enemies" of the capitalist world order.

While anti-Muslim judgments in the West thus misconstrue Western policy toward Islam, there is no doubt that persisting conflicts, both *within* the Islamic world and *between* Islamic countries and outside actors, have brought Islam front and center on the global stage. Such was the highly publicized case in Iran in 1979. There, highly mobilized Muslim revolutionaries cast off a Western-oriented regime that they castigated as un-Islamic as they simultaneously set out to build a new, Islamic political and social order. One of their main objectives was to end what they described as the forces of cultural imperialism which had introduced Western styles, ways of learning, acting, dressing, and being that the Muslim clerical establishment described as "Westoxication." One of the most telling slogans chanted by thousands of protesters in the streets in the final days of the crumbling regime was, "Neither East nor West, Islam!"[1] Of course, the Iranian revolution was not the first of such conflicts. The roots of the current Islamic revival extend back to Muslim political ideologues of the nineteenth century—to persons like Jamal al-Din al-Afghani (1838–1897) in the Persian and Turkish contexts; Muhammad Abduh (1849–1905) in Egypt; and Sayyid Ahmad Khan (1817–1898) in India—and to movements in the early twentieth century, such as the still influential Muslim Brotherhood, founded in 1928 in Egypt.

These struggles continue today. Muslim activists criticize the persistence of different forms of outside influence over Muslim governments and societies as well as regimes that they consider insufficiently Islamic. The growing power of Islamic political movements has led many formerly secularized regimes in Muslim settings to grant more and more symbolic and institutional support to the tradition. Indeed, since the recognition of the enormous power of Islam in the Iranian revolution, regimes throughout the Muslim world have made great concessions to Islamist agendas. Two important examples here are the "Islamicization" of the state and society in the Islamic Republic of Pakistan since the 1980s and the full adoption of Islamic law (the *shariah*) by Sudan in 1989. Pakistan, it bears mentioning, has been locked in ongoing conflicts with India, where Hindu religious revivalism has made significant headway against a strong secular national tradition. In addition, radical Islamist movements continue to challenge regimes whose practices they interpret as violating the requirements of Islam. These movements include the Al-Qaeda movement led by Osama Bin Laden, a wealthy exile from Saudi Arabia. In the 1990s, this movement launched an effort to end the United States' influence in the Middle East by approving attacks on American soldiers and embassies on the African continent. Bin Laden and leaders from several other groups have formed the International Islamic Front whose chief aim is to

[1] Ervand Abrahamian, *Khomeini's Populism* (Berkeley: University of California Press, 1993), p. 31.

eliminate the influence of the United States in the Arabian peninsula, the birth-place of Islam, where the world's largest petroleum reserves are also to be found. Islamist ideologies, in short, are shaping political power and conflict on a global scale.

A final reason for focusing on Islam stems from one of our earlier comments on Marxism-Leninism: We suspect that the reader of this book will have scant knowledge of Islam, "sharing the general . . . public's perceptions of Islam [that] have tended to be characterized by ignorance, confusion, and misinformation."[2] All of this being said, a word of caution remains in order. Islam is an incredibly complex religious, cultural, and political phenomenon. It contains a rich and extensive history that is hardly uniform in terms of practice or belief; it too has sub-divisions and divergent schools of thought, some of which we can only introduce here. Given the prominence of the late Ayatollah Khomeini's role in Iran and in world politics, it is inevitable that a book on ideologies should address him and his interpretation of Shiite Islam. It is necessary to remember, nevertheless, that while particular countries have established Islamic states, Islam—as articulated in the *Quran*—remains independent of the authority of any particular human being, or state: God alone is the sole authority. As authors, we are again in the uncomfort-able position of trying to make simple, albeit meaningful, statements in a single chapter about a vast and complicated subject matter. What follows is an attempt to present some major themes and terms of Islamism as a guide for understanding the action motivated by it.

The Abrahamic Monotheistic Background

The Arabic word *Muslim* literally means "one who submits to God." It con-veys the ideal of the righteous Muslim: one who submits in loving obedience to *Allah*, which is Arabic for God. According to Islam, this is the same God as Judaism's Yahweh and Christianity's Jehovah. Thus, Islam very self-consciously participates within these two, preexisting Abrahamic traditions. A short review of selected theological perspectives shared by all three traditions helps to under-stand the distinctness of Islam.

These traditions are "Abrahamic" because they all trace their beginnings to the figure of Abraham, who, according to the three traditions, made a covenant with God approximately 3,700 years ago to worship and follow Him alone as the path, guide, and final judge of righteousness. The exact forms of belief differ in important ways across these traditions, but the core abstract, ethical commitment is relatively consistent: All are based on the belief in a single, all-powerful, all-know-ing God who is the responsible creator and judge of all things in the cosmos, including humanity, and to whom all human beings have obligations. Abraham set the path for righteousness for each of the monotheistic traditions; their followers have been referred to as "the children of Abraham." Islam, like Judaism and Chris-tianity, maintains that human beings are the special creation of God, existing to

---

[2] Fred R. Von Der Mehden, "American Perceptions of Islam," in *Voices of Resurgent Islam,* John L. Esposito, ed. (New York: Oxford University Press, 1983), p. 18.

fulfill His will, and are thus held responsible for their earthly actions by God's judgment. God's will, moreover, has been revealed through a series of prophets—Adam, Abraham, Moses, and Christ—whose words and actions provide the standards for human conduct.

Muslims believe, however, that the will of God as revealed to Moses and Jesus had become distorted by Jews and Christians, particularly as their teachings became codified and embodied in formal religious institutions. Because of this corruption, there arose the need for a final prophet to whom God revealed His will in total form. That prophet—referred to in Islam as the "Seal of the Prophets"—was Muhammad ibn Abdullah.

The significance of Islam's reassertion of Abrahamic monotheism may be best seen by describing some of the central themes of the two preceding traditions that Islam also claims to incorporate. While members of these earlier traditions usually do not accept as authentic the Muslim claim to supercede them, it is useful for North Americans to consider the depth of this claim in order to understand some of the central ethical concerns of contemporary Islamist ideologies. Indeed, one source of the contemporary ideological struggle between Islam and the West is that Muslim activists understand their relation to Judaism and Christianity in ways that are often at odds with how Jews and Christians relate to them. This is true even though Islam very much borrows upon the central terms and premises of Judaism and Christianity, reinterpreting them to fit what it sees as the same imperative of monotheistic righteousness. More specifically, Islam views itself as restating the imperatives of righteousness initially found in the other traditions and can be understood by reflecting briefly upon the emphases on law and love found respectively in Judaism and Christianity. These traditions are themselves considerably diverse and each has various contemporary theopolitical manifestations. Our discussion focuses on specific doctrinal meanings of *righteousness* as expressed in each tradition's primary, authoritative texts: the *Torah* in Judaism, the *New Testament* in Christianity, and the *Quran* in Islam.

In its original, orthodox form, Judaism emphasizes a close relationship between righteousness and the fulfillment of God's law. The classic examples of this relationship are the Ten Commandments. They were part of the covenant concluded between the Jewish people and God after He, according to the tradition, freed them from slavery in Egypt around the year 1200 B.C.E.. In this covenant, God promised to insure their protection and everlasting prosperity in a land of their own in return for their unwavering righteousness and obedience to his laws; that is, in return for their promise to be a people of exemplary moral righteousness in God's eyes. The fulfillment of law thus had rich moral significance. Indeed, the Jewish tradition elaborates an immediate relation between righteousness and obedience to law as part of Abraham's earlier example; according to the tradition, Abraham's decisive moment of righteousness came when he obeyed God's commandment to circumcise all males in his house (Genesis 17). Hence, the Jewish population that had been freed from slavery followed Abraham's example when they agreed to keep God's laws. In addition to God's promises of greatness in exchange for their obedience, the Jews also heard His warnings of doom and destruction were they to go astray. Hence, for both its promise and its peril, the Jewish tradition stresses the fulfillment of law as a sign of righteousness. Indeed, Moses and the ancient Jewish kings who followed him promulgated laws that were to govern every aspect of social and political life. This is not to say that law is the *only* emphasis within Judaism, because Judaism contains extensive nonlegalistic philosophical tendencies in both its early and later forms that expound upon the meaning of righteousness in other ways. The multiple ethical insights contained in the biblical stories and the moral directives of the prophets, for example, demonstrate this tradition's diverse expressions. Nonetheless, the stipulated relation between law and righteousness as one of Judaism's foundations helps to understand its relation to the other Abrahamic traditions.

In Christianity, while Jesus' statements about the relation between law and faith found in the New Testament have also been open to varying interpretations and historical practices, the tradition in its origins clearly departs from the idea that righteousness is to be achieved through the observance of law as such. Looking back to the model of Abraham, the early Christians maintained that Abraham was faithful even before obeying God's command on circumcision and that his obedience to that command was only a sign of righteousness, not righteousness itself. Abraham expressed his righteousness in his love of God, a love that preceded any activity undertaken to comply with God's laws. According to Christianity, there is only one commandment that all must follow: to love God and one another. "The whole law is love," says Paul in his epistle to the Romans. This is not to imply that the Jewish tradition ignores the importance of love or that Christians uniformly interpret this central imperative. Our point in delineating the difference between Judaism and Christianity on the question of righteousness is to distinguish their foundationally different emphases concerning the obligations incumbent upon one who adopts the belief in the God of Abraham. Jesus—the son of God, according to the one tradition—declares that righteousness does not come "through deeds dictated by law." Rather, it comes through an ethic of love. Jesus thus blessed the weak and the downtrodden and praised those who cared more for the poor and peace than material wealth and worldly power. Crucially, unlike Moses before him, and Muhammad after, Jesus did not come to establish another political system in and of "this world." He came as Savior to the world, promising a better world—life in the "Kingdom of God"—for those who would follow him. His rejection of worldly power ran against the notion that all of the activities of God's community in this world should be directly governed by God's laws. The law of love would be sufficient to set things right. Indeed, like Islam after it, Christianity sees Christ's message as God's attempt to correct for the deviations in the ways of his children.

One additional development in Christianity requires comment before a discussion of Islam. Since Christianity maintained that righteousness is possible for everyone who has the faith of Abraham, it developed a concept of God's community that extended beyond the original Jewish concept. In the Jewish tradition, those who followed the laws and understandings embedded in the covenant became God's people—a nation distinct from, and unlike, others—for whom it would serve as God's model of righteousness. The Jewish people thus became God's "light" unto other nations with a "universal" role to play as the exemplar of Abrahamic righteousness. When Jesus claimed that righteousness demanded the fulfillment of the essence—though not the letter—of the law, he essentially affected an expansion of the monotheistic franchise and a new kind of Abrahamic "universalism." He said that faith in Jesus Christ, regardless of the laws one followed or the collectivity to which one belonged, was sufficient to become a member of God's community. Christianity's "universalism" thus lies in the idea that membership in God's community is open to all human beings, no matter what their national or other affiliations, so long as they believe in Christ.

The revelations from God that Muhammad received in the seventh century reflected some of these earlier understandings of righteousness. In creating a Muslim constitution in the Arabian city of Medina, Muhammad showed himself in particular, and Islam more generally, to be clearly committed to the central Judaic emphasis on the close relation between worldly power and righteousness as a model unto others for righteous behavior in this world. (God's law should become the law of humanity.) Yet, among the central messages in God's revelations to Muhammad was an ethic of love for fellow human beings along with the need to create a new, universal community of believers that would rekindle the essence of Christianity. We note these continuities in advance of a fuller discussion of them in order to underscore Islam's claim to be one of the traditions of Abraham.

According to Islam, Abraham was the first believer in God—the first Muslim—and Muhammad was a prophet in the great line of the prophets recognized by Judaism and Christianity. He criticized nonmonotheistic beliefs, asserted that the existing monotheistic communities had discernibly strayed from God's original purposes, and called on all human beings to adopt the straight path of righteousness. While Islam makes its own unique set of claims, it nonetheless absorbs elements of both Judaism and Christianity into its conception of righteousness. Primarily for this reason, Jews and Christians are referred to in Islam as "people of the book" and are, according to Islamic theology, permitted to practice their forms of worship of the same God without interference under Muslim regimes. (Muslims are required to attempt to convert only pagans and polytheists to the true path, and this, only under certain conditions and to a certain extent: God is the ultimate judge of all humans, even those who reject Him.) These shared ethical claims of Judaism, Christianity, and Islam are not insignificant when it comes to modern political possibilities. Indeed, they are foundations upon which members of the three traditions have attempted to discover bases for cooperation. Along these lines, an Iranian president visiting the Vatican in 1999 advocated "a dialogue of civilizations" based on a shared conception of God: "The hope," he declared, "is for the victory of monotheism, of ethics, of morals together with peace and reconciliation."[3]

---

[3] President Mohammad Khatami, quoted in "Iran's Leader and Pope Seek Better Muslim-Christian-Ties," *New York Times*, March 12, 1999, p. A11.

Basic Beliefs and Values of Islam

Before describing the distinct features of Islam, we note that just as there is no single Jewish or Christian tradition, there is no single Muslim tradition. This is true in what may be called "cultural" as well as theological terms: There are Muslims who, like many Jews and Christians, may not practice the rituals of the tradition, but still consider themselves "Muslim" in terms of culture. Theologically speaking, then, there is vast diversity within Islam around a common core set of beliefs. As John Esposito has put it, "[a]lthough Muslims maintain that there is one divinely revealed and mandated Islam, there have been and continue to be many Muslim interpretations of Islam."[4] It can be said, then, that monotheism has never exactly meant monolithism. There are, however, several basic beliefs and values that hold the different Muslim interpretations of Islam together. These include the significance of Muhammad, the Quran, the five pillars, and the ideal of an Islamic community.

Muhammad ibn Abdullah was born in Mecca in 570 C.E. (the Common Era, in the Western Christian sense of time) and spent most of his early life engaged in the commercial life of that prosperous city. At the age of forty, this introspective and contemplative man received the first of a series of revelations from God that was to continue for a period of more than twenty years. As the final chosen messenger of God, Muhammad spent the rest of his life spreading God's word and exhorting humans to turn to righteousness. The revelations varied in their concerns. Some were related to the existing society, such as those criticizing the greed and lack of morality and compassion of the Meccan upper classes. Others were rather abstract, calling on people to reject their polytheistic, idolatrous, or wayward ways and to purify their lives along the bases of monotheism. These revelations were gathered during and after Muhammad's life into one text, called the Quran. The Quran is the sacred scripture for all Muslims. It is considered to be the unfiltered, *literal word of God*, conveyed by God, in Arabic, to humanity through Muhammad. It contains 114 chapters (*suras*) and over 6,000 verses. In it, one may find descriptions of the moral and practical requirements for all Muslims.

In addition to being the recipient of God's word, Muhammad serves at least one other important purpose. His exemplary life of piety and perfection provides Muslims with a role model of the type of life all true believers ought to lead. His words and deeds—the *sunna* of the Prophet—are considered to be exemplary for all Muslims. The *sunna* were collected, sorted, and compiled in several collections of what are called the *hadith*. They serve as a permanent reference point concerning righteous faith and practice. Therefore, the early history of Islam under Muhammad's leadership becomes extremely important for understanding its current thinking and practice.

It is important to emphasize that in spite of Muhammad's centrality, he is considered to be a mortal human who was chosen by God to bring His word to humanity: Muhammad is to be neither worshiped as a divine figure himself nor

---

[4]John L. Esposito, *Islam: The Straight Path, Expanded Ed.* (New York: Oxford University Press, 1991), p. xiii.

thought of as the founder of Islam. Indeed, Allah alone is to be worshiped; He alone is the Creator of Islam, and Muhammad is only God's messenger. He has no divine powers: He cannot heal the sick; he cannot bring the dead back to life. While Islam recognizes the prophetic status of Jesus—indeed, like him, Muhammad was "bearer of good tidings and admonisher for all mankind" (Quran 34:28)—it nevertheless denies that Christ is the son of God. Central to the message that Muhammad conveyed from God was the idea of *tawhid*, or the singularity or unicity of God. "God has no associates," the tradition maintains. God is One Supreme Being. As the ninth-century Muslim theorist, al-Jahiz, put it in reference to the Christian view of Jesus, "God is too great to have paternity among His attributes. . . ."[5] The omnipotence of God is reinforced by His indivisibility. Indeed, this, according to the Quran, is the model of Abraham, who declared: "I am through with those you associate [with God]" (6:78). It is Abraham who set the standard for being a Muslim by rejecting all other objects of belief and submitting in loving obedience to God alone. Islam rejects the Christian notion of the Holy Trinity; that is, the notion of the union of three persons—the Father, the Son, and the Holy Ghost—in one Godhead.

The Muslim model of belief includes the famous five pillars or demonstrations of faith that are incumbent upon all Muslims: profession of faith, prayer, almsgiving, fasting, and the pilgrimage to Mecca. All Muslims profess the basis of their faith rests on the idea that "There is no God but Allah, and Muhammad is His prophet." They should pray five times a day. Prayers include very carefully prescribed bodily motions and may be performed anywhere. Mosques provide separate spaces for men and women. Only the Friday noon prayers are congregational. Muslims are required to give between 2 and 15 percent of their accumulated wealth for the support of the poor, the needy, or other community projects. Almsgiving thus expresses Islam's commitment to a well-balanced community of God. The fast of Ramadan marks the month of the revelation. Every able adult Muslim is expected to abstain from all bodily ingestion and activities from dawn to dusk as part of the ritual restoration of one's spiritual awareness. Similarly, all able Muslims are expected to perform the pilgrimage (the *hajj*) to Mecca at least once in their lifetime. There, they visit the sacred shrine—the Kaba, a large black stone— believed to have been built by Adam and rebuilt by Abraham and his son Ismael. The pilgrimage also includes a visit to the famous Plain of Arafat, where just before his death Muhammad called on all Muslims to live in peace and harmony. The visit reinforces Islam's "universalism"; like Christianity, it seeks to build a community among the pious, accepting all believers as members regardless of their particular national, citizen, or other cultural differences. Muhammad's call for harmonious relations includes an emphasis on love between the members of God's community. Perhaps aware of the tendencies of previous monotheists to divide among themselves, Muhammad, in his final sermon, called for all Muslims not to wrong one another: "Know that every Muslim is a Muslim's brother, and

---

[5] Al-Jahiz, "Refutation of the Christians," quoted in *Judaism, Christianity, and Islam: The Classic Texts and Their Interpretation, Vol. 1,* F. E. Peters, ed.(Princeton, N.J.: Princeton University Press, 1990), p. 254.

that (all) Muslims are brethren. It is only lawful to take from a brother what he gives you willingly, so wrong not each other."[6]

Politics and Struggle (*Jihad*) in Early Islam

The early days of Muhammad's prophecy were difficult; he preached the will of God to a small but ever-expanding body of followers in the city of Mecca, in present-day Saudi Arabia. He met with stiff resistance by the ruling community and, along with his earliest followers, was forced to flee to Yathrib, which—with its name changed to Medina—would become the first Muslim city of God. The movement to Medina provided more fertile ground for what was to become an extremely dynamic religious and political movement. There, in 622, Muhammad created a political community governed by God, who granted the Muslims the duty to resist, by militant means if necessary, their persecutors in Mecca. These developments set certain crucial political standards in Muslim history. Because of the establishment of a Muslim state, Muslims forever look to the prophet not only as a transmitter of God's will but also as a political agent for creating God's rule on earth. Under God's directive, the Prophet organized, mobilized, and struggled to fashion simultaneously political and religious space, such that all of life's activities were to express a dynamic relationship with God. Muhammad not only preached God's will, he established it in the Medina Constitution. As a result, Islam developed as a tradition which, according to the Prophet's model, decries any strict division between religious and political affairs, a theme we shall further discuss later in this chapter. Also significant is that the Islamic calendar adopts Muhammad's migration (*hijra*) from Mecca to Medina as its first year in order to commemorate the creation of the Islamic community as a sovereign entity.

While in Medina, the members of this political community were commanded by God to struggle militantly against their oppressors from Mecca who were blocking passage to the holy Kaba. God called on them "to fight those in the way of God who fight you, but do not be aggressive: God does not like aggressors" (2:190; cf. 22:39). Hence emerges one form—indeed, the most commonly understood form—of the Muslim doctrine of *jihad*. The word *jihad* literally conveys the idea that Muslims ought to strive, struggle, or endeavor in the way of God. It is intended to describe the disposition of the devout Muslim in all affairs of life. He or she should personally struggle to live righteously and to advance the global mission of teaching and spreading God's truth. *Jihad* also carries the meaning of "holy war" by the community. The command emerged during the formative years of Islam when the pagan and idolatrous rulers of Mecca outlawed and repressed Muhammad and his early followers for threatening the existing social and religious order. Islam describes the polytheistic and idolatrous ways of Mecca in the harshest terms—as the "era of ignorance"—because of the widespread worship of God's presumed "associates," rather than God alone. *Jihad* as "holy war" is to be carried

---

[6] Muhammad's "Farewell Message," quoted from Muhammad Ibn Ishaq's *Life of Muhammad*, in *Judaism, Christianity, and Islam*, Peters, ed., p. 239.

out in order to defeat the oppressors of God's community who "stand in the way of God." Insofar as the Muslim community envisions itself as God's final attempt to establish righteousness in the world, its defeat would constitute a monumental calamity.

In this way, Islam incorporates a doctrine of legitimate violence in defense of the *ummah al-Islamiyya*—the community of Islam. In contemporary political conflicts throughout the world, this doctrine has taken on renewed significance. Of course, violence is not new within Abrahamic monotheism—the Jews were commanded by God to carry out a conquest of the original inhabitants of their holy land and Christianity developed a tradition that promulgated doctrines of "just war." Nor is *jihad* the only form of "legitimate violence" that motivates ideological action within these traditions today. Each tradition has evolved to incorporate tendencies that legitimize the use of force or coercion as part of God's way. Nonetheless, the concept of legitimate force is profoundly at work in militant, resurgent Islamist movements, which view violence as one means at their disposal to defend the *ummah*. It should be noted that *jihad* includes God's command to be neither aggressors nor oppressors if those persecuting Muslims desist, for "God is forgiving and kind." This doctrine is obviously open to much interpretation—indeed manipulation—for Muslims are required by God to determine what constitutes persecution, aggression, and the appropriate extent of struggle under varying circumstances. Muslims in differing contexts often rely upon the most esteemed leaders among them to define each factor. Some Muslim jurists have ruled that *jihad* is only a last resort, that even under conditions of non-Islamic or oppressive government, Muslims ought to await God's judgment on the regimes before they risk the welfare of the community. Without a direct link to God, human judgment is inevitably involved in determining the appropriateness of *jihad*, and different political conditions and interpretations have shaped different human judgments. Still, one thing is certain: Any regime that clearly deviates from God's rule based on the pattern of Muhammad, opens itself up to condemnation as an oppressor of the community, and *jihad* remains an available and legitimate option for the community to defend its righteous ways.

At Medina, Muhammad legislated and preached a doctrine that by his death in 632 C.E. had spread to the entire Arabian peninsula. More significant for our purposes, this initial Islamic state established precedents and exhibited values of autonomous, sovereign, and distinctly Islamic governance that demonstrated the proper application of the will of God in the temporal world. It would be incorrect, then, to interpret the aforementioned "submission" to God to mean a quiet, fatalistic, or passive acceptance of His will: Muslims are morally obligated to do justice and to spread the ideals of God. The Islamic community under Muhammad's rule created an ideal model to be achieved by contemporary Muslim activists who criticize the loss of independence, deterioration of values, and secularization of politics in contemporary Muslim societies. Before examining the character of these contemporary Islamist ideologies, we must briefly attempt to explain the evolution of Islam, particularly in terms of its leadership after the death of Muhammad.

Leadership and Authority
after Muhammad

Each ideology we have examined posits some conception of leadership: the class-conscious revolutionary in Marxism, the accountable representative in liberalism, and the infallible leader in fascism. Leaders implement, define, and redefine the goals of each ideology. Significantly, conflicts over leadership can determine the very course that the ideology takes—in both theory and practice. Think of differences between Lenin and Stalin and what those differences meant to the history of Marxism. Or consider Madison's carefully argued defense of a trustee, as opposed to a reflector, model of representation and the consequences for democracy in the United States as a result of the adoption of the former, and not the later, model. Different understandings of leadership have meant a great deal in the historical practice of Marxism and liberalism.

After the death of Muhammad, a dispute over the nature of leadership shaped the most basic and fundamental division between the two major traditions of Islam: Sunnism and Shiism. So deep is this division that each group has not always recognized the other as legitimate. The Sunnis, who make up over 80 percent of the world's Muslim population—and whose name derives from the idea of the *sunna*, or the example of the prophet—believe that Muhammad left no specific provision for leadership of the greatly expanded community after his death. However, the principle of submission to the authority of God based on the model of His prophet was well established. While there could be no other prophetic successor to Muhammad, for he was God's final prophet, the Quran and Muhammad's model would serve to guide the future of Islam. To direct that effort, the position of the *caliph*, or successor to Muhammad as the representative of the community, was established in 632, whereby one elder of the community was designated by the existing leadership as the ruler. The Sunnis believe that Muhammad's successor as leader of the community should be selected through a process involving consultation, selection, and consensus (*ijma*) among its leaders. One basis of this view is the well-known *hadith* of Muhammad: "My community shall not agree on any error." Abu Bakr, a trusted companion and father-in-law of the prophet from Mecca, was the first caliph. The second caliph, Umar, added "Commander of the Faithful" to the title of caliph and led Islam into parts of present-day Iran, Iraq, and Egypt. The institution of the caliphate in this original form existed well into the thirteenth century.

But the watershed moment in the history of the caliphate came during the reign of the fourth caliph, Ali. He was the cousin, son-in-law, and one of the closest companions of the Prophet. Ali was renowned for his strict piety, and his followers—or Shiites, derived from the word meaning "faction" or "partisans"—believe, contrary to the Sunnis, that he had been designated by the Prophet as his successor. Their belief is based on a *hadith* that recounts Muhammad's designation of Ali as successor just before the Prophet's death. After completing his final pilgrimage and announcing his imminent death, Muhammad is said to have declared to the community, "Am I not nearer to you than your own selves?"

Without pausing, he raised Ali's arms and declared, "If I was near to anyone, thi Ali is near them! Oh God, befriend those who befriend him, and oppose those who oppose him! Assist those who assist him, and forsake those who forsake him!" According to Shiite Islam, then, this established a pattern whereby the existing leader would designate one of his male descendants as leader of the community When Ali was killed in 662, another Sunni caliph (Yazid) was appointed. This lea Ali's followers to rebel under the leadership of his son, Husain. The rebellion wa: harshly and quickly crushed; Husain was killed, and the basis for the split betweer the Sunni and Shiite Muslims was both established and intensified. To this day Shiite Muslims—who make up less than 20 percent of the world's Muslim popula tion, but are the majority in Iran and Bahrain, and comprise a significant part o the population in Lebanon, Iraq, and several Arabian peninsula states—recoun and lament the martyrdom of Ali and Husain (who, after all, was the Prophet' grandson) at the hands of their Sunni oppressors.

Thus, the Shiite Muslims believe that the leadership of Islam can come only from a certain lineage descended from Muhammad through Husain; and the Sunni Muslims believe that the leader was to be selected by the community. The lineage claim of the Shiites elevates their leadership to a higher theopolitical sta tus than the Sunni caliph. This results in differing political organizations and dif fering political terminology between the Shiite and Sunni traditions. The Shiite: describe the designated leaders of Islam as the *Imams*—the direct descendants o: Muhammad and the first Imam, Ali. Moreover, with the exception of the smaller Zayidi sect, they view the Imams as infallible interpreters of God's will whose authority in all worldly and religious matters is absolute. While the Imam is not a prophet, he is divinely inspired through his designated status within the family o the prophet. The Sunni caliph, by contrast, possesses great authority through hi. piety in upholding the tradition and his political esteem, but does not posses: divine inspiration or infallibility. In the Sunni tradition, an "Imam" means one who leads prayers. Among the roles of the Sunni caliphate in history was the suppor for an esteemed class of religiously wise scholars and jurists, the *ulama* (literally "those who know"), a term also employed in the Shiite tradition. The last widely recognized Sunni caliph was that of the Ottoman Empire, and the position wa: abolished in 1924 by the new Turkish republic. While there are current discussion: about reviving the caliph, the Shiite institution of Imam is alive and well, even ir the absence of a living Imam at this moment.

There are also different branches of Shiite Islam, the two main ones being the Ismaelis, or "Seveners," and the "Twelvers." Their differences stem from fol lowing different lines of descent from the sixth Imam, Jafar. Besides being the basi for the split, the Imam Jafar's other distinction in Shiite Islam is that he initiate the Shiite tradition of considering the sunna of Ali and the other previous Imam: as exemplary models of piety along with the model of the prophet. The "Twelver" tradition comprises the majority in the Shiite tradition and is the tradition tha took power in Iran in the 1979 revolution. The title Imam had been reserved to

[7] "The Hadith of the Ghadir of Khumm," in John Alden Williams, *The Word of Islam* (Austin: University of Texas Press, 1994), p. 171.

the first twelve Imams, but Ayatollah Khomeini claimed it as well, a feature of the contemporary resurgence of Islam that we shall discuss in a later section. *Ayatollah* means "emanation of God" or "sign for God." This title is reserved for the most eminent of the hundreds of *ulama* in this tradition called *mujtahids*. These theologians practice *ijtihad*, a term derived from the same root as the word *jihad*; it means to strive or struggle intellectually to understand the word of God. Among the most eminent of the ayatollahs is the Grand Ayatollah—the *Marja al-Taqlid*, which means "model to be emulated." There are very few Marjas in the world and, after the Imams, they are the highest religious authorities in the Shiite world.

While Shiites still differ on the question of descent, the general contemporary belief is that the line of direct descendants of Ali has been terminated and that there is no identifiable Imam. Nevertheless, according to Shiite theology, the last Imams did not die, but are absent "in hiding." In the Twelver tradition, for example, it is believed that the Twelfth Imam, although born in 869 (in the second century of Islam), is not dead. He is in occultation, or hiding, waiting to return in the future as *mahdi* (the "expected one," or divinely guided messiah), whereupon he will initiate a golden era of worldly justice in Islamic terms. Until that day, all political authority is fundamentally illegitimate, even though the *mujtahids* and ayatollahs serve in the *mahdi's* place. The absence of an identifiable Imam means that it is necessary to have members of the Shiite *ulama* interpret God's will for the community. We will return to this Shiite conception of leadership in the following discussion of contemporary Islam. For the moment, however, a brief discussion of developments in the Sunni tradition as well as the amazing successes of Islam in politics, scholarship, and culture throughout history seems necessary so that we may understand the contemporary view of many Muslims that Islam must return to the practices that made it so successful in the past.

	Selection of leadership	Major branches
Sunni	Caliph is chosen by consensus *(ijma)* among leadership	Hanafi, Maliki, Shafi, Hanbali
Shiite	Imam is a designated descendant of living Imam	Ismailis (Seveners), Twelvers, Zayidis

The Growth of Islam

We have already alluded to the fact that the early growth of the Islamic movement under Muhammad was extraordinarily rapid, continuing well into the sixteenth century. Armed with the Quran's teaching that the will of God is not abstract doctrine requiring simple belief, but rather a set of commands requiring action, Muslims expanded the borders of the Islamic community to include north Africa, central Asia, considerable portions of southern Europe, parts of India, and modern-day Indonesia. In battle, a mythology developed around Muslims who became known for their tenacity and willingness to sacrifice their lives for the cause, a sacrifice that would guarantee them eternal reward. Their military successes paved the way for tremendous achievements in culture. With Christian

Europe in the throes of what is commonly called the Dark Ages, Muslim scholar established centers of learning and inquiry which developed the cultural tradition of Islam; and in the Western Muslim world, they preserved, added to, and dissem inated the traditions of Ancient Greece and Rome. Religious scholars who headee many of these efforts, the *ulama*, eventually formed a sort of international Islami intelligentsia, and their scholarly achievements, particularly in the elaboration o Islamic Law (*shariah*), gave them a special status within Islam. These elaboration in the first and second centuries of the Islamic era (eighth and ninth centuries o the Christian Era) led to the development of the four different jurisprudentia schools of Sunni Islam: Hanafi, Maliki, Shafi, and Hanbali. After these school emerged, many of the Sunni *ulama* took the conservative step of declaring tha there was no further need for interpretation of God's requirements. They declaree an end to the practice of interpretation by closing "the gates of *ijtihad*." Eacl school has been influential in different parts of the Muslim world, thus creating a diverse, but relatively stable Sunni Muslim tradition. The differences betweel these approaches on personal, social, economic, and political matters can be sig nificant in the lives of ordinary Muslims. As Leila Ahmed has suggested in the context of laws regarding marriage, the differing interpretations make for quite different practices:

> For example, whereas all schools agree that marriage may be terminated unilaterall and extrajudicially by the male, Maliki law differs from the other schools as te women's right to obtain a judicial divorce. Maliki law allows a woman to petition no just on grounds of sexual impotence, as in Hanafi law, but also on grounds of deser tion, failure to maintain her, cruelty, and her husband's being afflicted with chronic or incurable disease detrimental to her. The differences for women obvi ously are fundamental. Similarly, Hanafi law differs radically from the other three in its view of marriage contracts and of a woman's right to stipulate terms such a that the husband may not take a second wife. The other three schools consider man's right to unilateral divorce and his right to marry as many as four wives [a stipulated in the Quran] to be the essence of marriage and therefore elements tha may not be altered by the specific contractual agreements entered upon by husbanc and wife. The Hanafi school, however, considered that the Quranic utterances or polygamy, for instance, were permissive, not mandatory, and that it was therefore not contrary to the essence of marriage for a man to have only one wife; and it con sequently saw the spouse's contractual agreement to this or other matters as valie and enforceable.[8]

As Ahmed points out, differing legal systems can create very different Muslin realities.

The scope and power of the international Muslim community in the late Middle Ages was unparalleled. Under the leadership of rulers called Sultans numerous Muslim empires were established throughout the world: the Abbasic (749–1258), based in Baghdad; the Ottoman (1281–1922), based in Istanbul; the Safavid (1501–1736) in Persia; and the Mughal (1526–1857) in India, to name few. While they were all united under the banner of Islam, much of their succes

---

[8] Leila Ahmed, *Women and Gender in Islam: Historical Roots of a Modern Debate* (New Haven Yale University Press, 1992), p. 91.

was due to the fact that these empires were able to accommodate themselves to varied local practices in the areas under their rule. In the Sunni contexts, strict adherence to the demands of Islamic law was accompanied by limited legal elaborations by *ulama* in fields where rules had not been previously stipulated. While the Islamic tradition provided a set of core beliefs and practices for all Muslims, its application to specific settings was quite varied. Such adaptation to the practices and customs of varying conquered areas resulted in a division between what has been referred to as the "orthodox" Islam of the urban, imperial "center" and the "folk" or "popular" Islam of the "periphery." The former was the Islam of the *ulama* who oversaw the Islamic courts and schools, while the latter became a more syncretic Islam that blended local traditions with the central requirements of the tradition.

One important development in this regard was the emergence of Sufism, named after early Muslims who rejected the growing imperial splendor attached to Islam of the center and believed that, in addition to following "externally" prescribed rituals, there were also intuitive or interior ways of reaching direct communion with God. Derived from the Arabic word meaning "coarse wool" to distinguish the Sufis from those who wore extravagant garments, Sufism (also called "mystical" Islam) grew out of contact between Islam and existing forms of mysticism in different settings. Sufism identifies a vast and varied set of puritanical practices in Islam. What all Sufi "orders" share is the belief that it is possible to reach a closer relationship with God through various extremely sophisticated and disciplined rituals designed effectively to remove one's consciousness from the world. Politically, Sufi orders have been significant bases of rule for Muslim governments over time.

We note before concluding this section that Sunni Islam did not elaborate a messianic doctrine like that found in Shiite Islam, even though the concept of a *mahdi* has been assimilated through popular belief. Nor does the Sunni tradition possess the institution of the Ayatollah. The duty of interpreting obligations incumbent upon Muslims is taken up by the *ulama* as well as by spiritually wise and respected *shaykhs* (literally, "elderly") and, more recently, by teachers or graduates from Muslim schools of learning who have been collectively referred to as "Muslim intellectuals."

That Islam eventually "declined" in its power and influence must be seen relative to the growth and power of the West with the Industrial Revolution and the emergence of European struggles to control resources and territory around the world. Throughout the era of Western imperialism, possibilities for sovereignty, welfare, and prosperity in Muslim societies became ever more tied to the interests of external powers: British, French, Italian, German, Dutch, Russian, Soviet, and the United States. As a result, Muslim jurists, intellectuals, and activists became ever more concerned not only with adapting external practices and customs to Islam for the enrichment of the tradition but also with Islam's potential weakening under the growing power of "the West." In the eyes of some, the recent tendency to incorporate cultural or political practices derived from other lands opened the way to inauthentic deviation from "the straight path"— the path of righteousness.

Theopolitics and Modern Ideology

No more than a generation ago, a section concerning "Islam and the mod ern world" would probably have raised some eyebrows among North American audiences: "Why discuss Islam in a book on ideologies?" "How can it possibly be relevant in modern politics?" Indeed, such questions might be asked about a range of religious traditions. Students and trained observers of politics alike would most likely have considered a section of an ideologies text devoted to religion and pol itics to be outdated.

Such assumptions are pervasive even today. People speak of religion as a "refuge" from the complexities of modern life, or a temporary response, indeed a reaction, to the rapid, disorienting changes brought about by processes charac teristic of the modern world. These assumptions are based on a widely shared belief among many people of the twentieth century that the outcomes of social and political change should be distinctly secular, in the sense of leading to the "priva tization" or total elimination of religion from the political realm. Such were the expectations of the great theorists of ideological movements of the seventeenth through nineteenth centuries, liberals and Marxists alike, who were deeply influ ential in creating modern expectations about liberty, equality, and opportunity. Among the most important of these expectations was that as societies became ever more complex (primarily through urbanization, industrialization, and education—what have been called "modernization" processes in social science), the religious and public spheres would become increasingly differentiated. Matters of gover nance would become limited to matters of regulating developing markets, or organizing the interests of a given society. Intimated here is what many theorists characterized as a transition from traditional to modern life, based on a particu lar understanding of history as a continuous, unfolding process. History may have some major bumps—wars and the like—but it would, over the long run, be a con tinuous process of linear transformation, where one stage of history would replace a previous stage, where the old would be superseded by the new, the traditional by the modern, the religious by the secular.

These assumptions are manifest in the ideologies we have discussed thus far. While not antireligious, liberal theorists suggest that religion should become a matter of private or social conscience in modern life, separated from matters of public policy. Recall that it was John Locke who, in his 1689 *Letter Concerning Tol eration*, was among the first in the West to call for this separation. The liberal tra dition sees itself partly as providing a solution to the history of religious conflict by encouraging people to separate out their beliefs on the question of God—upon which members of mass publics often greatly differ—from the interests which they share in common, such as stability, property, and liberty. This has never been an easy distinction to maintain in practice, but it has had success as a regulating prin ciple in polities where there is vast religious diversity. Liberal polities have proven that a general separation can be maintained by the mutual recognition among cit izens that any attempt to establish politically one authoritative view of ultimate reli gious truth poses a threat to the liberty of all—both in general terms, as a violation of free conscience, and specifically, as a violation of free religious belief. Today's classical conservatives recognize the problem of liberty, but tend to think that crises of morality require a greater infusion into society of religious understandings of morality. In fact, since religions are often understood by conservatives to be among the most honored and time-tested traditions of humanity, conservative ideologies often equate morality with religion, whereas liberals may draw on other, humanistic bases of morality (such as the Kantian idea that no human ought to use another as a mere means to certain ends). In contrast to this liberal view, Karl Marx never supported a separation between a private realm of conscience and a public political realm. This was not because he wanted to see a larger role for religion, but because he thought that to relegate matters of conscience to the private "inner self" was to perpetuate the alienated public sphere of capitalism. According to Marx, this was another ideological tactic that shielded capitalism from widespread public criticism. Against both religious liberals and conservatives, Marx was also harshly critical of the essence of the Abrahamic monotheistic belief in an all-powerful God. He described religion as "the heart of the heartless world" and reasoned that by submitting to God, people were placing their creative power outside themselves, a tendency that would only prolong their willingness to be dominated by each other and by capital. For humanity to be genuinely liberated, he maintained, it would need to see itself as the sole, creative, and responsible power over worldly affairs. Abrahamic monotheism, like capitalism, needed to be transcended.

Thus, to the surprise of many, late-twentieth century students of social and political change find themselves extremely puzzled about the dynamic role of religion and politics, and not only in Islam. In North America, this is due in part to the public debate about issues like reproductive rights for women, prayer in schools, and adultery. Why is this the case? The short answer may be that religiously centered institutions, leaders, and activists have not been uniformly inclined to follow the pattern of what liberals and Marxists once declared were their proper historical roles. Besides mobilizing their faithful to defend their specific, political, and material interests, they reject the logic of the inevitability of the secularization process and defend the belief in God as a moral outlook that better secures human dignity and accommodates the complexities of the modern life— including conditions of alienation and environmental destruction under capitalism. Indeed, modern religious social movements, such as the Liberation Theology movement in South America and the Sojourners in the United States, have led struggles against political injustice and grave economic inequalities. Even the Pope, as recently as 1999, condemned the vast and growing economic inequality as well as what he described as the "purely economic conception of man" that dominates capitalism. Religious groups often claim that religion provides meaning and a moral anchor that cannot be found in the other—merely worldly—political ideologies. Monotheists and other religionists are constituting their personal, social, economic, and political efforts as both righteous and religiously meaningful. In short, the late twentieth century witnessed a vitality and efficacy in theopolitical action that has surprised many. Perhaps theopolitical activists are not very different from other ideologically committed persons: It may be the tenacious character of ideological belief in general that makes it difficult for true believers to part with meaningful beliefs. Whatever the deeper human explanation, one thing is clear: At the beginning of the twenty-first century, the once settled matter about the inevitable secularization of political life has become rather unsettled.

For our purposes here, this leads to the questions: Why is Islam, in particular, so relevant in the modern world, and what is the source of its relevance? There are several reasons related to the effects of colonialism, mistaken notions about Islam's decadence, and the significance of new questions of cultural authenticity in the context of global capitalism. In some of these regards, the Islamist position is not unique, but, in what follows, we shall attempt to point to its distinct character.

Reasons for Islamist Resurgence

There is no doubt that one of the reasons for the Islamist resurgence lies in the history of Western colonial and imperial influence in Muslim societies. The story of this influence is long and complex; it need not delay our treatment of the ideas here. Suffice it to say that the resurgence of Islam has to do in large measure with the deepening effects of the expansion of Western influence and control across the surface of the globe since the nineteenth century (the French in North Africa, the British in the Middle East, both of them in South Asia, and the Dutch and British in Southeast Asia). After World War I, Western powers exerted considerable influence in creating a nation-state arrangement around the world that would serve their interests. When the Western powers did not engage in direct colonial rule, they secured their geostrategic and economic advantage through indirect political channels, and where they failed or were challenged in doing so, they often intervened directly or covertly to correct the situation.

This was especially the case in the Middle East, where the situation was aggravated by Cold War wrangling and competition for valuable petroleum resources located under the surface of Islam's most holy lands. Where local regimes threatened the power relations that were advantageous to Western powers, the latter reacted swiftly, and often forcefully—as in the CIA-backed restoration of the Shah of Iran in 1953; the joint French, British, and Israeli invasion of Egypt in 1956; and the Gulf War of 1991. In this context, Muslims throughout the world criticize the uneven Western support for the state of Israel. Established in 1948 as a national homeland for the Jewish people, Israel is viewed by Muslim revivalists as a Western colonial state implanted illegitimately in Islamic lands. The Islamist critique has expanded upon the more secular, Arab nationalist criticisms of Zionism (the Jewish nationalist movement that organized to create Israel); the Islamists systematically employ religious terms to describe themselves and their enemies. Thus strong denunciations of "Jews," along with others, like their "Crusader" patrons, pervade the Islamist discourse about the Arab-Israeli conflict. As long as the question of justice for the original, mostly Muslim Arab Palestinian population remains unresolved, this issue is bound to remain pivotal in contemporary Islamist ideologies. Conflicts continue to erupt between Western powers and opponents of the huge buildup of American and British military installations in the countries of the Arabian Gulf, very near to the holy sites of Medina, Mecca, Karbala, and Najaf. An end to the conflict over Western influence in the political affairs in those areas is difficult to foresee, given Western understandings of the strategic and economic importance of that region. In the heart of the Muslim world, therefore, the old story of Western domination has not yet ended. In the lives of Muslim populations throughout the world, it is an ongoing reality, especially when one also considers the additional factor of Western economic influence. Before we describe this, it is necessary to note an intellectual tendency dominant in the West that legitimated colonial rule of Muslim lands.

Throughout most of the twentieth century, many Westerners have believed that the only way that Muslims could survive in the modern world is if they abandoned their Muslim practices and adopted Western-style political, educational, and cultural ways. In the context of the study of Islam, the tendency to relegate Islam to irrelevance in light of modernity's challenges has been described by scholars as "Orientalism." The core idea of Orientalism is the notion that Islam is unable to generate the kind of innovative energies that are necessary to live well in modernity; consequently, for Muslims to become modern, they must abandon their understandings of the significance of Islam in personal, social, political, and moral life and adopt Western ways, including everything from political theories to styles of dress and habits of personal hygiene.

Critics of Orientalism—the scholar Edward Said, primary among them—have pointed out that Orientalists purport to describe the "Muslim mind" objectively, but their descriptions correspond very poorly with the actual diverse and dynamic reality of Muslim societies. (Indeed, they correspond poorly with the diversity of Western societies as well.) The Islamic resurgence of the early twentieth century provides a good example. At the moment when Muslim intellectuals and activists were mobilizing to repel colonial rule and to re-Islamicize their societies, Western "experts" on Islam were suggesting that Islam was a lifeless, obscurantist, reactionary, and helplessly immobile system. Critical of this perspective, Said has cogently argued that the claims of the Orientalists tend to say more about the identity of the Western observers—namely, how much they view themselves as the world's only innovators—than they do about those whose lives they claim to represent accurately. Moreover, he has pointed out how, throughout the history of Western imperial domination, this tendency to represent Islam as lacking all of the cherished characteristics in the West supports the historic logic of colonialism by making colonial rule seem necessary, desirable, and in the best interests of Muslims. By designating Islam as a timeless "Other" that is seemingly immune to historical change, Western Orientalists reinforce the twin ideas of their own superiority in a changing world and their moral right to impose their ways on others. Indeed, if one adopts the Orientalist perspective, it is easy to see how one might view Muslim identity as the indication of a flaw, and Islam as a static, rather than a rich, tradition. If one is an Orientalist, it is possible to see how colonialism might seem to be not only necessary in terms of naked calculations of geostrategic interest but also "good for the Muslims." Obviously, Orientalist thinking continues to shape much of what non-Muslims think about Muslims; and, since it stereotypes and devalues their tradition, it is a major component of non-Muslim, Western thinking that most disturbs Muslims, whether they are devout practitioners or not.

It is understandable, then, that twentieth-century Muslim activists interpreted the expansion and influence of Western political, economic, and cultural power as domination by imperialist and inauthentic forces. By cultural power, we mean the ability of influential agents—governmental officials, advertising executives, rock stars, Hollywood directors, actors and actresses—to shape the styles, hopes, tastes, values, meanings, and understandings of people. The Islamic resurgence rejects "cultural imperialism" carried out by both colonial powers and local movements interested in "Westernizing" Muslim societies. There are many dimensions to this critique. Islamists claim that the effects of cultural domination have permeated every sphere of society, from the structure of governance to the very self-understandings of individual Muslims. In some ways, the rise of the modern nation-state, derived out of the European experience, is in conflict with the supra-national bases of affiliation that, in principle, unite all Muslims. Islamists are aware of different national groupings that comprise the Muslim community, but these differences are not understood as grounds for sharp, antagonistic divisions. A Hasan al-Turabi, the Sorbonne-educated Islamist leader in the government of Sudan, has said: "an Islamic state is not a nationalist state because ultimate allegiance is owed to God and thereby to the community of believers—the *ummah*. One can never stop at any national frontier and say the nation is absolute, an ultimate end in itself."[9]

In general, one can imagine that the ideologically liberal emphases on individualism, the separation of the public and private, along with Western patterns of materialism, commercialism, and emancipation through technology, may be seen as components of cultural power that may engender tension in any society organized around different understandings. This problem is not unique to Muslim societies. For example, the Amish in the United States constantly struggle to keep their way of life insulated from the influences of "the English." A similar reaction develops in Muslim societies accustomed perhaps to more open and flexible borders, emphasis on strong communal and family bonds, a belief in God's social presence, and more fluid, personal administrative relations. Our goal here is not to create rigid differences between West and East, for, in the final analysis, they share many shared features. Our goal is to point out that various forms of cultural power are relevant to understanding why the Islamic revival is significant to students of ideology in this era, namely, because Islamists object to the imposition of cultural values derived from non-Muslim settings.

In the early years of the Islamic revival during the twentieth century, the special targets of this cultural critique were the educational policies implemented by new modernizing regimes in the Muslim world. In the 1920s, several nationalist regimes undertook plans to "modernize" their schools by introducing a less religious curricula that would cultivate national values as well as scientific skills useful to achieve goals of national economic development. The leaders of these reform hoped to create local engineering and technical skills for the integration of their

---

[9] Hassan al-Turabi, "The Islamic State," in *Voices of Resurgent Islam,* John L. Esposito, ed. (New York: Oxford University Press, 1983), p. 242.

industrial and agricultural sectors into the spreading market. This was seen as the path to progress and prosperity, much as it is today by proponents of global capitalism. The new curricula, designed by European-educated Muslims with the specific purpose of teaching the most recent developments in modern "positivist" science, conceived of scientific inquiry as a nonreligious pursuit. Positivist scientific inquiry views itself as an "objective" way of understanding nature, superior to theological modes of analysis. In Turkey, for example, the Kemalist movement, named after Mustafa Kemal Atatürk, created a new educational system that emphasized education in nationalism and the "positive" sciences. The Kemalists eliminated the previous Islamic school system and built a new nonreligious educational curricula designed to suit their new, national agenda. Kemal himself enthusiastically declared that "the torch which the Turkish nation is holding in its hand and its head marching on the path of progress and civilization is positive science."[10]

Islamists characterized such educational efforts as assaults on the authentic traditions of Islam. Hassan al-Banna, the founder of the Muslim Brotherhood in Egypt, suggested that similar Egyptian reforms amounted to "mental colonization" in which Muslims would be led to "demean" and "disparage" themselves and their traditions. The famous Turkish Muslim thinker of the time, Bediuzzaman Said Nursi, declared the Kemalists to be "Europeanized Turks," infected with the "disease" of "Europeanization." He condemned them for propagating what he called an irreligious "materialist philosophy" that neglected the concerns of believers, and, therefore, failed to prepare children for life's true challenges. Education based on the "drunkenness of nationalist patriotism" failed to teach "reliance on God" and "the submission of Islam." Without the latter values, children would not be able to "withstand awesome fears and situations of the world in the future." With them, they would "look eagerly to life."[11]

More recently Islamists have taken aim at the effects of cultural changes induced through other kinds of economic means. The end of the Cold War has led to a huge expansion of the markets for commercial capitalism, creating a great deal of social and cultural change as tastes of global populations have become increasingly organized around the same products. Although there are many exceptions, populations around the world have become consumers of McDonald's, Coca-Cola, TGIFriday's, Gap, and Bennetton as the world's most powerful corporations have extended their reaches into every metropolitan corner of the globe. One contemporary Western political theorist has defined this commercial dimen-

[10] Mustafa Kemal Atatürk, "Fifteenth Anniversary of National Liberation, 10th Anniversary of the Establishment of the Republic," from *Atatürk'ün Söylev ve Demeçleri (1906–1938)* (*Atatürk's Public Addresses and Statements*), Vol. II, Nimet Arsan, ed. (Ankara: Türk Tarih Kurumu BasImevi for the History of the Turkish Transformation Institute, 2nd printing, 1959), trans. and analyzed in Taha Parla and Andrew Davison, *Corporatist Ideology in Kemalist Turkey: Progress or Order?* (manuscript in progress).

[11] Bediuzzaman ("Marvel of the Times") Said Nursi, "Twenty-ninth Letter—Sixth Section, Which Is the Sixth Treatise," in Bediuzzaman Said Nursi: *Letters, 1928–1932* (Istanbul, Turkey: Sözler Neşriyat A. Ş., 1997), p. 495–96; and Hassan al-Banna, quoted in Ibrahim M. Abu-Rabì, *Intellectual Origins of Islamic Resurgence in the Modern Arab World* (Albany: State University of New York Press, 1996), p. 80.

sion of cultural power with the concept "McWorld." It describes the collection of market and political forces that is attempting to integrate the world and, as it does to create more uniform tastes, sensibilities, and ways of living. The corporate executives of McWorld, writes Benjamin Barber, consciously aim to create a loyal, "universal tribe of consumers" whose "needs" will be satisfied through material consumption:

> McWorld is a product of a popular culture driven by expansionist commerce. Its template is American, its form style. Its goods are as much images as matériel, an aesthetic as well as a product line. It is about culture as commodity, apparel as ideology. Its symbols are Harley-Davidson motorcycles and Cadillac motorcars hoisted from the roadways, where they once represented a mode of transportation, to the marquees of global market cafés like Harley-Davidson's and the Hard Rock Café where they become icons of lifestyle. You don't drive them, you feel their vibes and rock to the images they conjure up from old movies and new celebrities, whose personal appearances. . . . music, video, theater, books and theme parks . . . are all constructed as image exports creating a common world taste around common logos, advertising slogans, stars, songs, brand names, jingles, and trademarks.

McWorld promises, in the long term, to increase the economic advantage and cultural influence of Western economic actors and their local supporters throughout the world, even if it has also created tensions with defenders of local culture. Barber quotes the chief executive officer of Coca-Cola suggesting that "these new worlds of opportunity are not only heavily populated, but also culturally and climatically ripe for significant soft drink consumption" and describes Coke's "aggressive investment" strategy in Indonesia designed to prompt "societies that have traditionally consumed beverages like tea" to make "the transition to sweeter beverages like Coca-Cola."[12]

Prominent among those rejecting such consumer "campaigns" are Islamist movements interested in preserving what they call "cultural authenticity." This is not to suggest that all Muslim revivalists are anticommercialist or even that they refrain from consuming soft drinks. Islamist movements seek to promote trade, exchange, and innovation in an "authentic Muslim economy." We also do not mean to endorse the notion of a fixed, unchanging culture. We wish to emphasize that Islamists find the greed-driven, unchecked dissemination of Western tastes, styles, and morally offensive ideals, such as alcohol consumption or sexually charged entertainment, as an assault on their culture and religious values. The Quran explicitly prohibits the use of intoxicants and immodest bodily display for both men and women. (Contrary to some Islamist interpretations, it does not prohibit men and women from taking part in social activities.) Nonetheless, many of the billboard displays and television commercials displaying McWorld's cultural patterns are viewed as hostile to the ways of a more conservative Islamic order. That is, they are viewed as imposed cultural patterns. If the figurative meaning of TGIFriday's were conveyed in Islamic cultural terms, for example, it

---

[12] Benjamin R. Barber, *Jihad vs. McWorld: How Globalism and Tribalism Are Reshaping the World* (New York: Ballantine Books, 1995), pp. 15, 17, and 69–70.

would translate as, "thank God it is the day of congregation," since Friday is the traditional holy day of the week in Islam, and the last thing a devout Muslim would desire is to drink margaritas! Finally, it is important to note that the confrontation with McWorld appears to be an uneven contest: Islamists do not have the resources at their disposal to compete equally with the powers of McWorld who have the Internet, Hollywood, CNN, and Mickey Mouse to lead the way.

Another interesting ideological concept in this regard is Weststruckness (*Gharbzadegi*, which may also be translated as "Westoxication"), a term that was coined by the Iranian thinker Jalal Al-e Ahmad (1923–1969) in order to describe the "disease" of being "struck" by the West—both in the positive sense of being captivated with its advanced scientific and technological ways as well as in the negative sense of being captured or conquered by those ways in a process that leads inexorably to cultural corrosion. Even as it improved life in some ways, the disease of the "machine" civilization slowly eroded indigenous national cultural traditions:

> Our world is a world of confrontation between the poor and the rich in a world-wide arena. Our time is a time of two worlds. One is on the side of manufacturing, distributing, and exporting machines; the other is on the side of using, wearing out, and dismantling them. One is the producer, the other a consumer. And where is the arena of this conflict? The world market. And its weapons? Besides the tanks, artillery, bombers, and missile-launchers, themselves the manufactures of that Western world, here is UNESCO [United Nations Educational, Scientific, and Cultural Organization], FAO [United Nations Food and Agriculture Organization], the United Nations, ECAFE [United Nations Economic Commission for Asia and the Far East], and other so-called international institutions that seem to be international and universal, but the truth of the matter is that they're Western tricksters who bring colonialism to that second world in a new suit, to South America, to Asia, to Africa. And this is where the basis of the *Gharbzadegi* of all non-Western nations lies. This is not a discussion about rejecting or refusing machines, as the utopians imagined in the early nineteenth century. Not at all. The inundation of the world by machines is a historical inevitability. It's a discussion about the nature of our encounter with machines—as a growing nation . . . and about the fact that we don't make the machines; but because of economic and political necessity—and that international confrontation between rich and poor—we must be docile and humble consumers of Western products, or at best . . . poorly paid, contented, and submissive repairmen for whatever comes from the West. . . .
>
> And now, in addition to all this, gradually, the spiritual wealth of the East, of Africa, of South America has become a mental preoccupation for Western intelligentsia and educated people. It has now come to the point where the literate, cultivated man of the West enjoys "primitive" African sculpture and jazz music. In literature he reads the Upanishads, Tagore, Taoism, Buddism, and Zen. . . .
>
> At the same time, we Weststruck people in such times don't know our own music and hear it as useless noise. We talk about symphonies and rhapsodies. We've turned our backs on Iranian portraiture and miniatures. Imitating the Venice Art Festival, we paint heaps of color side by side, and in imitation of the Beinnale of Venice we even consider fauvism and cubism out of date. We've laid Iranian architecture aside, with its symmetry, its ponds, and foundations; its gardens, basements, bathhouses; and sash and lattice windows.[13]

---

[13] Jalal Al-e Ahmad, *Gharbzadegi* (*Westtruckness*), trans. by John Green and Ahmad Alizadeh (Costa Mesa, Calif.: Mazda Publishers, 1982 [1964]), pp 15–16, and 169.

Al-e Ahmad's critique, a relatively early expression of concerns about the los of culture in the context of global change, shows how the "universal" ideals in th West—such as the technological achievements—can be seen as culturally specifi odd, and destructive in relation to traditions elsewhere. And he points out th irony of how, at precisely the time when the products of Western commercial an technological culture are being adopted and imposed for profit on poor countrie around the world, the citizens of the rich countries are pursuing spiritual nour ishment in those eroded traditions. These traditions now appear, of course, i their salable, commercial form as the West's own cultural treasures fade from vie as well.

Al-e Ahmad was not an ideological Islamist. Indeed, his work can be viewe as a yearning to see a more authentic exploration of various aesthetic and cultur: possibilities globally. But his concept resonated so clearly throughout Iranian soc ety that it became part of Ayatollah Khomeini's criticism of the modernizatio drive of the Iranian regime in the 1970s, a drive that was conceived by the regim as requiring a separation between affairs of worldly business and those of religion Khomeini absorbed the concept of *Gharbzadegi*—using it more in the sense c Westoxication, and thereby calling forth associations with Quranic prohibition against intoxicants—into his critique. He observed that the fascination with, an adoption of, Western ways was leading people to abandon their Islamic politic: and moral foundations. These were the designs, he asserted, of "the enemies c Islam":

> As the imperialist countries attained a high degree of wealth and affluence—th result of both scientific and technical progress and of their plunder of the nations c Asia and Africa—these [Iranians] lost all self-confidence and imagined that the onl way to achieve technical progress was to abandon their own laws and beliefs. Whe. the moon landings took place, for instance, they concluded that Muslims should je tison their laws! . . . Let them go all the way to Mars or beyond the Milky Way; the will still be deprived of true happiness, moral virtue, and spiritual advancement an. be unable to solve their own social problems. For the solution of social problems an. the relief of human misery require foundations in faith and morals; merely acquirin, material power and wealth, conquering nature and space, have no effect in thi regard.[14]

Indeed, as Khomeini points out, not all Muslims have responded to th. global forces of cultural change in the same way. Many Muslims have participate in the expansion of Western ideals and influence, believing them to be desirable and sometimes powerful, tools of progress and emancipation from the influence of various forms of traditional domination, such as patriarchy or particularly st: fling Islamic interpretations of the just community. Like other religious tradi tions, the internal debate over the authentic Muslim interpretation of Islam i not new. In the contemporary period especially, many Muslims have welcomed fought for, and continue to fight on behalf of ideals and practices characteristi. of ideologically liberal or socialist goals, believing that they are fruitful t.

[14] Imam Khomeini, *Islam and Revolution: Writings and Declarations of Imam Khomeini* (Berke ley: Mizan Press, 1981), pp. 35–36.

enhancing the liberties and lives of people who have been systematically dominated in Muslim societies. Supporters of these aspects of the West are at fundamental odds with those religious revivalists whose interpretation of Islam makes little room for extensive liberty and full equality among all human beings. Again, we encounter the problem of generalization. We must stress that there is considerable ideological diversity and disagreement in the Muslim world. A difficult and delicate question to be answered is whether or not the welcome reception of Western forces by sectors of Muslim populations, or their explorations of cultural possibilities that are indigenous but not Islamic, truly constitute inauthentic responses to various forces of modern power? Nevertheless, traditionalists tend to consider them inauthentic, even as they adopt various practices and technologies themselves.

Puritanical and Reformist Tendencies

To Muslim revivalists, the Westernizing response is clearly inauthentic since it fails to conceive of Islam as relevant in social and political terms; and the welcoming posture of some Muslims toward radical cultural change is wrong because it diminishes the significance of the comprehensive and total moral outlook of Islam. At the core of the revivalist response is a rejection of the idea that Islam is some kind of dead tradition, that it is inefficacious for moral and political action in modernity. The revivalist's program for action includes several identifiable, conceptual, and practical requirements. At the risk of gross oversimplification, it may be stated that the modern resurgence of Islam has taken two different conceptual paths, distinguished largely by the degree of each's commitment to return to the "purity" of the seventh-century model. The more "puritanical" of the two paths believes that modernization and development have totally corrupted Islam; it calls for a complete transformation of contemporary Muslim states—a return to the traditional ideal Islamic community. This return, considered to be a reactionary denial of the reality of change by modernizers everywhere, is considered among purists to be an authentic restoration of the ideal. It should be noted that this puritanical response to rapid social change is not unique to Islam, although in the Islamist context it draws upon the ready made "golden-age" model of desert life in seventh-century Arabia. A second, less puritanical tendency also exhibits a desire to reinfuse their countries with traditional Islamic values and practices, but aims to do so by creating a dynamic, contemporary Islamic scientific, economic, and political order. Modernization does not require "Westernization," "Islamic reformists" (also called "modernists") argue, and they are working as government officials, university scholars, and economic actors to bring technology and prosperity to Muslim societies.

These categories should be seen only as rough analytical guides, not as exact depictions of the extremely complex reality of Islamist revivalism. Sometimes the tendencies that are at work are difficult to identify through simple observation. It is possible, for example, to mistake an Islamic reformist for a purist given that much of the Islamist revival involves adopting what are considered authentic cultural styles, such as apparel, that are very different from styles in the West

(although as the West diversifies, less and less so). Observers must be exception
ally careful not to reach unwarranted conclusions about the putative "reactionary"
tendencies in this regard based simply on apparent cultural differences. One
observer of the Iranian revolution has noted that clauses of the new constitution
of Iran dealing with scientific, technological, and economic development "seem
to have escaped the notice of Western journalists who claim that the Iranian rev
olution was carried out in the name of rejecting [a developed] society."[15] Even the
very socially reactionary Taliban leaders of Afghanistan use the Internet and pro
mote trade investment strategies. Indeed, the leadership of the most prominent
revivalist movements tend to have strong training in Islamic educational systems
that stress the comprehensive unity of religion and the affairs of the world.

The fundamental compatibility between Islam and scientific inquiry was
famously described in an 1882 lecture in Calcutta by Jamal ad-Din al-Afghani, one
of the early proponents for reform in Islam. Observing that "we see that the minds
of our Muslim logicians are full of every superstition and vanity, and no difference
exists between their ideas and the ideas of the masses in the bazaar," he criticized
Muslims' acceptance of the concept of a "European science." That the Europeans
have "put their hands on every part of the world" does not mean, he argued, that
they have a special claim to owning science. Scientific inquiry as such can be pos
sessed by no one. Reminding his audience that the Greeks and Romans had his
torically adopted knowledge from the East, al-Afghani noted that science is
independent of the grasp of any particular civilization. "[It] is constantly chang
ing capitals. Sometimes it has moved from East to West, and other times from West
to East." He believed that Islam was uniquely suited to incorporate science because
of the tradition's comprehensive concern to see all affairs of the world governed
by God:

> The father and mother of science is proof, and proof is neither Aristotle nor Galileo
> The truth is where there is proof, and those who forbid science and knowledge in the
> belief that they are safeguarding the Islamic religion are really the enemies of that
> religion. The Islamic religion is the closest of religions to science and knowledge, and
> there is no incompatibility between science and knowledge and the foundation of the
> Islamic faith."[16]

It is thus no accident that many reformist leaders come from professions like
teaching, engineering, law, and medicine. Defying Orientalist and non-Islamist
expectations about the inevitable secularizing interests of well-educated people,
they seek to re-Islamicize society—that is, to build a new society of Islamic justice
based on the Quran and the traditions of the Prophet. For some Islamists, this
no doubt means a simple "return." But for many others, it means engaging life
in the contemporary world as did the original Muslim community: by meeting its

[15] Ervand Abrahamian, *Khomeinism: Essays on the Islamic Republic* (Berkeley: University of Cal
ifornia Press, 1993), pp. 35-36.

[16] Jamal ad-Din al-Afghani, "Lecture on Teaching and Learning," in, *An Islamic Response to
Imperialism: Political and Religious Writings of Sayyid Jamal ad-Din "al-Afghani,"* (1839–1897)
Nikki R. Keddie, ed.(Berkeley: University of California Press, 1983), p. 106–7.

challenges and striving to build a righteous community under changing conditions. The key ideological concepts here are renewal (*tajdid*) and reform (*islah*), and the essential goal is to regain political and cultural sovereignty while restoring God's straight path of righteousness. Muslim revivalists reject the secularization of politics and society, emphasize the inseparability of Islam from all affairs of the world, and defend the vitality of the tradition.

Regenerating this vitality requires "re-Islamicization" through an earnest adoption of the principles of *ijtihad* and *jihad*. In general, the struggle being undertaken by Islamists is about identifying the resources within the tradition that can make it useful as a system of life today. In this context, Muslim revivalists insist that the gates to *ijtihad* are wide open once more. Again, there are varieties here. Both terms—*jihad* and *ijtihad*—mean endeavoring in the path of God, the former through practical activity and the latter through cognitive efforts of intellectual interpretation. *Jihad* encompasses different areas of practice, as we have seen, and only some Islamists carry out *jihad* in its sense of holy war. An example of this is the 1998 religious decree (*fatwa*) issued by the International Islamic Front, a coalition of groups led by Osama Bin Laden:

> The ruling to kill Americans and their allies—civilians and military—is an individual duty for every Muslim who can do it in any country in which it is possible to do it, in order to liberate the Al-Aqsa Mosque [in Jerusalem] and the Holy Mosque [in Mecca] from their grip, and in order for their armies to move out of all the lands of Islam, defeated and unable to threaten any Muslim. This is in accordance with the words of Almighty God, "And fight the pagans all together as they fight you all together," and "fight them until there is no more tumult or oppression, and there will prevail justice and faith in God."

This *jihad* strategy is not without risk, as many *mujahideen* ("strugglers") have discovered. Existing regimes in the Muslim world—many of which promote some aspects of the tradition themselves—are not willing to give up power to those who declare holy wars against them. Regimes have responded to calls for the militant form of *jihad* by marshaling all of their own practical and interpretive powers, using everything from coercive means like incarceration, exile, assassination, and torture, to reinforcing their legitimacy in Islamic terms by claiming that their governance is entirely consistent with Islam.

But *jihad* in its militant form is only one way Islamists have attempted to re-Islamicize society. The Islamist program of change calls for a "decolonization" of society at many levels. A new Muslim consciousness must be cultivated by eliminating all of the forces and effects of Western cultural power through a process of fundamental reform in politics, education, and other arenas of life. The objective of many social reforms—such as bans on alcohol and modest dress requirements—is to reverse the desires of Muslims to live in "un-Islamic" ways. From the Islamist perspective, Islam is not a mere component of culture. It is a way of living, a civilization unto itself, that unites many different cultures and national groups into one religious community. The active re-creation of an Islamic moral order must simultaneously reverse all of the social and psychological effects of Weststruckness: foreign modes of analysis and thought, attitudes, fashions and styles. In turn,

Islamism promises an end to the corrupt, dishonest, and manipulative ways of governance that dominate many Muslim societies. It offers just leadership that is responsible to God and to the general welfare of the community. As an alternative to authoritarian politics, Islamist reformists offer models of governance through consultation (*shura*), a concept in the Quran that has been developed to elaborate Islamic models of parliamentary governance; to those ends, "*din wa dawla*," in Arabic, is the common Islamist expression calling for the integration of "religion and state."

Islamists also offer alternative models of the economy based on Islamic norms. Islam, for example, forbids usury (charging interest on borrowed money); consequently, Muslims have historically designed ways to promote economic growth by managing money in various shared risk and responsibility plans. In general, contemporary Islamists argue that an Islamic economy permits personal earning and private property, but insist that at the same time Muslims fulfill their community obligations. An Islamic economy, they argue, does not tolerate grave social injustices and economic inequalities because it institutionalizes righteousness, not only material production, consumption, exchange, and accumulation. As one scholar has described it, the individual Muslim:

> is called upon to achieve salvation and ultimate fulfillment by living up to the terms of his covenant with Allah irrespective of the performance of other members of the community; the way to obtain Divine approval is primarily in the social field by performance of his social obligations. Islamic individualism is irreconcilable with the collectivism and moral relativity of socialist thought. The distinctive characteristics that the concept of private property has in an Islamic society must be understood in this context. In Islam no person has an absolute right to his property to use it as he will, except perhaps in the sense that he can use it for some purpose that has been accepted as lawful by the Quran. It is not the property which is in itself the source of trouble but it is the misuse of the property which causes unhappiness and unrest.[17]

Islamists thus promise a future of greater economic fairness as well as more adequate services in the basic necessities (sewage, water, electricity) that many poor throughout the non-developed world lack. Decolonization includes efforts to create centers of power—including Islamic banks—that will meet the needs of Muslims according to Muslim values. As they see it, reformists offer economic plans that correct for the separation between material and spiritual endeavors in Western capitalism, which, they also argue, creates wealth and prosperity for the few, both in the West and in the Muslim world, at the expense of the Muslim masses.

It is important to note, nonetheless, that the reformists' vision of an Islamic economy, while it is not compatible with unregulated "Western capitalism," is not antithetical to private property as such or to a competitive economy. This was significant in the context of the Cold War where the interests of Islamists and those of Western capitalism merged, at least temporarily, in several crucial

---

[17] Khalid M. Ishaque, "The Islamic Approach to Economic Development," in *Voices of Resurgent Islam*, Esposito, ed., p. 275.

global conflicts. One example was the covert collusion between the United States, the very conservative Islamic monarchy in Saudi Arabia, the Afghan mujahideen, and the Islamic Republic of Pakistan against the Soviet Union in Afghanistan. Both the Western capitalist and Islamist regimes are hostile to the "atheistic forces of communism" that promote collective models of ownership and full economic equality. Although there have been a few Islamist Marxist movements that link the requirements of general welfare to a radically populist economic agenda, they have not been the main currents in the contemporary revival.

Revolutionary, Participatory, and Socialization Strategies

While most Islamist movements share these general goals of re-Islamicization, the strategies they adopt to achieve them differ according to political context. At the expense of more oversimplification, but in such a way that hopefully clarifies important differences in ideological orientation, there are three primary strategies, what we shall call the revolutionary, the participatory, and socialization.

The revolutionary strategy seeks to implement a rapid and thorough alteration in the political and social structures of a society in which the ruling norms and institutions are deemed to be contrary to Islam. Revolutionaries are committed to radical organizational, mobilizational, and implementation tactics, including violence. The revolutionary strategy is often adopted in contexts where there are no legal opportunities for participation for the Islamist groups: Either they are barred from already carefully monitored electoral processes or those processes simply do not exist. Where participation is possible, the strategy adopted by modern Islamists may be better termed participatory. This strategy aims to use available electoral and associational forums to push—gradually or rapidly—the agenda of Islamic change. The goal of capturing power through the ballot box is not uniquely secular. Finally, in contexts where Islam is allowed free expression whether or not electoral procedures exist, many Muslim movements are implementing a sophisticated strategy of change that we refer to as socialization. This refers to efforts to spread Islam throughout society in order to transform society from the bottom up, as it were, through education and teaching. According to this strategy, as Hassan al-Turabi has noted, "social change takes place peacefully and gradually, and the Islamic movement develops programs of Islamization before it takes over the destiny of the state."[18] Socialization efforts include medical care delivery, Quran and textbook publication and distribution, new mosque construction, and social pressures to perform obligations incumbent upon Muslims.

These three strategies are not always distinct, and a single movement may pursue all three simultaneously or evolve from one strategy to another depending on conditions. Similarly, a socialization strategy may coincide with interests of states that are too weak to offer the kinds of services offered by those Islamist movements that are well-financed. In the early 1990s, the participatory strategy was dealt

---

[18] al-Turabi, "The Islamic State," p. 241.

a heavy setback in many places. In Algeria, the Islamic Salvation Front scored a huge victory in the first of two rounds of voting in the 1991 national elections. Before the second round, however, the government and military, fearing the consequences of a transfer of power to the Islamists, canceled the electoral process. While the government's reasons lie partly in concerns about the loss of economic and political power, many secular Algerians feared a variety of illiberal constraints on their freedoms that would result from the imposition of Islamic law. Although no one can predict a future that never was, the world did discover that large portions of the Islamist movement were prepared to adopt a violent revolutionary strategy in response to the closure of legal participatory procedures. Something rather different happened in Turkey in the mid-1990s. Here, the Islamist Welfare Party captured power, but a bit of historical background is needed to show the significance of this experience.

When Turkey was founded in the 1920s on the ashes of the Ottoman Empire, the new regime, headed by Mustafa Kemal Atatürk, abolished the caliphate, the Islamic law, and the Islamic school system. In their place it created a *laicist* nationalist republic, founded on a new civil and family code (adapted from Switzerland), and a new national educational policy based on the nonreligious positive sciences. The Kemalist regime also carried out a number of cultural policies designed, as Kemal put it, to gain "respect in the eyes of the truly civilized"—that is, the West. The alphabet was Latinized, the weekend was shifted from Friday to Sunday, women in state institutions were required to be unveiled, men could not wear religious garb outside of the mosque, and, in general, Western styles were strongly encouraged. The Kemalists adopted the term *laicism*, taken from the French anticlerical experience of the nineteenth-century, to describe their objective of eliminating Islamic symbols and practices from certain spheres of governance and society. The regime did not conceive of itself as entirely nonreligious, since it pursued its own religious strategy and supervised Islamic practice through a state Directorate of Religious Affairs. (Laypersons may be religious members of a community. They are not necessarily non- or antireligious, as "secularizers" may be.) Nonetheless, the Kemalist *laicization* policies stirred up a great deal of opposition from defenders of Islamic governance and culture. In open conflicts with devotees of various Sufi movements, the regime closed the Sufi meeting places and holy sites, and Kemalism went on to enshrine itself as the uncontested, and uncontestable, hegemonic ideology in Turkey. Yet, resentment over the *laicization* of the state and "attacks" on Islamic culture still runs deep. The leaders of the Islamist Welfare Party represented a clear response to this experience. The Welfare Party received the most votes in the 1995 elections. Its leader, Necmettin Erbakan, formed a coalition government and assumed the office of prime minister. However, after less than thirteen months in office, he was first forced from power—partly by pressures emanating from the staunchly *laicist* military—and then, in early 1998, his party was closed by order of the state's judiciary for violating constitutional provisions guarding *laicism*. The banning of the party was itself not unusual in Turkish politics. Turkey has experienced several periods of turmoil where the army has intervened, banned many different parties, and significantly readjusted the country's constitutional structure. What is significant is that, given its history, popular support, and the presence of an electoral system that it believes it can still use to its advantage, members of the former Welfare Party have not shifted strategies. Rather, they reconstituted themselves as a new party, the Virtue Party, and continue to pursue a participatory strategy that some analysts have compared favorably with "Christian Democratic" parties in Europe. At the local level, where the debate over Turkey's social and political life intensifies, the Virtue Party continues to use the reins of power to create an Islamist order.

While there have been many Islamist revolutionary movements that have gained attention in North America—the Taliban in Afghanistan, the Hizbullah (Party of God) in Lebanon, HAMAS (The Islamic Resistance Movement) in the Palestinian setting, to name only a few—the best symbol and example of the revolutionary Islamist alternative remains the Iranian Islamic Republic established in 1979 by Ayatollah Ruhollah Khomeini. Nowhere has the Islamist critique been so dramatically successful and consequential than in the Iranian context. Indeed, Islamists around the world celebrated the revolution as a real victory against the forces of imperialism.

We can make no attempt to assess the lasting impact of the revolution, but it is abundantly clear that it preached a total revolutionary Islamicization of the modernizing Iranian society—a cultural revolution—guided by the goal culture of revived Islamic governance. Steps were taken to transform education and legal codes, strict censorship was established, traditional Muslim customs including modest clothing and facial hair-styles were reintroduced, while political decision making and administration were placed in the hands of the *ulama*. In general, everything Westoxified was to be eliminated—including members of the secularized Muslim opposition who had helped to overthrow the shah. What must be emphasized in all of this is the charismatic leadership role of the Ayatollah Khomeini, the profound and widespread support he received from the masses of people, and the devotion to his memory after his death in 1989. This devotion is, of course, not universal among Iranians. Iran is an enormously ideologically diverse setting. But reverence for the Ayatollah remains a pillar of the Islamist revolutionary regime's durability. Khomeini was able to articulate concerns that reflected the interests, hopes, fears, and desires of several groups and classes whose fortunes had diminished in the context of the Iranian monarch's modernization drive. He masterfully appealed to the Islamic students, the small business owners of the bazaar whose livelihood was threatened by plans to develop new shopping malls, and the downtrodden—the *mostazafin*. ("Mostazafin of the world unite!" chanted the crowds in the streets.) His revolutionary discourse temporarily united groups whose ideological agendas ranged from Iranian nationalism and communism to forms of Islamic governance that differed from Khomeini's. The similarity between Khomeini and other twentieth-century revolutionary leaders is striking: Like Lenin, he started a revolution in exile and returned to lead it; like Ghandi, he tweaked the nose of the dominant imperialist power while he mobilized spiritual forces for political ends; and like Mao, he pushed beyond nationalism to an international ideological and cultural revolution.

Khomeini's authority on all matters was derived from the Shiite conception of a divinely inspired Imam discussed earlier. Although he was not a *Marja al-Taqlid*, his status of Ayatollah was more than sufficient to interpret authoritatively God's will under changing social, political, and cultural circumstances. Given his place in the tradition of Ali, Khomeini was not of the opinion that it was the role of the *ulama* simply to oversee religious worship. Like other Islamists, he considered the very ideal of separating the affairs of religion from those of the state to be a critical part of imperialist propaganda "formulated and propagated by the imperialists . . . and their political agents in order to prevent religion from ordering the affairs of this world and shaping Muslim society."[19] Although he did not claim to be one of the designated successors of the prophet, Khomeini described himself as assuming the same mantle of responsibility for the welfare of the Muslim community that any Shiite jurist inherits. His intense charismatic appeal cultivated by his deep understanding and commitment to Islam, his role in overthrowing a regime he described as reminiscent of the most tyrannical regimes in Shiite history, and his creation of a new government by what he called "rule by the just jurist" (*velayeti faqih*) led him to assume the kind of worldly religious authority and prestige enjoyed by the most admired Shiite *ulama* in history. Hamid Dabashi describes Khomeini's place within the Shiite tradition of leadership:

> An ayatollah does indeed occupy the highest position of religious authority in the Shi`i [Shiite] community. The years of learning, the mystic of devotion, and the concomitant spiritual presence they all inevitably attain give [them] . . . a certain air of genuine respect and lasting loyalty. Yet the mode and intensity of devotion afforded Khomeini by his followers, particularly in moments leading to the revolutionary crescendo, drive deeper into the collective consciousness of his mass of followers. He grasped something deeply disturbing, something deeply moving, in the midst of the misery, actual and imaginary, that defined his followers. He turned that mute anger against indignity into an articulate voice of dissent and then, being an ayatollah, put God's stamp of approval on it.[20]

After the revolution, Khomeini implemented his plan for rule in which he assumed absolute power. Today's Islamic Republic of Iran is governed by the just jurist and all-powerful groups of "Experts" and "Guardians" comprised of legal scholars and members of the *ulama*. There is also an elected president and an assembly (*majlis*) comprised of deputies whose commitment to the Islamist regime is scrutinized by the governing *ulama* before they are able to stand for election. These legal procedures, which enable popular participation but also stand side-by-side with the ongoing oppression of opponents of the system, conform to what Khomeni termed "constitutional" governance according to Islam:

[19] Khomeini, *Islam and Revolution*, p. 38.

[20] Hamid Dabashi, *Theology of Discontent: The Ideological Foundation of the Islamic Revolution in Iran* (New York: New York University Press, 1993), p. 417.

The Islamic government . . . is not a despotic government in which the head dictates his opinion and tampers with the lives and property of the people. The Prophet, may God's prayers be upon him, and Ali, the amir of the faithful, and the other imams had no power to tamper with people's property or with their lives. The Islamic government is . . . constitutional. However, it is not constitutional in the well-known sense of the word, which is represented in the parliamentary system or in the people's councils. It is constitutional in the sense that those in charge of affairs observe a number of conditions and rules underlined in the Quran and in the Sunna and represented in the necessity of observing the system of applying the dictates and laws of Islam.[21]

Just before his death, Ayatollah Khomeini issued a *fatwa*—a religious edict—calling for the death of the celebrated author, Salman Rushdie. Khomeini claimed that Rushdie had insulted Islam and the Prophet in *The Satanic Verses* and that it was the duty of all Muslims to kill him. The episode, which has yet to be entirely resolved, underscored the politically illiberal nature of Khomeini's version of Islamist governance. With the emergence in recent years of a power contest in Iran between clerical factions within the ruling regime, the future direction of the revolution remains unclear. Facing potential economic and, in particular, food crises of vast proportions, the regime has attempted to attract Western capital once again. Whatever path it takes, however, the Iranian revolution has had a profound impact on Islamist movements throughout the world as well as global politics.

The dimensions and outcomes of Islamic revival can thus be quite varied. In recent years, observers of Islamic politics have debated extensively whether or not Islamic governance and democracy are compatible. The experiences in Algeria and Turkey remain somewhat inconclusive. In both cases, the Islamist movement was repressed because it was viewed as a threat to the state. Perhaps the question is not appropriately posed. The more important question—both for regimes that claim to be Islamist and those that claim to be democratic—concerns the kinds of power arrangements that might enable coexistence between movements whose understandings about the relationship between Islam and public life radically differ. Neither holy war, nor draconian measures of control and coercion, seem to provide an adequate long-term answer to this question, a question that is relevant in other places in the world where theopolitical activists from within other traditions have made the political establishment of a divinely inspired vision their chief aim. Contemporary conflicts in the Muslim world suggest that Muslims await new ways of conceptualizing the relationship between Islam and power, ways that might allow Islam to occupy a place in social and public life for those who want it, without allowing it to dominate and determine the lives of those who have made other judgments about authentic ways of living. At the core of this persisting dilemma is the continuing relevance of the Islamic "totality" in ideologically diverse modern politics.

[21] Ayatollah Khomeini, "The Nature of Islam, Monarchy, and Colonialism," in Kemal Karpat, ed. *Political and Social Thought in the Contemporary Middle East*, (New York: Praeger Pub. 1982), pp. 509–10.

COMPARATIVE IDEOLOGICAL REFLECTIONS AND THE QUESTION OF ISLAMIC "TOTALITY"

As we have seen, Islamists have reasserted what they take to be the original Islamic ideal of the inseparability between matters of religion and affairs of the world. It may well be that this totality of the Islamist vision—its interest in thoroughly governing all affairs of life and death—is what most North Americans find striking. This vision raises two important comparative issues for students of ideology interested in the ongoing developments in Muslim ideological milieus. One concerns the place of the "individual" in contemporary Islamist thought in relation to liberalism and fascism; the other concerns the structural relationship between matters of the state and matters of religion. Islamists claim to unite the two, but recent research suggests that this claim is not always operative in practice.

In the Islamist vision, a Muslim is one who participates in fulfilling the ideals of the Muslim community by adopting the requirements of righteousness in all spheres of life. Righteousness therefore requires an organic understanding of the mutual obligations and duties incumbent upon all Muslims. This conception of the morally righteous member of the community is a tendency of the Islamist ideologies that greatly concerns many nonreligious Muslims living in Muslim society, since they are concerned that a restoration of the *sharia* and the re-Islamicization of cultural life will result in major constraints on their individual freedoms. Indeed, in contrast to the ideal of the individual we encountered in liberalism, Islam possesses no abstract conception of the individual independent of society. Even though there have been powerful existentialist and liberalizing approaches to Islam, the abstract "individual" conceived as independent of ties to the rest of the Muslim community makes little sense. Humans fulfill themselves as individuals only in and through the community of Islam. The ideal is a just, well-balanced community, not a "society" of "free individuals." Muslims must follow God's laws and practices as part of the maintenance of the social order. This may sound like a rather oppressive conception of society to liberals, but, within Islam, it is considered an emancipatory ideal that maintains one's righteous discipline and thus allows full, meaningful expression for the individual member of the *ummah*. A well-known Quranic verse expresses this ideal: "There is no compulsion in matters of faith. Distinct is the way of guidance now from error. He who turns away from the forces of evil and believes in God, will surely hold fast to a handle that is strong and unbreakable, for God hears all and knows every thing" (Quran 2:256). Indeed, North Americans who participate in theopolitics might find that this verse rings true for them as well.

In comparison with other ideologies we have discussed, while the Islamic vision of society does not rule out concerns for the general welfare of the people that bear some resemblance to Marxian concerns for economic inequality, it does not mandate full economic equality or commonly owned property. Moreover, the Islamic understanding of society bears some relation to the fascistic organic conception of relations between individual members of a nation. Here again, while there are overlaps that lead some Islamist expressions to approach fascism, the Islamist vision differs in principle from the fascistic. Islam requires that "just leaders" insure God's authority, which means that human beings are not to consider themselves omnipotent judges on human affairs. More significantly, the Islamic ideal, as we have mentioned, is not nation-based. It is international, expressing a universalist outlook similar to Christianity's. The fascist model cultivates an arrogant attitude toward power and fosters deeply hostile relations between different communities. While these may emerge in particular Islamist conceptions of politics, they are not essential to Islam or Islamism, as they are to fascism.

The second major issue we wish to address is the Islamist claim that Islam requires a fully integrative unity between matters of religion and affairs of the world. As we have seen, the original Islamic ideal fuses the spiritual and the mundane in politics, society, economy, and culture. We shall conclude by making a slight switch in analytical emphasis, because, in actual political practice, Islamic regimes throughout history, including Khomeini's, have not always maintained this strict unity. While the formula *din wa dawla* remains a powerful legitimizing tool— both for radical Islamist movements and for regimes trying to stave off their challenge—recent thinking about politics in Muslim societies suggests that there are at least two possibilities for separating religion from politics in Islamic contexts.

The first possibility stems from the logic of power that unfolded upon the death of the Prophet. Two prominent scholars of Islam suggest "that politics and religion become separable not long after the death of the Prophet with the beginning of dynastic rule."[22] With the Prophet gone, Islamic leaders began to base their rule on worldly political considerations, such as interests, status, and regime stability, in ways that did not replicate the model of Muhammad. This kind of separation does not mirror the interest in liberal societies of separating politics and religion, however. Insofar as Islam posits extensive rules for daily governance, the separate political considerations of Muslim dynasts were undertaken not to insure a religious realm free from politics. They were undertaken to insure a functioning Islamic totality—a realm of legality and social governance reserved for Muslim institutions that had a separate status apart from the worldly considerations of dynastic rule. The large Sunni Islamic empires, for example, established a cleavage between dynastic palace considerations and those of the tradition in order to secure Islamic governance in law and society. Leaders claimed the caliphate and carried out the *shariah*, which was developed and overseen by the *ulama*, who in turn supervised orthodoxy, education, and the application of the *shariah* in conjunction with the state. This kind of separation can also be seen in the practice of the late Ayatollah Khomeini, whose Shiite Islamic Republic derives its authority directly from God. Many observers of Iran noted with interest a speech Khomeini gave in 1988 to buttress the state's flailing image in the wake of a long policy stalemate and war with Iraq. Khomeini declared that the powers of the new Islamic state were so great that the rulers could, if deemed necessary, curtail the ritual obligations incumbent upon Muslims, such as pilgrimage to Mecca, fasting, and even prayer. "The ruler can close down mosques if need be . . . " he asserted.

[22] Dale Eickelman and James Piscatori, *Muslim Politics* (Princeton, N.J.: Princeton University Press, 1996), p. 46.

Thus, "inverting the commonly held assumption that the purpose of the Islamic state is to preserve and protect the *shariah*, [Khomeini] thus declared that the regime is empowered to curtail provisions of the *shariah* in order to protect the regime."[23] The speech seemed to emerge more from concerns about regime stability and legitimacy—as a result of choices of the leadership—than from the tradition itself. Khomeini's declaration was an expression of the will of a theopolitical actor trying to promote, preserve, oversee, and control a particular vision of an official Islamic order. That, then, is the first possibility for separating politics from religion in Islam. Unlike the liberal tendencies that developed in the Christian contexts of Europe, the separation here is not between the religious and the political; it is between the totality of the Muslim tradition and the political realm overseeing it.

The second possibility for separating worldly and religious affairs in Islam is a more secularizing possibility than the first, although it has not been a possibility that has established a fully nonreligious political realm either. In it, a separation is affected between the political and religious realms through the partial elimination of the official Islamic establishment and the construction of a legal and educational system based on nonreligious sources. The extent of this separation and elimination differs in different contexts. Moreover, given Islam's totality, political actors seeking to reduce Islam's role in governance in these contexts face opposition by those who see it as an attack on the tradition. The result is a political contest between those seeking to secularize certain spheres of governance—usually law and education—and those seeking to maintain the Islamic totality in those spheres. To meet the expectations of Muslim publics accustomed to the public role of Islam, the promoters of this second possibility often present themselves not as nonreligious secularists, but instead as Muslims interested in making possible what the Kemalist movement in Turkey called "pure Islam." As we have stated, the Kemalists established their own set of religious institutions to promulgate, oversee, and control an interpretation of Sunni Islam that was more compatible with their project of national, cultural transformation, and they did so while separating Islam from certain, specific spheres of governance and society. They described themselves as *laicists*, hoping to convey their interest in separating religion from politics in certain spheres without being fully secular. Indeed, the Kemalists established in the 1920s a pattern of religious governance that can be seen in other Muslim contexts, including Algeria and Egypt, although the extent of separation and the ways that power is organized between the state and Islam differ in different contexts. More generally, such *laicisers* use and promote Islam frequently to serve the political ends of rulership and regime stability, even as they act to sever religion's role in certain worldly affairs. They also, therefore, find themselves rivals of other theopolitical elites, who, on the pattern of the first possibility, seek to support a totalistic Islamic establishment rather than eliminate it.

In politics today, we see the intensification of both possibilities. There are *laicizers* who see themselves as separators of spheres, but maintain the tradition while

---

[23] Khomeini speech, January, 1988, quoted in Eickelman and Piscatori, *Muslim Politics* p. 50.

confronting a fully theopolitical opposition. So, they use the political means of the state (when they control it) to institutionalize less religious modes of governance. And we see those who use (or seek to use) politics to fully Islamicize it. The Prophet is gone, they argue, but it is still possible to maintain righteousness in all spheres of society through political action in the world. Both of these tendencies, and there are others, illustrate Islam's dynamic and adaptive variability in the politics of secularization, a dynamism that is ignored in Orientalist and journalistic discussions of Islam.

Research that is beyond the scope of our project here suggests that arguments exist in Islam that even advocate removing Islam from the hands of all politicians, secularly oriented or theopolitical. King Hassan of Morocco, who referred to himself as the President of the Believers and the Commander of the Faithful, is nonetheless on record as having denounced certain (other) theopolitical actors in the following way: "We should resort to what the Christians say: render unto God that which is God's and unto Caesar (*Hiraql*) that which is Caesar's."[24] Others—who are in no way mere imitators of the European Christian experience—agree, although they disagree on whether such a separation can take hold with patriarchal dynasts like Hassan or other authoritarians in power as they are throughout the Muslim world today.

If Muslims agree on the need to separate spheres—and it is not at all clear that they will—the resulting separation will no doubt be one that preserves its vision of righteousness. Historical experience from other parts of the world suggests that religious commitments are not easily relegated to the dustbin of history. Like the faithful of other traditions, Muslims continue to find the tradition relevant in meeting the challenges of the modern world. Separated or integrated in governance, theopolitical activists in various traditions energetically assume the right to judge rulers if they transgress or threaten their vision of the divine good. The full secularization of personal, social, or political life is a compromise that few monotheists appear to be willing—or, as active submitters to an all-powerful, creator God, able—to accept.

SUGGESTED READINGS

ABU-RABI, IBRAHIM, *Intellectual Origins of Islamic Resurgence in the Modern Arab World*. Albany: State University of New York Press, 1996.

AHMED, LEILA, *Women and Gender in Islam: Historical Roots of a Modern Debate*. New Haven: Yale University Press, 1992.

ARKOUN, MOHAMMED, *Rethinking Islam: Common Questions, Uncommon Answers*. Boulder, Colo.: Westview Publishers, 1994.

BARBER, BENJAMIN, *Jihad vs. McWorld: How Globalism and Tribalism Are Reshaping the World*. New York: Ballantine Books, 1995.

BEININ, JOEL, AND JOE STORK, eds., *Political Islam: Essays from Middle East Report*. Berkeley: University of California Press, 1997.

[24] Quoted in Eickelman and Piscatori, *Muslim Politics*, p. 52.

DABASHI, HAMID, *Theology of Discontent: The Ideological Foundation of the Islamic Revolution in Iran.* New York: New York University Press, 1993.

DAVISON, ANDREW, *Secularism and Revivalism in Turkey: A Hermeneutic Reconsideration.* New Haven: Yale University Press, 1998.

EICKELMAN, DALE F., and JAMES PISCATORI, *Muslim Politics.* Princeton, N.J.: Princeton University Press, 1996.

ESPOSITO, JOHN, *Islam: The Straight Path,* expanded ed. New York: Oxford Uuiversity Press, 1991.

KEDDIE, NIKKI R., ed., *An Islamic Response to Imperialism: Political and Religious Writings of Sayyid Jamal ad-Din "al-Afghani" [1839–1897].* Berkeley: University of California Press, 1983.

PARLA, TAHA, AND ANDREW DAVISON, *Corporatist Ideology in Kemalist Turkey: Progress or Order?* (work in progress).

PETERS, F. E., *Judaism, Christianity, and Islam: The Classical Texts and Their Interpretation,* 3 Vols. Princeton, N.J.: Princeton University Press, 1990.

al-Quran, A Contemporary Translation by Ahmed Ali. Princeton, N.J.: Princeton University Press, 1984.

SAID, EDWARD W., *Orientalism.* New York: Vintage Books, 1979.

12

Ideological Conflict in the Twenty-First Century

History [is] the slaughter bench at which the happiness of peoples, the wisdom of states, and the virtue of individuals have been sacrificed.

G. W. F. Hegel

The twenty-first century, like the twentieth, will be a time of tremendous ideological conflict—a competition for the hearts and minds of people. Recent historic events such as the collapse of the Soviet Union and the "end of the Cold War," the opening of China to the West, and efforts at self-determination in Eastern European countries, have consequently led some to proclaim an "end to history" because the ideological conflict between two of the idea systems we have discussed appears to be over. That is, recent watershed events are said to "prove" that liberalism and capitalism have not only triumphed over socialism and communism but also will eventually prevail over all other ideological competitors. We think that conclusion is wrong. While there have historically been periods when ideological conflict among idea systems has been temporarily muted—leading some to proclaim the "end of ideology" or "end of history"—the competition among belief systems and their respective visions of the ideal human society always seem to reemerge. To be sure, many nations have turned to Western states and huge transnational corporations for technology, scientific information, consumer goods, and capital. Some of these same countries, however, have shown considerable reluctance in the wholesale adoption of capitalism as an economic system and endeavor to reject it as an ethical and social system: They appear to want wealth and consumer goods, but not capitalism as a social system with its possessive individualist cultural requirements. Indeed, many of these same issues continue to be debated in the West as well.

Perhaps, as Plato believed, that is inevitable: humans—like the ancient Greek gods—will always quarrel about values, visions of history, and human potentials. Today, the struggle includes variations of the original ideologies: neoliberalism, post-Marxism, postsocialism, and ethnonationalism, to name a few. Nevertheless, as the memories of the Vietnam War begin to fade from the collective consciousness and new generations come to adulthood ignorant of all but the cinematic horrors and CNN images of war, it becomes increasingly important to recall all the people—well over 100 million—who have died during the past century at the hands of their fellow beings, the result of well-intentioned efforts to make the world safe for *a* particular vision of the good life.

Although individuals may kill for a variety of reasons—passion, self-defense, jealousy, revenge—it has only been groups of individuals (sects, classes, factions, tribes, nations) who kill other groups of individuals over questions of philosophy. Quite often it seems to be words and ideological visions, neither territory nor economic power, that supply the dynamic, motivating force behind groups of humans attacking other groups. In order to understand why this occurs, it is important to remember our assertion in the introduction that each of the ideologies studied adamantly believes (1) that it alone knows what the human essence is, (2) that it alone knows how humans can reach their full potential, and (3) that it alone possesses the appropriate vision of "the beautiful."

At a general, ethical level, then, each idea system believes that it contains the seeds that will allow for or ensure the full flowering of humanity. Small wonder that so many have willingly fought, suffered, and died in these modern crusades to establish the City of God on earth. Arthur Koestler, examining pathological trends in human history, appropriately argued that

> we are thus driven to the unfashionable conclusion that the trouble with our species is not an excess of *aggression*, but an excess capacity for fanatical *devotion*. Even a cursory glance at history should convince one that individual crimes committed for selfish motives play a quite insignificant part in the human tragedy, compared to the numbers massacred in unselfish loyalty to one's tribe, nation, dynasty, church, or political ideology, *ad majorem gloriam dei*.[1]

There is at least one additional chilling feature of our time that makes it unique—we live in the postnuclear age. Since August 6, 1945, humanity has tried to adapt itself to the horrific reality that it now possesses the capacity to commit *species suicide*. With the collapse of the Soviet Union as a superpower, the potential of nuclear disaster has nevertheless increased as nonnuclear nations rush to develop the nuclear technology that they believe will give them national security as well as a place at the bargaining table of nuclear powers. Both India and Pakistan have recently demonstrated nuclear capabilities; their ongoing, often heated ethnic, religious, and national tensions illustrate the precarious nature of today's nuclear politics. However, what originated as solely nuclear threats to our existence has, in the intervening years that closed out the last century, been upgraded to thermonuclear technology and supplemented with chemical and biological weapons of mass destruction. The potential of a self-inflicted global holocaust is both ironic and tragic: The same species that so often appears desperately to want to build appropriate societies where all people can freely develop their humanity is also quite capable of completely obliterating itself in the process. Perhaps, as Sigmund Freud tried to warn us, it may be humanity's tragic fate simply to bring an end to its psychological suffering through war rather than continue to struggle for the creation of the beautiful. As Nietzsche asked, "How much did this people have to suffer in order to become so beautiful?" Or, perhaps, we will remember Aristotle and *logos*, reasoned speech, and elect to begin an *informed dialogue* with others over the meaning of freedom, the essence of humanity, and the nature of the beautiful.

SOME THOUGHTS RECONSIDERED: LIBERALISM'S CHALLENGE

One of the questions left unanswered in the introduction to this book asked about the relationship between idea systems and political action. There it was asserted that although no causal relationship between ideologies and political acts could be proven, common sense seemed to indicate that they were indeed connected. The debate over the question of ideology and action has intensified in recent years, in proportion to the waves of political activism that continue to sweep over the world. The student activists of the 1960s and early 1970s in North America and in China in

---

[1] Arthur Koestler, *Janus: A Summing Up* (London: Pan Books, Ltd., 1978), p. 14.

the 1980s, the average citizens throughout Eastern Europe in 1989, and the *Taliban* in Afghanistan in the 1990s, all demonstrate clearly that few periods in recent history have witnessed a greater concern with political ideas and their implementation.

The United States now stands as the most potent, hegemonic power of the century. We noted earlier that liberal democracy, as well as any other ideology, can be separated from the imperfect attempts of any particular state to put those ideas into practice. Indeed, toward the end of the twentieth century, the prime charge against both the United States and the then-existent Soviet Union was that they continued to talk as though they had succeeded in constructing the ideal goal cultures of a liberal democratic and socialist society, respectively, while in fact they both were a long way from realizing their exemplary ends. The price the Soviet Union paid for this discrepancy was enormous: Its experiment in building a socialist state collapsed of its own weight. The United States also faces major ideological problems to be confronted in terms of the credibility gap between its universal liberal democratic ideals and political reality. While economic ideologues and "beltway" politicians proclaim the United States a free and equal society, domestic and foreign critics argue that it has systematically denied people of color, women, and the poor a fair place in its economic system and has developed a body of customs and laws that ensure that they can be neither free nor equal. America, it is argued, is imperialist, racist, sexist, and classist.

From within its own ideological camp, democratic elitists and advocates of "alternative liberalism" accuse the United States of having a rigid class structure that benefits the few at the expense of the many, precluding once again the possibility of achieving the espoused ideals of liberal democracy. As the never-ending body count from hate crimes, homelessness, substance abuse, social diseases, environmental pollution, and urban lifestyles reminds us, the fulfillment of the ideals of *The Declaration of Independence* for all Americans remains out of sight for the foreseeable future. From outside the confines of this ideology, critics argue that the United States, often using the United Nations and/or NATO as its ideological cover, will do anything it deems necessary to maintain the security of the "free world"/"free market" and will continue to foist upon all segments of the globe an economic system that is primarily designed to fill the pockets of a small group of capitalists. To be sure, capitalists live around the world, but their "high-tech" police force takes its orders from Washington and Wall Street. Even the United Nations worries about global economic trends: The rich are getting richer while the poor are quietly dying. The combined wealth of the world's three richest families accounts for more than the annual income of the 600 million poorest people; the wealthiest one-fifth of the globe consumes 86 percent, the bottom one-fifth just 1 percent, of global commodities. How can such stark inequalities be justified with liberal democracy? How long can such tendencies continue?

Nevertheless, the United States has remained remarkably silent in terms of ideological development. In part, this is understandable since it has become the undisputed, globally dominant, ideology. Exhibiting all the conservative traits of *the status quo* ideology, it is logical to ask: If liberalism continues to fail to respond substantively to the alienation among its own citizens, will it ever respond to issues of global economic injustice? If it fails to adapt to change, will its reign continue through this century?

Competing Ideological Claims

The American political scientist Robert Dahl observed: "There is no Democratic theory, only democratic theories."[2] In a historical sense this is certainly accurate. Democracy has meant different things to different individuals at different times in history. For Plato and Aristotle, democracy was considered one political option, albeit highly undesirable, for a type of rule—rule by the *demos*, the people. Although neither philosopher thought very highly of the idea of democracy, both thought of it as not merely a type of government but also a *type of society* with a certain quality of life associated with it. Indeed, it was because democracy could not, in their view, provide the *good life* for all of its citizens that both philosophers opposed it.

Still, in its earliest foundation democracy was conceived as class rule and this, as we have shown, is also how Marx thought of it. To Marx, the liberal bourgeosie would eventually be overthrown by the class-conscious proletariat, who would temporarily govern in the objectively best interest of all. With the emergence of international capitalism, Lenin expanded Marx's analysis to include the entire world. Once the global transition from capitalism to communism was completed, all members of the community would be able to reach their particular fulfillment as species beings. Although the Soviet Union has collapsed, Marxism as an ideology and its post-Marxist variants remain viable. Their quest, moreover, continues to be to free humanity from the irrational and outdated capitalist economic system which structurally denies the majority of humanity the real chance to reach its potential. And the growing global economic discrepancies make it clear that the Marxian analysis of international capitalism is anything but *passé*.

Liberal democracy, like the other ideologies, also claims a monopoly on understanding humanity. Originally the democratic franchise was tacked onto liberalism to meet the pressing demands of the working class. Today, the dominant school of liberal democratic theory—pluralism—continues to view democracy primarily as an electoral mechanism for choosing between political leaders. Contemporary political scientists who subscribe to this view do not consider democracy as a type of society with a certain quality of life associated with it. Rather, democracy is reduced to questions concerning who rules and how these rulers are selected. In this conception, to be a democratic nation means to have relatively open elections between two (or more) political parties where no single party has a disproportionate chance of winning. Many political theorists scoff at even this limited notion of democracy. After all, what difference does it make if you choose among candidates X, Y, or Z if each is a capitalist? And as the power-elite critics ask, can elections as they are presently structured insure political equality *among* citizens and *between* voters and their candidates?

---

[2] Robert Dahl, *Preface to Democratic Theory* (Chicago: The University of Chicago Press, 1956), p. 1.

Within the liberal democratic tradition there continues to exist a small but tenacious movement that argues that liberal democracy is more than a question of governmental rule—it is a matter of quality of life. We have referred to this movement as possessing an "alternative vision" of a liberal democratic society. This scholarly community argues that if liberal democracy could be extricated from the capitalist market system, and if its theorists could restore the earlier commitment to a notion of democracy as a type of society that values political and civil liberties and relative (if not substantive) economic equality, then liberal democracy could meet its most noble goals.

Still, much of the nonaligned world remains reluctant to adopt either communism or liberal democracy. These two ideologies appear to be inappropriate to the particular cultural and historical needs of many nations. Rejecting what they view to be the crass materialism and excessive competitiveness of capitalism as well as the ideas of atheism and class struggle behind official Marxism, these nations find more appealing variations of Italian (or generic) fascism and Islamism. Even within these societies, however, defenders of the new ideals struggle for full equality, individual liberty, and democratic civil society.

With the notions of corporativism, leadership, will, emotion, and organic national community, fascism has proven itself a powerful ideology for pulling together a collection of diverse groups and individuals even if the term *fascism*—for obvious political reasons—is used by few people today. Moreover, the continuing importance of the nation-state and nationalism in general gives at least partial support to Mussolini's early contention that nationalism and collectivism would be dominant themes of the twentieth century. While both liberalism and communism also utilize nationalism and the state for the achievement of their goals, it is only in fascism that the nation-state is central and all embracing. Hence, in spite of the absence of individuals willing to proclaim themselves "fascists," the doctrine is alive and well as a competing ideology. And, of course, racism is not dead even though it has not returned in the form of National Socialism.

Finally, we have all too briefly introduced the phenomenon of Islamism into the ideological debates of the late twentieth century. Islamists are at the forefront of struggles claiming cultural authenticity on their side, even though the "authentic" requirements of the ideology are vastly contested among the Islamists themselves. While noting the surface similarities between Islamic and fascist thought, we concluded that Islamism could not be properly called "fascist" in that it is international in its scope and finds ultimate authority not in the nation-state but in the word of God. Whatever label one chooses to attach to it, it seems obvious that Islamism is and will continue to be a powerful competitor for the hearts and minds of people, for it too believes that it possesses the truth.

SHADOWS OF THINGS THAT WILL (OR COULD) BE: SOME FINAL THOUGHTS

Recall Plato's cave. Perhaps we are still prisoners in it. However, you have now been exposed to the "puppet shows" that each ideology claims mirrors reality. Each ideology purports to know the good, the beautiful, and the truly human.

Each is convinced that it—and it alone—is best for humanity. Which is true? Which an illusion? Which has the answer(s) to the important questions of the human condition? What visions of the future are correct? An answer: They all believe they are. But what is the Truth?

As we said at the outset of this presentation of ideologies, we recognize the human longing for the comfort and security of a world with few questions and readily comprehensible, easily accepted values—the original fool's paradise of Plato's cave where individuals believe they are free because they remain ignorant of their own enslavement. Little has changed since the time of Plato and his imaginative allegory of the cave. This book will conclude with a modern variation on these Platonic themes through a discussion of Fyodor Dostoevski's ingenious "The Grand Inquisitor on the Nature of Man" from *The Brothers Karamazov*.

This paradoxical tale takes place in sixteenth-century Seville during the infamous Spanish Inquisition. According to the story, Jesus Christ has decided to revisit the earth for a brief time. The masses of Seville instantly flock to him as he moves quietly among them. After Christ has performed several miracles to the delight of the crowd, the Grand Inquisitor—who is a ninety-year-old man, a cardinal in the Church, and the leader of the Inquisition—enters the scene, merely points his finger at Christ, and the guards take him away. Christ complies. The people do not protest. Late that night, the Grand Inquisitor starts to interrogate his prisoner about deeply personal and ideological issues: What is the nature of humanity? Do humans want freedom or happiness? What is the meaning of life?

While Dostoevski's allegory can be read narrowly, as a story about Roman Catholicism in particular or organized religions more generally, it can also be interpreted as a broader, philosophical parable. From this latter perspective, the Grand Inquisitor represents *absolute* political power and Christ, the Son of God in Christianity, can be seen as representing *absolute*, objective Truth. Whether or not this was the author's intention does not concern us here: To paraphrase the contemporary novelist Italo Calvino, it is the eye that commands the story, not the pen.

Returning to the allegory, the Grand Inquisitor confronts his prisoner and asks him a simple, albeit critical question—"Is it Thou?" Before the Inquisitor can possibly receive any response, he snaps at the prisoner, "Don't answer, be silent." If the prisoner had answered this question, either positively or negatively, the elderly cardinal would have had a far greater degree of knowledge (and certainty) than that produced by the silence. He would at least have known who the prisoner thought he was. After all, perhaps this was not Christ but rather a case of mistaken identity? Or, perhaps this was only a hallucination from an old and troubled man. But there is no audible response. This profound silence begins an escalating series of unanswered questions, leaving the reader perplexed by, yet questioning of, the story's action.

As the minutes turn into hours, the Inquisitor presents to his prisoner a scathing indictment of Christ—his teachings and his actions. He tells Christ that he does not understand human frailty and that he failed humanity forever when he refused to seize political power in order to control the masses when he had the opportunity to do so centuries before. The Inquisitor boldly maintains that he, and a few select others, had to "correct" Christ's work. And, because of Christ's "mistakes," the elite had to seize power, lead the people, and occasionally perform horrendous actions like the Inquisition in order to maintain control of the hearts and minds of the people and fulfill God's plan. Human beings, the Inquisitor insists, cannot live with moral freedom. They cannot live with the knowledge that the power to define the content of their lives belongs ultimately, and only, to them. In the Grand Inquisitor's version of history, humans are weak creatures who want to be fed and forgiven, deceived and led. The last thing people want is to be free and responsible for their lives. As the Inquisitor puts it, "people are more persuaded than ever that they have perfect freedom, yet they have brought their freedom to us and laid it humbly at our feet."[3] Ironically, through his actions the Inquisitor gives the people a very real kind of freedom. It is freedom that can best be conceptualized as *freedom from*—freedom from hunger, from guilt, from responsibility, from anxiety, from uncertainty and from chaos. These are not insignificant things. Does anyone genuinely enjoy feeling chaos and uncertainty, guilt and responsibility? This, however, in Dostoevski's account is Christ's freedom—*freedom to* experience all of the uncomfortable states-of-being against which the cardinal through organized religion tries to shield humans and thereby give them happiness.

The Grand Inquisitor lectures Christ that there are three universal human desires: first, to find something or someone to worship; second, to worship what is established beyond doubt; and third, to organize a universal state of true believers around that which is to be worshiped. This trilogy of human desires is about human value systems, belief systems—ideologies. Humans want to do "the good." We want to know that we have lived a meaningful and moral existence. So desperate is this need, that we want those around us, indeed everyone, to agree with our choice of how to live and in what to believe. Individuals appear to find comfort and security in mass affirmation. Moreover, we find it intolerable to have challenges to our life choices. If others live differently, or embrace different belief systems, what does that imply? Does it mean that perhaps we are wrong? Or, maybe we are right and they are wrong, but who ultimately knows? To avoid this uncertainty, humans long for a belief system that is the absolute, objective Truth. To make sure that it is the Truth and remains beyond question, we will struggle to organize a universal state established on our beliefs. Humans, it seems, do not like questions or doubts surrounding what they believe in when it comes to their ideology. (Yet, it was Plato who first told us that values are what the gods quarrel about endlessly.) The final goal of a universal state of true believers springs from both the human yearning for community and the craving for the comfort of universal unity.

By the end of his soliloquy, the Grand Inquisitor has worked himself up into an existential frenzy. He wants Christ to say something—anything—to him. At this moment of personal crisis, the Grand Inquisitor would even willingly accept Christ's ridicule and rejection since that would provide him with some sort of an answer to his personal doubts. What the cardinal cannot tolerate, in spite of his claims to the contrary, is the uncertainty of not knowing the Truth. This is understandable. Given the many deeds he has carried out during his life, the cardinal is deeply troubled not knowing if he was correct in his life choices. Will he go to

---

[3] Fyodor Dostoevski, *The Grand Inquisitor on the Nature of Man*, trans. Constance Garnett, (Indianapolis: Bobbs-Merrill, 1978), p. 26.

heaven or to hell? Was he right to cultivate illusions of freedom for those he chained to the wall with shadows of bread and hope? Does he really understand the nature of humanity? Is there a Truth? And if so, what is it?

At this critical moment in the text, Dostoevski brilliantly elects to have Christ remain silent. He speaks not a word. Silence cannot be spoken for. Rather, Christ simply yet dramatically rises, kisses the old man, and leaves. The reader of the story cannot help but try to impose meaning on this ambiguous action. Why does he do this? What does the kiss mean? Does it symbolize love or forgiveness or understanding or betrayal, or something else altogether? Of course, we do not know the answer(s) to these questions. We do believe, however, that Dostoevski constructs the parable in this manner to cause the reader to experience uncertainty, to realize that humans inevitably seek meaning, and to cause us to wonder further about the allegory.

But, remember that from our interpretative frame of reference, the character of Christ represents absolute, objective Truth. As such, his kiss cannot have any meaning. It cannot "mean" any of the things readers would like it to "mean": It cannot mean love or responsibility or betrayal or forgiveness; nor can it "mean" any combinations of the above—a kind of pluralism of truths; nor can it "mean," even, that truth is simply in the eye of the beholder. More significantly, the kiss cannot "mean" there is no Truth and that there is only uncertainty and the void: If that were *the meaning* of the kiss, Christ—representing absolute, objective Truth—would have established that particular "Truth"; that is, he would have authoritatively established that there is "no Truth"—as the absolute, objective Truth. If that were the case, Christ simultaneously would have robbed humanity of experiencing the totality of *freedom to*: We would now know at least this much— there is no Truth—that chaos, uncertainty, the void, is the Truth. This meaning, however, would have deprived us precisely of experiencing the fear and trembling we all inevitably feel during moments of profound doubt. It seems that Dostoevski chose to have Christ exit the dialogue in order to leave us, the reader, in the unbearable position of existential chaos, uncertainty, and not knowing.

Returning to Plato's parable, perhaps there is no way out of the cave. Then again, perhaps there is. Perhaps it ultimately does not matter whether or not humans can leave the cave: What matters may be the journey to look for, and always ask questions of, the "answers" to life's essential paradoxes. This, of course, applies to ideologies as well. It is now your chance—and your responsibility—to try to carry on your own dialogue with the shadows on the wall in hopes of better understanding them and perhaps finding a way to live a more fully human life inside of, if not out of, the cave. If you recall our introductory discussion, it was precisely at this point that we parted company with Plato and looked to John Stuart Mill for further inspiration for our investigations. Plato seemed sure that the path to the sun lay open to at least a few human beings if they were willing to engage in the extraordinarily difficult process of education that he prescribed. Plato appeared positive, in other words, that at least some members of the species were capable of achieving absolute knowledge about reality. We are less sure.

Our time is characterized by a noteworthy suspicion of absolutes. The contemporary French political philosopher Jean François Lyotard described this as the "postmodern condition." People no longer believe in the grand ideological absolutes of the modern age, such as the inevitable triumph of reason, the emancipation of labor, or a qualitatively better life through the development of technology. At the beginning of the twenty-first century, these quests seem to many to have created more harm than good. After all, "reason" was used to rationalize colonization of "different," "other" cultures; scientific knowledge to build gas chambers and nuclear weapons; class struggle to justify oppression. Few contemporary political theorists posit universal notions of human nature or human potential. Considerable doubt abounds about the possibility of ending either domination or injustice; skepticism exists about the generalizing of circumstances from one person or group to another. Every generalization seems to leave something, or someone out.

With humanity's highest ideals thus in doubt from the postmodernist perspective, attention has shifted from the grand stories of human emancipation to concern with new, complex forms of power on a local scale. Individuals and smaller communities strive to insure that they are not dominated by ideals that they instinctively consider foreign to their lives and troubles. They resist universal explanations for social problems, and tend to think that less social organization is always better than more, even as more and more societies experience similar problems of social and economic inequality, ecological destruction, racism, sexism, and general estrangement. It is deeply ironic that this new skepticism about universals is itself rapidly becoming the most powerful universal of our time. (Indeed, to be consistent, one should be skeptical of skepticism, but that seems to be a position some postmodernists find unacceptable.) But despite the efforts of proponents to resuscitate the higher ideals of each ideology, the foundational schemes of liberalism, Marxism, fascism, and Islamism no longer seem to have the all inclusive grip that they once enjoyed. To our minds, the postmodern condition—if there is one—need not end the desire for large-scale solutions to large scale problems, but it does define those solutions as essentially historical: They are our choices, made within history, not solutions for all time.

Perhaps in the final analysis no one can offer you, or any other person, ultimate answers to the important questions that have been raised throughout this book. We can, however, tell you that we believe that only after you are able to understand critically your own belief system and, as Mill would have it, empathetically to see the world through the eyes of other belief systems can you even begin to develop grounds for judgments—both empirical and moral—on how humans do and ought to live. As Immanuel Kant so eloquently put it, "The death of dogma is the beginning of morality." We also know that action based on informed judgment is necessary. That is why *political literacy*—not computer literacy—is *the* critical need of the new century.

This book has attempted to present several ideologies in a relatively sympathetic manner in an effort to encourage you to understand the concepts, themes, and justifications that constitute the ultimate contests of political life. As such, we have tried temporarily to suspend judgment concerning each of them while engaging in this "academic" exercise. Human beings, particularly in an age of ideology, must constantly make choices among competing values—they must act in the real world even if it is a world of shadows. And at a time when humanity seems perched precariously on the edge of self-destruction from nuclear, chemical, biological, or ecological sources of its own creation, such choices and actions are even more important. Human beings are, after all, purposive creatures. We are capable of directing our thoughts and actions toward the achievement of the goals we desire. In the twentieth century we became extraordinarily adept at inventing countless and miraculous *techniques*—weapons of mass destruction being perhaps the ultimate ironic statement of that capability. However, we have, in our judgment, been far less successful in the creative construction of our *goals*. We continue to resist the critical self-examination of our belief systems, forgetting Mill's warning that such a practice not only robs us of the chance to learn from other alternative visions and to substitute truth for error but also turns what we think we believe into dead dogma. It seems we still prefer to hug our comfortable chains of enslavement rather than face the responsibility and uncertainty of freedom. While this behavior may be all too human, it is a denial of our humanity nevertheless. And, as Nietzsche reminds and encourages:

> A very popular error: having the courage of one's convictions; rather it is a matter of having the courage for an *attack* on one's convictions!!![4]

SUGGESTED READINGS

DOSTOEVSKI, FYODOR, *The Grand Inquisitor on the Nature of Man*, trans. Constance Garnett. Indianapolis: Bobbs-Merrill, 1978.

FRASER, NANCY, *Justice Interruptus: Critical Reflections on the "Post-Socialist" Condition*. New York: Routledge, 1997.

FREUD, SIGMUND, *Civilization and Its Discontents*, trans. James Strachey. New York: W.W. Norton & Company, 1962.

KARIEL, HENRY S., *Beyond Liberalism*. New York: Harper & Row, Publishers, 1978.

KOESTLER, ARTHUR, *Janus: A Summing Up*. London: Pan Books, Ltd., 1978.

LEOTARD, JEAN FRANÇOIS, *The Postmodern Explained*. Minneapolis: University of Minnesota Press, 1993.

MACPHERSON, C. B., *The Real World of Democracy*. New York: Oxford University Press, 1975.

THOMPSON, E. P. AND DAN SMITH, eds., *Protest and Survive*. New York: Monthly Review Press, 1981.

TRUMBO, DALTON, *Johnny Got His Gun*. New York: Bantam Books, 1970.

[4] Friedrich Nietzsche, quoted in *Nietzsche: Philosopher, Psychologist, Antichrist*, by Walter Kaufman (Princeton, N.J.: Princeton University Press, 1974), p. 19.

Index

A

Abbasid empire, 264
ABC of Communism, The (Bukharin), 168
Abduh, Muhammad, 252
Abraham/Abrahamic traditions, Islam and,
    253–56
Abu Bakr, caliph, 261
Abu-Rabi, Ibrahim, *287*
Action orientation, 6
Adorno, Theodore W., *248*
Afghanistan, 251, 279
Age of Ideology, 9
Ahmed, Leila, 254, *287*
Al-Afghani, Jamal ad-Din, 252, 276
Al-Banna, Hassan, 271
Al-e Ahmad, Jalal, 273
Alexander II, Czar, 149
Alexander III, Czar, 149
Algeria, Islam in, 280, 283
Ali, caliph, 261–62

Alienation, 7, 16, 126–30
Al-Jahiz, 258
Alternative liberalism, 22, 294
    of Dewey, 106–11
    of Jefferson, 98–106
    of Rousseau, 95–96
Althusser, Louis, *142*
Al-Turabi, Hasan, 179, 270
Andropov, Yuri, 179
Antagonistic contradictions, 197–98
Anti-bolshevism, fascist, 221–22
Anti-intellectualism, fascist, 225
Anti-liberalism, fascist, 219–21
Anti-Semitism, 243–44, 245–46
Anti-Zionism, 228
    Islam and, 268
Arendt, Hannah, 10, *20*, 98
Aristocracy, natural, 45
Aristotle, 7, 20
Arkoun, Mohammed, *287*
Articles of Confederation, 52

Aryan race, 237, 238–40
   struggle between Jews and, 240–41
Atatürk, Mustafa Kemal, 271, 280
Aufheben, 120
Auschwitz, 248
Autarky, 222
Autumn Harvest Uprising, 191
Avanti (newspaper), 215, 217–18
Avineri, Shlomo, *142*
Ayatollah, meaning of, 263

B

Bacon, Francis, 26–27
Ball, Terence, *20*
Barber, Benjamin, 272, *287*
Barker, Sir Ernest, *47*
Bayreuth/Bayreuth Circle, 237–38
Beam, George, 69
Beinin, Joel, *287*
Belief system, ideology as, 7
Bentham. Jeremy, 40, 126
Beria, Lavrenti, 174
Berlin, Isaiah, *47*
Berman, Marshall, *112*
Bernstein, Eduard, 146, *162*
Bin Laden, Osama, 252, 277
Bismarck, Otto Edward von, 146
Bolshevik faction, 151, 155, 157, 164
Bonapartism, 168
Boorstin, Daniel J., *86*
Bourgeois class, 134–35, 154
Brest-Litovsk, Treaty of, 156
Brezhnev, Leonid, 175, 178, 179
Brothers Karamazov, The (Dostoevski), 295–97
Buchenwald, 248
Bukharin, Nikolai, 168–69, 180
Bullock, Alan, 242, 244–45, *248*
Burke, Edmund, 42–46

C

Calhoun, John C., 66
Caliphate, 261–62
   abolition of, 262, 280
Capitalism
   alienation of labor under, 127–29
   class conflict under, 130
   competition in, 128–29
   decline and fall of, 135–41
   exploitation of labor under, 127–28
   fascism and, 222
   history and development of, 130–35
   individualistic liberalism and, 40, 111
   Locke and, 33–34
   peaceful coexistence of socialism and, 178–79
   as possessive market society, 31–32
   profit in, 136, 137–39
   revisionist Marxism and, 145–46
Capitalism, Socialism and Democracy
      (Schumpeter), 81
Cave allegory of Plato, 2–4, 17, 294–95, 297
Censorship, 71
Chadwick, Owen, *20*
Chamberlin, Houston Stewart, 238, 241
Checks and balances, 62
Chernenko, Konstantin, 179
China. *See* People's Republic of China (PRC)
Chinese Communist Party (CCP), 190, 191
Christianity
   Aryanization of, 246
   German romanticism and, 235
   Islam and, 255–56
   Judaism distinguished from, 255–56
Civil Society, Hegel on, 123
Class
   bourgeois, 134–35, 154
   bureaucratic, 246
   in Maoist China, 195–96, 195–98, 197–98
   Marx on, 131
   natural aristocracy, 45
   Rousseau on, 90–91
Class consciousness, 140, 154, 156–57
Clinton, William J., 70
Cohen, G.A., *142*
Cohen, Stephen, *187*
Coleman, Frank M., *86*
Collectivization, 168
Comintern, 172
Communism
   fascist view of, 221–22
   international, 155–56, 161–62, 171–73, 176–78
   Leninist themes, 152–62
   Marx's vision of society under, 135, 140–41
   See also People's Republic of China (PRC);
      Soviet Union
Communist Manifesto (Marx & Engels), 7, 13,
      157–58

Communist party, 171, 172
　Chinese, 190, 191, 192–93, 199, 200, 205, 206
　Lenin's concept of, 152–54, 156–58
　Soviet, 171, 172, 186
　Yugoslavian, 177
Community of Islam, 260
Compradore bourgeoisie, 194
Condition of the Working Class in England in 1844
　　(Engels), 120
Conservatism, 42–46
Constant capital, 138, 159
Constitution, U.S., 7, 46, 52–57
Constitution Convention of 1787, 52–53, 67
Contract. *See* Social contract
Contradiction, Mao on, 196–98
Cooke, Jacob E., *86*
Copernicus, 18
Corporativism, 222–24
Cultural power, 270
Cultural Revolution, 202, 203, 204, 207
Czechoslovakia, 177

D

Dabashi, Hamid, 282, *287*
Dahl, Robert A., *86*, 293
Dallmayr, Fred R., 20
Das Kapital (Marx), 116, 117, 135
Davison, Andrew, *288*
Declaration of Independence, 52, 69, 96
Declaration of the Rights of Man, 96
"Decolonization," in Islamist action program,
　　277–78
Demand, as function of ideology, 7–8
Democracy
　Dewey on, 109
　direct, 58
　as electoral mechanism, 96
　factions and, 54–57
　irony of, 83–84
　Islamic governance and, 283
　Jacksonian, 70
　Marx on, 293
　normative democratic elitism, 81–83
　Schumpeter on, 82
Democracy in America (Tocqueville), 50
Democratic centralism, 154–55, 169
Democratic socialism, 74, 110
Democratic Wall campaign, 207

Democratization, Soviet, 176
Deng Xiaoping, 195, 203
　fall of, 207–8
　rise of, 204—207
De-sacralization of Mao, 204
Descartes, René, 26–27
De-Stalinization, 174–76
Deutscher, Isaac, *162, 187*
Development of Capitalism in Russia, The (Lenin),
　　150
Dewey, John, 73, 83, 87, 106–11, *112*
Dialectical materialism, 124
Dialectics, 118, 120–21
Diamond, Martin, 59
*Difference Between the Democritean and Epicurian
　　Philosophies of Nature, Economic and Philo-
　　sophical Manuscripts, The* (Marx)), 117
Direct democracy, 58
*Discourse on the Origin and Foundations of Inequal-
　　ity Among Men* (Rousseau), 88
Doctrine of Fascism, The (Mussolini), 218
Domination, defined, 3
Dostoevski, Fyodor, 295–97, *299*
Dunn, John, *20*

E

Eastern Europe, communism and, 173, 177
Eckhart, Dietrich, 238
Economics, conditioning effect of, 131
Economic Theory of the Leisure Class, The
　　(Bukharin), 168
Education, 2–4, 64
　Islamic revival and, 270–71
Eickelman, Dale F., *288*
Eisenhower, Dwight D., 79
Electoral College, 70
Elite theory, 77–84
Elitist leadership, 216, 226–27
Emotionalism
　fascism and, 244
　rationalism *vs.*, 234–36, 245
Engels, Friedrich, 13, 115, 116, 131, 165
Enlightened self interest, 64
Enumerated powers, 62
Equality
　liberal notion of, 38–39, 49–51
　of opportunity, 76

Equality, *continued*
    tension between liberty and, 75–77
Erbakan, Necmettin, 280
Esposito, John, 257, *288*
Essay on Government, An (James Mill), 41
Essay on the Inequality of Human Races (Gobineau),
    236
Estates, Hegelian, 123
Estrangement, alienation as, 129–30
Evolutionary Socialism (Bernstein), 146
Extended republic, 59

F

Fabian Society, 146
Factions, 54–57
    artificial, 66
Family stage, in Hegelian theory, 123
Farr, James, *20*
Fascism, 211–30, 284–85
    anti-bolshevism and, 221–22
    anti-intellectualism and, 225–26
    anti-liberalism and, 219–21
    characteristics of, 217–24, 228–30
    continuing appeal of, 294
    corporativism and, 222–24
    definitional distinctions, 212–15, 229–30
    evolution of doctrine of, 215–17
    generic, 214
    Islamism and, 37, 294
    Mussolini on, 211, 213, 214, 225
    national goals of, 224–25
    National-Socialism as distinct from, 214
    nation-state and, 218–19
    race and, 227–28
Fatwa, 277
    against Rushdie, 283
Federalist papers, 53
    No. 10, 53–55, 58–59, 65
    No. 39, 60, 61
Federal system of government, 62–63
Fest, Joachim C., 245
Feudalism, 22–23
    liberalism contrasted with, 23–24
Feuerbach, Ludwig, 124
Finance capital, 159
Finer, Herman, 223, *230*
Fischer, Louis, *162*

Forces of production, 132–33
Foundations of Leninism, The (Stalin), 170
Foundations of the Critique of Political Economy
    (Marx), 116
Four Cardinal Principles, in PRC, 205
Four modernizations, in PRC, 205
Fraser, Nancy, *299*
Freedom
    economic, 100–101
    of expression, 18–19
    Hegel on, 122–23
    Marx on, 130
    natural rights and, 38–39
    political, 101
    Rousseau on, 89–90
Free will, Rousseau on, 89–90
Freire, Paulo, 202, *210*
Freore, Paulo, *20*
Freud, Sigmund, *299*

G

Galileo Galilei, 18
Gay, Peter, *162*
General will, 93–94, 95, 221
Gentile, Giovanni, 222, 227
German Ideology (Marx), 117
German romanticism, 232–36
    racism and, 239–40
Gharbzadeghi, 273–74
Glasnost, 181–85, 207
Goal culture, 155
Gobineau, Joseph Arthur de, 236–37, 238, 240
Gorbachev, Mikhail Sergeyevich, 163, 174–75,
    179–85, *187*, 198–99, 207
Government
    Burke on, 44–46
    federal system of, 62–63
    Hobbes on, 30–31
    Jeffersonian, 97–100
    Locke on, 36–37
    Madisonian, 57–64
Great Depression, 72
Greene, Nathanael, *230*
Gregor, A. James, 212, 213–14, 230
Grundrisse, The (Marx), 116
Guenther, Hans F.K., 238
Guerilla warfare, 193, 194

H

Hadith, 257, 261
Hanson, Russell L., *20*
Happiness, Jeffersonian concept of, 96, 101–2
Harrington, Michael, 114
Hartz, Louis, *86*
Hassan, King of Morocco, 287
Hegel, G.W.F., 7, 110, 235, 289
    critiques of, 124–25
    philosophy and politics of, 118–24
Heilbroner, Robert L., 114, *142*
Help Book, The, 7
Heraclitus, 119
Hermeneutics, 13–16
History of the Communist Party of the Soviet Union (Bolsheviks): A Short Course (Stalin), 170
Hitler, Adolf, 7, 8, 13, 172, 214, 231, 232, *248*
    on communists, 10
    on democracy, 243
    differences between Mussolini and, 243
    on emotionalism *vs.* rationalism, 235
    life of, 241–42
    on Marxism, 265
    propaganda as tool of, 245–46
    racism of, 239, 240, 243–44, 246–48
    speeches of, 244–45
    Wagner's influence on, 237–38
Hobbes, Thomas, 21, 27–32, 106
    individualism and, 38
    Locke and, differences between, 36–37
    possessive market society and, 31
    on social contract, 29–31
    on state of nature, 27–29
Hook, Sidney, *162*
Horowitz, Asher, 93, *112*
Horowitz, Gad, 93, *112*
Hough, Jerry, *187*
House of Representatives, 63
Human nature and condition
    Hobbes on, 21, 28–29
    Jefferson on, 102–4
    Madison on, 54–55
    Marx on, 27, 125–30, 133–34
    Mussolini on, 27
    Plato's insight into, 8
Human will, Mussolini on, 217
Hume, David, 30, 55, 64
Hundred Flowers campaign, 207

Hungary, 177
Husain, 262
Hu Yaobang, 207

I

Ideology(ies)
    action orientation of, 6
    defining, 4–5
    distinguishing features, 5–9
    functions of, 6–8
    mass movements and, 9–20
    Mill on, 18
    Plato's cave allegory and, 2–4, 17, 294–95, 297
    political, origins of, 1–20
    reasons for studying, 11–16
    in 21st century, conflict over, 290–99
    uncongenial, reasons for tolerating, 16–17
Ijtihad, 263, 264, 277
Imams, 262
Imperialism
    Lenin's theory of, 159–62
    Mao's rural strategy and, 192–94
Imperialism, the Highest Stage of Capitalism (Lenin), 159
Imperialism and the World Economy (Bukharin), 168
Increasing misery, law of, 139
Individualism
    Islam and, 284
    liberalism's roots in, 23–25, 38–40
Industrial Revolution, 125–26
Inequality, private property and, 124–25
Inherited rights, 44
Instability of governments, avoiding, 71–73
Institutions, control of majority tyranny through, 62–63
International communist movement, 155–56, 161–62, 171–73, 176–78
International Islamic Front, 252–53, 277
Iran, 10
    Islamic revolution in, 252
Iranian Islamic Republic, 281–82
Irony of democracy, 83–84
Islam, 38, 250–88
    Abrahamic monotheistic background, 253–56
    basic beliefs/values, 257–59
    early, politics and struggle in, 259–60

Islam, *continued*
  fascism and, 284, 294
  five pillars of faith, 258
  governance, compatibility of democracy and, 283
  growth of, 263–65
  leadership and authority after Muhammad, 261–63
  Marxism and, 284
  public-private dichotomy, 38
  reasons for focus on, 251–53
  relations between state and, 284–87
  resurgence of puritanical/reformist tendencies in, 275–79
    as reaction to Western influence/control, 268–75
    strategies for, 279–83
  Shiite. *See* Shiite Islam
  Sunni. *See* Sunni Islam
  totality of Islamist vision, 284–87
Islamic Salvation Front, 280
Italian fascism. *See* Fascism; Mussolini, Benito
Izvestia, 168

J

Jackson, Andrew, 70
Jafar, Imam, 262
Jahn, Father, 234
Jefferson, Thomas, 8, 83, 87, 126
  alternative view of liberal democracy, 96–106
Jesus Christ, 255, 256
Jews, struggle between Aryans and, 240–41
Jiang Jieshi (Chiang Kai-shek), 173
Jihad, 259–60, 277
Joes, Anthony, 214, 230
Judaism
  Christianity distinguished from, 255–56
  Islam and, 254–55
Judicial review, 62
Justice, social contract for, 84–86
Justification, as function of ideology, 8–9

K

Kant, Immanuel, 298
Kariel, Henry S., *299*

Kaufmann, Walter, *142*
Kautsky, Karl, *162*
Keddie, Nikki R., *288*
Kemalist movement, 271, 286
Khan, Sayyid Ahmad, 252
Khomeini, Ayatollah Ruhollah, 8, 11, 250, 253, 263, 274, 281–83, 285
Khrushchev, Nikita, 174–75, 176, 178
Knox, Henry, 52
Koestler, Arthur, 291, *299*
Kramnick, Isaac, *47*
Krupskaya, Nadezhda, 150
Kuomintang (KMT), 192

L

Labor
  alienated *vs.* unalienated, 126–29
  exploitation of, 127–28
  Hegel on, 121–23
  necessary, 135
  in possessive market society, 31
  property ownership and, 34–35
  surplus value of, 135
  wage-slave, 128, 137
Labor theory of value, 39, 135
Laicization policies, in Turkey, 280–81, 286–87
Laquer, Walter, *230*
Laski, Harold, *47*
Leadership
  Aryan, 238–40
  Communist party/revolutionary, 152–55
  elitist, 216, 226–27
  Islamic, after Muhammad, 261
  in mass movements, 11
Legislator
  Madison's concept of, 60–61
  Rousseau's concept of, 94
Lenin, V.I., 8, 11, 114, 141, 143, 164, 166, 175, 218
  democratic centralism, 154–55, 169
  distrust of Stalin, 167–69
  imperialism, theory of, 159–62
  life of, 149–52
  Marxism of the left and, 147, 148–49
  permanent revolution doctrine, 154–55
  power struggles following death of, 167–69

role of Communist party, 152–54, 156–58
    state socialism concept, 158
Leninism
    Marxism and, 143–62
    themes from, 152–62
    See also Marxism-Leninism
Leotard, Jean François, 296, *299*
Letter Concerning Toleration, A (Locke), 37–38, 266
Leviathan (Hobbes), 28, 65
Lewis, Sinclair, *230*
Liberal democracy, 40–42, 293–94
    Dewey's alternative view of, 106–11
    elite theory and, 77–84
    Jefferson's alternative view of, 96–106
    Madison and, 65–66, 67–69
    majoritarian, in America, 74–77
    Rousseau's alternative view of, 95–96
Liberalism, 21–47
    British tradition of, 38–39
    challenge to, in 21st century, 291–93
    conservatism and, 42–46
    historical roots of, 22–47
    Hobbes and, 27–32
    individualism and, 23–25, 28, 38–40
    Locke and, 32–38
    majoritarian, rise of, 70–74
    preliberal *vs.* liberal society, 23–24
    in religion and science, rise of, 25–27
Liberalism in America, 45–46, 48–86
    context for, in late 1970s, 49–51
    egalitarianism and, 49–51
    Madison and, 52–69
    majoritarian, 74–77
Liberation Theology, 267
Liberty, tension between equality and, 75–77
Lifton, Robert J., *210*
Locke, John, 15, 32–38, 96, 105, 135
    individualism and, 38–39
    influence on American egalitarianism, 50
    on invention of money, 34
    on property, 33, 34–36
    on state of nature, 32–33, 36–37
    on toleration, 37–38, 266
Logic, Hegel on, 120–21
Logos (reasoned speech), 20
Long March, 191–92
Luther, Martin, 25–26
Luxemburg, Rosa, 147, 153, 218
Lysenko, T.D., 13

M

Macpherson, C.B., *20*, 31, *47*, *112*, *299*
Madison, James, 7, 8, 12, 41, 42, 48
    on central dilemma of liberal democracy, 49
    Constitution of 1787 and, 52–53
    criticisms of system of, 66
    on extended republic, 59
    on factions, 54–57
    political system of, 57–64
    republican remedy of, 65–66, 67–69
    on voting rights, 67–68
Magdoff, Harry, *162*
Mahdi, 263
Majoritarian liberalism, 70–73
    in British tradition, 73–74
Majority tyranny, 41
    control of, Madison on, 54, 57–60
Mandel, Ernest, *142*
Mandeville, Bernard, 40
Manifesto of the Communist Party, The (Marx & Engels), 116, 117
Mannheim, Karl, *20*, 42
Mao Zedong, 11, 173, 177, 189, 190–91
    on contradiction, 196–98
    life of, 191–92
    rural strategy of, 192–94
    as symbol, 201–3
    Thought of, 190, 192
Marcuse, Herbert, *142*, *187*
Marja as-Taqlid, 263
Market socialism, 208
Marx, Karl, 5, 8, 13, 113, 233
    on alienation, 7, 126–30
    on bourgeois class, 134–35
    on class structure, 131
    on decline and fall of capitalism, 135–41
    on democracy, 292
    on history and development of capitalism, 130–33
    on human condition, 27, 125–30
    life of, 114–17
    on religion, 131
    on revolution, 139–41, 144–45
    on role of state, 59
    vision of communist society, 135, 140–41
    writings of, revisionist *vs.* orthodox interpretations, 117–18
    See also Hegel, G.W.F.

Marxism, 5
  capitalism and, 130–35
  of the center, 145–46
  Chinese, 190–95
  divisions within, 117–18, 144–48
  Islamism and, 284
  of the left, 147
  method of, 161–62
  orthodox, 117, 145–46
  power-elite analysis and, 79–80
  praxis of, 165
  revisionist, 117, 146
  of the right, 146
  Russian, 148–49
  Soviet, 164–88
Marxism-Leninism, 141, 162, 169–70
  Stalin's contributions to, 169–73
Mass culture, 82
Mass movements, 9–20
  See also Revolution(s)
Matthews, Richard K., *86, 112*
May 4 Movement, 191
McCarthy, Thomas, *20*
McDonald, Lee, 93
McMurtry, John, *142*
Mecca, 257, 259
  hajj to, 258
Medina, 256, 259, 260
Mein Kampf (Hitler), 7, 13, 232, 243
Merleau-Ponty, Maurice, *187*
Meyer, Alfred B., 116, *162*
Michels, Robert, 77, 78
Miliband, Ralph, *142*
Mill, James, 40–41, 73, 126
Mill, John Stuart, 1, 18–19, *20,* 42, 126,
  298, 299
Mills, C. Wright, 79, *86*
Money
  invention of, 34
  power of, 80
Monopoly, 139
Moody, Peter R., *210*
Mosca, Gaetano, 77, 216
Moses, 255
Mosse, George L., 233, *249*
Mughal empire, 264
Muhammad, 254, 256, 257–59, 260, 261–62
Mujahadeen, 251, 277
Multinational corporations, 160

Muslim, meaning of, 253
Muslim Brotherhood, 252
Mussolini, Benito, 8, 11, *230,* 294
  anti-bolshevism and, 222
  anti-intellectualism and, 225–26
  on anti-liberalism, 220, 221
  on corporativism, 223
  differences between Hitler and, 243
  elitist leadership and, 216, 226–27
  on fascism, 211, 213, 214
  on human nature, 27
  on human will, 217
  life and early thought of, 215–17
  on nation-state, 219
  position on World War I, 217–18
Myths racial, 241

N

National bourgeoisie, 195, 196
National liberation, wars of, 161–62
National-Socialism, 231–49
  fascism as distinct from, 214
  Hitler and, 241–48
  propaganda as tool of, 245
  rise of Nazi party, 242
  volkish tradition/spirit and, 232–36
Nation-state
  in fascist ideology, 218–19, 294
  orientation, 161
NATO, 70
Natural aristocracy, 45
Natural law, Hobbes on, 30
Natural rights, 29
  freedom and, 38–39
Nazis/Nazism. *See* Fascism; Hitler, Adolf;
  National-Socialism
Nazi-Soviet Pact, 172
Necessary labor, 135
Needs, wants and, 89
New Economic Policy (NEP), 158, 168–69, 180
"New open door" policy, in PRC, 205
Nietzsche, Friedrich, 217
Nolte, Ernst, 229, *230,* 243
Nomenklatura, 179
Nonantagonistic contradictions, 197–98
Noncontradiction, principle of, 118
Normative democratic elitism, 81–83

Nursi, Bediuzzaman Said, 271

O

October Manifesto, 151, 154
Ollman, Bertell, *142*
On Liberty (J.S. Mill), 18, 41
Oppression, defined, 3
Orientalism, 269
Origins of Totalitarianism, The (Arendt), 10
Orthodox Marxism, 117, 145–46, 148
O'Sullivan, Noël, *230*
Ottoman empire, 264

P

Pahlavi, Shah Reza, 10
Pakistan, Islamicization in, 252
Pareto, Vilfredo, 77, 216
Parla, Taha, *288*
Participation
    as basic value, 51
    Rousseau on, 95
Payne, Stanley G., 213, 222–23, *230*
Peaceful coexistence doctrine, 178–79, 200
Peasantry
    Chinese, 193–94
    Russian, 154, 193
Pedagogy of the Oppressed (Freire), 202
People's Liberation Army (PLA), 207, 208
People's Republic of China (PRC)
    after Mao, 203–9
    economic development, 208–9
    founding of, 192
    path to socialism in, 195–98
    Soviet Union and, 198–201
Perestroika, 163, 179–85, 187
Permanent revolution, doctrine of, 154–55, 198
Peters, F.E., *288*
Plato, 5, 8, 18, 290
    Cave allegory of, 2–4, 17, 294–95, 297
Plekhanov, Georgi V., 148
Pluralism, 59
Polanyi, Karl, *47*
Polis, 49, 58
Politburo, 168
Political literacy, need for, 298

Political parties, 66
Politics, Jeffersonian, 104–6
Positive state, 73, 74
Possessive market society, 31–32
Power
    Hobbes on, 31
    Locke on, 37
Power-elite analysis, 79–81
Pravda, 151, 168
Praxis, defined, 165
Presidency, U.S., 62–63, 69–70
Primogeniture, 101
Professional revolutionaries, 152–53
Profit, 136, 137–39
Proletarianization of PRC, 196
Proletariat
    dictatorship of, 156–58
    readiness for revolution, 147–48
    in Russia, 148, 153–54
Propaganda, 71, 245–46
Property
    factions and, 56
    Jefferson on, 96, 100–101
    Locke on, 33, 34–36
    private
        Hegel on, 124–25
        liberalism and, 39
    Rousseau on, 90
    voting rights and, 36, 40, 49
Protocols of the Elders of Zion, The, 241
Public and Its Problems, The (Dewey), 108
Public-private dichotomy, 37–38, 266–67
Putin, Vladimir, 186

Q

Quotations from Chairman Mao Zedong, 202
Quran, 253, 257, *288*

R

Racism
    in Germany, 236–41
    Italian fascism and, 227–28
    in 21st century
Racist internationalism, 246–48
Ramadan, fast of, 258

Rationalism, emotionalism *vs.*, 234–36
Rawls, John, 84–86
Reflections on the Revolution in France and on the Proceedings in Certain Societies in London Relative to That Event (Burke), 43
Relations of production, 132–33
Religion
  liberalism and, 25–27
  as "opiate of the masses," 131
  relations between state and, in Islamic revival, 284–87
Report on Investigation of the Peasant Movement in Hunan (MAO), 191
Representation
  elite theory of, 77–78
  Madison's view of, 60–61
  virtual, 45
Republic, 60
Republic, The (Plato), 3
Revisionist Marxism, 117, 146, 148
Revolutionaries
  characteristics of, 9–11
  professional, 152–53
Revolution(s)
  American, 53
  avoiding, 71–73
  bourgeois, 154
  of 1848, 147
  French, 122
  Iranian, 252
  Jefferson on, 99, 101
  peaceful *vs.* violent, 144–48
  perestroika as, 179–85
  permanent, doctrine of, 154–55
  readiness of proletariat for, 147–48
  of rising expectations, 9
  Russian, 151, 155–58
  wars of national liberation, 161–62
Rhodes, Cecil, 160
Ricardo, David, 135
Righteousness, 254, 255
Rights
  inherited, 44
  natural, 29, 38–39
  voting, 36, 40–41, 49, 111
Romanov abdication, 151
Romanticism, German, 232–36
  racism and, 239–40
Roosevelt, Franklin D., 70, 79

Rousseau, Jean Jacques, 83, 87, 88–95
Rubenstein, Richard L., *249*
Rural strategy of Mao, 192–94
Rushdie, Salman, *fatwa* against, 283
Russia
  revolution of 1905, 151
  Russian Marxists, 148–49
Russification, 167

S

Safavid empire, 264
Said, Edward W., 269, *288*
Satanic Verses, The (Rushdie), 283
Schneider, Herbert W., *230*
Schram, Stuart R., *210*
Schumpeter, Joseph, 81–82
Schurmann, Franz, *210*
Science
  Dewey's use of, 107–8
  Islam and, 276
  liberalism and, 25–27
Second Discourse, The (Rousseau), 91
Second Treatise on Government (Locke), 35, 96
Selected Works of Mao, 190
Self-alienation, 129
Self-interest, 32, 39–40
Self-realization, 121–22, 127
Senate, U.S., 63
Separation of powers, 62
"Seveners," in Shiite Islam, 262
Shared values concept, 39
Shariah, 264, 284
Shays, Daniel, 52
Shays Rebellion, 52, 99
Shiite Islam, 253, 261, 262–63, 282, 285
Shirer, William L., *249*
Simplification, as function of ideology, 6–7
Size principle, 62, 65
Smith, Adam, 13, 39, 135
Smith, Dan, *299*
Smith, William, 99
Snow, Edgar, *210*
Social contract
  Hobbes on, 29–31
  for justice, 84–86
  Locke and, 36–37
  Rousseau on, 91, 92–96

Social Contract, The (Rousseau), 92
Social Darwinism, 225
Socialism
    democratic, 74, 110
    different paths to, 177
    fascism and, 222–24
    market, 208
    Nazis on, 247
    in one country, doctrine of, 170
    in PRC, 195–98
    state, 158
    Tito's brand of, 173, 176–77
Sojourners, 267
Sorel, Georges, 217
Soviet Marxism, 164–88
    after Stalin, 173–79
    Stalin and, 164–73
    Yeltsin and, 185–87
Soviet Union
    Bolshevik revolution in, 151, 155–58
    economic development of, 156–58
    as first totalitarian state, 170–71
    glasnost, 181–85
    peaceful coexistence doctrine, 179
    perestroika, 179–85
    post-Soviet Marxism, 185–87
    primacy of Soviet interests, 171–72
    relations with China/PRC, 172–73
    transfer culture in, 155, 156, 158
    Twentieth Party Congress, 174, 177
Species being, man as, 127, 293
Species suicide, 291
Staggered elections/terms of office, as check on
        tyranny, 63
Stalin, Joseph, 117, *188*
    Lenin's distrust of, 167–69
    life of, 166–67
    posthumous denunciations of, 174–76
    rise to power of, 164–69
Starr, John Bryann, *210*
State
    Hegel on, 123, 124–25
    Marx's critique of, 125
    See also Nation-state
State and Revolution, The (Lenin), 157
State of nature
    British liberal tradition and, 38–39
    Hobbes on, 27–29
    Locke on, 32–33, 36–37

    Rousseau on, 86–91
State socialism, 158
Stork, Joe, *287*
Substructure, in Marxism, 131
Sudan, adoption of *shariah* in, 252
Suffrage. *See* Voting rights
Sufism, 265
Sultans, 264–65
Sunni Islam, 261, 262, 263, 265, 285
Sun Zhongshan (Sun Yat-sen), 191
Superprofit, 160
Superstructure, in Marxism, 131
Supreme Court, as check on tyranny, 63–64
Surplus value of labor, theory of, 135, 137

T

Taliban, 276, 281
Tawhid, 258
Tawney, R.H., *47*
Teleology, Hegel's political theory as, 123–24
Theopolitics
    modern ideology and, 266–68
    revival of, 251
    See also Islam
Theory of Justice, A (Rawls), 84–85
Thompson, E.P., *299*
Three Faces of Fascism (Nolte), 229
Tiananmen Square, 207–8
Tito, Joseph Broz, 173, 176–77
Tocqueville, Alexis de, 50, 53, 62, *86*
Toleration, 18–19, 111
    Locke on, 37–38
Tory party, 22
Townsend, James R., *210*
Traditionalism, 42
Transfer culture, 155, 156, 158
Transnational corporations, 160
"Trickle down theory," Locke's early form of, 35
Trotsky, Leon, 153, 154, 166, 168, 169, *188*
True believer, 10, 11, 19–20
Trumbo, Dalton, *299*
Trustee relationship, 36–37, 61
Tucker, Robert C., *142, 162, 188*
Turkey, Islam in, 262, 271, 280–81
"Twelvers," in Shiite Islam, 262–63
Twentieth Party Congress, 174, 177

U

Ulama, 262, 264, 265, 282
Ulyanov, Vladimir Ilich. *See* Lenin, V.I.
Umar, caliph, 261
Ummah al-Islamiyya, 260, 284
Unalienated labor, 129
United States, status quo ideology in, 292–93
    See also Liberalism in America
Utilitarianism, 41

V

Variable capital, 139
Versailles, Treaty of, 218, 242
Violence, Islamic doctrine of legitimate, 260
Volkish tradition/spirit, 232, 233–34
    Christianity and, 235
Voluntarism, 217, 224–25
Voting rights, 36, 40–41, 49, 111
    Madison's view of, 67–69
Vozhd, 164, 179

W

Wage-slave labor, 128
Wagner, Cosima, 238
Wagner, Richard, 237–38

Wagner, Siegfried, 238
Wakeman, Frederic, Jr., *210*
Walker, Martin, *188*
Wants, needs and, 89
Ward-republics, 97–99
Wars of national liberation, 161–62
Weber, Eugen, *230*
Westoxication, 252, 273–74
White, Morton, 107, *112*
Wilson, Edmund, *162*
Wilson, Woodrow, 70
Wolfe, Bertram D., *162*
Wolin, Sheldon, *47*
Woltmann, Ludwig, 241
Womack, Brantly, *210*
Woolf, S.J., *230*
World War I, 151, 217–18
    Russia's withdrawal from, 156

Y

Yanan Hermitage, 204
Yeltsin, Boris, 185–86
Yugoslavia, 173, 176–77

Z

Zhao Ziyang, 207